CU00793967

MAKE ME!

Understanding and Engaging Student Resistance in School

Eric Toshalis

HARVARD EDUCATION PRESS
CAMBRIDGE, MASSACHUSETTS

Youth Development
and Education Series

Series edited by Michael Sadowski

OTHER BOOKS IN THIS SERIES

Schooling for Resilience
Edward Fergus, Pedro Noguera, and Margary Martin

I Can Learn from You
Michael Reichert and Richard Hawley

Portraits of Promise
Michael Sadowski

Second Printing, 2016

Copyright © 2015 by the President and Fellows of Harvard College

Library of Congress Control Number 2014949035

Paperback ISBN 978-1-61250-761-3
Library Edition ISBN 978-1-61250-762-0

Published by Harvard Education Press,
an imprint of the Harvard Education Publishing Group

Harvard Education Press
8 Story Street
Cambridge, MA 02138

Cover Design: Joel Gendron

Photo Credit: Ronnie Kaufman / Larry Hirshowitz / Blend Images / Getty Images

The typefaces used in this book are Adobe Garamond Pro and Legacy Sans.

CONTENTS

For the troublemakers;

for everyone who has ever been in a classroom,
imagined it differently,
and tried to do something about it;

and for Mason.

CHAPTER 1

Why Examine Resistance?

I LIKE TO tell people I was losing my patience, but really I was losing my cool. It happened when I was in my second year of teaching middle school. My students came from a range of backgrounds, some low income, some wealthy, most middle class. Many came from families with adults who worked as migrant laborers, several were English language learners, and some had parents who were recent immigrants working in the hospitality industry or high-tech companies nearby. The majority of my students were what you would likely call "good kids." Javier wasn't.[1]

Javier was disruptive. Javier was angry. His home life was a story of broken promises, fractured relationships, and neglectful caregivers, and his experiences at school weren't much better. That he came to school at all was sort of a miracle, but I am ashamed to admit that I found myself relieved some days when he didn't. As I said, Javier was angry, and that made him scary. Though he was often quite funny and charismatic, he was also mean to his classmates, he started several fights, and he seemed to relish disturbing classroom routines by distracting peers, challenging my directives, and generally opposing my agenda nearly every day. And one day, I couldn't take it anymore.

Javier was seated in the front row where I had put him so I could better monitor his misbehavior. But this day, I was in the back of the classroom distributing worksheets while checking in with students. The class was loud and off-task despite my pleas to quiet down and focus, and Javier was using the chaos as an opportunity to take the stage. I had been fighting all period long to garner and redirect my students' attention, but Javier had command of the room with his jokes, his interruptions, and his de facto mocking of my authority. I was afraid to confront him individually because I knew he'd flare, make a scene, and further distract the class, so I tried to coerce his peers into paying attention to me. I cajoled them with promises of less homework, warned them that they would need to know stuff because it was going to be on the test, and told them I was disappointed with their lack of effort. None of my pleas worked. Having exhausted my weak set of classroom management tricks while watching the class grow in its resistance to academic work, I walked to the front of the room where I could see everyone, particularly Javier, and that's when it happened.

I turned to face the class, looked Javier in the eye, and suddenly heard myself bellow, "Everyone! Shut! Up!" The room collapsed into silence as all eyes turned to watch me, especially Javier. I have no idea what I said after that point. I don't even remember what we were studying or whether we accomplished anything for the rest of the period. All I know is that my disruptive, insensitive, angry, and desperate command achieved the compliance I had craved. Like Javier, I had successfully forced others to watch and listen to me, no matter the cost. I had finally won something, but was about to lose everything.

I spent the remainder of the class period and the rest of the day scared. Not scared of Javier or the kids, but of myself and what I was becoming. Out of frustration, exhaustion, and desperation, I had to face the fact that I had told my students—*shouted* at them—to shut up, and I had done it while staring down a student who needed anything from me but more threats. I did that. And I'm that guy who went into teaching because I was going to be the kind of educator who inspired kids, like Javier, to find their voices, see their power, and make the world their own. And now I was confronting the idea that I was a fraud and a failure, one who may have silenced and alienated Javier if not many others, just for a few moments of obedient silence.

Driving home that evening, I had nothing but questions. What had I done? Why had I done it? Why weren't my students doing what they were told? Why didn't they seem to care about learning? And why was Javier so resistant to nearly everything I tried? By the time I pulled up to my apartment, I realized I hadn't just lost my cool or run out of patience; I had reached the limits of my understanding. I didn't know what to do, because I didn't know what I was seeing. I didn't know how to relate to Javier, because I didn't understand him. And I didn't know how to respond to my students' resistance, because I had no idea where it came from.

I have been trying to figure these things out ever since. This book is what I have discovered.

What Is This Book About?

This book is about how to understand student resistance in school, not how to control it. That's an important distinction to make up front because many who struggle with oppositional student behaviors will come to this book with the question "How can I stop it?" Fortunately, a lot of material in these pages will answer that question. But strategically, and I would argue more importantly, this book targets a different question, one as analytical as it is practical: "What is happening when students resist?" The goal in focusing on this latter question is to provide educators with the level of sophistication they need to *read* adolescent student resistance rather than merely *react* to it. The chapters that follow will make clear that students resist because they need to, because they can, and, often, because they should. This book examines why that is the case and what we can do about it.

Who Is This Book About?

We call them troublemakers. Delinquents. Insubordinates. Pains in the ass. We say they're being rude, defiant, or disrespectful. We conclude that some of our students just don't want to learn, that they're more interested in disruption, goofing off, and socializing than getting a proper education. This is how we often describe students who resist in school.

Sure, we know that our students are people with complex lives and diverse needs who deserve our best, but we also know we can't let them self-destruct or destroy the learning environment. So we do what we can to convince them to change their behavior or attitude while holding them accountable for their choices. We talk to them after class, tell them how worried we are, call home, and provide various forms of "tough love." We seek advice from colleagues, and we consult written sources for hints on how to deal with our students' misbehaviors. We try to be fair, consistent, and proactive, but we know the disruptions and disturbances have to stop. We find ourselves spending an inordinate amount of energy and time on those students who resist, and we therefore worry about our more compliant kids who may get neglected as a result. So we find ourselves using reprimands, referrals, detentions, and suspensions to send strong messages and convince students to behave. Sometimes these approaches seem to work, but often they don't. And every year, the patterns seem to repeat with the same set of students.

This book is about those students, the ones who oppose what we try to do in school or who disengage and withdraw from activities we design to help them succeed. But because education depends on relationships, this book is not only about them—it's about us, too. It's about who we are as educators, what we think is important, what we accept as true, and what we do to our students ostensibly in the name of education, motivation, encouragement, discipline, care, and accountability. To better understand why students resist the way they do, we will need to challenge a host of supposedly commonsense approaches and bust a variety of myths that tend to drive forms of thinking and decision making that are ultimately counterproductive. As a result, some of what you will find in this book may confirm what you suspected all along, and other insights may challenge previously held beliefs. If you relish learning as much as you hope your students do, my hope is that you'll find the topics invigorating.

Why Is This Book Needed?

Working with adolescents who seem to be working against us can be vexing. We care deeply about our students and dedicate the best parts of ourselves to helping youth achieve their potential, which is why we're sometimes incredulous when they oppose us. Depending on the form their resistance takes, we can be irritated, frustrated, and confused, or we might be shocked, scared, and offended. We might even get irate. This is because student resistance messes with things. It messes with us.

Not surprisingly, then, we are often at a loss for how to respond to resistance, much less understand it. Making stuff up as we go, we sometimes respond to student opposition in ways that are not the shiniest moments in our professional careers. Perplexed, angry, or hurt, we occasionally react harshly, thinking only about expediency, as I did in the vignette above. Though it may be painful to admit it, we sometimes ostracize, humiliate, shame, and threaten students to bend to our will, and we get away with doing that because the institutions in which we work tend to prefer submission over opposition. "Show 'em who's boss," our colleagues might tell us. "Don't take any guff."

We might subsequently reflect on our responses to student resistance and how our actions affect ourselves and others—we may even regret what we've done—but without the right tools, knowledge, and support, we sometimes end up with problematic conclusions and approaches. The way we think drives the way we act, and if our thinking is polluted with misconceptions, ill-advised approaches, and disproven assumptions, we may encourage the very forms of student resistance we're trying to reduce. And when we are confronted with new information or methods to address student resistance, we might even resist that novelty if it challenges our current belief systems, particularly if we already feel confident in what we do. In such cases, our own resistance—and not the students'—might be the problem.

Consequently, how we frame and respond to student resistance is often insufficient. Many of us underperform when we confront student resistance, despite the clear connection between it and important school-based outcomes such as academic achievement, school discipline, student alienation and marginalization, propensity for drop-out, educator job satisfaction, teacher attrition, antisocial school climates, and violence. Seeking help, many of us take precious time to consult scholarship for guidance. Unfortunately, the research literature on student resistance is scattered across multiple fields, with no single source or theoretical tradition to provide coherence. Insights from empirical studies in neuroscience, educational psychology, sociology, and anthropology abound, as do theoretical explanations from critical pedagogy, critical theory, critical race theory, and postcolonial, feminist, and queer theories.

The practical utility of such scholarship is further undermined either by overly complex academic treatments or by outright inaccessibility to readers because of research journals' use of online paywalls or other restrictive subscription policies. While countless handbooks and textbooks on classroom management are offered to address this problem, many suffer from simplistic, outdated, or single-theory approaches that fail to provide practitioners with the nuanced, multifaceted treatment the subject deserves. In short, scholars have made many valuable observations about student resistance in the classroom, but this knowledge has rarely made it into the hands of those best positioned to do anything about it—educators.

This book is an attempt to rectify that problem. It seeks to bridge the enormous chasm we sometimes build between theory and practice, and between research and policy. Because resistance is somewhat overtheorized in the research literature and sometimes woefully undertheorized by practitioners, the chapters that follow are my attempt to bring the two sides into conversation.

Who Is This Book For?

I have written this book for the educator I was and wanted to be, and for the preservice, in-service, and veteran educators I have known since. The analyses and examples I provide are designed to address the concerns of all educators of adolescents: middle school and high school teachers, counselors, school psychologists, social workers, administrators, coaches, paraprofessionals, parents, youth advocates, after-school leaders—anyone who works with adolescents in educational settings.

I also think of educators as public intellectuals, as learned professionals whose insights and contributions illuminate important aspects of the human condition and are therefore crucial to the collective well-being of schools, communities, and societies. Intellectuals are often well versed in the theory of their discipline, and I believe educators should be no different. If we start with theory and research, we provide ourselves with powerful criteria for judging the merits of a particular approach beyond the simplistic "it either works or doesn't" expediency. In contrast, when we follow an "act now and think later" approach, we tend to grope for explanations about why our methods seem successful in some instances but not in others. This approach can lead to blaming kids and can exacerbate inconsistencies in practices that produce inequities in outcomes—and I don't have to tell you how bad some of those trends have gotten.

So, if you're the type of educator who rigidly adheres to rules without analyzing their efficacy or ethics and who tends to fault kids whenever anything goes wrong in the classroom, this book will challenge your worldview on nearly every page. But if you feel as if something is wrong but you can't quite pin down what it is or how to think differently about it, this book is for you.

Those who are as baffled by student resistance and misbehavior as they are tired of simplistic educational "tips and tricks" will likely find a lot that speaks to them in these pages. The research-driven insights I provide may affirm your hunches or give a name to what you had suspected all along, just as they may sometimes push you out of your comfort zone and force you to consider what you've been doing poorly. My goal throughout is to push the envelope and provide sufficient support to get you where you need to go.

Does that mean this book is all about theory? No. Because I teach classroom management, I know well that school-based professionals need real-life techniques to handle the dicey situations they will face the very next day. This book is replete with such techniques. But supplying specific approaches can lead to problems. For example, if I answer educators' pleas to "just tell me what to do!" my experience suggests that they will do exactly what I describe, and that's not good. Whether the newly learned technique was appropriate for that situation or not, many educators will deploy it, often unsuccessfully, as if unique and complex interactions with diverse students all can be handled by a singular response. To me, that's not applying theory to practice; that's throwing hastily grabbed approaches at poorly understood circumstances. We can and should do better than this.

Besides, easy answers won't get us where we need to go. Nor will overcomplicated and alienating abstractions. We can promote higher academic achievement, diminish behavioral problems, and practice more sophisticated interventions only if we approach our work with the same rigor, inquiry, curiosity, and risk taking we expect from our students. The theories I present may sometimes seem rather removed or lofty for school-based professionals who need immediate solutions, but I include them because educators need rich material to handle complex situations. When educators possess a strong foundation of research-based analyses and a level of theoretical sophistication that allows them to see how some solutions are appropriate and others can make things worse, they will choose powerful and liberating responses to address challenges like student resistance. In short, educators will do what's right when they know what's up.

Of course, some educators may not merit that trust, because of the way they operate in their work and because too little of their decision making is informed by theory and research. However, I'd rather trust and empower educators than participate in our culture of relentless blame that targets them for all things wrong in public education. We educators are the solution, not the problem. But if we're to be the solution, we need a complex understanding of why students resist, so that we can effectively choose which approach from our bag of tricks will best support a resistant student's optimal development and academic achievement. To me, that's the work. That's our job.

Why "Make Me!"?

The title of this book has multiple meanings. In one sense, it's what students often say to us when they challenge our directives. "Make me," they dare us. "Make me do what you think I should do, because I may not do it at all unless I feel like it." Challenges like this remind us that schools are among the most restrictive environments we have created for youth and that the experience of being contained or controlled within them inevitably produces resistance. All of us, adolescents in particular, need to feel in control of at least part of our destiny. As we will see, a primary origin of the "make me" response occurs when that self-control is suppressed.

But at another level, "make me" also means "create me" or "build me." This secondary meaning illuminates the way we effectively construct others when we attempt to control their behavior. If who we are is determined largely by what we do, then those who shape our decisions are actively participating in *making* us who we become. This is particularly true in educational settings like classrooms and schools where educators are forever making kids do things that are ostensibly for the students' benefit. When students sometimes resist those attempts, it can be frustrating (or disappointing or infuriating) for the adults, but if we respond from frustration more than curiosity, if we use discipline more than inquiry, we squander one of the most precious insights our students give us. Resistance is a message that something isn't right; an educator needs preparation, courage, and practice to hear that message and channel it into something productive. Doing so changes students, our relationship with them, the context of that relationship, and us. In other words, how we make students makes us.

What Do You Mean by Student Resistance?

For the purposes of this book, *student resistance* really means "student resistance in school" or "student resistance in the classroom." I define the concept as follows:

- Any behavior by one or more students that is perceived by the educator or the student or students to initiate a course of action that differs from, alters, inhibits, or prevents the general direction or intention of activity in the classroom or school
- Any student verbal or nonverbal communication that withdraws from, questions, critiques, refutes, or refuses a perspective, a norm, knowledge, or an implication presented by the educator, by peers, or by the school
- Any situation in a school setting in which a student decides not to comply with an implicit or explicit expectation

This definition suggests that student resistance is rarely reducible to uncomplicated and easily dismissed misbehavior. The complexity of the definition requires us to begin asking questions about origins before we plan our response.

In addition, the definition purposely does not take a stand on whether the resistance must have at its root a known and understood social, political, or moral purpose. Students sometimes resist on impulse, only later discovering what's at stake for them in their opposition (adults do this too). But the lack of a stated or even a conscious moral or political manifesto should not be taken to indicate that a student's resistance is bereft of critique or merit. Student resistance is often propelled by strong motivational undercurrents and political indignation. Something always happened before the resistance occurred; some set of circumstances, relationships, and communications—for whatever reason—compelled the student to resist. Though we as adults may not perceive these conditions or understand them, we have to admit that students often have good reasons for resisting. Therefore, we should have equally good reasons for responding to their resistance the way we do.

How Is the Book Organized?

In my experience, most educators conceptualize student resistance as "the behavior that must be thwarted or suppressed through manipulations, incentives, and punishments so that order and productivity may be maintained." This characterization paints resistance as the antithesis of academic achievement, the opposite of good behavior. This book is organized to suggest that this perspective is extremely limited.

To this end, I have divided the book into the four domains of inquiry—theoretical, psychological, political, and pedagogical—that most inform a nuanced understanding of student resistance in school. Each of these domains, considered separately, is inadequate to address resistance and would simply reproduce the problems that created the resistance in the first place. For example, if we analyze resistance using only the theoretical literature, we ignore psychodynamic processes that strongly influence individual decision making and social relationships. If we go solely psychological in our approach, we ignore institutional, cultural, and political forces that direct individual actions and meaning making, forces that are best illuminated in the theoretical and political domains. Likewise, if we approach resistance only pedagogically, we will likely adopt the objectives, curricula, activities, and classroom management techniques that may achieve short-term goals but will chronically fail to integrate important psychological needs and political realities in students' lives. And if we think about resistance only in political terms (i.e., how resources, status, access, and sanctions are distributed to different racial, social, cultural, and ethnic groups), we fail to see that the true test of our response to resistance lies in how we actually teach, provide counseling and other support services, and create learning environments in which inequities are either reinforced or dismantled.

Student resistance, and our response to it, is therefore a problem that is theoretical, psychological, political, and pedagogical—simultaneously. Resistance can distract, demean, and destroy valuable educational outcomes, but it can also (and, I would argue, should) be used to promote high academic achievement, prosocial behaviors, and school and community reform. In this way, resistance is also simultaneously a theoretical, psychological, political, and pedagogical *solution*. Seeing it this way reveals the educator to be a pragmatic theorist, a political strategist, an educational psychologist, and a state-sanctioned disciplinarian, all rolled into one.

Contrary to much of what standards-based reforms have come to represent, the power in educators' work comes not from what we are able simplify, count, and reward, but what we are able to understand, integrate, and apply. This is why each chapter contains multiple classroom- and school-based examples of how the theories and research relevant to student resistance might be applied in real-world situations. Additionally, between each chapter, you will find a brief vignette. These vignettes depict many of the concepts and research findings found in surrounding chapters. Though none of the vignettes refers to actual people, the characters and situations in the vignettes are composites of students and adults I have known and with whom I have worked over the past two decades. You can use the vignettes to reflect on how the research might be applied in real-life situations, or you can use them as a springboard for conversations with colleagues. You might pause between chapters to consider your and others' initial response to the vignette and then return to it after more reading to reconsider how theories and research apply.

To further support the educator in moving from theory to application (and back again), each chapter concludes with a "Promising Practices" section. Those sections contain broad, schoolwide interventions; classroom-based approaches; and one-on-one techniques that can be used to understand and engage student resistance in a productive manner. Some methods will appeal to classroom teachers while others may be more appropriate for administrators, counselors, school psychologists, or social workers. Whatever the method, the goal is to demonstrate that the thorniest questions about student resistance have actual answers that can and do work in today's schools.

A Note About Terms

Most of the time I will be writing about educators, students, schools, and research. But sometimes I will use the first person and write about myself. So who am I? I am a teacher, a researcher, a teacher educator, an author, a public school devotee, and a youth advocate. I have taught at various grade levels in several environments: middle school kids at a public K–8 in a rural community, eighth-graders in a gifted and talented program at a suburban public junior high school, and freshman through seniors at an under-resourced, diverse urban high school. I have also taught undergraduates and graduates whose ages ranged from late teens to early sixties. And truth be told, with these varied audiences and decades of experience, I have made nearly every misinterpretation and mistake described in this book. In fact, I wrote it partly because I needed to understand why I was confronting the same types of resistance, year after year, and not getting much better at handling them.

Since serving as a full-time teacher, I have spent years researching resistance while working as a teacher educator in five teacher education programs in three states. As a professor, I have always had one foot in teacher education and another in developmental psychology, each informed by anti-oppressive pedagogies and critical literatures that question the assumptions on which much of modern public education is built. Because I teach both adolescent development and classroom management, I am always seeing connections between the two disciplines and how relevant they are for preservice and in-service educators. This book represents much of that integration.

Who am I referring to when I say "we"? If there is a single, consistent, and pervasive challenge I have seen in the classroom, in my research, and in graduate teacher preparation, it is how to understand and engage student resistance. I struggled with this challenge when I was in the classroom, I still struggle with it today, and every one of my interns struggles with it every semester. So when I say "we" or I talk about "educators" in this book, I include myself and the many school-based professionals who work so hard to positively affect the lives of our youth and the next generation of educators we prepare to serve them.

Will I be using some academic mumbo jumbo in this book? Yes, I will. Scholars have dedicated their lives to studying educational phenomena and have made powerful discoveries that directly address some of the toughest problems in public education. In doing so, they use weird words and complex ideas to convey novel approaches and complicated situations. This is why I wince whenever I hear practitioners complain about the jargon of their profession, as if a few fancy words here and there are too much for folks who just want to keep things simple. Educating youth is not simple! As a comparison, physicians aren't using jargon when they name a broken ankle a "lateral malleolus fracture" or a stomach ache as "acute appendicitis"; they're being descriptive. And engineers aren't being elitist or inaccessible when they use terms like cantilevers, trusses, spandrels, and gussets; they're being precise. The same goes for educators. We need to stop being anti-intellectual in our work and learn how to apply with facility the terms and theories that drive our profession. The job of being an educator is just as analytic and intellectual as it is interpersonal, political, and practical. I believe it's time we own that.

What Are the Recurring Themes?

There are a host of major takeaways I will present in the chapters that follow, and I don't want to spoil the fun by giving them all away here. But you will see a few recurring themes woven throughout the book:

- Resistance is normal and healthy.
- Resistance can be productive for students and for educators.
- Resistance is guaranteed whenever we highlight differences in ability.
- Resistance is often rooted in inequity.
- Resistance is a symptom of a problem, not the problem itself.
- Misunderstanding resistance hurts everyone, including us.
- We frequently provoke resistance through our practices.
- We need to be careful not to romanticize resistance.

Each of these themes will be explored, explained, and applied in multiple ways using insights from the four domains. As you begin to recognize these themes in your work and consider changing your approaches with students, I recommend returning to this brief listing to see how your own thinking may have changed. How has your understanding of these themes shifted? What practices may need revision as a result? And as you ponder your own development and practice, you might consider using these themes as conversation starters with curious colleagues. As with anything exciting or challenging, an idea is often enhanced when shared.

A Contradiction and a Promise

At the meta-level, this books stands against the backdrop of relentless pathologizing that pervades our culture's depictions of and rhetoric about youth. Our "kids these days" are marketed to as hapless consumers, exploited as cheap labor, recruited as cannon fodder, feared as criminals in the making, objectified as sex symbols, overmedicated as unruly patients, and dismissed as mindlessly self-indulgent. Understood as subhuman, they are to be controlled. Add to this the observation that adults often project their own anxieties and desires onto those whose lives are still mostly in front of them (jealous anyone?), and it's no wonder the mechanisms and institutions we create to serve youth seem more guided by distrust than anything else. To argue for an increased attention to student resistance—not to silence and punish it, but to listen to and integrate it—may seem countercultural, and that's because it is.

It's also why, in some sense, I will be arguing a contradiction: *when we engage student resistance, we should neither demand that students comply nor comply with students' demands.* This statement will strike many as unrealistic if not dangerous. We need students to comply because we're in charge of their safety, security, and growth. Indeed, that is true, but human beings have done some rather horrific things over the millennia in the name of safety, security, and growth, and I don't think education gets a free pass just because its focus is learning. We demand that students comply with all sorts of things even though a cursory analysis reveals our purposes are sometimes suspect and the impacts are often inequitable. "But isn't student resistance often destructive?" you might ask. Absolutely, it is. It can be misguided, self-defeating, annoying, and downright oppressive. But the same can be said about compliance. This is why we need the resources of resistance as much as we need the predictability of compliance. We need to be more curious about the causes of resistance and less dedicated to its eradication.

In the end, by questioning our kids-these-days rhetoric, I want to show that we cannot create a better world if we make our students into quiet, compliant vessels of our own factoids and insecurities. Student resistance offers a collective opportunity to make education relevant, responsive, and rigorous. And in that opportunity is youth's chance to emerge into adulthood prepared to handle the challenges that face us all. In essence, our students' pushback will move us forward. That's the contradiction of resistance. That's its promise.

PART I

UNDERSTANDING RESISTANCE THEORETICALLY

Determined

Though she is ashamed to admit it, Karen is starting to think of career options outside education. She feels that she is losing a battle, but she isn't even sure what she is fighting. Teaching the lower-track biology classes at her high school, she is well acquainted with the challenges of convincing her students that classroom activities, homework, and tests are worth their effort. Karen knows she has a knack for relating well to her students, especially those considered "academic priority" by her district, and she enjoys the uphill struggle that work represents. She writes good lessons, makes things fun, keeps standards high, provides a lot of support, avoids giving detentions and referrals for misbehavior, and makes frequent calls home. Karen is confident she is a good teacher.

But lately she feels as though her students and the system are conspiring to fail. Many of her students of color, her English learners, and those from families struggling with poverty seem almost determined to disappoint. She doesn't even like to hear herself think that word, *determined*, but some days the word seems appropriate, as if students' behavior is intentional.

"Why do I try so hard when they won't?" she remarks to a colleague. "And I am talking about both my students and my colleagues."

When she looks at the sources of support available in the district and community and examines school resources, policies, priorities, and staffing decisions, she feels the same word creep into her thinking—*determined*. The more she looks, the more it seems as if the school is determined to fail the neediest kids just as much as those kids seem determined to fail school.

When she expresses these sentiments to her fellow teachers, one colleague advises her, "Just teach the ones that want to learn, and forget about the rest," while another admits in a whisper, "It got easier for me when I just lowered my expectations."

Knowing such approaches are wrong but not entirely knowing why, Karen believes she is at a tipping point in her career as an educator. Unsure about whether to try to change the system or her students (or both) and feeling doubtful about whether either effort will yield significant results given the resistance on both sides, Karen knows she needs to change the way she thinks or change jobs. She just doesn't know where to begin.

CHAPTER 2

"Making Trouble Makes It Worse"
Theories of Social Reproduction

WE TEND TO act as if the way we perceive the world is the way the world is. We also tend to respond to people as if they are (in actuality) who we think they are (in theory). Sometimes we're right and our theories match reality. Other times we're wrong and things get messy. Whatever actions we choose and whichever beliefs we retain, they're always driven by our assumptions and directed by our interpretations. To claim that theory is somehow separate from practice or that our practices are somehow distinct from our theories is to miss an important point: all of us are constantly operating according to some theory. It behooves us to explore those theories a bit to see whether they're capable of doing the work we need them to do in our schools. As we'll find, they often aren't.

We therefore begin our analysis of student resistance by examining key theories at the foundation of educators' work in schools. To do this, we will need to ask questions—challenging questions—about the beliefs and assumptions that shape our responses to student resistance. For example, one of the toughest questions we can ask about public education is whether it exacerbates or ameliorates social inequities. Does schooling tend to worsen society's stratifications, or does it generally enhance social mobility and opportunity? More specifically, do the differences in academic achievement that we observe across various subgroups (based on race, ethnicity, socioeconomic class, gender, linguistic heritage, immigrant status, sexuality, and disability) tend to increase or decrease as a result of public school education?

In my experience, we are often reluctant to ask questions like these. Even though the questions contain a set of assumptions about the influences and outcomes of resistance, who is most affected by it, and who is responsible for it, our need for immediate and pragmatic "solutions" often overrides our curiosity about causes, effects, and ethics. We prefer quick answers over tough questions, short-term fixes over long-term struggles. In our rush to get things done, we regularly triage what to do from moment to moment and seldom take time to examine the larger forces and ideologies that are always shaping circumstances in and around the classroom. Those of us who are somehow able to take precious time and energy to consult scholarship can end up mired in esoteric and inaccessible texts written by scholars who seem far too removed from the day-to-day realities of the classroom to offer much help. Or the literature describes educational issues in a way that may be too complex or too bleak for those of us who need a simple boost to get through the next day. So we rationalize that avoiding scholarship is the right thing to do, or we dismiss the value of intellectual inquiry so that we can go about our business as usual. Unfortunately, when it comes to reading and responding to student resistance, this is a dangerous trend.

The findings and theoretical assertions in educational scholarship require our exploration for a host of reasons, chief among them their ability to reveal systemic problems that are often invisible to those of us who are embedded within "the system." Basically, we can't see many of these problems because we're immersed in them. Once we step back to gain the larger view, we're able to see what's happening and recognize where to act to produce the best outcomes. In other words, to understand why students resist us and why they resist the systems we represent, we first need to recognize what might be worth resisting. This chapter is designed to do just that.

A Theory of Cyclical Origins and Outcomes

There are two theoretical traditions largely responsible for framing and investigating resistance in school settings, and the two sides don't exactly get along. On one side are the *social reproductionists*. They argue that schools should be theorized not as even playing fields on which merit is awarded based on effort and accomplishment. Instead, social reproductionists understand schools to be one of the chief institutions that reproduce if not exacerbate preexisting social hierarchies. These theorists point out that if you enter school poor, you are likely to finish school poor, and that if you enter school wealthy, you are likely to finish school wealthy.

Resistance theorists, on the other hand, argue that schools do indeed perpetuate social inequity but that resistance and change are also inevitable. For these theorists, learning in a democracy requires learning how to *be democratic*, which involves critique, deliberation, inclusion, and resistance against the social order—not just blind deference to it.

Both the social reproductionists and the resistance theorists are right, and in some ways, both are wrong. This chapter outlines why the theory of social reproduction is valuable for professional educators even when its assertions may overstate the situation. Chapter 3 then conducts a detailed investigation of resistance theories that have emerged in part as a response to the social reproductionists. The conversation between these two camps supplies a theoretical backdrop for the psychological, political, and pedagogical inquiries in later chapters.

The Myth of Meritocracy

Let's start with an historical example. Horace Mann, the great educational reformer and politician of the mid-nineteenth century, wrote the following in his annual report to the Massachusetts State Board of Education in 1848: "Education then, beyond all other devices of human origin, is a great equalizer of the conditions of men—the balance wheel of the social machinery. I do not here mean that it so elevates the moral nature as to make men disdain and abhor the oppression of their fellow men . . . But I mean that it gives each man the independence and the means by which he can resist the selfishness of other men. It does better than to disarm the poor of their hostility toward the rich: it prevents being poor."[1]

In Mann's (gender-exclusive) view, schools represent the highest ideals of a free, democratic society, in which all citizens can achieve their aspirations in direct proportion to their effort and developed talents. If you want it, this message says, all you have to do is work hard to get it and public schools will be there to facilitate your ambitions, regardless of your background. This, in essence, is the promise of a meritocracy.

Just over fifty years later, in an address to the New York City High School Teachers Association, Woodrow Wilson, the president of Princeton University and the eventual governor of New Jersey and two-term president of the United States, said this:

> We want to do two things in modern society. We want one class of persons to have a liberal education, and we want another class of persons, a very much larger class, of necessity, in every society, to forgo the privileges of a liberal education and fit themselves to perform specific difficult manual tasks. You cannot train them for both in the time that you have at your disposal. They must make a selection, and you must make a selection . . . [W]e should not confuse ourselves with regard to what we are trying to make of the pupils under

our instruction. We are either trying to make liberally-educated persons out of them, or we are trying to make skillful servants of society along mechanical lines, or else we do not know what we are trying to do.[2]

The juxtaposition of these two quotes illustrates a long-standing tension in public education. As educational historian David Labaree frames it, the tension arises from simultaneously wanting our schools to promote equality while also expecting them to preserve advantage.[3] We try to meet both desires by preparing students for the different roles they will need to play in society and in the economy. In the process, schools examine, sort, and rank students so that we can distinguish students who will give orders from those who will take them. Through teacher nomination, testing, curriculum differentiation, ability grouping, and discipline, schools are expected to identify who will be the CEO and who will work on the factory floor. The differing allocation of resources to schools and the varying distribution of teaching talent also help channel some students into the upper echelons of society while sending others into the working class (or working poor).

Up until the middle of the twentieth century, scholars generally assumed that such decisions about allocation were based largely on talent and effort (this, despite centuries of resistance by those who were least rewarded by these decisions).[4] But by the 1950s and 1960s, evidence began to accumulate that education was far less successful at promoting equality of opportunity than it was at reinforcing inequalities based on race, class, gender, ethnicity, disability, and other demographic factors. Wilson's statement quoted above suggests that this reinforcement of social inequities was not just a by-product of an imperfect system but rather was an intentional component of its mission. The 1954 *Brown v. Board of Education* decision by the U.S. Supreme Court and the succession of legislative reforms that followed it were enacted precisely because evidence was abundant that schools needed significant modifications if they were to realize Horace Mann's equalizing vision.[5] Since then, countless studies in the twenty-first century have confirmed that schools continue to rank students according to injurious social categories and teach differently, and have different expectations for, racially, ethnically, and socioeconomically stratified student populations.[6] Because of this history and because the current landscape suggests serious inequities in educational practices and outcomes, the claim that schools are meritocracies may represent a myth more than reality.

Seeing the System: Structural Analysis

If the claim that schools are meritocracies should be entertained with suspicion, what then explains the disparities in achievement between different groups? What causes inequity? For most of the last half of the twentieth century, educational philosophers and critical theorists tended to answer these questions through *structural analyses*, that is, through examinations of the formal, institutional, legal, procedural, and economic systems that frequently shape people's lives and their location in social hierarchies. These scholars concluded that schools are structured—designed and organized—to mirror and subsequently reproduce the divisions and ranks evident in society. Educational philosopher Henry Giroux asserts that schools should not "be analyzed as institutions removed from the socioeconomic context in which they are situated." Instead, schools should be viewed as "political sites" actively invested in the control of language, the construction of meaning, and the generation of implicit and explicit rules about how groups are to understand one another. For Giroux, the seemingly "commonsense values and beliefs that guide and structure classroom practice" are not universal givens but rather are social inventions based on specific and traceable assumptions designed to maintain the status quo and benefit the ruling classes.[7] Though this characterization of schools may sound like some insidious plot by moustache-twirling evildoers bent on world domination and the subjugation of the masses, the inequity-sustaining character of schools is much less obvious but far more pervasive than this. Without the theoretical preparation, however, most of us won't be prepared to see just how extensive the problem is.

Structural analyses suggest that if the inequities of education are intentional, they arise from the systemic features of language, culture, and institutions more than any conspiratorial leaders within them. Schools naturally reference and transmit the prevailing sentiments and expectations of society. If we consider those components discriminatory, then it makes sense that schools would reproduce such discrimination in the absence of efforts to the contrary. Change is prevented by manipulating language, by introducing divisions between groups so that each will see the other as dangerous or uncivilized, and by denigrating those who resist (as troublemakers, deviants, rebels, etc.). When someone violates prevailing norms within an institution, in this case a school, people use language to frame the student as totally at fault, a practice that renders the school and society blameless. We rarely consider that systemic circumstances may have compelled the student to act against school norms (e.g., unfair practices, discriminatory tests, inequitable distribution of resources), because to do so would require us to question our own assumptions about the seeming neutrality of our schools. Instead, we often explain the behavior by claiming that the student has a bad attitude, comes from a troubled family, or is too attached to a culture that doesn't value education.

The structure of schooling—how it is designed, organized, and rationalized—makes it difficult for individuals to claim that being poor, rejected, humiliated, or oppressed is the reason for their resistant behavior. This is because the structure itself (which includes the belief that schools are meritocracies) makes that poverty, rejection, humiliation, and oppression seem like it was chosen, like it was deserved.[8] In this way, structural problems get framed as personal failures.

Analyzing the structure of things can get us out of this trap. For example, imagine an English language learning student of color from a low-income, "working poor" family. Now imagine that the student attends an under-resourced school in a neighborhood with high rates of crime, poor air quality, limited social services, and a lack of nutritious food options, and is taught by underprepared teachers who use outdated curricula and culturally exclusionary forms of pedagogy. A structural analysis of that student's propensity to struggle in and potentially resist school would reveal that the student's behavior is not a personal failure but rather is a personal *effect* of how society has structured his or her experience. This structural analysis flips the causality to reveal context as the primary instigator of individual student decision making. As we will see, this shift in causality makes all the difference when we are interpreting student resistance in the classroom.

Being Named and Normalized

French philosopher Luis Althusser makes an important contribution to structural analysis with his theory of the "ideological state apparatus." Influenced by Marxism, Althusser attempts to make sense of how different social classes relate to one another and how social stratifications seem to persist (if not strengthen) over time. Explaining how capitalism reproduces itself in each subsequent generation despite its glaring inequities, Althusser draws a distinction between what he calls "state apparatuses" and "ideological state apparatuses." He theorizes that state apparatuses are the components of a society that keep order primarily through threat of punishment or violence. Examples include the police, the military, the FBI, courts, and prisons. Ideological state apparatuses, on the other hand, are the institutions that maintain control over the population mostly through less overt but still coercive means. Churches, temples, professional organizations, unions, country clubs, families, and the media are all examples of ideological state apparatuses. Whereas state apparatuses accomplish their goals by threatening or causing pain, ideological state apparatuses function by using ideology. And for Althusser, the most dominant ideological state apparatus is education.

According to Althusser, what makes education so dominant is the way ideology presents itself. To those within the system, the ideology does not appear to be ideological. It does not feel imposed or even invented. It feels customary, right, normal. It is taken for granted as "the way things are." For example, schools routinely segregate students according to age. Seventh-graders are separated from eighth-graders, and freshmen never take classes with seniors. Why? Is this the best practice? Should some subjects or concepts be taught across grade levels? Should we accept the theory that age should be the main criteria for sorting kids? Other examples: school is canceled during the summer; girls who get pregnant in high school are diverted to alternative educational programs; students who get in a fight are automatically suspended; class clowns are sent to the principal's office. Again, why?

We continue to do each of these "normal" things—even when confronted with evidence that they may work contrary to our expressed goals—because the ideology in schools makes them seem commonsensical if not self-evident. We might look out and see that older and younger kids are different, so it makes sense to group them according to those perceived differences. We may think holding school in June, July, and August is just un-American. We maybe perceive pregnant girls in high school as a distraction, so we send them away. We might believe that students who fight need to be taught a lesson, so we send them home for a day or two to think about it. And we may think class clowns just want attention, so we send them down the hall, where they won't receive any.

Althusser suggests that the power to convince students and educators to internalize these norms is what makes public education an ideological state apparatus. When these norms become *normal* they appear to be obvious or true. And if an individual spends enough time working within an ideological apparatus, the constructedness of such norms becomes hard to see. The ideology becomes our reality, and we stop questioning it. As a result, people do not feel like they are internalizing or deciding to believe anything, because *it is the way it is.* According to Althusser, those who internalize the ideology and who remain consistently compliant with regard to its expectations may actually experience the apparatus as a place of freedom. To them, everything "just feels right" and they therefore become invested in the system's perpetuation. Those who question it are told, "Stop rocking the boat. This is how we do it here."

This normalizing process shapes not only how educators understand students' needs but also who those students become. For example, researchers have long noted that schools tend to teach working-class kids in a more regimented fashion, emphasizing discipline, obedience, punctuality, and behavioral control. It's what those students need, we reason, so that they will be prepared for factory or service-sector jobs in which the necessity to follow orders is crucial.[9] In middle-class or upper-class schools, however (or in tracked classrooms where most of the students come from such backgrounds), the pedagogical approaches tend to be far more open. Students in these contexts are encouraged to explore their own questions, negotiate meanings, express their perspectives, and take more electives. Direct supervision is rare in these settings, and behavior is controlled less by rewards and punishments and far more by stated and unstated norms that students are expected to internalize as "normal." These students are prepared for leadership. *It is not just that schools teach different students differently as a way of preparing them for their predetermined positions in society; it is that schools convince teachers, students, and communities that those differences are natural instead of invented.* We will return to this foundational insight in subsequent chapters.

Hailing

One way the ideological state apparatus of education convinces people of the naturalness of their positions is through what Althusser calls "hailing." Hailing is the addressing of someone within and through an ideological apparatus. This practice of naming broadcasts how a person will be understood and is expected to behave. Hailing, therefore, shapes how individuals will choose to act and, crucially, how they understand themselves.

Althusser gives the example of a police officer shouting at a citizen, "Hey, you there!" But for our purposes, let's imagine it is a student being addressed by school security in this way. Regardless of whom this exclamation was directed toward, most students within earshot will likely turn to see if they themselves are the one being hailed, even if they know they have done nothing wrong. They might even get a sinking feeling that they are in trouble as they turn to see if the shouting school official is looking at them. That very turning is evidence that students have internalized an ideology of security, surveillance, and punishment and, to some extent, have accepted their relationship with the school as subjects. If a school official yells, students know they should turn to see if they are the one being addressed because that school official's function is to provide order and discipline, whereas the students' function is to be watched, directed, and potentially reprimanded.

Being hailed in this manner automatically and immediately places the student in a specific relationship with the school, and if the hailing is repeated often enough and in sufficiently varied ways (through curricula, discipline, greetings, nicknames, parent-teacher conferences, dress codes, etc.), the relationship is strengthened such that it becomes natural. Likewise, when educators refer to students as "class clowns," "gang bangers," "at-risk," "prom king/queen," or "student body president," the terms are far more than labels. In an ideological state apparatus, the labels become roles.

Althusser proposes that if public education is largely run by the ruling classes, then it makes sense that the system would reflect the ideologies typically found in those cultures. And it would also make sense that the structures of the resulting system would produce expectations that privilege the worldview and behaviors of the dominant group. Hailing is the way ideological state apparatuses name their compliant participants (who display "appropriate" and "respectful" behavior) and their rebellious detractors (who may be "inappropriate" or "disrespectful") so that decisions can be made about who will play which roles and how the institutions should respond. Hailing creates the role of "good student" or "bad student" and assigns people to that role. Again, there is no evil intent here—just a natural outcome of a system's membership and design. Educational philosopher and activist Paolo Freire puts it this way: "It would be tremendously naive to ask the ruling class in power to put into practice a kind of education which can work against it . . . [F]rom the point of view of the ruling class, of those in power, the main task for systematic education is to reproduce the dominant ideology."[10]

In the end, Althusser suggests that if beliefs drive people's actions, then the construction and propagation of beliefs will determine what people think they can do with their talents. And if institutions can use ideology and hailing to control what people believe about themselves, those institutions don't have to worry too much about controlling how those individuals will behave—people will control themselves.

How the Rich Get Richer Through Cultural Capital

The French philosopher Pierre Bourdieu also wanted to explain how social disparities between classes seem to continue from generation to generation. Like Althusser's theories, Bourdieu's theories directly pertain to public education. Bourdieu's explanation of social reproduction involves the inequitable distribution of what he terms "cultural capital." Analyzing how the economic system of capitalism structures opportunity, he observes that the accumulation of financial wealth is the result of an individual's access to monetary and material capital as well as his or her ability to leverage those items to produce more wealth (i.e., "You have to have money to make money"). Bourdieu notes that the same process occurs with culture. If an individual's modes of speaking, acting, and relating are favored by the dominant group, that individual will tend to be more successful than someone who does not possess those characteristics. Those who win possess the cultural capital that makes them look like winners, and those who lose by failing to acquire the required cultural capital look like losers. Social disparities are therefore rooted in individuals' and groups' ownership of, or access to, the desired forms of cultural capital. If you have a lot of cultural capital, you get access to more of it, and if you have little cultural capital, you have less opportunity to accumulate more—and you may even be punished for that deficit. As we will see in later chapters, school discipline is often a key contributor to this process.

Bourdieu argues that social reproduction occurs in each subsequent generation not because youth necessarily want to live the same lifestyle as their parents but because access to specific behaviors, types of knowledge, activities, appearances, and the spaces in which those components are taught provide pathways into jobs that are inextricably linked with a person's social class. If you grew up among auto mechanics and housekeepers, you have a pretty good idea of how to act around people in those positions and how to attain and sustain that lifestyle. The same is true for the child who was exposed regularly to financiers, senators, doctors, or the leaders of industry. Your familiarity with the expectations within a particular culture becomes a form of capital that can be used to gain additional access, greater legitimacy, and a higher status within that culture. In short, if you know how to act the part, you will likely get the part.

For Bourdieu, it makes no sense to assert that one culture is better than another even though society clearly rewards some cultures far more than others. Bourdieu observes that all cultural rankings are arbitrary. Anytime we travel abroad or interact with cultures different from our own, the arbitrariness of those norms becomes obvious. Bourdieu also says that these arbitrary rankings tend to become normative, as if they are descriptive rather than invented. For example, driving on the right side of the road feels normal to those who learned to operate a vehicle in the United States, but it feels weird if not unsettling when these same people try to navigate London streets from the left side. The decision to drive on one side or the other is wholly arbitrary, but it *feels* normal once you internalize its rules and behaviors.

Borrowing from Althusser, Bourdieu proposes that true power arises from the ability to make a decision seem like it is part of the natural, objective order of things, to make it seem normal. To achieve this naturalization, those with significant cultural capital point to "objective" divisions in society (e.g., those between men and women, Whites and Blacks, wealthy and poor, old and young, immigrants and naturalized citizens) to justify the continued separation and ranking of such groups. "Those people," they might argue, "don't have what it takes." And because cultural capital is unevenly distributed, which allows some people to have much more of "what it takes" than others, the statement that some people don't have what it takes can seem descriptive. Though the system is structured to provide cultural capital to some more than others and to allocate rewards according to that distribution, the failure to procure "what it takes" is seen as an individual flaw rather than a predetermined systemic outcome. The genius of this normalization is that the established order that created these divisions and then ranked some forms of cultural capital over others appears self-evident, taken for granted, invisible.

So how does this relate to education? Though there are multiple implications of Bourdieu's work for schools, I suggest two main takeaways.[11] First, those from the middle and upper classes tend to be highly invested in the ranking mechanisms of schools because those systems provide tremendous justification for the privileges that middle-class (and White, heterosexual, Christian, English-speaking, able-bodied, etc.) members already receive as a result of that system. The naturalization of cultural capital makes the beneficiaries feel like they earned and deserve the privileges they enjoy, while it makes those who have less cultural capital look as though they chose that situation. Consequently, Bourdieu's analysis suggests that the system will be perpetuated less through people's conscious and cynical manipulations of resources and more through the "normal" everyday actions of those working within schools doing what they think is best.

The second implication is that educators will tend to reject criticisms of the system and suppress attempts to resist or reform it because that same system is what likely made the educators successful in the first place. "If it ain't broke, don't fix it," they might say, because to them, it doesn't seem broken at all. To expose its arbitrariness would be to question the very system that approves of and rewards their culture, their work, and their identity. In this way, Bourdieu shows how *social reproduction in schools can proceed as much from bland deference to norms as it can from overt forms of social control.* Again, this crucial insight will inform much of the analyses in later chapters.

Stacked Decks and Class-Based Determinism

While Bourdieu's theory shows how schools can rationalize the social mobility of some and normalize the failure of others on the basis of students' different accumulations of cultural capital, the theory begs a question: How do schools actually accomplish this sorting and ranking? In *Schooling in Capitalist America,*

Samuel Bowles and Herbert Gintis attempt to provide an answer. Their highly influential study traces the way schools emulate the economic system in which they reside. Bowles and Gintis observe that the economy is structured in layers with executive classes that preside over industry, government, and finance; managerial classes that occupy middle-level positions; and the labor classes that make up the workforce. According to Bowles and Gintis, schools largely correspond to this layering. They mirror the larger economy by using structures, expectations, practices, and decisions that track working-class youth into workforce employment, channel middle-class kids into managerial positions, and propel the elite into executive-level roles. For example, Bowles and Gintis describe how schools serving middle-class and upper-class students often present curricula as inquiry, offer an array of electives and pacing options, refrain from direct forms of supervision, and provide opportunities for extracurricular enrichment (field trips, clubs, "gifted and talented" education, advanced placement classes, international baccalaureate programs, etc.). In these school environments, knowledge is constructed more than it is received and rules are learned so that they may be manipulated and rewritten. Schools like this teach students to lead.

In contrast, Bowles and Gintis show that schools serving low-income and working-class families typically adopt more regimented approaches to curriculum, classroom management, and discipline. Through required uniforms, security- or police-patrolled hallways, strict school-day and classroom routines, top-down disciplinary procedures, mandated content delivery, and didactic pedagogical techniques, students in these environments are prepared to be bossed rather than become bosses. Trained to receive knowledge more than construct it, students in these contexts are encouraged to learn the rules in order to follow them, which subsequently leads the students to assume lower-status positions in the economy. Bowles and Gintis show that schools justify this class-based differentiation by basing it on students' apparent "gifts." Even though the procedures used to measure these supposed merits are established and endorsed by those who most benefit from the rankings, the structure of schooling socializes students into accepting the existing social order through its own self-perpetuating logic. In essence, the economy produces school structures that produce roles that produce people who (re)produce the economy.

Though compelling, *Schooling in Capitalist America* does present a closed, all-encompassing system, one that seems to determine, not just influence, an individual student's social location. Bowles and Gintis's argument, however, overstates the power of economic and educational systems to lock individuals into the same social locations their parents occupy. Some scholars following Bowles and

Gintis have therefore sought to explain the attempts by groups and individuals to undermine or overcome this supposedly closed system. Paul Willis's *Learning to Labour* represents one of the first and perhaps the most influential of those accounts.

The Trap of Resisting School

Learning to Labour is an ethnographic examination of the subculture of working-class English teenage boys, particularly their behaviors in, and beliefs about, school. Similar to the factory-floor tactics that their parents sometimes used to slow the pace of work in their industrial jobs, Willis's youth were observed to disrupt classroom routines using jokes, various forms of misbehavior, and aggression. "The lads," as they were known, were highly critical of the meritocratic messages their teachers and community conveyed. Because the school represented middle-class values and conventions that the boys felt devalued their working-class neighborhoods, homes, and families, the lads repudiated the education being offered to them. Setting themselves up and against the more wealthy and academically successful students in their school and the teachers who the lads perceived as favoring those students, the lads chose behaviors that conflicted with the school's prevailing culture. Determined not to be perceived as snobs, they engaged in fighting and staged various classroom disruptions, always looking for opportunities to "have a laff," typically at the expense of the students they perceived to be full of themselves due to their greater status and success in school. The lads also took a decidedly anti-intellectual stance against the curriculum and how it was taught, dismissing the value of lessons, neglecting assigned work, or deliberately underperforming in the classroom rather than risking broadcasting their compliance with a system they felt could not guarantee any upward mobility.

Though they recognized that conforming to teacher expectations might allow some of their group to rise up and out of their working-class origins, the lads reasoned that the chances of improving their social location were so remote that making fun of other students, interrupting class routines, and getting in fights offered better opportunities for social bonding. Rather than trade their compliance for grades, or their working-class pride for their teachers' middle-class knowledge, the lads preferred the comradeship and power they generated with their peers through "having a laff," partying, and fighting. In the process, the lads often amplified their masculinity and expressed their perceived racial superiority by oppressing girls and denigrating ethnic minorities. They also failed school.

Many theorists and researchers have claimed that Willis solves the problem that Bowles and Gintis present, namely, how to account for resistance within a closed and determined system.[12] These scholars argue that Willis drastically departs from reproduction theory and creates an entirely new field of inquiry now generally understood as *resistance theory*. In doing so, Willis helped to generate a fresh area of exploration that focuses less on structural aspects of schooling and more on individuals' and groups' resistance to it (he is largely credited with inventing the field of critical ethnography). He also shattered the overly deterministic view of the passive and ignorant student who is duped into following class-based rules. But in the end his analysis still indicates that the lads reinforced if not totally reproduced the very same class divisions they rejected in the first place. In this way, *Learning to Labour* provides a detailed account of how student opposition can sometimes reproduce social stratification rather than dismantle it. This is why some have called *Learning to Labour* the story of "how the winner loses."[13]

The Hard Truths of Social Reproduction Theories

There can be little doubt that the social reproduction theories just discussed cast schools in an unflattering light. They also portray resistance as hopeless if not self-destructive. Social reproductionists understand schools as indispensable components in (or even the main drivers of) a social and economic machine that oppresses many to privilege a few. Whether their theories present this outcome as intentional, accidental, or natural, the educational system has an insidious agenda: the system either sustains or makes worse the disparities so often bemoaned in our society. Social reproductionists therefore crack open the shiny veneer of public education's promise to equalize opportunity and enhance social mobility. In doing so, they give us good reason to be wary of rhetoric that schools are places where "all children can learn" or "no child [will be] left behind." Bleak as it may be, social reproduction theories provide us with necessary suspicion.

Why Educators Resist Social Reproduction Theories

Regrettably, the revelations from social reproduction come at a price. Unless we look elsewhere for alternative explanations, the educator and the student can be left stranded in a cascading, no-win situation:

1. Schooling is unfair, structured by and biased in favor of those with privilege.
2. Marginalized students resist the unfairness of school, oppose the way they are labeled and tracked within it, and reject the exclusion that

occurs when those with more cultural capital are provided with more advantage.

3. But by resisting this unfairness in a way that refuses school, students reproduce (or worsen) their lower status by cutting themselves off from the primary mechanism of their social mobility—their education.

In this model, teachers, counselors, school psychologists, administrators, social workers, and parents are all depicted as cogs in a larger oppressive system. Students fare no better—they are helpless dupes. Even students who recognize the unfairness and act to subvert it engage in forms of resistance that are, self-defeating, system-perpetuating, and counterproductive. Their valiant and often ingenious forms of opposition serve only to anchor them in their social strata. Even if a student's resistance is experienced as personally gratifying and intellectually honest, the result seems hopeless.

At this point, you may feel the desire to retreat from these theories to go think about something a little more promising. Gardening perhaps. Maybe a romantic comedy on TV. Or just a long walk. Admittedly, the rather depressing implications of social reproduction theory can offend the convictions and aspirations of most if not all educators. We want to—*need* to—believe that the work we do matters, that it makes a positive difference. Who wants to be shown that individual educators and students, despite their good intentions and best efforts, perpetuate an unjust and closed system with a predetermined, exclusionary outcome? Who wants to be a cog in an oppressive machine? And what's the point of doing anything if the system is so pervasively rigged and all efforts are compromised from the very beginning? Questions like these suggest that Henry Giroux is right when he calls social reproduction theory "a blue-print for cynicism and despair."[14]

Indeed, the pessimism and determinism of social reproduction theory is its fatal flaw.[15] The claim that the structural, cultural, and behavioral components of education all conspire to produce institutions and individuals that are incapable of mounting any effective challenge to the status quo has been roundly critiqued for decades now, largely because of its defeatist themes. In fact, scholars from nearly every conceivable subdiscipline of educational research outright reject the contention that the system is totally foreclosed or that no one can change it. The notion of powerless educators contradicts the research findings regarding who is most likely to innovate, reform, and improve schools (the answer: it's educators). The idea that curricula can only serve the interests of the dominant culture completely ignores the kind of culturally responsive, progressive, rigorous, and justice-enhancing materials that educators create daily. And the assertion that school practices and procedures only constrain students' potential overlooks the many ways educators, administrators, and parents collaborate to build schools that cultivate each student's unique possibilities.

Some educators intentionally ignore social reproduction theory, employing an ignorance-is-bliss attitude. Others may consult theories of social reproduction only to end up immobilized by despair, resulting in a "read 'em and weep" response. But we should not let the pessimism accompanying such scholarship be an excuse to remain passive or to refrain from joining others in the hard work of teaching and learning. The theories may be hopeless, but the real-life work most definitely is not.

The Importance of Overcoming Pessimism

Picture a sailboat on the ocean on a day with sustained wind. Left alone, the boat will go wherever the wind blows it, eventually drifting far out to sea or crashing onto the shore. To sail the boat, the crew members need to understand the wind and manipulate it to make the boat go where they want to go even if the wind is directed elsewhere. After all, sailing would be somewhat pointless if a boat could only go where the wind pushed it. The power and beauty of sailing lies in the way the crew harnesses the wind for its purposes, and crews can do this even though the wind itself is invisible. To use the wind (and not be used by it), the crew has to pay attention to its signals—its sound, its feel on the skin, and how it ripples the water, ruffles the sails, and tosses gulls around in the sky. If sailors can read these signs and know how to position their sails, rudder, and keel, they can take the threat of wind and turn it into a thrill.

If social reproduction is the wind, educators are the crew. Without educators' critical analyses and careful interventions, social reproduction will likely push education toward the status quo or, worse, toward increased inequity. But just as sailors can actually steer sailboats *into* the wind, educators too can reverse the trends that social reproduction theories imply. For this to happen, educators, like a sailboat crew, must learn to recognize the signs and work hard to use the available tools to react accordingly. When they do, they can steer education in the direction they need it to go—even if they have to zigzag a bit to get there.

Similar to Howard Zinn's observation that "you can't be neutral on a moving train," the sailboat analogy attempts to depict how our actions as educators are forever occurring inside institutions that are headed in some direction, toward some goal. If we are not vigilant, we may default uncritically to the system's priorities and proclivities, which, as shown in this chapter, are often unjust and marginalizing. For example, educators who persist in the dominant belief that merit alone determines students' fates will likely adopt practices and support institutional routines that blame students for their failure rather than scrutinize components of the school that made such failure likely. Focusing on the students is crucial as long as that focus does not prevent us from analyzing larger institutional trends and cultural forces that shape the schools themselves. To know which classroom techniques can best overcome inequity and to know how to develop the relationships that best resist constraining ideologies, we must take the larger view—the structural view—and enable ourselves to oppose what we observe. Educational theorist Michael Apple outlines some of the steps we need to take:

> Understanding education requires that we situate it in the unequal relations of power in the larger society and in the realities of dominance and subordination—and the conflicts—that are generated by these relations . . . Rather than simply asking whether students have mastered a particular subject matter and have done well on our all-too-common tests, we should ask a different set of questions: Whose knowledge is this? How did it become "official"? What is the relationship between this knowledge and the ways in which it is taught and evaluated, and who has cultural, social, and economic capital in this society? Who benefits from these definitions of legitimate knowledge and from the ways schooling and this society are organized, and who does not?[16]

Social reproduction theories are one key part of that larger view, overdetermined and pessimistic as they are.

These insights have great consequence for how educators perceive and react to student resistance in the classroom. When educators neglect the social reproduction perspective, they may mistakenly identify student resistance as evidence of bad attitudes or poor motivation rather than strategic actions designed to oppose ideological assimilation. It is very easy to frame students as the problem whenever larger contexts are ignored. The danger of this myopia is especially acute when we consider educators' responsibility for testing, identifying, and ranking students according to criteria typically developed far from the context in which the criteria are ultimately applied. Willis argues for the enduring value of social reproduction theory despite its message of futility: "Schools may be about many things other than 'Reproduction' . . . But so long as the burden of selection/ sorting/examination is placed on schooling in an unequal and class[-stratified] society, then the 'Reproduction' perspective must be taken into account."[17] We can better understand the importance of resistance when we realize that institutions are never indifferent, that they have agendas that typically default to social reproduction, and that our actions within them always fall somewhere between complicity and defiance.

Promising Practices: Countering Social Reproduction

When we struggle to understand students' resistance and respond to it productively, we typically draw from a "bag of tricks" to try to reverse the situation. But in doing so, we often encounter only more resistance. When this downward spiral begins to happen, we sometimes confront the possibility that both the students and the system seem to be determined to fail each other, even though that prospect challenges common understandings of the purpose of education and runs contrary to what we think ought to be our students' goal. And when we look to our colleagues for support, we sometimes find that they seem more prepared to lower their expectations or simply accept failure from "students who do not want to learn" than to analyze the contexts in which that failure occurs. This can create a feeling of hopelessness and it can make us question both our own skills as educators and the capacity of our schools to meet the needs of our most disadvantaged students. To help us make sense of these situations and move from hopelessness to hope, we need both a new theoretical frame and some concrete practices.

Luckily, we educators can act in innumerable ways to make visible the patterns of social reproduction that often operate in classrooms and schools. Rather than massive, pie-in-the-sky campaigns of social change, which are sometimes too big and unattainable for those who need more immediate solutions, it's often best to choose practices that help raise local awareness of larger social forces at play in our schools so that we can prevent these forces from predetermining the outcomes of our efforts. To raise this awareness, we need a two-pronged approach. First, we need to question institutional priorities and procedures. Second, we need to examine the extent of our own participation in problematic trends and identify responses that most promise to reverse them.

Forming Critical-Friends Groups

To integrate both approaches, educators can form interdisciplinary critical-friends groups (CFG) at their school. CFGs are an intentional and sustained gathering of colleagues who meet regularly to analyze issues of context and practice in a focused, collaborative, and reflective setting.[18] The groups can be organized around specific topics, shared readings, examinations of practice, reform efforts, or any number of classroom- or school-related issues. CFGs tend to function best when facilitated by someone with CFG training and are often enhanced by the use of protocols (agreed-upon guidelines for a conversation). Protocols help keep the participants' attention focused on specific questions and help educators make highly nuanced transitions from theory to practice (and back again). Pressed for time and pressured to achieve results, educators often move too quickly to the technical, quick fixes (i.e., "Just tell me what I need to do in my class tomorrow"). Such expediency, however, can sidestep important theoretical analyses that might otherwise place such decisions in context.

When they are run well, CFGs help us see which of our practices might result from problematic ideologies or institutional assumptions we've taken for granted. The groups provide regular opportunities for us to ask hard questions about our students, our classrooms, and our schools' structural components that may (or may not) be contributing to academic failure. And when CFGs read and discuss scholars' explanations of how social reproduction can occur in and through school, educators can begin unpacking the assumptions, routines, and relationships that sometimes exacerbate inequities.

Conducting Participatory Action Research

Depending on what is discovered and discussed in a CFG, educators might extend the work further into participatory action research. An umbrella term for a range of activities, participatory action research generally describes a process of integrating work with data-driven research and eventual action that is aimed at enhancing social justice. Choosing to research *with* stakeholders rather than conduct research *on* them, participatory action researchers typically involve rather than just observe those who are most affected by institutions. As an example, educators might gather groups of students to ask them what most encourages and discourages them to succeed in school. Those same students may then take part in efforts to identify institutional, cultural, or ideological factors that hinder their achievement, and this can lead to collective actions that alter practices and reframe assumptions. At each step in the research, educators and students blend their experiences in the community with their observations to take concrete steps to produce positive change. Factors that contribute to social reproduction can therefore be identified, resisted, and ultimately overcome.

These practices (and many more that will be detailed in subsequent chapters) suggest that only when we are brave enough to recognize that schooling sometimes exacerbates social inequity can we begin to see the patterns and develop solutions to resist them. Though social reproduction may always loom as a persistent threat, countless examples of critical inquiries and collaborative actions in schools and communities demonstrate the capacity of individuals and groups to generate momentous change. The remainder of this book can be read largely as a testament to this exciting possibility.

Dance Moves

Midway through the tenth-grade spring standardized mathematics test, Mr. Hernandez looks over to see Shayla making silly faces at her classmates and silently performing dance moves in her seat. Standing up to get her attention, he walks over to Shalya's seat to find that she has drawn geometric designs instead of neatly filled-in bubbles on her Scantron form. He picks up her answer sheet and motions for her to accompany him into the hallway.

"What are you doing?" he asks quietly but firmly.

"Nothing," Shayla answers. "It's my test and my score and my pencil, so I can do what I want with it."

"But why don't you care about your score?" Mr. Hernandez asks.

"'Cause I don't. You know I'm gonna go to my junior year whether I pass or fail this thing. This test is for the school, not me."

Thinking about how to get back into class as quickly as possible to make sure this type of behavior is not spreading, Mr. Hernandez tells Shayla that her behavior is "disrespectful, disruptive, and disappointing." After telling her to retrieve her things, he goes to his desk, pulls out a referral, checks the boxes on the form for "insubordination," "disruption," and "one-day suspension" and sends Shayla to the office. She rolls her eyes, clicks her teeth, waves at her friends, and repeats the dance moves on her way out the door.

Later in the conference with the vice principal, Ms. O'Neil, Shayla is asked why she refuses to take the test seriously. Getting only an "I dunno" as a response, Ms. O'Neil asks a follow-up: "Are you worried you might not pass so you purposely made a joke of it?"

Shayla sighs then explains, "There's no point in the test, Ms. O'Neil. It's not required for graduation, and it's really only a test of the teacher. Besides, all we do is drill and practice and take quizzes in that class. It's so boring and I'm never gonna to use this stuff again in my life. And anyway, I am passing the class! I can do what I want on the test—freedom of speech!"

Mr. Hernandez then enters the office and catches up on the exchange. When it looks as though Ms. O'Neil may disapprove of the suspension, he offers this characterization: "Shayla does not respect my authority, does not value mathematics, does not care about succeeding in school, and is a negative influence on her peers. For other students' sake, I cannot allow this to continue, which is why I wrote the referral."

Picking up the phone, Ms. O'Neil wonders how she's going to communicate the situation to Shayla's parents.

CHAPTER 3

"You're Not the Boss of Me"
Resistance Theory

THE PREVIOUS CHAPTER presented social reproduction theories that trace schools' tendency to reinforce rather than reform social inequity. Though it may be a hard pill to swallow, an understanding of these theories helps vaccinate us from the disease of systemic cluelessness. Social reproduction theory reminds us that we are part of school systems, social systems, cultural systems, and political systems that profoundly influence our decision making, particularly when we're faced with students who resist. Knowing the tendencies within those systems— and within ourselves—can help us realize when resistance is appropriate. But we can't stop there. We need to keep moving to see how social reproduction can be reversed.

This chapter describes theories that counter the closed systems of social reproduction so that specific, productive, and emancipating practices can flourish whenever resistance is encountered in the classroom. As public intellectuals, we educators engage every day in the important work of translating theories into practices (and back again). A deeper analyses of complex theories can help us examine "commonsense" approaches that may be neither common nor sensible once subjected to closer scrutiny. Throughout these efforts, the point is to construct and possess good theories, not be constructed and possessed by them. Resistance theory shows us how that's done.

Resistance theory also serves as the counterpoint to the pessimism and determinism that pervades reproductive accounts of schooling. It focuses on the nature of student opposition, its antecedents and consequences, and how resistance can dismantle and remodel existing structures rather than simply fortify them.

Recognizing that all social life entails aspects of dominance and subordination, resistance theory asserts that absolute freedom from restrictions is just as impossible as absolute control over others. The theory also shifts our view of causes and effects so that we can learn to read student resistance authentically, critically, and productively. For these reasons and more, its value to educators is immense.

Escaping the Trap of Social Reproduction

As described in chapter 2, schools are often set up to privilege arbitrary standards of conduct and culturally exclusive forms of knowledge, and when students reject those requirements, the system points to their resistance as proof that the more "civilized" students deserve their predetermined rewards. Meanwhile "the rebels" are effectively cut off from the information and relationships they most need to extricate themselves from second-class status. In this view, resistance is framed not as a way out, but as part and parcel of the way the ruling class retains its status and the underclasses cement their subordinate location in the social hierarchy. As we'll see below, it's not so much that the social reproductionists were wrong; it's that they overstated their case.

Recognizing the Patterns but Rejecting the Conclusions

Scholars debate whether Willis's *Learning to Labor* refutes or reinforces Bowles and Gintis's *Schooling in Capitalist America*.[1] Both volumes, along with the theories of Althusser and Bourdieu, have been accused of framing marginalized youth as "merely cannon fodder for the capitalist factory" or as "dummies, dupes, or zombies" who rebel only to haplessly strengthen the system's fortress-like defenses.[2] By implication, educators are similarly cast. In reinforcing arbitrary norms, pathologizing resistant students' behaviors, and suppressing youth opposition, teachers and other educators are depicted as automatons capable of neither questioning nor challenging the status quo.

But anyone who has spent any amount of time in schools knows this is not (entirely) true. Certainly, the potential for social reproduction is there. What's more, the patterns of cultural exclusion and systemic marginalization are fairly obvious if you know where to look and dare to do so. The truth, however, is that students and their educators can and do successfully resist all the time. Institutions and individuals undoubtedly rely on problematic norms to label and punish "deviance," but they also encourage people to take control of their destinies, transform institutions, and produce more equitable outcomes. Social reproduction theories help us to see the cultural and structural features that necessitate (if not provoke) resistance, but the system those theories describe is not closed. People's life trajectories are not determined. Change is possible. Resistance makes a difference.

Cause and Effect

Moving from theories of social reproduction to more nuanced analyses of resistance changes how we view the school and students' occasional opposition to it. Figures 3.1 through 3.3 illustrate the progression of this logic. In figure 3.1, the belief that schools are meritocracies produces a specific cause-and-effect dynamic. The presumption that schools are equitable institutions and that student success depends solely on individual will, talent, and effort positions the students as the cause of any problems. By this logic, if the institutional context is understood to be normal and therefore innocent, those who disrupt or challenge it will be considered abnormal, guilty, the problem. Student resistance, in this case, is painted as deviance. Accordingly, school-based professionals who adhere to this perspective will likely seek to fix the "problem" by changing the students (or removing them from the institution) to avoid disturbing the status quo. This effectively holds only the students accountable for failure while it lets society, communities, schools, and educators off the hook.

Conversely, when the myth of meritocracy itself is questioned—that is, when theories of social reproduction are considered plausible—the cause-and-effect dynamic effectively reverses. The shading in figures 3.1 and 3.2 highlights how this change in perspective can shift where educators tend to locate the "problem." Where students were once considered deviants, figure 3.2 now suggests that the conditions within the school are considered the source of inequity. As a result,

FIGURE 3.1 When schools are understood to be meritocracies

The "problem" is located in the *student's* attitudes, behaviors, beliefs, upbringing, values, motivations, identity, or culture.

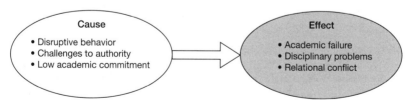

Student resistance = *deviance*

student behaviors previously understood to be *deviant* are now classified as *defiant*. This small change of just one letter nevertheless symbolizes a big shift in thinking.

When one asks, "What are students doing when they are resisting?" there is a big difference between the answer "They're *deviating* from an accepted norm," and "They're *defying* an unacceptable context." This shift from deviance to defiance is momentous because the causes of resistant behaviors are effectively relabeled as institutional rather than individual. Deviant students are thought to possess some enduring dysfunction that may be named using cultural references ("those people don't value education"), biological labels ("typical raging hormones," "looks like undiagnosed ADHD to me"), or psychological pseudodiagnoses ("anger management issues," "poor self-esteem"). But defiant students, on the other hand, are understood to be reacting against something. They have a personal, political, or moral agenda undergirding their opposition. Neither sick nor unstable, they're struggling against domination. Educators who adhere to the perspective depicted in figure 3.2 will likely seek to change the school more than students.

To carry this analysis further, figure 3.3 shows what can happen when theories of social reproduction are enhanced by theories of resistance. In this situation, educators and students may identify multiple causes of resistance as they examine how and why schools sometimes perpetuate inequity. But depending on whether that resistance is met with suppression or engagement, there are two quite divergent effects. On the left side of figure 3.3, we can see that the effects of suppression mirror those in the shaded regions of figures 3.1 and 3.2. That is, depending on our theory of schooling and resistance, we can read the same behaviors and events as either causes (figure 3.1) or effects (figure 3.2), or even as mediators that both have causes and produce effects (figure 3.3).

FIGURE 3.2   When schools are understood as contributors to social inequity

The "problem" is blamed on the *school's* attitudes, assumptions, community relations, history, values, practices, goals, and culture.

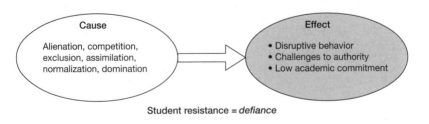

Student resistance = *defiance*

Take, for example, Willis's subjects in *Learning to Labor*. The lads' opposition apparently did nothing to politically inform or morally enlighten the educators, and Willis presented no evidence that their behaviors produced any social change. His point, in fact, was quite the opposite. The resistance Willis observed in his subjects only cemented their second-class status while the institution continued to reinforce business as usual. But was this the lads' fault? At some level, the school and the community are to blame for not engaging that resistance more productively. When the teachers, administrators, and support personnel framed

FIGURE 3.3   When resistance to schooling is understood as a response to inequitable contexts

Both the problem and the solution are located in *educators' and students'* attitudes, assumptions, culture, privilege, beliefs, values, goals, and/or practices.

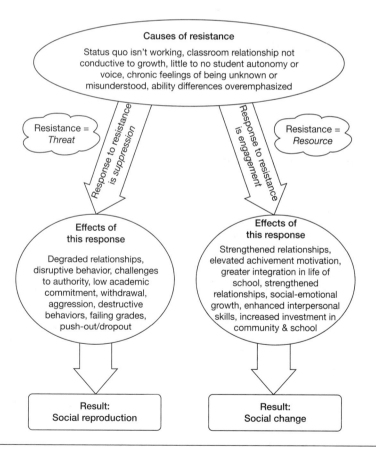

the students as the problem, the lads' resistance could only be read problematically. Were the lads' critiques heard, considered, and engaged by the community in a more substantive manner, the school might have transformed into a space in which the lads could be both working class and academically successful, where they could hold on to their roots and still attain the advantages that education offered. This suggests that educators often fail to properly respond to resistance either because they can't see the patterns of inequity or because they won't do the work to change those patterns.

Social reproduction theory helps us to see that when resistance is deemed a threat and suppression is the strategy used to deal with it, institutions will tend to duplicate or exacerbate social injustices. However, the analysis doesn't go far enough; resistance theory can also show that if individuals and institutions consider resistance a resource and respond to it with engagement, then social change can occur. In this case, the educators and students together represent both the problem and the solution. Resistance theory shows us how this is possible.

Resistance Theory or Theories?

To be fair, however, it is probably best to characterize resistance theory in plural form. Because of ongoing debates among scholars and practitioners, a single unifying definition, methodology, or characterization of resistance simply does not exist. Thus, we often refer to a multiplicity of resistance *theories* rather than a single theory. Nevertheless, several components appear consistently in characterizations of the field and will be described in the following sections. Knowing them will help us understand why student resistance is often an outcome of circumstances we constructed and relationships we formed—contexts that actually encourage opposition more than compliance.

Agency: Making the Self, Making the World

Framing the purposes of resistance theory, the educational philosopher Henry Giroux asserts that "resistance must be situated in a perspective that takes the notion of emancipation as its guiding interest."[3] A closed theoretical system in which individuals have no autonomy and produce little or no change would be incompatible with this purpose. As an alternative, resistance theorists present *agency*. Agency is both something that individuals possess (i.e., a capacity) and something that people do (i.e., a behavior).[4] Closely related to the concepts of volition, initiative, and intrinsic motivation, agency is a socioculturally mediated phenomenon: it does not exist in a vacuum but instead is always influencing and influenced by culture, institutions, and relationships. Students and teachers have agency when they can translate their intentions and desires into actions that have real consequences for themselves and others even when those actions are shaped by social forces beyond the individual's control. Resistance is therefore an expression of the individual's agency and an exercise in his or her ability to make things happen.

Authorship: Writing Your Own Story

In *Understanding Youth: Adolescent Development for Educators*, a book I cowrote with the developmental psychologist and researcher Michael J. Nakkula, we explore how identity formation in teens may be conceptualized as an "authoring" experience.[5] As children emerge into adult ways of knowing, being, and behaving, they typically seek to make their own way in the world, to be distinct, and to act in a manner that feels authentic to their self-understanding. Engaging a complex world, youth want to write their own story rather than have it written for them. "Let me do it!" they demand. "You're not the boss of me!" they assert. Adolescents also seek to belong, to feel connected, and to join others in collective action. Attempting to find the satisfying middle ground between isolation and enmeshment, youth are forever balancing internally felt desires with externally imposed messages and expectations. Thus, their identities (and ours) may be understood to be coauthored, and their actions co-constructed.

To illustrate the importance of agency to this authoring process, consider a thought experiment. After reading the next sentence, pause for a moment to reflect on your reaction.

You will resist this sentence.

What happened when you read that sentence? Did you say to yourself something like:

I will? No, I won't. Or wait, I guess I just did. Don't tell me what to do! But that sentence *did* tell me what I'd do, and I sort of did it, so I guess it's right. But by resisting it, I am also breaking its expectation, so it's also wrong. Who's in control here? *I* am. *Am* I?

If you felt somewhat trapped by the statement even as it accurately named your reaction, that hints at your desire to be the author of your own experience. When we are told what to do or how we will experience something, it can strip us of our agency and make us want to resist. This reaction is often intensified in teenagers, given how much of their daily lives are predetermined by adults.

Resistance theories consider the human desire for self-determination a central concern. For this reason, most resistance theories imagine students as authors more than marionettes. But because authorship takes place within cultures, ideologies, and institutions that expect some measure of compliance, *resistance is inevitable*. Individuals are always using, taking, rejecting, reformulating, inventing, and resisting the messages and demands society delivers, because individuals are much more than passive receivers of culture and ideology. Agency exists precisely because socialization is not merely absorption. It is in those resistant moments when students (and educators) create self-determining experiences that the individual's attempt at authorship is readily apparent.[6]

The Need for Assent in the Classroom

Extending the concepts of student agency and authorship further, sociologist and critical ethnographer Mary Haywood Metz describes "teachers' ultimate dependence on their students."[7] She observes that because the results of teaching reside in the minds and behaviors of students, it is the students who have the ultimate control over the relative success of teachers' efforts. Her contention is that anything accomplished in the classroom is radically dependent on student cooperation. No matter what the teacher does, if the students say no, it will not happen. Though "commonsense" depictions of classroom power dynamics trace a teacher's ability to win students' assent to his or her control and engagement (and we'll see in chapter 5 how there is still some truth to this), Metz shows that "students may be persuaded, dominated, intimidated, bribed, or manipulated, but in the end, they decide whether to grant the teacher control."[8] This assent-side approach (versus a control-side one) makes resistance an issue of agency as opposed to one of domination.

Metz's analysis suggests that many students resist not because they are given too much power but because educators fail to recognize how much power students already have. In fact, Metz argues, it is in those moments when the student decides *not* to comply—when resistance occurs—that the teacher's dependence on student assent rapidly becomes visible. Situations in which students refuse to obey can be among the most stress-inducing experiences teachers endure because such instances reveal how little the teachers actually control, how much the students really determine, and how close teachers are to "classroom chaos" whenever students express their agency through defiance. And because of their cultural and personal proclivities, students vary in their tendency to cooperate, just as teachers differ in their cultural dispositions and managerial skill-sets that may be used to obtain that cooperation. Regardless of what the teacher does, to achieve academic success in whatever fashion the student must decide to devote energy to the task at hand. The student's agency, not the teacher's, is the deciding factor.

In the end, if we take seriously the prioritizing of agency, authorship, and assent in resistance theory, we must understand that students have the power to deny what we seek to do. If this realization produces despair, we may be clinging too tightly to tired and problematic notions of the teacher as ruler and the student as subject. Resistance theory helps us see that our dependence on student assent does not diminish our practice but instead acknowledges how much more can be gained if we emphasize relationship and cooperation over control and manipulation. This insight will be foundational in our work in later chapters.

The Importance of Agency in Understanding Resistance

When we place agency in the foreground of our analysis of student resistance, we have to consider whether our responses to student behaviors are more emancipatory or authoritarian. In doing so, we may face tough questions and even tougher answers. Though ample cultural and institutional resources are available to justify our responses regardless of their outcomes (i.e., few in the teachers' lounge will blame colleagues for student misbehavior), the central role of agency in resistance theory reminds us that our actions in the classrooms and schools sometimes fall far short of democratic ideals. By extension, student opposition is therefore sometimes politically and morally prudent. In short, *students resist us for good reasons*.

The flourishing of human potential in any context depends in large part on whether individuals experience autonomy, authorship, and assent. Just as nations demand sovereignty, so too do students demand agency, and rightfully so. Students need their learning to be theirs; they need behavioral expectations to be negotiated; they need school-based relationships to be collaborative. Resistance is a signal that those experiences may be lacking, that a change in the terms of engagement may be needed. Framed in this manner, agency highlights how resistance is often a form of participation in rather than a departure from collective activity.

Power: Rebuilding a Key Concept

The move away from the pessimistic theories that trap individuals in replicating systems of domination coincides with the move toward optimistic theories that demonstrate the power of resistance to create change. Understanding this power and how it functions, however, can present some tricky questions for educators. For example, if we need resistance to create meaningful change, who then has the power in our schools and classrooms? Does this mean we should let students run the schools? If we reclaim resistance as these theories seem to suggest we should, how will our classrooms operate? Shouldn't we enforce rules and maintain high academic expectations despite student resistance? In a standards-based environment with its many high-stakes assessments, how should we use our power to make sure students perform well?

Questions like these indicate that our old ideas about how power is obtained, expressed, and sustained cannot take us where we need to go. Recognizing that resistance is crucial to a well-adapted individual and to a functioning democracy only gets us so far; to truly integrate resistance into our ideologies and practices, we need to reformulate power too.

Power Produces

Sociologist Max Weber defines power as the ability to carry out one's will despite resistance. He asserts that if you can force others to comply with your desires, you have power. Conceived in this way, power implies rank—those at the top have greater influence and control over situations than those at the bottom. For Weber, power is therefore a form of domination realized through forces of control. If you don't have control, you don't have power.

Political theorist Hannah Arendt framed it differently. To her, power comes from people's ability to work together to achieve collective goals. Power is not an individual possession so much as it is a shared potential. Groups, organizations, and whole populations may seem less powerful than states, militaries, or even corporations, but that is only because the possible power of collective will and action has not yet been realized. For Arendt, the power is always there as potential; it just has to be recognized and organized to produce the results people want to see.

We can observe these constructions of power all the time in teacher-student interactions in the classroom. Some teachers exert enormous amount of energy trying to quell student disruptions and contain student expressions. Such teachers often believe that for whatever reason, they themselves are the rightful owners of power in the classroom. When a student tries to take power from these teachers, they consider the action an insurrection that must be repressed if academic progress is to be maintained. They fear that the potential power of the students may grow if it is given opportunities to express itself or is allowed to organize. Through coercion, exclusion, reprimands, embarrassment, threats, and punishments, the teachers attempts to control the behaviors of the student in hopes that order will be maintained. They rationalize that this control is necessary for progress and achievement. Of course, such efforts frequently elevate students' desire to resist, and this can perpetuate all sorts of problems for teachers and students alike and can actually undermine progress and achievement.

Sociologist Michel Foucault challenged such depictions of power. To build a theory of resistance grounded in the agency of the individual, Foucault had to distinguish his idea of power from more repressive definitions. According to Foucault, power is neither exerted by the powerful onto those who resist it nor determined by a zero-sum calculation (wherein one person's gain of power results in another person's equivalent loss). Foucault rejects these ideas by maintaining that power is not a substance or a possession but is instead a *relation*. Power is created dynamically, not distributed incrementally. It is produced by individuals and groups in a vigorous interplay of constraints and possibilities where questions of "Who has the power?" become less important than concerns about where and when people create opportunities for themselves to achieve envisioned goals.

For example, we can produce power by being loud, silent, strong, clever, compelling, attractive, cool, threatening, funny, charismatic, or disciplined, or through countless other behaviors. We can also produce power by controlling resources, possessing valued knowledge, attaining formal positions in established hierarchies, writing or enforcing rules, forming alliances with others, appealing to people's hopes and fears, or claiming divine guidance.[9] As a result, power is not found solely in those monolithic and supposedly durable structures such as governments, militaries, corporations, or schools; nor is it reserved for those who attain positions "above" others. In Foucault's analysis, power is everywhere and ever-changing all the time.

Applying this definition to the classroom, it's not that the teacher has (most of) the power and students struggle to wrest what they can through subterfuge and defiance. Instead, both teacher and student create and use different kinds of power that interact in different ways depending on the context. This is why Foucault's revised definition of power is so relevant to student resistance. If power is dynamically produced in situations and relationships, then resistance is not just a struggle of the powerless against the powerful. Instead, *resistance is the production and use of power, an invention and expression of the individual's or group's struggle to be an agent.*

Depending on the situation and the relationships within it, student resistance can function in an infinite number of ways. It can reinforce an individual's autonomy, confer status among peers, explore the boundaries of permissible conduct, experiment with possible identities, and challenge prevailing assumptions. It can even affirm social bonds that may be used at a later time to collaborate for further action. The point is, *power produces not just results but people.* Foucault's analysis shows that the self is always being constructed in and through exercises of power, and so too are social relationships and institutions. This is why adolescent resistance in the classroom is so intimately intertwined with identity formation, peer relationships, self-determination, and the motivation to achieve one's self-constructed goals. Students' power to define themselves depends on their capacity to resist how others want them made. In this sense, the often-heard youthful assertion "You're not the boss of me!" is quite descriptive.

Power Organizes

As we saw in Althusser's and Bourdieu's work in chapter 2, power can be produced by naming who or what is "normal." The power to name and have that naming accepted produces relationships and situations that bestow normality on some while conferring abnormality on others. Ideologies and beliefs set the terms by which these normalizing claims are determined, and this process typically yields rankings and delivers privileges. From the high school baseball team that prefers fast and accurate throwers to the after-school chess club that finds such athletic skills irrelevant, the arbitrary rules of each game form the context that determines what and who will be valued and how power and status will be produced. The power to name what behaviors and characteristics are normal becomes the power to organize who will be invited and included, and who will be alienated and dismissed.

Building on foundations laid by Althusser and Bourdieu, resistance theory contends that some of the most potent forms of power are produced through assumptions, beliefs, and practices. Power is communicated and enacted by what we consider normal and abnormal. In this sense, power organizes: it organizes our attention, our understanding, our values, and our actions. It takes an array of possibilities and reduces them to a narrower set of norms that, if they are allowed to go unquestioned for long enough and are accepted by sufficient numbers of people, become our realities. Recognizing that some forms of power are only accepted to the extent that they are concealed, Giroux identifies a peculiar form of normalizing power prevalent in educational settings. He calls that organizing power the "hidden curriculum."

Schools have always used curricula to organize meaning. From the Common Core to professional organizations' recommended standards to state frameworks all the way down to district content objectives and recommendations from department heads, educators use curricula to construct the scope and sequence of their subject areas. In essence, these curricula say, "Here is what is important to learn and how it ought to be taught."

The same is true for the hidden curriculum, with one crucial difference: whereas traditional curricula are largely explicit and readily accessible, the hidden curriculum, says Giroux, is composed of "unstated norms, values, and beliefs embedded in and transmitted to students through the underlying rules that structure the routines and social relationships in school." Though the hidden curriculum is neither posted on walls nor detailed in textbooks, it remains a "vehicle of socialization . . . that functions to provide differential forms of schooling to different classes of students."[10] When certain forms of testing are preferred, particular forms of authority are favored, or specific kinds of behaviors are indulged, there is a hidden curriculum. Whenever one student feels normal and accepted but another feels marginalized and excluded, there is a hidden curriculum. And when educators who raise doubts about the purposes and effects of tracking are told not to rock the boat, there is a hidden curriculum. Therefore, if the traditional curriculum is an attempt to organize content, the hidden curriculum is an attempt to organize people.

For example, teachers often establish the rule "be respectful" in the classroom, ostensibly to prevent offensive behaviors and to promote regard for others' needs. On the surface, this traditional curriculum of respect seems like a perfectly reasonable, productive, and normal thing to do. We want people to be nice to each other; case closed. But the command to be respectful can only be enforced successfully in those contexts where the definition of *respect* is agreed upon, and the rule can only be policed effectively by those who possess the authority to define *respect*.

When an educator's definition of *respect* is contested by students or when the students do not trust the educator's ability to use the term as they understand it, the educator will find it difficult to convince students to "be respectful," and resistance will almost certainly ensue. The same is true when students feel chronically disrespected by the way they are sorted, labeled, examined, instructed, and otherwise treated in schools. In general, the power to control people's "respectful" actions, therefore, comes from the ability to name and to normalize what is considered respectful; that is, it comes from a hidden curriculum. And even a hidden curriculum needs assent if it is to be successful.

What we too often forget—and what resistance theory helps us remember—is that this normative category of respect, like all normative categories, is always relationally determined and subject to contestation, negotiation, and reformulation even when it is hidden. Evidence of the contested nature of respect can be observed in myriad classroom interactions. Consider a situation in which a student is being disciplined by a teacher. Is eye contact considered respectful or disrespectful in that situation? Clearly, it depends on the actors, what they value, and how that relationship is negotiated. When students are talking with one another before class and one "disses" a friend's favorite basketball team, is this a sign of disrespect? Who do we trust to determine what is and what isn't respectful there? Or when a student neglects to raise a hand but offers an opinion in class regardless, is that an example of disrespect? What about when a student interrupts a peer—is that rude? What if the interruption occurred because the previous statement was considered by the student to be offensive? Would silence in that case have been more respectful? Likewise, is it respectful to ask a student who is an atheist to say the Pledge of Allegiance? These examples illustrate why Foucault defined power as "that which organizes multiplicities."[11] Power organizes the meaning we make as well as the meanings that make us.

Resistance Is to Be Expected

Theorizing power in this way helps us to see that resistance should be expected all the time, not just when obvious repression occurs. In a diverse society, normative claims will always be opposed by those who feel excluded by them. In a multicultural community, laws and regulations will be forever contested by those who do not feel protected by them. In a heterogeneous classroom, the prevailing behavioral expectations will be continually resisted by those who reject the assumptions on which they are built. Those examples of resistance are all occasions in which power is being produced precisely because attempts are afoot to make sure it is denied. When we view resistance as the outlying blip on an otherwise normal distribution of compliant behavior, we deny the inevitability of differently held beliefs about what is true, right, fair, and just. If diversity and agency are core components of human flourishing, resistance is unavoidable. Schools should therefore expect resistance, prepare for it, and even welcome it because in many ways, both the educator's and the students' sense of dignity and freedom depend on it.

The Tensions in Resistance Theories: They're a Good Thing

Where social reproduction theory created a closed and determined system, resistance theory presents a tension—a dynamic and constant negotiation between agency and control. Resistance forces individuals and institutions to acknowledge what may have been excluded, to recognize a neglected, forgotten, or denied need. By their very acts of opposition, resisters reveal that so-called finished institutions or complete systems of thought are inadequate and need transformation. This is why resisters are so often considered threats. The normative "that which is" will always be understood by some to be "that which shouldn't be," and this produces tension. But it's a good kind of tension, one that opens possibilities. Just as you cannot make an omelet without breaking some eggs, we cannot make schools more equitable unless we break open foreclosed ideas to reveal the tensions they contain. Resistance shows us where we might begin that work.

Analyzing Without Romanticizing

As explained in the introduction and reinforced throughout the chapters, one agenda of this book is to reclaim resistance as a resource, as a positive contribution to a thriving school. In doing so, however, we risk romanticizing it. We must admit that not all acts of student opposition in school are productive and many should not even be categorized as resistance in the first place. Sometimes students' (mis)behaviors do not emerge from a desire to transform their conditions or from an attempt to assert their autonomy.[12] Sometimes goofing off is just goofing off. As we examine the benefits of resistance in learning communities, we must avoid equating every act of transgression with the Boston Tea Party, the Seneca Falls Convention, the Montgomery Bus Boycott, the Stonewall Uprising, the United Farm Workers' Strike, or Occupy Wall Street. We must keep active the tension between repressing resistance and romanticizing it, because the most powerful analyses typically occur somewhere in between.

The Myth of Pure Agency

Just as we need to remember that resistance can be both a resource and an impediment to justice, so too do we need to problematize agency. Resistance theory helps us do this. Agency is always complicated, contingent, and contradictory because acting and being acted upon are seldom if ever extricable. We never end up in a perfectly free state, where we exist with no outside influence and where agency is total and complete. We can only experience and express agency in relationship to some social force or social connection. Agency is always contextual.

This means that the relative "success" of resistance depends on its reception, not just its expression. A student who desires more agency in a restrictive environment is not inherently resistant. Rather, the student is resistant *to* something or someone; he or she is resistant *relationally*. To consider a student's resistance isolated from the context or relationships that produced it is like trying to understand a two-car collision by only gathering information from one driver and only examining the damage of one car. Resistance is always an interaction in context.

Furthermore, the teacher and student are always in a relational dynamic of interdependence; each needs the other to be effective. The statement "Either I am totally free to do what I want to do, or I am repressed," creates a self-defeating dichotomy because neither the teacher nor the student ever exist outside the relationships that shape them. Engagement, therefore, is crucial for both parties. Students must engage the teacher at least partly on their own terms, and the teacher must engage students at least partly on his or her own terms. After all, to be entirely self-determined is to be completely cut off from the powerful learning that is occasioned by relating to others, to culture, and to institutions that actually facilitate (not just limit) our growth. For these reasons, to understand resistance, we should not search for supposedly pure, unaffected experiences of agency. Instead, we should explore how opposition functions, who benefits from it, and how various participants are affected by it. This shift is subtle but crucial.

The Myth of Total Domination

If agency is never pure, it follows that domination is never total. Systems, ideologies, and institutions can and do exert a profound influence on who we become and what we do, but these structures are never in full control of how individuals and groups interpret their experiences. This is a key contribution of resistance theory. Just because resistance may not be apparent does not mean it is not occurring. Outward compliance may be a cover for spirited inward rebellion or may mask the simple, freeing act of daydreaming. Likewise, countless forms of passive resistance are generated by people in situations where they feel their agency is being diminished. Educational researcher Kathleen M. Nolan puts it this way: "Where enthusiasm is expected, there will be apathy; where loyalty, there will be disaffection; where attendance, absenteeism; where robustness, some kind of illness; where deeds are to be done, varieties of inactivity . . . each in its way, a movement of liberty."[13]

Promising Practices: Methods Derived from Resistance Theory

According to Giroux, resistance theory calls on "educators to unravel the ideological interests embedded in the various message systems of the school, particularly those embedded in its curriculum, systems of instruction, and modes of evaluation."[14] This requires that we question not just students' behaviors but our interactions with them and the environments we create ostensibly to support their learning. Such broader questioning reveals the power dynamics and the implicit and explicit expectations that shape relationships in school. Students' behaviors are too complex to simply be characterized as "good" or "bad" because the behaviors involve multiple interactions with an array of participants and circumstances. Students' oppositional actions can be both a critique and a mockery, a disturbance and a demonstration, an example of self-determination and of self-destruction.

How we educators respond to student resistance can reveal a lot about the hidden curriculum that drives our decision making. When we claim that students disrespect our authority, do not value our content, do not care about succeeding in school, and are a negative influence on their peers, we are using a pathologizing approach that is unlikely to reveal the assumptions, policies, curricula, or practices that give rise to resistant behaviors in the first place. What resistance theory helps illuminate is the students' power to express their dissatisfaction with the conditions of their learning and how their opposition is an opportunity for educators to engage rather than squelch this expression. The school has the repressive power to punish students for their "insubordination" and "disruption," but students have the power to inform and influence their peers and community about how discipline is being carried out. Regardless of the result, student resistance offers the possibility of transformation: transformation in their relationships with us, transformation in their relationships to what we teach, transformation in their relationships to the school, and transformation in the school's relationship to larger societal trends. Student resistance makes things happen.

Interrogating the Hidden Curriculum

So what sorts of school practices might help us better address student resistance? The critical-friends groups suggested in chapter 2 would help here too. Such groups might eventually evolve into a deputized subcommittee at the school and be tasked specifically with analyzing how the school sometimes exacerbates social inequity and other times overcomes it. Part of the groups' work would be to examine practices and policies, but another part might be to look for the unstated assumptions and beliefs that form the hidden curriculum at the school.

A key resource to help educators identify those elements would be the students themselves. Individual and group interviews as well as student-led forums on contested matters surfacing in the school community could enhance the transformative potential of resistance and possibly diminish the destructive potential of other forms of opposition. When students are enlisted as agents rather than controlled as subjects, they will be more invested in solving their school's problems because they are involved in generating the solutions. Understood as coauthors of a school's ongoing transformation, students will be more likely to assent to institutional objectives because those goals will be shared more than declared.

Codeveloping Classroom and Schoolwide Norms

In individual classrooms, teachers might capitalize on students' need for agency by codeveloping class norms *with* them rather than posting class rules *for* them. If norms are ideologically constructed and eventually mediated through unstated but often contested expectations, one way of raising awareness and building community in the classroom is to have students practice identifying and naming their assumptions about what "good" and "bad" behaviors actually look like. Classroom management textbooks and online resources provide a multitude of ways such introductory exercises might be facilitated, but listing activities, guided discussions, Socratic seminars, dialogue circles, and occasional refining sessions are all excellent ways to enhance agency, authorship, and assent in even the most resistant students. They are also excellent ways to illuminate the power students already have to make themselves and their communities more responsive. Following these introductory activities with, say, twice-per-quarter class meetings where terms and practices can be renegotiated will reinforce the students' roles as coauthors and agents. At some point, students might be trusted to facilitate those meetings themselves and generate recommendations for the collective, including the teacher.

Enhancing Opportunities for Students to Critique

Finally, if we wish to make resistance transformative rather than reproductive, students need regular opportunities to critique the environments in which they are expected to learn. They need practice articulating their opposition and organizing their actions, experiencing themselves as active builders of their circumstances rather than passive receivers of somebody else's plans. Through debates, the arts, journalism, spoken word, video documentaries, podcasts, and many other avenues, students can voice their discontent as well as their gratitude. If we protect opportunities for students to do this by providing spaces in which their critiques can be refined and by inviting community members to receive these critiques, we will give youth a reason to stay engaged and participate in meaningful change. Sometimes students are so hungry for such opportunities that all we need to do is unlock the door and turn on the lights—they'll take it from there.

PART II

UNDERSTANDING
RESISTANCE
PSYCHOLOGICALLY

Heavy Situation

Gravity acts on all objects, massive or minuscule, with the same force of acceleration. Ms. Jackson has been teaching science long enough to know that this concept, while relatively simple, is rarely accepted by most students when it is first introduced. Asked about which dropped item will strike the ground first, a bowling ball or a feather, students rightfully predict it will be the bowling ball.

"How come?" asks Ms. Jackson.

"Because heavier things fall faster," her students respond. "Gravity doesn't pull on the feather as hard as it pulls on the bowling ball."

Having confronted these fallacies every year she has taught this concept, Ms. Jackson knows she has to do more than display equations, describe laws, and explain concepts. Just telling students the science won't do it—she has to unpack their naive understanding, overcome their disbelief, and convince students of new knowledge. So she puts them in groups of four and gives each group two pieces of printer paper, one white and one blue.

"Experiment with your materials until you can get each piece of paper to hit the ground at the same instant when dropped from six feet off the ground," she announces.

She encourages students to use the video app on their cell phones to record and replay the moment the papers hit the ground, and she urges them to discuss, debate, clarify, experiment, observe, revise, and do it again. In the process, she watches students crumple the papers into tight wads or fold them repeatedly until the sheets are dense squares. One group even forms the sheets into cone-shaped darts. When she hears students gradually begin to account for air resistance in their experiments, Ms. Jackson throws them what she likes to call "a cognitive curveball." She stops the class, gathers their attention, and asks them to discuss what they think would happen to the papers in the experiment if they were to somehow take the air out of the room.

She gives them a minute or so to talk it over in groups, then writes on the board, "With the air gone, what shape would likely allow the paper to drop the fastest?"

A variety of hypotheses emerge, many of which are wildly erroneous, but a few students begin to suspect problems with the question itself. "That's a trick question, Ms. Jackson!"

Smirking a little, Ms. Jackson replies, "How so?"

"Because with no air, the shape doesn't matter," says one student, after which a debate ensues about the nature of mass, weight, gravity, acceleration, friction, and the vacuum of space. When the debate starts to get repetitive, she cues up a YouTube video of a bowling ball and a feather being dropped inside a tall tube, first with regular atmosphere inside it and then with all the air vacuumed out.

After showing the video (twice, actually, because several students did not believe the result the first time), she tells them, "Raise your hand if you still think heavy objects fall faster than lighter objects."

With no hands in the air, Ms. Jackson knows it's now time to introduce Newton's law of universal gravitation.

CHAPTER 4

"This Should Be Different"

Cognition and Imagination at the Foundation of Resistance

THROUGH ADVANCES IN neuroscience and brain imaging, we are getting clearer and clearer pictures of what our brains actually do when we learn something. Even though the brain remains one of the most complex and possibly least understood objects in the universe, one thing is sure: in the brain, learning is about making connections. For the growing adolescent, those connections form increasingly sophisticated networks of understanding and webs of relationships that allow powerful new ideas, identities, beliefs, and actions to materialize. Sometimes these cognitive developments produce epiphanies and inventions that lead to personal or collective breakthroughs. At other times these profound cognitive changes necessitate forms of resistance that may impede the progress we're trying to foster. Exploring research from cognitive developmental psychology and neuroscience, this chapter will illuminate why resistance is such an important cognitive activity for youth, how that resistance might be understood in the classroom, and which educational responses might best promote continued school engagement and academic achievement.

Learning as Building, Not Packing

Computers store and process data as a series of on/off switches coded as zeros or ones. Tap certain keys or click your mouse on a button, folder, or file, and the computer pulls up that data and presents it to you through programs that interpret millions of zeros and ones as pixels and sounds. The brain, however, does not do things this way. It is organic, not digital.

Brain cells, called neurons, send signals through their treelike branches of dendrites and synapses in far more complex ways than simple open-or-closed gates. Depending on which neuroscientific accounting method you consult, the human brain possesses somewhere between one and two hundred billion neurons. That's a big number, to be sure, but the most revealing number is the total possible *connections* among those billions of cells. The brain contains ten thousand times as many connections as it has cells. Our heads thus contain something in the neighborhood of 10^{15} neural connections in them, which translates to at least a quadrillion pathways a signal can travel.

This is why it doesn't make much sense to say that the brain stores data, at least not in the way a computer does. Rather, *the brain attaches meaning to experience* by connecting new information to previous knowledge and the theories, ideas, feelings, and memories that grow from it. When it comes to the human brain, knowledge is therefore not the same thing as data. This is because knowledge is not stored; it is made. Knowledge is not inputted; it is built. Knowledge is not absorbed; it is *constructed.*

The theory and science of constructivism begins with these core observations to suggest a radical reframing of learning, one that continues to challenge older but incredibly durable (and highly problematic) conceptions of the teaching and learning process. Instead of framing the learner as a passive receptacle of information—an empty vessel to be filled—constructivism understands the learner as an agent. When something, let's call it X, is taught, the learner doesn't reproduce X within his or her mind precisely as the teacher delivered it. X is changed when it is learned because the learner has to connect it to previous understanding and make meaning of it in a way that is usable in that learner's context. The learner's knowledge of X is not really a thing so much as it is a dynamic, an interaction between experiences, desires, feelings, and ideas that are unique to the individual and the environment in which the individual is learning.

For example, a student bases her understanding of X on the nearly infinite array of neural connections that arise when she considers what X means to her. X might make immediate sense to her because it maps onto a previous understanding of Y and Z very well, or X might be utterly confusing if Y or Z contradict it. For another student, X may be constructed into a different conception because X connects better with his experience A, theory B, and feeling C. Both students can be said to "understand" X, but the understanding (effectively X_{YZ} and X_{ABC}) is qualitatively different in each student's brain because *each student does something different to that knowledge.* The great Swiss developmental psychologist Jean Piaget puts it this way: "Human knowledge is essentially active . . . To know is to transform reality in order to understand [it] . . . By virtue of this point of view, I find myself opposed to the view of knowledge as a copy, a passive copy, of reality . . . [K]nowing an object does not mean copying it—it means acting upon it."[1]

What does this idea of learning as building mean for the educator? One clear implication is that the knowledge offered by a teacher is always meeting—and being transformed by—the knowledge brought by the learner.[2] In other words, teachers are in control of what they deliver but they are not in control of how that delivery is understood. Confronting this realization, many of us may feel a sense of loss because we can never be sure the student is apprehending the content the way we taught it.

But isn't it actually better this way? In the old model of education, what Paolo Freire calls the "banking method," in which the teacher deposits information into the students' minds and later withdraws it in the form of regurgitated homework and tests, the learner is rendered passive and relatively powerless. All of the heavy intellectual lifting is done by the teacher; the student needs only to pay attention and receive (and later return) the deposits. This model reduces knowledge to data, and pedagogy to transmission, and any educator worth his or her weight in Scantrons knows that learning is far richer than this.

Because of constructivist theory and research, we now recognize that all knowledge must pass through the individual learner's beliefs, experiences, and feelings. Because all knowledge is altered in this process, there is no perfect correspondence between what is taught and what is learned. This does not mean the student has an eternally flawed understanding of the teacher's perfect knowledge. Rather, the learner is a knowledge builder, a meaning maker, a self-constructor, and a world changer. Echoing this insight, the educational philosopher Deborah Britzman describes learning as "the self's own [internal] work of art."[3] If constructivism frames learning as a kind of art, then curriculum is never simply transmitted because students are never completely passive in its reception. They're agents throughout the process. Accordingly, constructivism understands educators not as conveyors of content but as facilitators of understanding. We educators are called to provide meaning-rich experiences that encourage learners to build an ever more complex understanding of their world and themselves.

Why Students Refuse Knowledge or Resist Learning

If the process of understanding something is active and constructive, then the learner is always making decisions about what to do with the new knowledge, where to put it, how to categorize it, and why it's worth knowing. However, if the learner does not know what to do with the knowledge, has no idea where it might connect to previous understanding, is unsure how to categorize it in light of earlier learning, or is not convinced that the new knowledge is worth knowing in the first place, the knowledge will likely be rejected.

Resistance, it turns out, isn't just a negative outcome of bad learning conditions but rather is fundamental to the learning process. To understand something, the learner must accept new knowledge from a source external to the self. The key word is *acceptance*. Even when the context around learners compels them to accept something, if the knowledge presents enough conflict with learners' pre-existing understanding, the learner will likely resist. Curriculum theorist Charles Bingham explains it this way: "The act of learning depends primarily on the acceptance that the knowledge of someone else [or something, or some situation] deserves a spot in one's own scheme of things. When one learns from a teacher, for example, there must be either a conscious or an unconscious acknowledgement that the teacher has something to offer that is actually superior to that which one knows at present."[4]

In other words, learners must release their attachment to their previous understanding if they are to accommodate new knowledge that challenges it. They must trust the new information and its source enough to let go of their understanding and alter or replace it with what is being presented. This causes a momentary (or sometimes long-standing) experience of instability. Educational psychologists call this experience *cognitive dissonance*.

French philosopher Jean-François Lyotard recognizes the psychodynamic tensions that can arise during experiences of cognitive dissonance when he states, simply: "Thinking and suffering overlap."[5] Heeding this comment, we would do well to remember that learning often necessitates *un*learning. When we observe in the classroom furrowed brows, shaking heads, doubtful glances among peers, or an audible "Nuh-uh" or "Wait, what?" we can interpret such resistance and the momentary "suffering" it may represent as a sign that learners are preparing their brains to receive new knowledge. It doesn't mean they will accept that knowledge, but they might, depending on how well we cultivate safe environments for such learning.

A student's resistance to letting go of old understanding or integrating new knowledge may be his or her attempt to preserve the status quo when the change being offered doesn't feel conducive to the student's sense of well-being, sense of consistency, comfort, or a positive self-understanding. Depending on how much the new knowledge threatens previous understanding, how much learners trust the source, or how stressed learners might be when they are confronted with the new information, learners may find it easier to refuse knowledge than accommodate it. Thus we may confront students who are as invested in rejecting knowledge as they are in accepting it. When students choose to resist learning rather than work to reformulate their neural networks to allow for new understanding, this isn't being lazy so much as it is being protective. We need to remember that students may resist not because they don't want to learn, but because their resistance may reduce internal conflicts and diminish their suffering, if only for a moment.

Even though cognitive dissonance can generate internal and outward resistance, it's one of the most productive and powerful experiences we can inspire in learners. It may seem counterintuitive to endeavor to inspire confusion, refusal, and resistance in the learner, but cognitive developmental psychology and neuroscience have shown that authentic, complex, deep, and long-lasting learning seldom occurs without struggle. This is because cognitive dissonance forces a decision in the mind of the learner: "Do I accept the new knowledge or work to reject it? And if I accept it, what needs to change in the way I think about things?" The learner's challenge of integrating the knowledge that *comes in* with the knowledge *already possessed* forces the brain to make comparisons, weigh perspectives, consider options, evaluate plausibility, and judge merits. When the learner is compelled to make these sorts of determinations, the process activates and strengthens the most complex parts of the brain. The result? Resisting knowledge makes people smarter.

Because building new understanding frequently depends on the demolition and remodeling of previous understanding, the context in which learning occurs must welcome doubt, encourage inquiry, support risk taking, and accept resistance. Summarizing this constructivist approach, educational philosopher Maxine Greene makes a poignant observation: "Most of us know enough to recognize that the young are not empty vessels but centers of energy in search of meaning. The point [of meaningful education] is to address them as persons in crisis."[6] This doesn't mean we should allow learners to persist in their rejection of new knowledge—to do that would be to encourage forms of denial that impede growth. But classrooms and schools tend to function optimally when we cultivate, rather than avoid, dissonance in students. According to psychologists George Slavich and Phil Zimbardo, "at the heart of all types of active and student-centered learning . . . is the constructivist notion that students generate knowledge and meaning best when they have experiences that lead them to realize how new information conflicts with their prevailing understanding of a concept or idea."[7] By focusing students' attention on the conflicts that surface between their current understanding and the new knowledge they are considering, and then guiding them to more nuanced or accurate explanations that will resolve those conflicts, we can transform resistance into learning. Resistance can therefore be more than productive—it can be fun.

Attitude, Adolescence, and the Advent of Abstract Thought

Attitude. It is perhaps the leading trait adults name when they bemoan the supposedly sorry state of "kids these days." Whether it's teens' rolled eyes, slouching postures, irreverent clothing, snarky tone, or "whatever" dismissiveness, adults often grow tired of adolescent expressions of resistance. Teens' so-called bad attitudes can make us feel unappreciated, mocked, ignored, and undermined—feelings that can lead to diminished job satisfaction if not burnout. As a result, we find ourselves reasoning that if our students would just quit it with their "attitudes," we could get things done more efficiently and avoid the sorts of unnecessary drama that distract us from our objectives. Sound familiar?

But adolescent attitudes signal an important change in cognition that, if properly addressed, gives us much more to celebrate than lament. In fact, one of the reasons working with adolescents can be so rewarding is precisely *because* of their attitudes. That annoying and exhausting contrariness we often observe in our students' behaviors comes bundled with a host of intellectual and critical capacities that make it fun to "mess with their heads." The ability to generate hypotheses, appreciate irony, apprehend juxtaposition, explore variability, exercise logic, infer causality, craft arguments, and discern fact from opinion comes alive in adolescence. And the curricula in middle and high schools are largely designed to capitalize on these new talents (or at least they used to be, before high-stakes testing—more on that in chapter 12). When we ask sixth-graders or seniors to "describe the protagonist's motivation" or "solve for *x*," those activities depend on the intellectual sophistication that comes with abstract thinking. Luckily, it is during adolescence that this power most rapidly advances, which is what can make working with teens so satisfying. Even when their new cognitive powers are accompanied by attitudes we adults may find distasteful or rude, it is helpful to remember that such instances of resistance are not just regrettable and avoidable by-products of growing up; they're necessary expressions of, and experimentation with, newly empowered minds.

Comprehension and Apprehension: Brain System 1 and the Need to Protect the Self

The development of abstract thought or *hypothetical thinking* occurs as part of a maturation process that mirrors the evolution of our species. Tracing the development of life on earth from primordial slime to fish, to mammals, and all the way to early hominids and the eventual appearance of *Homo sapiens*, scientists have revealed the coinciding development of ever more sophisticated brain systems. Parts of our brains look a lot like a crocodile's brain, and other parts closely resemble a pig's, because at some point in the tree of our evolutionary past, our branches converged. This means that as complex and powerful as the human brain is, it still relies on some fairly primitive functions to help us get through our days.

Cognitive scientists have located these specific brain functions in a variety of regions of the brain and are discovering new ones all the time. For example, we know the areas of the brain that are responsible for maintaining our autonomic functions like breathing and digestion; regulating our hormones; controlling our voluntary actions like moving our limbs; and making sense of visual, auditory, tactile, and linguistic information. Scientists have even mapped how, when, and where we process music versus understand poetry.[8] Because a full accounting of these discoveries and their relevance to classroom resistance would take volumes, we will rely on a widely accepted and rather elegant explanation popularized by psychologist Daniel Kahneman in his book *Thinking, Fast and Slow*.[9]

Kahneman is a proponent of what has come to be known as *dual-process theory*. This theory characterizes the many functions of the brain into two basic systems that Kahneman calls, simply, system 1 and system 2. These systems run in parallel, both reliant on the other but each operating with very different assets and liabilities. One way to grasp how and why students sometimes demonstrate resistance in the classroom is to understand the demands and limitations of these two systems.

System 1 is the older, more primitive part of the brain—the part located in or near the brain stem. It's often referred to as the *reptilian brain*, because it closely resembles the brains of alligators and komodo dragons, and because it is largely responsible for the fight-or-flight response. Primarily tasked with processing experiences and producing reactions, system 1 is incredibly fast because it relies on easily accessed memories, free associations, quick assumptions, and rapid reflexes (see table 4.1 for a comparison of systems 1 and 2). It uses instinct, intuition,

TABLE 4.1 A comparison of system 1 ("experiential") and system 2 ("analytic") thinking

	System 1	System 2
Defining characteristics	· Fast, instinctive, largely unconscious · Automatic, efficient, fight-or-flight responses; reactionary, reflex-driven, makes simple conclusions · Runs on generalizations and trained responses; has immediate access to a vast store of memories · Similar to instinct in how it operates often behind conscious thought, but its judgments and decisions are learned rather than preprogrammed	· Slow, deliberate, self-aware, mostly conscious · Highly sophisticated in its ability to calculate, evaluate, judge, feel, relate, create · Capable of analyzing abstractions and possibilities, hypothesizing, deducting, imagining · Highly susceptible to input and experience; capable of enormous growth in complexity over time
Optimal conditions	· When effortless and rapid situational appraisal is needed and the costs of mistakes are low · When efficiency and speed of reaction are paramount · Superior in directing everyday behavior, but inferior in thinking abstractly, comprehending cause-and-effect relations, delaying gratification, and planning for the distant future	· When complex situations require careful deliberation and weighing of options, and when time and energy to process this information is abundant · When relationships, emotions, ideas, and multiple perspectives must be integrated · Superior in abstract/critical thinking, but inferior in automatically and effortlessly directing moment-by-moment behavior

Examples	• Knowing whether it's a mountain lion or a squirrel one hears in the bushes • Immediately identifying the difference between "Uh-huh" or "Nuh-uh" in someone's response • Recognizing people's faces, immediately accessing memories of them, then planning how to react when they approach • Distant memory of a terrifying clown in a movie you saw when you were eleven years old; current reaction when you see a clown today: you loathe clowns	• $E = mc^2$; spoken-word poems; debate; coordinate proofs; jazz; architecture; inventions • "I understand what you're communicating and can empathize with your situation"; "What do you want to do this weekend?"; "I prefer Jay-Z over Mozart" • Forming a hypothesis based on careful and critical review of evidence, then testing that hypothesis through experiments, situations, and reflections • Criticizing a policy or practice and using imagination and argument to suggest alternatives
Drawbacks	• Little to no voluntary control; difficult to retrain • The most readily accessible memories tend to be those associated with strong emotions such as fear, pain, and hatred; consequently, snap judgments may be highly biased and impulsive • Relies on shortcuts, i.e., bases decisions on little information and a lot of conjecture • No capacity for complexity or nuance	• Difficult to activate, energy intensive, prone to distraction • Requires relative comfort, quiet, safety, and willful intent to fully engage • Sustained focus is often hindered by diverting attention to less energy-intensive and more immediate and automatic tasks associated with system 1 • Needs significant preparation and ample time to function optimally • Very, very slow (and maybe a little lazy)

and reflex to make nearly instantaneous judgments that prioritize the organism's safety. Our distant mammalian relatives probably evolved the ability to make such hasty decisions from limited and fleeting information so that they could survive attacks by large, hungry predators.[10] As the millennia unfolded, system 1 evolved the ability to quickly distinguish the footfall of a predator from the scurrying of a sparrow and then act accordingly without waiting for slower, more conscious parts of the brain to deliberate and decide.

System 1 is so powerful that we may actually owe our evolutionary existence to its efficiency and effortlessness, but its success does come at a cost. Because system 1 reacts rather than ponders, its judgments are often wrong. Any brain system that depends on generalizations, stereotypes, and partial (or skewed) recollections will be prone to make snap judgments and errors, and our brains are no different. If you had a bad experience with a spider when you were a child or saw a scary movie with spiders when you were young, chances are you'll negatively react to any perceived arachnids in your environment. Your reactions to a spider will be biased and impulsive, not considered and nuanced, even though the spider may be harmless and may be helping rid your area of biting or stinging insects. The more conscious and analytic parts of your brain may know better, but system 1 makes the initial call on how to react.

In evolutionary terms, being wrong is an acceptable downside. When predators are afoot, it is far better to be wrong and quick rather than be right and slow. But in our day-to-day interactions, in which immediate threats from looming predators are (mostly) rare, system 1's fight-or-flight response can get in the way. For example, when students make public academic mistakes, their survival is rarely if ever in question. No saber-toothed tiger is going to eat them for lunch because they answered a teacher's question incorrectly or wrote a problem on the board that contained errors. As far as the food chain goes, they'll be fine. However, their dwindling self-worth, shaky social connections, and fear of looking dumb might be experienced as threats if their wrong answer is accompanied by ridicule, embarrassment, or shame. In such instances, a student's fight-or-flight response may be activated, and when it is, most of the thinking being done by the individual in that moment will be processed by system 1—the very system least capable of complex thought and most likely to make judgments based on reductive thinking, overgeneralization, bias, and impulse. And the troubles with system 1 don't stop there.

To be able to act quickly in light of knowledge already attained, our brains must access memories efficiently. System 1 is very good at this, again, as long as the speed of decisions is more important than their correctness. Experiences and the meaning we make of them move from short-term to long-term memories according to a variety of factors, chief among them the extent to which those memories are "coded." Memories assigned just a few codes will be recalled only if we happen to remember those limited triggers that are capable of calling up the memories. No code, no recall. We often teach our students mnemonic devices to memorize information, precisely because these techniques offer multiple access points to the knowledge being stored. We do the same thing when we provide rich, invigorating, and interactive classroom activities during which knowledge can be connected to a variety of intellectual, social, and emotional experiences. In this way, the student has a host of access points that create robust code networks in the brain so that knowledge can be recalled and skillfully applied in later situations.

But this enriched learning opportunity only happens when threats are nonexistent. When threats arise, system 1 needs information fast. The quicker the knowledge can be accessed, the quicker the decisions can be made. It turns out that the most readily accessible memories we have—the ones most easily recalled by system 1 during a fight-or-flight response—are those we associate with our strongest emotions. Emotional reactions activate multiple regions of the brain, creating an array of code networks and access points. This multiregional activation of emotions in the brain is especially true of strong feelings such as fear, agony, and hatred (and also comfort, pleasure, and love). Experiences of pain, danger, injury, or abuse are remembered richly so that the brain can access those experiences quickly and therefore avoid those situations when they might present themselves again. Kahneman calls this tendency to base decisions on strong, easily recalled memories the "availability bias." Rather than wait to examine a bigger set of less vivid recollections, system 1 accesses our most forceful experiences and then reacts. As a result, system 1 tends toward the extreme whenever threats are perceived, even if the threats present no real danger to the individual. Basically, system 1 cries wolf a lot.

What do the intricacies of system 1 have to do with learning? How is it related to resistance? Basically, when learners feel threatened, they can act like reptiles. Students (and educators) who feel unsafe, preyed upon, stressed, or otherwise endangered either physically, socially, or intellectually will tend to respond using system 1. In such cases, they don't think so much as they react. Relying on snap judgments and emotional impulses, threatened learners are most prepared to battle or bolt, not delve and deliberate. The parts of the learner's brain that evolved to react so swiftly to predators will sometimes react to things like humiliation, mockery, and stress as if the individual's survival were at stake. Trained by millions of years of evolution, learners operating primarily in system 1 will seek to fight or flee before relaxing or relenting. In short, they will resist.

Too often, these reactions are interpreted by educators as defiance. This defiance, however, should not be construed as a rejection of learning but instead should be viewed as a self-preserving stance against perceived threats. When brain system 1 perceives danger, it will reject the context or individuals that represent the threat. And once brain system 1 goes into survival mode, learning is a luxury. Any reaction stemming from this fight-or-flight impulse does not mean the student does not *want* to learn; it means he or she *can't*. In those moments, "I'm outta here!" or "F—— you!" may not be the learner's most productive response in terms of academics or relationships with others, but system 1 isn't interested in making friends or building new knowledge at that point. System 1 wants to survive. Educators who locate the problem in a student's attitudes or behaviors fail to realize that it's the situation we should blame. Threatening the already-threatened student with punishment, failure, public humiliation, banishment to the principal's office, or suspension may only exacerbate forms of resistance born of the fight-or-flight response. It would be like trying to put out a fire by dousing the flames with gasoline.

When we rank some students above others (with grades, tracked classes, test scores, and labels like "SpEd" or "gifted and talented"), or when we allow students to make fun of one another, to mock others' mistakes, or to ridicule those who invest themselves in academic activity, we cocreate unsafe classrooms. When we look the other way while instances of bullying and ostracism occur in our hallways, locker rooms, cafeterias, bathrooms, and bus stops, we force learners to take defensive postures when they attend school. And when we create classroom cultures, testing regimes, and disciplinary procedures that make students feel like we're hunting for their weaknesses (rather than building their strengths), we encourage them to run or resist. Because it is arising from the least sophisticated parts of the brain, this type of resistance isn't nuanced, critical, or complex. It isn't a form of political opposition meant to alter systems of oppression. It's a blunt, reactionary instrument designed to keep the organism alive so it can fight another day. When system 1 is running the show, apprehension and aggression trump comprehension every time. Therefore, if we want our students to learn and learn deeply, we simply must provide contexts that support them to move their thinking out of system 1 and into system 2.

Executive Functioning: Brain System 2
and the Power of Abstract Thought

System 2, humans' newest cognitive evolutionary achievement, is the last part of the brain to mature. This most sophisticated part of our brains is found primarily in the cerebral cortex, which is the large, undulating gray matter above and behind the eyes and extending all the way to the back of the head. System 2 is responsible for the many executive functions humans are capable of performing. *Executive functions* are the things the brain does that lead, manage, and direct the voluntary actions of the individual.[11] Educators have called these functions "higher-order thinking" or "critical thinking" and have used tools like Bloom's Taxonomy to target the development of those synthesizing and evaluating skills that blossom in adolescence. For the most part, executive functions are what we commonly understand as "thinking" (you used system 2 as you read and understood that sentence just then, and you're doing it right now). If system 1 basically reacts, system 2 plans, organizes, strategizes, prioritizes, evaluates, solves problems, manages emotions, delays gratification, negotiates with others, decides what to pay attention to, and generally regulates the flow of ideas (table 4.1). System 1 may be able to walk and chew gum at the same time, but system 2 can write novels, debate issues, do calculus, dance the tango, and make sense of subatomic particles. If there is such a thing as "the mind" that is somehow separate from the brain, system 2 is where we'd likely find it.

Whereas system 1 is experiential, system 2 is analytic. That means system 2 is far superior in its calculating potential and level of sophistication. Need to read social cues or manage emotions? System 2 will handle it. Working to interpret or create symbols? System 2 is up to the task. Need to assess risk and act accordingly? Well, in that case, adolescents sometimes come up a little short—more on that later. Regardless, system 2 can appraise the actions of system 1, correct mistakes that may have been made there, and revise how knowledge will be coded and networked with previous understanding. System 2 can then plan responses, coordinate perspectives with others, and direct actions all while judging and revising and organizing as it goes. Its executive function even allows it to inhibit the reactionary responses of system 1 so that the brain can devote energy to more analytic processes. Paradoxically, at the same time that these executive functions are flowering during adolescence the human brain actually prunes millions of unused neurons. This pruning allows nutrients to flow more efficiently to the most frequently used neurons, thereby strengthening the neural networks used most often. This pruning and strengthening is why "practice makes better," particularly during childhood and adolescence because it is during that developmental era that the brain is reinforcing and fortifying the connections the person most needs. All this consolidation and contemplation makes system 2 burn much more energy than system 1. System 2 also makes the brain run much, much slower.

Take, for example, Isaac Newton's apple. The legend of its falling from a tree and striking him on the head is apocryphal, not because it didn't happen but because it's ludicrous to think that such an event would somehow instantaneously inspire his theory of gravity. The truth is, Newton had been working on that problem for years. He needed to invent calculus and identify a series of other laws of physics before gravity would even make theoretical sense.[12] Newton's example illustrates that the work of system 2 requires a bunch of preparation and a lot of time. To initiate and sustain focus, the individual must have the will to activate system 2 (we'll explore this further in chapter 5), be in an environment of relative safety (so that system 1 doesn't kick in and take over), and be free from, or able to manage, distractions. Only then does system 2 really kick in.

Even though humans have had eons to develop these higher cognitive capacities, system 2 doesn't just switch on effortlessly; it needs the right conditions and the appropriate motivations, and it is sometimes only activated if prodded and prepared. This makes system 2 fairly needy and, frankly, a little lazy. Because we were hunters and gatherers far longer than we were house-dwelling, museum-visiting, Internet-surfing citizens, our brains are hardwired to look for energy-saving shortcuts whenever they might become available. In our distant evolutionary past, we were never sure about the availability of food, shelter, and safety, so we had to conserve resources and be ready to fight or flee whenever possible.

Think of the simple act of making a grocery list. Cognitively speaking, it's a shortcut we've developed to externalize our thinking onto paper, where our thinking will wait for us to retrieve it when we need it. To try to remember those items amid the thousands of other things we do each day would be to tax system 2 beyond its capabilities (and system 1 is too busy just trying to survive), so we take shortcuts. Likewise, we use calculators and calendars and computers. We make maps, invent symbols, and set clocks. Many of our bodily systems are also designed to take shortcuts, to save rather than expend energy whenever they can. This is why our brains will tend to revert to system 1 when the option to do so is presented. System 2—because of its enormous cognitive power—requires considerable mental effort, which is costly in time and energy. But system 1 burns fewer calories and runs almost effortlessly. So, we tend not to activate system 2 unless we have exhausted the alternatives, like checking our email, texting, watching a YouTube video, updating our Facebook page, and making a snack.

Our students are no different. In the classroom, they resist initiating academic work and easily entertain distractions because adolescents, like adults, are hard-wired to drop their thinking into system 1 to preserve energy. Presented with classroom opportunities to compare the meaning of two sonnets, solve a differential equation, debate a complicated law, or conduct a challenging scientific experiment, students often take their sweet time to get started. And once they get going, they frequently allow social or behavioral disruptions to take them off task. Getting students on task can be quite a challenge, not because they want to avoid learning but because system 1 wants to be in charge. We might be tempted to label this tendency to be off task as being lazy, as if to suggest that some people possess a character flaw that other, more motivated folks do not. But from a cognitive perspective, it's more accurate to say that the brain tends to prefer efficiency over power. All learners, students and educators alike, are predisposed to use their most efficient and least sophisticated brain system over their far slower, energy-intensive, but significantly more complex one. Therefore, to take full advantage of the benefits and extraordinary powers of system 2 in the classroom and to effectively override the human tendency to neglect it, we need to appeal to its most worthwhile and gratifying aspects. To do that, we need imagination.

Hypothetical Thinking, Imagination, and Opposition: Resistance as Exercise

Perhaps the hallmark achievement of an adolescent's cognitive development is the advent of hypothetical thinking. The acquisition of this fundamental capacity transforms the relationship between the individual and his or her world. No longer limited to the concrete realities or the fantasies of childhood, adolescents can take conceptual and experiential givens and imagine them otherwise. With the ability to think hypothetically, youth can theorize reality itself as only one expression in a range of possibilities. "Things could be different," the adolescent reasons, "because I can now picture those prospects."

The ability to see the world as constructed (and to understand one's own thoughts as constructions) affects nearly every intellectual, emotional, social, and behavioral process that adolescents undertake. Their judgments become more nuanced, reasoning becomes more sophisticated, feelings are contextualized differently, and decisions get made with a greater awareness of impact. Learning itself takes on whole new powers as the adolescent can consider multiple perspectives, pathways, and solutions simultaneously. Highlighting the importance of this cognitive transformation, developmental psychologist Eric Amsel lists some of the capabilities the adolescent develops as hypothetical thinking emerges. With proper support and encouragement, the adolescent can:

- Treat alternative event sequences as possibilities
- Logically infer consequences from possible worlds
- Reason counterfactually
- Experience or anticipate regret
- Critically reflect on possible worlds
- Make systematic inferences about those possible worlds
- Objectively interpret reality in light of other possibilities
- Regulate system 1 reacting and system 2 thinking and distinguish experiential from analytic processes
- Form mental models and interpret reality in light of them[13]

The notion of possibility runs throughout Amsel's listing because that's what hypothetical thinking is all about—imagining what *might* be, what *could* be, and maybe what *should* be. When the adolescent compares such possibilities to what currently *is*, resistance is a probable and often quite productive outcome.

Hypothetical Thinking as an Imaginative Exercise

There is a bumper sticker that reads, "Imagine a world without hypothetical thinking." Though surely intended to be ironic, the sentiment underscores how crucial the advent of hypothetical thinking is to the individual and to our species. During adolescence, humans first begin to practice this uniquely human form of cognition, the products of which represent our most vital achievements as a species. Art, music, literature, science, mathematics, and civilization itself would likely never have developed were it not for the imagination that springs from our hypotheses.

According to Amsel, hypothetical thinking is "the ability to reason about alternatives to the way the world is believed to be."[14] He goes on to identify three actionable components implied in that definition. To think hypothetically, individuals must (1) recruit the imagination, (2) make inferences about imagined state of affairs, and (3) interpret the real-world consequences of the states imagined. Each of these actions demonstrate just how inseparable imagination is from the higher-order, critical cognitive faculties that we educators are supposed to inspire in our adolescent learners. They also suggest the necessity of resistance whenever the students' need to imagine is being suppressed.

Our students are naturally curious about how the world works, partly because they know it can work differently. They're inquisitive, speculative, and suspicious, but those precious dispositions can vanish whenever we teach as if the authorities are the only ones with the answers. If classroom texts yield only adult-sanctioned interpretations, if science labs are predetermined, if math problems can only be solved in one way, and if opinions about historical events are constrained to whatever the experts declare, adolescents will divert their imaginations away from academics and into activities where they themselves can flourish. In class, we might see such diversions in various forms of inventive (mis)behavior: a preference for drawing or doodling during lectures or even a constant background hum of social chattering when students are supposed to be listening. All these actions may be attempts to create moments where possibilities are imagined, where the brain doesn't have to just sit and receive but instead can fly off and explore.

Think of the daydreaming student, staring out the window and thinking of some imaginative possibility outside in the real world where such activity might be allowed. Educational philosopher Peter McLaren calls daydreaming a form of "mental mutiny." In the students McLaren observed, such behavior "was a scandal of absence, a silent insurrection, a withdrawal into the dark interiority and [spontaneously playful] caverns of imagination. Sitting motionless and pretending to be thinking about an assignment was more than just a policy of clandestine provocation, it was fundamentally an ontological rebellion, a breaking free from a constrictive and crippling moral perfectionism divested of the [freedoms available outside] . . . Staring straight ahead into blank space was not vegetative. Rather it became a mental mutiny, an inert agitation, a silent upsurge against extermination of the corporeal being: it was to shriek soundlessly against the betrayal of the mind and flesh."[15]

In many ways, daydreaming is a form of resistance we ought to expect given what the adolescent brain is capable of (versus what we actually have it do). To the adolescent, a correct answer may be far less interesting and inspiring than a good question or a great idea. Activating and challenging the imagination is what youth yearn to do.

Unfortunately, if we're honest with ourselves about how we often teach in our middle and high schools, we have to admit that many of the back-to-basics curricula and the no-nonsense pedagogies we've adopted in the era after No Child Left Behind sometimes reinforce intellectually stultifying experiences that crush creativity and exacerbate resistance. The ever-present test-prep activities, for example, are rarely exercises in the facilitation of hypothetical thinking. The point is to learn what the test wants and deliver it with minimal mistakes. No room for imagination, no expectation of curiosity, no need for creativity. Noting this tendency, Robert Sternberg, dean at Tufts University and a renowned researcher on intelligence, observes: "Try being creative on a standardized test and you will get slapped down just as soon as you get your score."[16] Students resist this stuff not because the knowledge isn't valuable or the answers the material provides aren't correct, but because the way it's being taught is telling them that their imagination is not welcome. The smart response in that context, especially in light of the brain developments detailed above, is to take one's imagination elsewhere or use it subversively.

Children Pretending, Adolescents Using Pretense

You might be wondering, "How is an adolescent's hypothetical thinking different from a child's? Don't six-year-olds imagine all kinds of worlds, creatures, situations, and stories all the time?" Absolutely, they do. But there are categorical differences between a child's way of imagining and an adolescent's way of hypothesizing. The possibilities young children create are typically limited to their real-world knowledge, experiences, and beliefs. Their make-believe worlds are rich and imaginative, to be sure, but when it comes to living in and interacting with others in the real world, children tend to derive their ideas from concrete experiences and their many limitations. As Amsel puts it, children's "imaginary worlds are not possible worlds by which reality can be understood."[17] For them, possibility is constrained by reality. Children know their imagined characters and scenarios are framed by the real world, not the other way around. In essence, children pretend.

Adolescents, on the other hand, use pretense. A pretense is an idea we may know is untrue but we want to act and think, if even for a few moments, as if it were true. Adolescents often love to use pretense because they are interested in claims and stipulations that contradict or reformulate how we understand reality. One reason they do this is because so much of reality is presented to them as a given. Through schooling experiences and the many rules and procedures we establish to keep them safe and compliant, we sort of say to them, "Here's the world, kids. As is."

For adolescents to feel that they have any agency, they need a future that is *not* given. They need a world that is malleable, open, indeterminate, capable of being built rather than simply received. Pretense breaks open the "given-ness" of things and poses alternate possibilities. "Suppose there never was a Civil War," says the eighth-grader. "What would happen if the moon were only 240 miles away instead of 240,000?" asks the sophomore. "If Huck Finn were Harriet Finn, a lot would have to change," asserts the junior. "I'm never gonna need to know the quadratic formula later in my life!" claims the freshman. Statements like these illustrate the powers of conjecture to pose questions and challenge the status quo, pushing systematically at the boundaries of the real to expose the limits of the concrete and reveal the possibilities of the abstract. When ostensibly educational spaces and relationships do not allow for such explorations, resistance is inevitable.

Adolescents as Impertinent Explorers of the Great What-If

When adolescents make conscious or unconscious decisions about how new information is to be categorized and stored, they see something first the way it *is*. But if they're in environments that support the new information, their minds can also rather quickly appreciate, sort, and store information as it *might* be. This helps explain why adolescents are often obsessed with the way things *should* be, since their imagination can now conceive of it against the way things *are*. Early adolescents in particular are just beginning to experience the power of their own imagination and the beauty of the well-considered what-if that can expose the gap between how things are and how they should be. Not surprisingly, when that gap is encountered in school or in the classroom, it can produce not just imagination and curiosity, but outright resistance. The complaint "That's not fair!" might therefore be read as "I imagine something different here, and I want to talk about it!"

The trouble is, adolescents are not very practiced at offering their theories and posing their hypotheticals in ways that will be well received. We could likely do better at translating adolescent outbursts into the sentiments and developmental moments they suggest, but anyone who has spent much time around teenagers knows they can be an impertinent bunch. They are sometimes impulsive and naive, often self-righteous, and frequently self-absorbed. This is not because they have bad attitudes per se; rather, it's the result of the slow process of acquiring new cognitive abilities. Hypothetical thinking does indeed emerge in adolescence, but it isn't perfected there. A fully developed thinking machine of that complexity takes some time. Part of being a lifelong learner is realizing that we are never done with exercising the possibilities of our own minds, that we can always grow, that we are forever integrating knowledge, experiences, meaning, and feelings into new understanding and skills. Adolescents have had less than two decades to amass their cognitive wealth. They're immature because they're *not yet mature*.

Here's an example of that immaturity: their propensity for risk taking. Whether the activity involves alcohol, drugs, fast cars, unprotected sex, or the accepted dares that can lead to tragic injury, stories about reckless and risky adolescents are commonplace. Explanations for risky behaviors range from simple, dismissive claims about peer pressure or raging hormones to complex ideas about the differences between adolescent and adult ways of thinking. But plenty of misconceptions swirl around why, where, when, and with whom teens often take dangerous risks. Developmental psychologist Laurence Steinberg lists some of these erroneous conclusions: "Among the widely held beliefs about adolescent risk-taking that have *not* been supported empirically are that adolescents are irrational or deficient in their information processing, or that they reason about risk in fundamentally different ways than adults, that adolescents do not perceive risks where adults do, or are more likely to believe that they are invulnerable, and that adolescents are less risk-averse than adults. None of these assertions is correct."[18] Instead, adolescents' occasional predilection for risk taking is a chemical matter connected to the old problem of the slow (but bright) brain system 2 falling behind the fast (but dim) brain system 1.[19]

First, there's the chemical: dopamine. Dopamine is manufactured in the brain and assists in the transmission of signals across neurons. Basically, it's a chemical messenger that works throughout the body in different organs in different ways. In the brain, dopamine is intimately connected with how we perceive and process rewards. More or less, when you do something that produces pleasure—that is, when you are "rewarded"—you get a squirt of dopamine in certain areas of the brain, and that feels good. Feel-good activities produce feel-good dopamine, which compels the individual to do more of those feel-good activities so that he or she continues to feel good. Addictive drugs actually amplify the effects of dopamine (though, because the effects are muted over time, addicts must take higher and higher doses to achieve the same high), and all addictive behaviors can be partly traced to the dopamine cycle. It's powerful stuff.

Here's the clincher: researchers have discovered a rapid increase in the development of dopamine delivery and reception systems during puberty, a process that occurs largely in brain system 1. This, scientists believe, is presumed to lead to increases in reward seeking during adolescence. The problem is, system 1's elevated desire to experience rewards happens *before* system 2 fully matures. The executive functions of self-regulation, delayed gratification, and impulse control develop at a much slower pace than the reward-seeking processes. System 2 actually develops over the course of adolescence, which, according to many neuroscientists, now extends well into one's twenties (look no further than the antics of undergraduates for confirmation of this ongoing developmental process). Steinberg explains that this gap between the arousal of system 1's reward seeking "and the full maturation of [system 2] . . . creates a period of heightened vulnerability to risk taking.[20] As a result, youth may choose or invent activities that offer social and experiential rewards without any deeper deliberations regarding consequences or justification. In doing so, they're not thoughtless—they're thought-*delayed*.

If adolescents are theoreticians, experimenters, meaning makers, knowledge builders, and experience inventors, a refusal to do what they're told to do is a brilliant way to take a risk and try to learn from it. Sometimes, in a single act of resistance, they are able to resist the status quo, garner personal and social rewards, and invent possibilities for themselves. Combine that with an imagination that can perceive of possibilities far preferable to the reality these young people confront, and you sometimes get rejections and refusals that occur on a whim. Adolescents are certainly capable of well-planned, considered, and strategic responses to perceived problems, but the lagging development of system 2, coupled with the robust reward structure of system 1, sometimes pushes them to jump before looking. Consequently, they may resist impulsively.

In situations where an adult brain might use caution and a careful weighing of options, the adolescent mind prefers instantaneous responsiveness and the possibility of a reward. Observing them act on that impulse, we often ask them incredulously, "What were you thinking?" When they respond with variations of "Um, I kinda wasn't. I'm only starting to do that now," we are faced with a choice. We can reprimand or punish them, which typically forecloses discussion and analysis with the vague hope that they'll somehow "stop and think about the consequences of their actions" while they sit alone in the hallway or in detention. Or we can see later interactions as opportunities to help adolescents develop the analytic capacities of system 2 and engage them in dialogue that evaluates both their decision making and their interpretations of events. When we decide to respond as a sounding board and safety net rather than as judge, jury, and executioner, we participate in the parts of risk taking and resistance that open up cognitive and social possibilities while we simultaneously diminish the need to scold and penalize.

The fact is, adolescents are going to take risks, and they are going to resist. It is therefore just as important that we consider the consequences of our actions when *we* respond to that inevitability as it is that that they think about the effects of their behavior when *they* try to realize their imaginations.

Acting Out Versus Acting Out of Curiosity

Educators often claim that their students' (mis)behaviors are evidence of resistance, that students are trying to obstruct something in the classroom that should not be refused. And we educators are often correct in this assumption. Students do try to undermine what we try to accomplish in the classroom. They do try to disrupt and destroy our plans. They are often resisting us. When student behaviors get in the way of our intentions, we may be right in calling their actions some form of reprehensible misbehavior. But it's when we move too quickly to ascribe intent that we often get the interpretation wrong. We say, "They're acting out," as if that explains the behavior, or we claim, "They're just doing this because they want attention" as if wanting attention from caring and more knowledgeable adult mentors were a bad thing. Because of the cognitive developmental achievements and challenges noted above, adolescents will sometimes (mis)behave to get noticed and will sometimes detract from others' learning to entertain themselves. But we will never really know what they're trying to do just by looking at what they're doing. The key is to investigate, not guess at, their intention. We need to be curious.

When we approach student resistance with curiosity instead of condemnation, we emulate some of the cognitive activity that motivates the resistance in the first place. Adolescents' newfound powers of hypothetical thinking turn them into active theoreticians who need to test ideas, explore boundaries, and create opportunities to expand their understanding. They grow reticent to accept others' claims just because the claims are given by authorities or accepted by others. They need to see how things work for themselves. The act of resistance translates hypothetical thinking into acting, helping the individual to move from passive reception of things as they are to active participation in changing things to what they could be. Resistance is a way of acting as a curious agent, not a submissive object. Peter McLaren puts it this way: "The theater of agency is *possibility*."[21]

Because students are young, inexperienced, and still developing, they may be unsure of the effects and outcomes of their actions, so their (mis)behaviors are often designed as experiments. They are asking, "What is possible here?" Even the simplest forms of resistance have an element of curiosity built into them. "I wonder what will happen if I ignore my teacher right now and turn to talk to my seatmate instead. Will I get caught? Will it matter if I miss something being discussed? Will I earn social points from my peers? How much will it harm my relationship with my teacher?" There are strong undercurrents of inquisitiveness in many moments of classroom resistance; in analyzing these moments, we need to recognize that they can have quite complex origins. Dismissing students' actions with casual labels or assuming we know the intent when we haven't worked to understand the students' perspectives only pushes them further away, thereby increasing the likelihood that their resistance will grow. Student (mis)behavior may be impulsive, problematic, and even annoying, but it's certainly not bereft of imagination, creativity, curiosity, and possibility. Consequently, to learn from student behavior and grow as responsive educators (just as we hope our students will learn and grow when they analyze their actions), we need to be as interested in their intentions as they are in the results.

Promising Practices: Engaging the Cognition of Opposition

It turns out that engaging resistance as a way of promoting cognitive development isn't that difficult. As described, we can use resistance productively by changing how we view adolescent actions and the brain processes that inspire them. When we think differently about what adolescents are thinking, we'll act differently in response to their actions. Let's look at some practices we should try (and a few to avoid) if we are to directly address forms of resistance that emerge from adolescent hypothetical thinking, imagination, and curiosity.

Avoiding Ire from the IRE (Initiate, Response, and Evaluate) Process

Students are sometimes at their most disruptive and resistant during classroom discussions. Sometimes, they are not interested in what we may be talking about, but more often, the *way* we are talking shuts down their imagination. Far too often, teachers teach by structuring interactions with students in an almost-digital, turn-by-turn manner. We initiate an inquiry or a demonstration, we solicit responses from students, we evaluate those responses, then we repeat. This initiate, response, and evaluate process, or IRE, can produce just that: ire. It can be maddening. And if allowed to proceed unchecked, it can actually deter hypothetical thinking.

Adolescents want to explore the edges of things, to imagine possibilities that are not restricted by reality. They need experience in testing hypotheses, posing questions, tackling complexity, and collaborating across differences to translate ideas into actions. The IRE technique positions the teacher as the sole authority and evaluator in the room and forces students into passive roles. In elicitation sequences like this, students must present their knowledge to the teacher, one at a time, so that it may be evaluated. Peers' perspectives are rendered irrelevant; tangential connections are not welcome; questions about meaning, purpose, or possibility are not encouraged; and creativity in expression is not appreciated.

To maintain the rules of this exchange, teachers spend inordinate amounts of time shushing students, waiting for their attention, reminding them of the one-at-a-time rule, and policing seemingly off-task behaviors to make sure students are adhering to the IRE process. That can turn even the most intriguing concepts and lessons into mind-numbing drills of knowledge regurgitation. And then teachers wonder why they get only monosyllabic responses from students even after careful and polite encouragements.

When you compare the IRE format to the types of informal conversations adolescents (and adults) commonly engage in when they're not forced to sit and receive information, there are marked differences. When talking with friends, people listen some, interrupt a little, stop to ask questions, clarify misconceptions, add stories that connect to what others are saying, tell anecdotes about how something reminds them of something else, and generally let dialogue go where it goes organically. These exchanges are rich with opportunities to share perspectives, generate ideas, solve problems, hatch plans, and form relationships. Their very lack of rigid structuring is what makes them so productive.

If you were to enter such a conversation with your friends and impose a one-at-a-time rule mandating that everyone must raise a hand before being acknowledged as the sole speaker, it would make your friends go elsewhere to converse. They'd hate the hassle, and your relationships would likely deteriorate. And guess what: our students often hate it too. Their off-task talking or speaking out of turn or their offering of thoughts without first raising their hands may be their attempts to break open a closed system of dialogue. One way of looking at their (mis)behavior during IRE exchanges is that they are taking the risk to undermine IRE to prepare themselves and their peers for more authentically democratic and cognitively enriching forms of communication in which learners are agents rather than vessels. Resisting IRE may be their attempt to initiate an actual dialogue in which imagined possibilities can be shared and theories of the world can be thoroughly examined, not just received and regurgitated.

I see this time and again in my own classroom. The moments when I open the conversation to linger and wait for students' unprompted thoughts, anecdotes, and connections is precisely when students lean in, sit up, take notice, and engage. Soon after moments like these are allowed to unfold, the third and fourth waves of hands start to go up as students seek to join in the dialogue, and then suddenly hands are no longer necessary, because the room is electrified with all kinds of imaginative meaning-making activity. Teachers who get students questioning and responding to each other like this, who encourage frequent connections and comments, who steer conversations not toward predetermined destinations but toward uncertain inquiries and imagined possibilities—those teachers are elevating anticipation and curiosity in ways that best allow hypothetical thinking to flourish. If we truly want to develop hypothetical thinking in youth and are committed to allowing them to practice their executive functions, we need to provide novel and uncertain modes of interacting so that they can experiment, imagine, and grow.

Making Meaning, Not Taking Notes

Students may resist a class activity because the way it is presented makes them feel dumb, inadequate, or incompetent. Teachers try to diminish this possibility by having students record information in various ways so they can return to it and use it for later academic work. Having students store information on paper rather than in the brain effectively externalizes memory retention. Teachers frequently require their students to take notes as a way of facilitating this memory-enhancing technique, but many teachers also use note-taking to occupy students with busywork while otherwise boring information is being dispensed. If done poorly, this method can produce more problems than solutions.

If we expect students to take notes during a lecture, for example, they may have trouble simultaneously listening, writing, and thinking about the material. Doing all three at once is asking a lot of the adolescent brain. Learners will often miss some of what was said, write only portions of what they heard, and will form only partial thoughts about the content as the brain shuffles back and forth between listening, writing, and thinking about what was heard and written. (Well-seasoned adult learners often have trouble with effective note-taking, too.)

Even when our students write down the information accurately and completely, they might not use the material effectively. If we don't pause occasionally, our students might not have time to let the knowledge sink in or to connect it with prior knowledge. Consequently, they can get anxious or angry because they know they will not do well when asked to recall what they just learned. They know they don't know the material, even when the information is on the paper right in front of them. That anxious realization can push learners' cognitive activity from the executive functions of brain system 2 into the reactionary and simplified responses of brain system 1.

The stress or confusion produced by note-taking practices like this effectively squanders students' powers of imagination and restricts their capacities for hypothetical thinking. As a result, the students are left with words they didn't understand, notes they don't remember, and concepts they never dissected. To make things worse, when the lecture or demonstration finally ceases, we might try to check for understanding by cold-calling on students. When that efforts yields only confusion or misconceptions, or if off-task (mis)behavior starts to emerge (as it usually does when students worry about looking stupid), some of us will dumb down the questions in hopes that at least one correct answer will be given. We might even ask the simplest one: "What did we just talk about?" But if our students' brains are preoccupied with the stressful challenge of simultaneously listening, writing, and thinking, and if they are afraid of looking dumb when they don't have a clue about what was just presented (much less what it might mean), they're not being impudent when they answer, "I dunno." They're being honest.

Taking notes has its educational value, to be sure. But to maximize its potential and minimize the possibility that students will resist the activity, information needs to be presented in bite-size pieces with frequent pauses. This allows the brain to catch up and make meaning of what it is seeing and hearing, to do the building and connecting that learning requires. To strengthen the connections between the just-acquired knowledge and the preexisting knowledge in the minds of the learner, we must provide time for review, discussion, and application. We must also slow down, ask higher-order questions that require synthesis and evaluation, and provide opportunities for students to talk things over with their peers. These formative assessment techniques and methods of checking for understanding are crucial not just to a well-planned lesson but also to a well-engaged brain. After all, recording information is not learning it. To know something, we have to be able to use it.

Asking "What's Going On?"

When students do resist and when we think their (mis)behavior merits a conversation, we would do well to approach those interactions psychologically, not just disciplinarily. If students build knowledge rather than absorb it and if brain system 2 needs the right supportive contexts to fully initiate, we need to know what students were thinking and trying to do before we provide guidance or render judgment. To do this, one favorite technique I recommend to preservice and in-service educators is to begin all disciplinary conversations with a question. My favorite is: "What's going on?"

This question invites students to share their experiences, perceived causes, and intended effects. It also gives the educator a glimpse into how students think and what they know (and don't know) *before* disciplinary decisions are made.

The conversations that ensue from open-ended questions like "What's going on?" lend themselves to interventions that encourage students to practice their executive functions. When we help adolescents prioritize a different set of goals and reflect on a different array of effects, including larger social or political issues related to their behavioral choices, we are providing them with rich developmental opportunities. Under such encouragement, students can stretch their cognitive capacities, revise their self-understanding, improve their social relationships, and imagine different outcomes. In this way, resistance may be transformed from an impediment to learning to an opportunity for growth.

School Is Not His Thing

Courtney Harris is eating lunch with her social studies department colleague, Ted Kirk. As often happens, the conversation turns to their problem students, and that's when Courtney mentions Martin.

Ted remembers the student. "Yeah," he says, "I had him in my class last year. Nice kid, but a C student at best."

Finishing her bite of salad, Courtney tries to take a hopeful tone. "I think he could do so much better if he wanted to," she says, "but he just doesn't seem to want to. And lately, he's been in an academic nosedive. Getting a C would be a big improvement." She pauses for a second to think about what she has done to try to convince Martin to do his best. "I mean, I tell him he's smart all the time. I tell him I know he can do it. I try to be as encouraging and friendly as I can, but he never asks for help and he never raises his hand anymore. I can't figure out why he doesn't seem to care about school."

Ted asks, "Do you think it's a self-esteem thing?"

"Yeah, maybe," Courtney says, "except that he is so confident with his ideas when you talk with him one-on-one, and he seems so well liked by his friends. In small group work or debates, he'll offer his opinions, but he just won't do the written work when it's required. When I confronted him about it one time, Martin actually said to me that he didn't see the point in doing the assignment. He actually said he didn't care about the topic and then he said, 'I'm only gonna get a C on the worksheet anyways.'"

As Courtney's words jog Ted's memory about Martin's performance in his class last year, Ted says, "I think his homework grade last year was almost a zero. The only reason he scraped by with a C was due to group projects, simulation performances, a few mediocre test scores, and his participation grade. Even though he's such a nice kid, I had to look pretty hard for reasons to give him reward tickets. And when I did, it felt like charity and never seemed to motivate him to do more."

"I know," Courtney agrees. "Several weeks ago he turned in two homework assignments back-to-back, and I wanted to encourage him to keep it up so I gave him a Student of the Week badge. But he sort of crumpled when I announced it, and I never heard back from his mom when I sent the letter about it home."

Hearing this, Ted concludes, "I think he just doesn't care about learning. School's not his thing."

When the bell rings, Ted and Courtney pack up their bags and head off to their afternoon classes. But for the rest of the afternoon, Courtney can't help wondering if she and Ted are missing something. At the end of the school day, Courtney walks to her car and sees Martin and his friend practicing free throws on the basketball court next to the faculty parking lot. As she gets into her car, she watches Martin take ten free throws while his friend rebounds; then they switch. Curious about what she is witnessing, she sits in her car and watches the two boys go through three more rotations, clearly practicing their technique and getting better. The scene makes her wonder: why is Martin so committed to this activity but seldom so motivated in his schoolwork?

CHAPTER 5

"Why Should I Try?"

The Motivations That Drive Opposition

EDUCATION, LIKE ALL social activities, necessitates conflict. It requires the educator and the student to manage the tension that is produced whenever "what I want" and "what is expected of me" don't align. Internal desires, hopes, and goals are forever challenged by outside expectations, norms, and responsibilities. Even though old Enlightenment notions of liberty often frame schooling as the primary means by which individuals become "free," anyone who has ever been forced to sit in a boring classroom listening passively to a lecture about a topic of no interest knows that this claim may be a bit stretched. In many ways, education is obligation. From the moment the alarm goes off earlier than the student would like to get out of bed to the last page of homework completed during what might otherwise be an evening's worth of free time, education can feel like a constant demand to comply. And because it asks students to suspend their individual desires and supplant them with somebody else's, education will always carry the potential for resistance.

This chapter examines the role that internal processes play in shaping adolescent resistance in school. The goal in this treatment is to reveal the powerful undercurrents of motivations, mind-sets, emotions, and skills that direct student's feelings and behaviors and often prompt students to resist. Here, the conflicted nature of education is understood not as an impediment to learning but as an essential component of healthy processes in which students find meaning, form identities, and build relationships.

Resistance and the Inner Drive to Feel Safe and Free

Many of us became educators because we loved our content area, enjoyed working with youth, wanted to make a difference in our community, and/or liked the lifestyle afforded by an academic calendar. We didn't necessarily choose the profession because we wanted to get involved in the messy work of dealing with people's feelings. But try as we might to "stick to the basics" and avoid the "touchy-feely" stuff, the fact of the matter is that we work with people—people with desires, fears, and countless other complicated emotions, people who do strange and challenging things based on psychodynamic forces that are difficult to fathom. To do our jobs well as educators of people, we need to recognize that we are also students of psychology.

Learning is not solely a cognitive activity. From a psychoanalytic perspective, learning is a *psychic* event. That is, learning involves an individual's ideas, emotions, drives, wishes, and fears. Learning is super cognitive, to be sure (see chapter 4), but it also involves interpersonal, intrapersonal, and affective components. That's why learners are often thrilled by what they learn, excited by new skills, frustrated by difficult knowledge, or angered by an awareness of injustice. We *feel* knowledge as much as we think about it.

Learning is a psychic event because it enlists the many conscious procedures that are used to feel and make sense of new knowledge, but also because it involves an array of processes that are, at best, only partly known by the learner at any given moment. This partly known aspect of our internal mental selves is called the *unconscious*—the powerful but largely hidden undercurrent of intuition, apprehension, and desires that drive our emotions and reactions. The unconscious guides our inclinations when we are awake and creates our dreams when we sleep. Through focused introspection or various forms of therapy, individuals can approach the unconscious and sometimes learn what's at stake for it and what it wants from one situation to the next, but, as the theory goes, the unconscious is largely a destination we never quite reach. We run after it more than we catch it. (In fact, many of us spend a lot of our adult lives trying to figure out why we do what we do and feel what we feel!) The classroom implication here is that students (and educators) are not fully the masters of their self-knowledge. Though learning is often presented as the individual's process of getting to know the world, it is also the process of getting to know oneself.

Why Education Must Interfere

Scholars who have applied psychoanalytic thought to the classroom have identified the way education, if it is to be successful, must interfere with the student's self-understanding. This disruption is necessary because a person's conscious self prefers to operate in a sort of self-centered mode, as if the conscious self were in total control of one's thoughts, actions, and environment. Psychoanalysts variously refer to this tendency as the narcissistic, omniscient, and omnipotent self, or the parts of our conscious and unconscious processes that mistakenly believe we totally know what we're doing, totally know who we are, and totally know how the world works. But when new knowledge is confronted, the self is forced to realize that it doesn't know everything, that previous understanding may have been inaccurate, and that neither the self nor the world functions as theorized.

Though the disconnect between a person's unconscious understanding and reality is often understood primarily as a cognitive challenge, it's an emotional and existential one too. New knowledge sometimes shakes learners' perspectives and their conclusions about themselves, their relationships, and their world. In those moments when new knowledge threatens old understanding—when learning effectively injures the learner—feelings like confusion, anxiety, anger, or fear may surface from the unconscious, and the learner may not know entirely why (i.e., "I'm not sure why I feel this strongly about X in this moment, but I do!"). Educational philosopher Deborah Britzman understands this as a moment of confrontation that produces interference in the mind of the learner: "In psychoanalytic terms, for the self to be more than a prisoner of its own narcissism, the self must bother itself. It must learn to obligate itself to notice the breaches and losses between acts and thoughts, between wishes and responsibilities, between dreams and waking life. To think is to haunt one's thoughts, to be haunted by thoughts."[1]

A frequent outcome of this interfering, bothering, or haunting is to pull away from new knowledge or push back against it—to resist. Britzman elaborates:

> Consider what education asks of students: to listen, to pay attention, to stop talking, to hold the whisper, to stay with the subject, to concentrate, to risk a mistake, to correct a mistake, to talk in front of their peers, to take a test, to go play, to be serious, to stop laughing, to consider things which would not occur to the self, to debate a belief, to encounter strange theories; indeed, it asks students to confront perspectives, situations, and ideas that may not just be unfamiliar but appear at first glance as a criticism of the learner's view. In all these demands, education seems to be asking selves to risk their resistance

even as educators have difficulty tolerating the forms working through resistance takes. These demands directed outward return to the teacher in contested forms: as questions, hostile notes, gossip, hurt feelings, forgotten details, failure, incomplete sentences, baffling behavior, falling asleep, sexual innuendo, boredom, slips of the tongue, jokes, irrelevant comments, silence, indeed as all other sorts of ambiguous and puzzling gestures. Our educational demand actually comprises two: we demand that the self consider its own wishes, desires, and needs—to think for itself—precisely in the same moment that we demand that the self think about the requirements of others.

Of course, students want to learn, to attain new knowledge and skills that enhance their understanding and ability to interact with the world in a way that makes them feel confident, connected, and happy. But students are also motivated to avoid displacing their needs with others' and to dodge any experiences that will produce confusion, embarrassment, guilt, shame, anxiety, or pain. In the mind of the learner, some knowledge is therefore worth resisting. For example, the notions "I'm dumb," "I won't be successful," or "Nobody likes me" can be disturbing if not terrorizing, which is why the learner might (and maybe should) refuse any experiences that generate such thoughts. The trick in understanding resistance is to recognize when we create or allow such experiences in the learning environments we lead.

Learners readily accept new knowledge when it is experienced as confirming or when it adds value to preexisting knowledge, but when new knowledge is emotionally or existentially difficult, the learner may use various mechanisms to defend against it (hence, "defense mechanisms" such as denial, withdrawal, humor, projection, and aggression). In those moments, the learner has what educational scholar Jennifer Logue calls "an affective investment in ignorance"—the learner would prefer *not* knowing because a lack of knowledge is less psychologically threatening than accepting the knowledge.[2] This willful ignorance is most often a fleeting, situational refusal of a specific type of knowledge, but it can endure if perceived threats persist. Unfortunately, even tragically, educators often misread such temporary resistance as an indication of a pervasive unwillingness to learn anything new, as if the student's resistance to some threatening knowledge is evidence of resistance to learning writ large. Nothing could be further from the truth.

Responding to the Threatened Learner

Recognizing that students are resisting should at the very least tell us that they are frightened.[3] Something happened before or during the activity that the learner has interpreted as a threat. The new knowledge being offered, its context, or both might have made the student feel frustrated, inadequate, insecure, mocked, or unsafe. Or the new knowledge might have required significant revision of preexisting ideas to which the student was attached. This may have made the individual fearful of the cognitive and emotional changes needed to accommodate the new knowledge. (For an exploration of the racial, ethnic, and class implications of this phenomenon, see part III.)

For example, we often try to encourage students to learn by offering incentives in the form of gold stars, candy, prizes, pizza parties, or monetized point systems that students can redeem for goods at school or businesses nearby. Or, we bestow Student of the Month types of honors on those who have distinguished themselves in some positive way. We believe that the knowledge of these potential rewards will motivate students to do their best. But for some students, such knowledge is a threat. Students who emerge from collectivist cultures in which selfhood is constructed around family and community, where service and deference to the collective is prized far more than individual distinction, the knowledge that hard work will be labeled with "I'm better than all other students this month" or "I won and you lost" awards can greatly interfere with their psychosocial well-being. To be singled out is to be separate from the collective, which is why individualized rewards can be experienced as shameful for students whose worldview is more collective than individualistic. A student confronting this no-win situation at school would be rightfully hesitant in, if not resistant to, activities that may lead to these awards. Resistance offers protection from a psychosocial threat like this even when the cost may be cultural misunderstanding and diminished academic achievement.

For the educator to be annoyed or inconvenienced by this resistance would be like a physician being irritated or disrupted by a patient's pain. Both the resistance and the pain tell the professional that something important is happening. A doctor uses pain—where it's located, how it presents, when it occurs, the way it feels, when it goes away—to figure out what might be wrong. Doctors treat pain as a *symptom* of something wrong, not the wrong thing itself. Resistance in the classroom might be approached in the same manner. Although resisting students may be attempting to withhold their best efforts, to undermine the teacher, to avoid cooperating with others, or to disrupt the flow of a lesson, these students are also conveying a good deal of information in their opposition. Like pain, resistance is often only a surface indicator of deeper issues that require professionals' attention. Educators' first reactions might be to lament resistant behavior or try to suppress it, and that's understandable given adults' own fears, drives, desires, and unconscious needs (i.e., we too prefer unthreatening environments and types of knowledge that confirm rather than deny our essential goodness). But psychoanalytic theories teach us that if we can remain curious about the emotional, conscious, and unconscious dimensions of students' behaviors, we can shift our practices from suppression to investigation.

Mind-Sets: The Beliefs Underneath the Refusals

Part of the hard work of dealing with student resistance occurs when we push ourselves to better align our practices with what we know about student motivation. We will explore many of those practices shortly. But one of the more difficult challenges of engaging rather than suppressing student resistance is to let go of some "commonsense" notions we adopted long ago, ones that may be continually supported by our colleagues and institutions. To reveal what motivates resistance and what might channel student behaviors into more productive arenas, we sometimes need to rid ourselves of old fantasies and do some resisting ourselves. This section examines how the beliefs that students hold (and the way we influence those beliefs through our practices) impact the decision to resist in the classroom. You might be surprised at what it suggests.

Avoiding the "You're So Smart!" Trap

Educational psychologist Carol Dweck and several other scholars have radically altered a whole list of dominant assumptions about achievement motivation. In doing so, they have exposed multiple reasons why students often resist and withdraw rather than invest and engage.[4] Perhaps her biggest insight pertains to intelligence. Long believed to be an intrinsic quality that stays more or less constant throughout an individual's lifetime, intelligence, we now know, is anything but fixed. The numbers can range a bit, depending on which researcher you talk to, but most scholars in the field estimate that around 70 percent of our intelligence is malleable. That means the vast majority of our "smartness" can be improved simply by practicing things, trying new problems or activities, challenging ourselves, and applying good old-fashioned effort. Given this, it no longer makes much sense to try to capture our "IQ" in a single number using a single test at a single moment in time. Intelligence is an activity and a process far more than it is a quantity.

What do these conclusions about intelligence have to do with learning, students, and resistance? Wondering the same thing, Dweck set up a series of experiments involving manipulatives and decision points and watched as kids of various ages interacted with them. In one experiment, students were asked to solve a series of puzzles. When they completed each one, they were given the option of attempting to solve either a similar or more difficult puzzle in the next round. When the students completed a puzzle, half of them received praise for *how hard they had tried*, while the other half received praise for *how smart they were*. The differences in subsequent behaviors between those two groups were striking. The majority of those who received praise for having "worked hard" or having "tried very hard" chose a more difficult puzzle in the next round. Those who were praised for having been "so smart" tended to choose a puzzle of equal or reduced difficulty in the next round. That is, the students who were praised for their effort tended to request more challenge and displayed more investment in learning when they were asked to choose the next puzzle. On the other hand, the students praised for their intelligence tended to refuse the opportunity to learn more and resisted trying harder. The second group essentially chose to withhold effort and underperform, and they did this immediately after being told how smart they were. Why?

To answer that question, Dweck interviewed students about their beliefs and learning experiences and discovered how the messages that educators communicate can profoundly influence what she calls a student's "mind-set." Because of the way they had been praised, encouraged, and evaluated, some students developed a "growth mind-set" while others developed a "fixed mind-set." Those with a growth mind-set believed they could improve their skills in certain activities if they tried. For them, the determining factor was not an inherent quality they possessed; instead they believed their performance hinged on whether they devoted sufficient focus, time, and effort to the activity. In short, they believed not just that practice makes better, but that practice makes *smarter*. In contrast, the students with a fixed mind-set believed that either they had the prerequisite intelligence to accomplish a task or they did not. When an activity was easy for them, that meant they were smart. But when they struggled or faltered at another task, they considered the difficulty confirmation that they somehow did not possess the required intelligence. "I'm a hands-on learner," they might claim, "not a math person." Because the intelligence was hypothesized to be innate and immutable, students with fixed mind-sets often maintained that they could do nothing to change their intelligence. They believed they were either smart or not so smart (i.e., dumb) and that their achievement would reflect this level of intelligence.

Amazingly, all it took to get one group of students to withdraw effort and resist challenge was praising them for their smartness. To see how this works, put yourself in that student's shoes. Nobody wants to look stupid, and everyone wants to feel smart, so when someone praises you for *being* smart, you want to reproduce the circumstances that generated that acclaim. You've just received an assessment of a fixed quality you possess, and your goal is now to confirm it. In fact, when a teacher praises how smart you are, this is how you may hear it:

- Look smart! Don't risk making mistakes!
- If you really are smart, you shouldn't have to try very hard—it should be easy for you.
- And if you have to work hard, it means you aren't that bright.

Trying more challenging activities exposes you to the possibility that you will fail the next time and that you might not be told you're smart again. Or worse, you might even be told you're dumb (or "college prep" or "academic priority" or "at-risk" or "not GATE/TAG material" or "not ready for AP classes" or any other of the many fixed mind-set labels we routinely apply to students). So you stick with the same level of difficulty or even choose an easier task when you can, as a way of preserving the impression that you're not dumb, as hollow as that achievement may be. And when opportunities arise for you to demonstrate your proficiency on a summative assessment or final project, you might get anxious or look for ways to withdraw or resist if the difficulty of the task appears to be above where previous success was guaranteed. Basically, you're motivated to stay where you are, to avoid challenge, and to protect yourself from the possibility of looking and feeling dumb.

Now, when you're praised for *trying hard* (whether you succeeded or not), you're motivated by a different logic. The message you're getting is that your intelligence is malleable, that you can get better at something—smarter at it—if you apply effort and develop your capabilities. So you want to keep trying because the praise you're receiving is linked to your effort more than your performance, plus the more you try the more you can see incremental results. You eventually become motivated not so much by the praise but more because you want to try harder to figure something out. Or maybe you even attempt a more difficult challenge to stretch yourself and see what you might be able to do, especially if your friends are doing the same. You're growing because you believe you can. Mistakes and stumbles are just part of the process of getting better and smarter, not confirmation that you will never have what it takes to succeed. You might even ask for help on occasion, but not too much! You just want a hint, then you want to figure it out on your own through your own hard work. At this point, if you're resisting anything, you're resisting doubts about your capabilities or worries about your eventual success. Cognitively and motivationally, you're on fire.

So what should we do as educators to promote these forms of engagement and prevent these forms of resistance? First, we need to stop praising students for their intelligence. It's neither motivating nor helpful, and it creates conditions that are ideal for withdrawal, diminished effort, resistance, and even bullying. Dweck and her colleagues' research shows that in an environment in which intelligence is understood to be something you either have or don't, image maintenance quickly becomes the primary concern—not learning, collaboration, or compassion. By telling students how smart they are in an attempt to get them to work harder and engage more, we actually produce resistance and virtually guarantee that students will underperform, shy away from challenges, and be more invested in tearing others down than building one another up.

To avoid the pitfalls of a fixed mind-set, we need to recognize and encourage students' persistence, their grit, or their stick-to-itiveness.[5] We should note how mistakes or lapses in success are opportunities for enhanced performance on the next try. We must remind students (and ourselves and our colleagues) that errors are only indicators of where learners are now, not where they will always be. We need to stress the incremental nature of human capabilities and how each of us will become more proficient at anything we choose as long as we persist. We should share stories of how we experienced difficulty in some activity at first but then worked at it, sought help, stuck with it, and eventually became competent at it, with room to improve even today. And whenever we can, we need to reinforce the fact that none of us were born competent at anything, that everything we are able to do with proficiency we achieved through effort, over time.

Second, we need to maintain high expectations and refrain from dumbing things down to give struggling or resisting students an easier time. Typically, students don't need academic work to be easier for them to be successful; they need more support, encouragement, and resources to motivate their persistence. Removing challenges does not produce growth; it encourages stagnation. Conversely, when we keep standards high, we build trust and confidence by conveying the message that we believe students possess the skill and the will to rise to the occasion.

Telling students we know they can get there and that we will show them how is far more motivating than telling them we've made their work easier. Students know when they're being pandered to even when they are often willing to accept—or may actually request—lowered expectations. They tolerate this pandering or plead for less rigor because they know that lowered expectations usually come bundled with diminished work. (Again, in the mind of the adolescent, less work = more free time = more autonomy, which can be quite a lure especially when immediate desires are allowed to eclipse future aspirations.) The long-term effects of these lowered expectations are well known and tragic, particularly for racially marginalized or low-income students. Consequently, to keep all students engaged in our activities rather than resisting them, we may have to provide extra support, alter our approaches, and modify assignments, but we must always make sure we challenge our students and encourage their persistence. No one gets better at anything without challenge and persistence.

Third, when giving feedback to students about their work, we cannot be afraid to be critical. We don't have to tell them they are doing great to encourage them. Often, we don't have to evaluate their work at all. We are often far too loose in the way we dispense empty accolades like "Good job," "Nice work," or "Well done." What do any of those assessments even mean? How do they help students know what they did right and how they can improve on it? As an alternative, being solely descriptive about what we see is often the only feedback students need to go back to their desk and make their work better. The student who is reluctant to apply his or her best effort doesn't need to be told "You're awesome" or "You're really smart." That student needs to see where the work meets expectations and where it needs to go next if it is to be better. For example:

> I see in these first two paragraphs, Johnny, that you're using transition sentences and proper punctuation, but toward the end of your essay, I see less of that. I also see that your conclusion wraps up a few main points but names several items you did not cover earlier in your essay. I can also see that you've worked hard on this so far. How do you feel about it? Where do you think it needs revision? How can I help you improve on your efforts thus far?

Statements and questions like these don't need to be dressed up with bland and vacuous praise for them to be successful. And truth be told, many of us deliver that praise because it makes *us* feel good not so much because it makes the students do any better. It's a message we send to ourselves that *we're* doing a "good job," that *we* are competent. Part of the lesson here is to remember that teaching is not about our needs—it's about theirs.

If we have cocreated a culture of risk taking and have codeveloped a learning community in which mocking comments and hurtful smirks are not allowed, students will experience no shame when areas that need improvement are noted. They will be motivated to make their work better because they can feel their knowledge growing and their skills improving, and they can see the results in their enhanced performances over time. This is reward enough; it doesn't need to be sugared with unnecessary praise. As a result, we should try to eliminate those comments about how smart a struggling student is or how intelligent a successful one must be. And if it takes us a while to get into this new habit, we don't need to beat ourselves up about it. Challenge and persistence is good for us as much as it is for our students. But if we still feel the occasional need to use praise to motivate, we need to make sure it's (1) specific, that is, based on some skill or talent the student is developing; (2) sincere, namely, not vacuous or meritless; and (3) spare, or it loses its punch because of its ubiquity. In the end, to sustain the motivation required to achieve academic success, students need forms of encouragement that make them want to persist, not resist.

Getting Better Versus Being the Best

Educators commonly try to motivate students by getting them to focus on the result of their efforts. "Are you ready for the test?" "What grade will you achieve in this class?" "What's your GPA?" These performance goals makes sense because we want students to link present actions to future outcomes and see themselves as agents in that causal process. In an effort to assess learning and motivate students to do their best, schools sometimes send the message that the sole reason to engage in academic activities is to demonstrate one's ability.[6] However, grades and other measures of achievement can become major sources of anxiety, especially for peer-preoccupied youth operating in competitive environments. Many students rightfully wonder, "How do I compare with others? Do I measure up? What grade did they get? Am I dumber than they are?" When a letter or a number is assigned to their performance and praise is attached to how high that letter or number goes, we reinforce the message that outperforming others should be students' objective.

This is the major disadvantage of what has come to be known as a *performance goal orientation*. Whether explicitly stated or not, the hidden curriculum of performance goals tells students to broadcast to their peers that they are more able than others (or at least not less able than some) or to hide their performance altogether out of a fear that theirs is deficient. Either way, the student is being trained to resist collaboration and refrain from helping peers, all in an effort to attain public recognition for their efforts by being "better" than their classmates. In fact, researchers have found that students who are encouraged to adopt performance goal orientations are less likely to seek help themselves.[7] Clearly, this is not a desirable outcome.

In contrast, a *mastery goal orientation* shifts the attention away from relative ability and toward learning, understanding, self-improvement, and the development of knowledge and skills over time. Like Dweck's growth mind-set detailed earlier, students are less likely to feel threatened when their teachers and peers are focused on progress rather than product. When classrooms are dedicated to developing proficiency rather than capturing ability, the worry of making a mistake and having it "count" disappears. Students will be less likely to resist academic work because there are no academic or social penalties for temporarily failing.

To move toward more mastery orientations, we don't have to abandon graded final products or other forms of summative assessments, but we might restrict their usage to those instances when students have already demonstrated, through multiple formative assessments, that they "get it." When we do this, final performances are transformed into positive opportunities to show what students know rather than stress-inducing exercises to catch their mistakes. Academic activities are no longer opportunities for students to claim they're "the best" compared with their peers; rather, classwork becomes an occasion to get better at whatever they try, alongside their peers, while being helped by learned educators in a community dedicated to growth.

Motivation: (Not) Doing Something for a Reason

Whereas psychoanalysis is mainly concerned with the emotions that emerge from unconscious drives, educational psychology is often concerned with the behaviors that arise from motivation. Why do students choose to do one thing but neglect or resist another? What helps to increase motivation, and what might diminish it? What are the cognitive, social, cultural, and affective components that influence decision making? Or, more pointedly, where should we locate blame for motivation problems that manifest in resistant behaviors? Should we target unmotivated students or unmotivating contexts?

Numerous psychological and neuroscientific studies suggest that students are generally most motivated to invest energy in activities that promise growth, success, challenge, and better relationships; they are least motivated to invest when contexts run contrary to this. Therefore, to begin to understand how resistance and motivation are connected in the mind of the adolescent learner, we may have to admit what youth already know: school isn't always motivating.

Some school activities are not enjoyable, some content is not interesting, some knowledge is not valued, and some experiences are not welcome. "Duh," a student might say in response to this observation. Despite what may seem to be a self-evident statement, educators often forget the demotivating aspects of school and we exacerbate rather than ameliorate student resistance when we think of motivation in simplistic, problematic, or "commonsense" terms. Thus, an in-depth analysis of motivation can help us respond to resistance more productively. In short, to understand why students say no, we need to understand what motivates the yes.

Self-Efficacy (Not Self-Esteem)

Researchers have identified multiple factors that shape students' achievement motivation, many of which demonstrate an intermingling of intrinsic and extrinsic forces. A student's sense of perceived self-efficacy is an important one of these factors, in part, because it helps to explain why many students resist. Perceived self-efficacy is the student's personal judgment of his or her capabilities to plan and carry out a course of action that will achieve the student's goals. It's the part of the student's psyche that says, "I think I can do this and I think I know how." Students who believe they are capable of accomplishing a task and can identify the steps needed to do it are far more motivated to undertake the activity than those who doubt their capabilities or who cannot name the steps required for success. Educational researcher Barry J. Zimmerman explains that "self-efficacious students participate more readily, work harder, persist longer, and have fewer adverse emotional reactions when they encounter difficulties than do those who doubt their capabilities . . . Students' beliefs about their efficacy to manage academic task demands can also influence them emotionally by decreasing their stress, anxiety, and depression."[8]

If the student's goals include pleasing the teacher, avoiding punishment, or garnering the praise of a parent, then the student's self-efficacy may be driven by extrinsic forces. However, whether those forces are internally or externally derived is less important than what individuals *believe* about their capabilities. Educational psychologists George Slavich and Philip Zimbardo assert that self-efficacy beliefs influence the extent to which students "are optimistic versus pessimistic, make resilient versus detrimental attributions for successes and failures, apply appropriate coping strategies for dealing with difficult situations, and persist in the face of challenge." Slavich and Zimbardo therefore conclude that self-efficacy beliefs "are a strong determinant of students' academic success."[9] This is a crucial point: regardless of whether the teacher is telling students to do something or the students are intrinsically motivated to do it, if there is sufficient doubt in the students' minds as to their capacity to succeed, they will likely resist.

Giving up during an academic task or refusing to begin it in the first place is a common form of resistance in the classroom and is often rooted in students' perceived self-efficacy. In such situations, it isn't so much that students don't *want* to do something; it may be that they don't believe they *can* do it. If this is the case, they (and others) may need to be convinced that they are capable. Only then will their resistance wane. A productive approach here would be to focus on enhancing students' perceptions and skill-sets so that students believe in the possibility of positive outcomes and can see how they are achievable. To that end, Slavich and Zimbardo identify three sets of expectations that must be managed if students are to become self-efficacious: (1) the students' own beliefs about their likelihood of success; (2) the beliefs that others (e.g., peers, parents, and principals) have regarding the students' potential for success; and (3) the teacher's beliefs about both the students' likelihood of success and the teacher's own self-perceived potential to guide students to that success.[10]

Focusing solely on the individual student's self-efficacy is helpful, but it's only one part of the ecology in which that self-efficacy is constructed. Students who are surrounded by disbelieving peers and discouraging adults, or who suffer from institutional labels that predict underperformance (such as "remedial," "SpEd," or anything other than "gifted and talented" or "advanced placement"), may find it difficult to generate the motivation to attempt challenging tasks. Therefore, it's important that we manage those social expectations, too, through strong and responsive classroom management techniques and reflections on our own beliefs about what's possible for our students and for ourselves. We might even need to reconsider and reform the way we test, sort, and rank students by "ability." After all, no learning environment will be successful if students don't believe they will succeed.

When we respond to forms of student resistance that emerge from low self-efficacy by scolding students for being unmotivated, or when we issue reprimands, threaten detentions, or dispense referrals when they defy our directives, we demonstrate to students that their core motivational problem is less important to us than their behavioral compliance. Sure, when students experience low self-efficacy, they may say in a defiant tone something like "I don't feel like it," but internally what they mean to say is, "Convince me I can do it." Though many of us may want to respond to the student who says, "I don't feel like it," with a lecture on the pitfalls of bad attitudes, a better approach might be to provide additional encouragements and demonstrations of how the student might achieve the success he or she desires. Sometimes to engage resistance well, we have to listen closely to hear what our students are too scared or too immature to say, and then respond to that resistance not punitively, but generously.

Before moving on, I want to offer one quick observation to help dispel the way the preceding insights are often misconstrued. Self-efficacy is not self-esteem. For far too long, educators have erroneously stressed the importance of student's self-esteem, largely due to a cultural shift toward that approach in the 1970s, 1980s, and 1990s. Unfortunately, self-esteem, or how one feels about oneself, has little to no correlation with a person's actual qualities or talents. Some people can feel horrible about themselves and be remarkably talented, caring, and productive, whereas other folks can think the world of themselves and be complete jerks. This is why self-efficacy is a far better concept to organize our work than self-esteem. When our goal is to improve self-efficacy, we will necessarily focus on students' capabilities and what they believe they can do (as opposed to how "Awesome!" they are). When educators target self-esteem, however, they often shift their practices toward empty forms of praise that effectively train students to expect accolades from others (more on that later) or encourage self-centered "Me, me, me!" responses to interpersonal difficulties. In the classroom, chasing self-esteem leads nowhere. If we truly want to motivate our resistant students, we will be far more successful in the short and long term if we focus on elevating students' perceived self-efficacy rather than indulging them with empty promises of self-esteem. In the end, we want students to do well and then feel good about it, not feel good and hope for the best.

(Dis)Interest

Students sometimes resist academic activity by expressing a lack of interest in the topic being studied. "This is boring," they say, or, "Why are we even studying this?" they ask. If they don't possess sufficient concern for or curiosity about the content, their motivation to focus and apply effort will typically weaken, and (mis)behavior usually isn't far behind. Good teachers know this. They know it because they have seen time and again the causal link between a good anticipatory set (or "hook") and their students' engagement, and they know how well-sequenced lessons peppered with novelty, experimentation, and social interaction can elevate students' motivation to stay focused and eventually succeed. Even when teachers work hard to demonstrate the relevance of their content and draw connections to students' real-life situations either now or in the future, it's important to recognize that when students express disinterest, it's a sign that the lesson isn't working for at least some of them. In those instances, it will be far more productive to alter our pedagogy than it will be to blame students for being bored.

But sometimes even interested students can appear resistant. The act of generating and sustaining interest can lead students to behave in ways that we may misinterpret as disengagement or refusal. It's counterintuitive, but it's true, and here's why: according to research conducted by educational psychologist Ann Renninger, a student's interest in a topic, activity, or skill develops through four phases, each of which possesses a particular set of characteristics, wants, and needs.[11] Students initially have what Renninger calls "triggered situational interest," in which the learner is open to being told what to do as long as such direction is given concisely and the student's ideas and the difficulty of the new knowledge is respected in the exchange. As discussed earlier, new knowledge can produce emotional responses, both positive and negative, and to keep moving the learner into deeper forms of interest, the teacher must acknowledge and appreciate those reactions.

If conditions support it, learners soon move into the second phase, "maintained situational interest," in which they develop their interest by making connections to previous knowledge and experiences. Here students need an environment conducive to exploration. They become open to being told what to do so that they can make sense of the material, especially when confusions arise. For students' interests to be maximized, however, their efforts must be recognized and their ideas must be integrated. Entertaining a student's incorrect assumptions or errant calculations for a few moments can often inspire much greater interest and engagement than simply offering a correction. Personalized instruction has to contain a personal component. We might ask students, "Why do you think that?" "How did you get to that conclusion?" "What makes you so sure?" This second phase of interest development underscores that what we do in schools can't just be about learning isolated knowledge and decontextualized skills. It must also be about the unique learner who is building that new knowledge onto previous understanding and integrating those new skills into preexisting capacities.

In the third phase, what Renninger calls "emerging individual interest," there is a subtle but critical shift. As learners move from their dependency on teacher-driven suggestions and content explanations to more self-driven and individualized forms of inquiry, they need space to play with ideas independently. At this point, the student's own curiosity about the content is felt as more vital than the teacher's inquiries. The teacher has done a terrific job in getting students to this phase but now needs to shift tactics and fade somewhat. Students may get frustrated if the teacher's questions and directions persist into this phase, because students' interest levels have risen to the point that they are ready to assume responsibility and do the intellectual work themselves. During the third phase of interest development, students' intentions in the activity and their goals for any resolution in the learning are experienced as self-generated, and they typically want to keep it that way. In a sense, students are taking ownership of the content so that their interest becomes internally motivated rather than externally inspired. Consequently, in this phase, students do *not* want to be told what to do. Nor do they want to be told how to revise their thinking; they want to be left alone to figure it out, to make it work, to connect their new knowledge to previous understanding, and to do all of this *on their own*.

Teachers who drop by a student's desk when he or she is in the emerging individual interest phase may find themselves confronting an individual who seems standoffish if not annoyed by their presence. If we miss cues like these and instead lean in to the student's personal space to point out mistakes or areas that need improvement, the student may get irritated if not angry, not because the student is uninterested or disengaged but precisely because he or she is occupied and absorbed. As well-intentioned and correct as our guidance may be in those moments, such interventions may produce forms of student resistance that can be misinterpreted as evasion, dismissiveness, ingratitude, or rudeness. If we respond to the student with the assumption that the behavior is destructive rather than productive, the relationship between the student and the content (and between the student and us) can quickly sour.

Only during the fourth phase, when students demonstrate "well-developed individual interest," are they again receptive to constructive feedback and further challenge. Although students in the first two phases of interest may appear to be the most receptive to feedback, it is only when they make the transition to later phases that they are positioned to work effectively with it. If we come in too early or too strong with error corrections or suggestions for revisions, we might actually turn an interested student into a resistant one. Again, it seems counterintuitive, but sometimes our most interested students can be our most resistant if we misinterpret their motivations and mishandle our responses.

Running the Numbers: Is It Worth My Time?

When students are deciding which activity to undertake (or how hard to try when they have no choice), they often calculate the probability of their eventual success. Before investing time and energy, they "run the numbers" on two main questions: "To what extent can I expect to be successful at this activity?" and "Compared with other things I might be doing, how much do I value this activity and its likely outcomes?" The field of research investigating this internal motivation calculation is known as *expectancy-value theory*.[12]

This relatively simple but highly useful concept can be used to explain and better respond to student resistance in the classroom. When students do not believe they will be successful at something, they are likely to resist complying with any directives that compel them to risk failure, especially when that failure will be public. Their resistance can arise from any number of sources, including perceived skill deficits, a lack of sophistication in their understanding of needed concepts, discomfort with the level of support being offered, or a general distrust of teacher encouragements such as "You can do this!" when students' efforts have been followed by disappointing performances in the past. Whatever the cause of their resistance, students who don't expect to succeed will seek to protect themselves from their predicted failure. They will often do this in impulsive and inappropriate ways. They may act out, ask to go to the bathroom, turn to seatmates and start talking, mess with a neighbor's backpack, take out their cell phone and begin texting friends, or create some other diversion that will keep them from having to play a game whose odds they don't like. And that's just if they don't believe they will be successful. The same behaviors can sometimes materialize when students do not value the activity or its outcomes. "Sure, I *could* do that," they think, "but I don't *want* to, because I don't care about what results from it, so I'll do this other thing instead."

Teachers who notice off-task or resistant behaviors in the classroom can sometimes address the problem best not by seeking to curtail it through coercive means (typically through reprimands, cold-call humiliations, detentions, referrals, etc.) but by inquiring about how students are feeling about the task ahead. This effectively engages their resistance rather than trying to overpower it. Using techniques like *fists of five*, in which the teacher asks for students to rate the level of their expectancy of success on a continuum from zero to five (five fingers indicating "I got this, no problem," on down to a raised fist with no fingers indicating "No way, never, nuh-uh, not gonna make it"), can provide rapid and revealing information about whether observed (mis)behaviors stem from expectancy-value issues or something else. We could use the same method to generate quick feedback regarding the level of worth students perceive in the activity.

It takes a little courage to ask students to disclose whether they care about something we've created for them, but this bravery is nothing compared with what we expect from students when we demand they attempt something publicly despite their belief that it is nearly impossible for them to succeed. To ask someone to be vulnerable while we are unwilling to show such vulnerability ourselves is the very definition of an unhealthy relationship, and kids know it. Finding out how much students value the work and whether they think they will be successful in it can reveal the reasons for resistance before problems even start.

Self-Determination (Not Self-Extermination)

In addition to self-efficacy, interest, and expectancy value, researchers have identified three other intertwined factors that motivate students to achieve in school and, conversely, may contribute to students' tendency to resist when they are lacking. Combined into a single concept called *self-determination theory*, the three factors are competence, relatedness, and autonomy.[13] Researchers Edward Deci and Richard Ryan have shown that learners need all three of these experiences on a regular basis to maintain the motivation to achieve. Students need to feel competent, meaning that they must be able to identify consistent, smaller successes or recognize their developing skill-sets in ways that lead them to believe in their capabilities (this is connected to the mind-set, self-efficacy, and expectancy-value phenomena described earlier). They also need to feel that they belong and have affirming relationships with peers and significant adults (chapters 9 and 11 will cover this notion of relatedness in greater depth). And finally, students need routine experiences of autonomy in which they have a personal and internal level of control over their choices, actions, and environment (the concept of agency covered in chapter 3 has much to do with autonomy).

Though this need to feel self-determined in order to be motivated comes from a complex interplay of these three factors—competence, relatedness, and autonomy—it is the suppression of autonomy that can most rapidly incite student resistance in the classroom. Experiences of autonomy help build students' motivation because they answer the question "Who's in control here?" with a resounding "Me!" When outcomes and conditions are dictated by distant forces or by someone else, an individual's locus of control shifts to external sources, which can be experienced as disempowering. As discussed in chapter 4, the development of the adolescent's executive functions creates the desire if not the need for experiences in which the learner can weigh options, exercise discretion, and identify self-directed courses of action. Students want to take the theoretical and imaginative parts of their developing brains out for test drives, and to fully develop these capacities, adolescents need to be allowed to do so.

If we place students in situations in which decisions are made for them, responses are scripted by others, and choices are limited if not nonexistent (e.g., test prep), we force them to make a tough decision: either comply and forgo autonomy, or resist and create autonomous opportunities of their invention. When students opt for the latter experience, we often interpret that decision as a move away from learning, as a rejection of academic work. But self-determination theory suggests that students may be resisting because they want *more* learning, not less. They want to bring their full executive faculties to the task, to experience their own agency, and to learn how to act autonomously. They want to use more of their brains, test more of their capabilities, and develop more of their skills. If students are in autonomy-suppressing environments, their resistance might be read as a request for deeper engagement and a more personally authentic, self-driven form of learning. In this case, resistance is almost something to cheer.

Because all students are to some extent subordinated in school, they all, to some extent, seek experiences that provide greater autonomy.[14] When it comes to classroom-based, lesson-driven interactions, however, students' need for autonomy should not be confused with a desire to be left completely alone. They might want us to step back, but they don't want us to go away (at least not entirely or for very long). Students still want and need guidance—sometimes a lot of it when academic mistakes or problematic behaviors are rampant—but the advice, supervision, and direction we provide may need to be restrained somewhat so that autonomy can flourish. Opening space for students to experience learning at least partly on their terms (and to make sense of the mistakes that their autonomy can produce) motivates curiosity and personal investment in the task at hand because it is *their* choices that are most shaping the outcomes. Students learning autonomously want to see what will happen with their theoretical or material creations, and they want the results to be great. If we properly set them up and then get out of their way, the only thing our students will resist will be failure.

Educational psychologist Candice Stefanou and her team of researchers determined that autonomy can be supported in the classroom in at least three ways:

- *Organizationally*: encouraging student ownership of the environment by having students choose evaluation procedures; set due dates; and participate in creating, sustaining, or revising class rules
- *Procedurally*: encouraging student ownership of form by having them choose the topics of inquiry, the materials to use, the way competence will be demonstrated, and how to spend their time
- *Cognitively*: encouraging student learning by having students discuss multiple approaches and strategies, find multiple solutions to problems, justify the solutions, formulate goals, and debate the options[15]

In contrast, what we've done institutionally and educationally over the past few decades has directly conflicted with this research. In some districts, class sizes have swelled to forty or fifty students, which can force teachers to prioritize the maintenance of order over the facilitation of autonomy. Mandated high-stakes standardized testing has also compelled schools to increase their level of control over students' (and teachers') behaviors and how they spend their time. Such a focus has led to reductive rather than expansive curricula, and widespread "teaching to the test" rather than inspiring curiosity and supporting inquiry. Students in such contexts are right to wonder why work has been separated from creativity, experimentation, imagination, and play, and why academics have become synonymous with compliance, docility, and adult-driven agendas. Looking for unfettered opportunities to grow and express themselves, students confront schools where recess has been eliminated; where lunches and passing periods have been drastically shortened; and where physical education, art, and music have been severely curtailed. Concurrently, they find themselves immersed in schoolwide behavioral modification programs that have grown in popularity in recent years (Positive Behavioral Interventions and Support chief among them). Many of these programs include monetized prize regimes designed to incentivize obedience rather than encourage autonomous decision making (more on the pedagogical problems with these approaches in chapter 12).

Adolescents newly endowed with incredible cognitive, interpersonal, and creative capacities are rightfully frustrated in environments that have permitted these changes because opportunities for autonomous thinking and acting have been significantly reduced. When students choose to decline classwork, to socialize rather than focus on class activity, to be tardy, to skip school, or to drop out entirely, they may be attempting to preserve some semblance of autonomy in their lives, to do *something*, even a reprehensible thing, *as they wish*. Their need for self-determination may be so strong, in fact, that some may select self-defeating behaviors just to experience choice (this relates to the "dangerous dignities" we will explore in chapter 10). To reverse this possibility and protect students' need for autonomy from increasing institutional encroachments, we need to cultivate relationships and provide school-based opportunities for students to experience themselves as autonomous individuals capable of making decisions and handling the outcomes.[16] This will not only elevate their achievement motivation; it will prepare them for adult responsibilities, too.

Promising Practices: Motivating the Resistant

Several of the research findings and theories explained in this chapter were accompanied by explanations of practices that educators can adopt to better engage student resistance in the classroom. Many of these practices focused on how we might revisit classroom expectations, revise implicit messages, and rework interpersonal approaches to motivate students toward academic achievement. The intent has been to focus our attention on the powerful and positive changes that occur when we attend to students' motivations, mind-sets, and beliefs. Below, I provide a few suggestions for shifting other perspectives—our own.

Updating Our Beliefs About Learning

In *Motivating Students Who Don't Care: Successful Techniques for Educators*, Allen Mendler provides a helpful list of conclusions, drawn from research, that educators need to understand before they can proceed with the tough work of motivating the unmotivated. This compelling list represents the state of the field and serves well as a description of the beliefs teachers must possess if they are to productively engage student resistance in the classroom. According to Mendler, if we are to motivate youth to achieve their potential, we need to be motivated by the following basic beliefs:

1. All students are capable of learning when they have the academic and personal tools to be successful.
2. Students are inherently motivated to learn but learn to be unmotivated when they repeatedly fail.
3. Learning requires risk taking, so classrooms need to be safe places physically and psychologically.
4. All students have basic needs to belong, to be competent, and to influence what happens to them. Motivation to learn most often occurs when these basic needs are met.
5. High self-esteem should not be a goal, but rather a result that comes with the mastery of challenging tasks.
6. High motivation for learning in school most often occurs when adults treat students with respect and dignity.[17]

Educators might consider reading this list regularly as a check on their thinking. Expanded to poster size, it might also serve well as a classroom culture-setter and discussion item with students, or it could be reproduced in handout form to distribute and examine with colleagues. The list might even be excerpted and included in schoolwide documents such as mission statements, back-to-school-night materials, or messages from administration.

Revising the (Infamous and Always Misspelled) Three Rs: The Six Rs

For nearly two centuries, education has referred to the basics we're supposed to teach as the *three Rs*: reading, writing, and 'rithmetic. As an alternative, I want to offer an expanded list of areas we might focus on in our work. These areas apply the aforementioned research and theory on inner drives, motivation, and mind-sets and help draw clear connections between these concepts and the many forms that classroom resistance can take. I would urge educators to attend to the following six Rs.

Relevance. Too often when teaching content, we introduce our lessons with statements like, "We have a lot to cover today so please sit down and pay attention." Or when teaching something we think is important, we say, "Hold on to your questions and comments—we need to get through this." When students ask us why we are studying a particular topic, we might even glibly respond, "Because you need to know this."

Responses like these indicate to students that the relevance of the material to their lives is less important than other concerns, that adult interests effectively trump youth curiosity. This is the wrong message, as common as it is. In fact, the late educational researcher and expert on motivation, Jere Brophy, once studied 317 teachers and observed that only a scant 1.7 percent of them ever explained the relevance of the lesson to their students. And he found that none of them—zero—actually explained how the lesson would help students develop more useful knowledge or skills.[18] To help connect students to the lessons they're learning right now, not in a distant future, when cellular mitosis or the quadratic formula or iambic pentameter or the Northwest Ordinance will supposedly make or break their success as an adult (and really, will it?), we need to show why the topic is relevant, why it matters, why they should care. Failing to do this is a recipe for diminished motivation and outright resistance.

Results. As discussed, when students are choosing whether to allocate time and energy to an academic task, they need experiences of competence. These experiences need to occur regularly, not just on tests or on project presentation days. To stay motivated and reduce resistance, students need "little wins" as they go along. When we highlight or facilitate incremental results, we emphasize that the students' effort is paying off in the present, right now, right here. We can do this by checking for understanding and then noting when students have demonstrated growth or by recalling where they were previously in their understanding and comparing it with where they are now. We can also raise their level of concern and their interest in the task at hand simply by offering teasers like, "By the middle of class today, you will have learned a new way to factor binomial equations," or "Before the end of the week, you will know why capitalist economies don't want everyone employed." Regardless of how we do it, it's crucial that we make sure students occasionally pause to experience themselves getting smarter and more sophisticated in their use of new skills. These pauses for self-reflection remind students why they're there—to learn and to grow.

Relationships.   Education is essentially a social enterprise. Students learn from others, with others, and in spite of others. They tend to learn the fastest and most deeply from those with whom they have a connection. Parents, guardians, mentors, coaches, friends, and teachers who have connected meaningfully with youth are often the most influential in young people's development. We often forget this as educators, focused as we have to be on making sure the content is delivered, schedules are followed, discipline is reinforced, and tests are administered. But students won't learn from us if they don't want to be in our presence, if they don't want to be in relationship with us.

Of course, some students care little whether they like us or want to know us, since they're in the class for the content or the grade and we're sort of just part of the pedagogical furniture. Or perhaps they were assigned to our caseload by their position in the alphabet and not by choice. But for most students, the relationship matters and can matter a lot (we'll be exploring the racial, ethnic, and class implications of this in part III). More than teachers of content, we are teachers of people, and people are social. The same goes for counselors, administrators, school psychologists, social workers, and all other school-based professionals— without relationships, nothing would ever get done. To motivate students and to prevent forms of resistance that may be personal or targeted toward perceived relational slights, we have to initiate, sustain, and occasionally repair our relationships with students. We're not their friends, we're not their parents, but we are in relationship with them, and that means we need to take time to address the "touchy-feely" stuff.

Reciprocity.   If autonomy is critical to students' achievement motivation (and it is), and relationships are crucial to students' willingness to learn from us (they are), then it makes perfect sense that students would want relationships in which they get to experience autonomy. Perhaps the best way of establishing this with teenagers is to cultivate reciprocity. Those unilateral "my way or the highway" approaches we hear too often in schools rarely increase learner motivation. Students know (though we sometimes forget) that our social reality is mutuality, which is why acknowledgments of the give-and-take of relationships can motivate students to invest in, rather than reject, their connections to others and to school. This is not to say that we should relax standards or ignore the need for clear and consistent boundaries; indeed, keep that stuff. To occasionally share power, to negotiate rules and procedures, to open conversations in which students get to name their concerns and needs, or to actually *apologize* to our students when we have made a mistake—these things communicate that students are agents in their relationships with us, not objects. An attention to reciprocity communicates to students that the relationship is a two-way street, that they share in something they partly control and for which they are partly responsible. Reciprocity can therefore build confidence, competence, and connection as well as provide relational resources to draw on when the time comes to address instances of resistance.

Rigor (not remediation). Learners are motivated by achievable challenges, not easy tasks. Giving students little wins does not mean dumbing things down. Students may not say it, but they know at some level that it's intellectually insulting to be given work that is beneath them. (Again, in their minds, easier work = more free time = more autonomy, and what we need to show them is that challenging work + support + autonomy = growth = freedom.) Students who struggle academically do not need remediation as much as they need rigor and more varied and consistent support so they can develop and catch up. Grouping and tracking underperforming students into environments of lower expectations and reduced autonomy is the exact opposite of what research suggests they most need (more on this in chapter 12).

When we read students' academic struggles as evidence that they're not cut out for honors or AP or GATE/TAG, or whatever other upper-echelon classes we offer to those lucky enough to have attracted the right attention over the years, we are falling back into fixed mind-sets and conveying to students and the rest of the world that we do not believe they can do it. Why are we surprised when they prove us right? Struggling students need to be shown they can do it, and then challenged to prove it, while being inspired by attentive guides, encouraged by collaborative peers, and recognized by a welcoming community. Motivate, don't remediate.

Responsiveness. We'll go much deeper into this idea in part III, but suffice it to say here that cultural differences shape what students value and how they like to learn. They also shape learners' receptivity to new information and unfamiliar teachers. To establish schools, classrooms, rules, curricula, procedures, and behavioral norms based on limited and exclusionary standards that basically privilege the privileged will invariably alienate and eventually demotivate the marginalized. Students tend to be most motivated to learn in settings where familiarity and safety are pervasive. When they're treated as "others" in a learning context, they may become resistant to what that context asks of them. That's not to say that we should never push students out of their comfort zone or avoid asking students to consider other ways of doing or thinking about things; such experiences are essential to learning and growing in the twenty-first century. But we need to be careful of carelessly or relentlessly advocating White, middle-class, heterosexual, English-speaking, Christian norms while failing to solicit and honor students from other backgrounds. To motivate all students to want to learn from us and to diminish the possibility that their resistance will take the form of underachievement, we need to be responsive to the variety of home cultures and the many insights, skills, and other contributions that spring from this variety.

Keeping a Motivating Checklist on Motivation

One last list here. This one is inspired by material in Jeb Schenck's terrific book, *Teaching and the Adolescent Brain*.[19] In it, he provides dozens of suggestions for how to motivate adolescents to achieve academic success. I have culled, paraphrased, and revised several favorites to hone in on those that might also prevent classroom resistance. The following items might serve well as a checklist for educators to self-reflect on their own practice. Or the list might be something to consider more collaboratively, perhaps with other teachers in a critical-friends group dedicated to analyzing and improving one another's teaching. It could also serve as a jumping-off point for small-group discussions in a faculty meeting. Regardless of how it's used, the list summarizes some of the main points of this chapter.

- When students have options, they perform better. Give them choice in the direction and level of challenge whenever you can. Autonomy works.
- When we label a student, it sends powerful messages about our expectations. Be careful with labels, and question any form of ability grouping.
- Never quit on students. There's no quicker way to get students to give up than showing them we already have.
- Be judicious in using rewards. Manipulation is not the same thing as motivation.
- Vague and frequent praise, such as "Good job" or "Well done," is rarely motivating. Don't confuse recognition, encouragement, evaluation, and feedback with praise—they function very differently in the mind of the learner. Kids are often more motivated by criticism than kudos.
- Match every increase in challenge with an increase in support, and differentiate both to make sure students are neither bored nor overwhelmed.

- Set clear and specific goals, and show the incremental steps that students will take to reach them. When they reach a step and achieve a goal, note it (but see the comment on rewards and praise above).
- Teach students how their brain works.
- Stop any derision, mockery, or scorn the moment it occurs in the classroom, then cobuild a culture of risk taking, inquiry, and growth with your students. No one will be motivated to learn in an unsafe environment.
- Connect with learners, find common ground, share experiences and perspectives, smile and laugh. Students are motivated to learn from those they like.
- Never tell students how "smart" or "intelligent" they are.
- Reinforce the belief that competence comes from effort.
- Get students interested in a lesson with a good hook and a description of the topic's relevance, get them started on something meaningful, check for understanding, guide when requested, then fade. Circle back later to see how they're doing or what they've done, but try not to interrupt interest, autonomy, and inertia when it's happening. They can do it themselves. Show them how, then get out of the way.

Super Busy

Ms. Harris is dismayed at what she sees. After weeks of preparation and reminders, she can tell that Maria hasn't even started her history project—and it is due the next day. Ms. Harris has been worried about Maria's progress but has felt the need to protect her from embarrassment because of Maria's obvious shyness. Maria does her best to disappear in class, rarely jumping into class discussions and almost never asking any questions. So Ms. Harris typically uses those moments before and after class to check in with her, to try to develop a personal relationship with Maria so that she will want to engage more in class. Unfortunately, things have been so busy recently that Ms. Harris hasn't had the chance to pull Maria aside to see how things are going. But today, after Maria spends the period in silence and makes it clear she has nothing prepared for tomorrow's project presentation day, Ms. Harris asks Maria to talk for a minute at the end of class.

"You've had over a month to work on this, Maria. Why haven't you made any progress?" Ms. Harris asks.

Knowing as soon as she was asked to stay after class that she was going to be asked about this, Maria answers quickly, "I'm sorry. I've been super busy with soccer practice and other homework. I haven't had any time."

Just then, Maria's smartphone makes a noise Ms. Harris recognizes as an alert that a text message was being received. Seeing Ms. Harris's look of annoyance about this, Maria quickly looks at her phone to see who just texted her before hitting the silence button and putting it back in her pocket. Maria then adds, "I sat down to try to start it a couple of times but always had other things that came up, so I never got going on it. I'm sorry."

Growing frustrated at the cell phone and at the excuses, Ms. Harris asks Maria, "Why didn't you ask me for help? You know this project is a big part of your grade, and you have known for a long time that you were going to present it in class to everyone. How do you plan to pass this class if you fail this project?"

Maria thinks for a second about what Ms. Harris has said, then thinks about her friend's text message, then thinks back to the question Ms. Harris has just asked. "I dunno," Maria replies, "I guess I'll work harder on stuff the rest of the semester."

Unsure of how to respond, Ms. Harris lets Maria know that if she failed the project it would likely be the main topic of discussion at their upcoming parent-teacher conference.

Maria listens, shrugs, mumbles "Okay," and then turns, takes out her phone to text her friend back, and walks to her next class.

CHAPTER 6

"What? I Wasn't Listening"
The Passive No of Disengagement

SOME OF THE best parts about working with adolescents in schools occur when we get to accompany them on journeys of discovery, when we get to push and pull them toward new meanings and new skills that open the world to them. When their passion for life, justice, inquiry, ideas, or invention gets turned on—and it happens because of something we did with them—it is a thrill to behold.

The magnitude of the opposite experience can be just as great. Middle and high school educators often express the most despair about their work after confronting students who seem to have given up. We know what bad things await those who turn off, push away, and drop out, and we become frustrated when we observe students disengage from the possibilities that education provides. "They have so much going for them!" we'll say. "Why are they quitting?" The energy we expend in fretting about our students and trying to convince them to change their behaviors can sometimes produce the turnaround stories we crave, but sometimes such attempts have little effect. In those cases, the problem that may have begun with the student's hopelessness now ends with the educator's hopelessness.

The situation is not hopeless, however—not by a long shot. Student disengagement is a complicated phenomenon and its causes and components are myriad, but one thing we know about it for sure is that it is reversible. Students disengage for reasons, reasons that researchers have been studying for decades, reasons that have clear antecedents and obvious implications for practice. In this chapter, we will explore that research to learn how disengagement may be understood as the activation of a subversive (and sometimes shortsighted and self-harming) skill-set

123

that is designed to protect the individual from negative experiences. In this way, disengagement is a form of resistance and our response to it is an opportunity to repair the damage and reverse the trend.

Disengagement: A Quiet Form of Resistance

Some forms of resistance are outwardly expressed and immediately evident. Telling off a teacher, smoking in the restroom, destroying school property—behaviors like these let us know the student is in some sort of crisis, has some need for aggression, or may be requesting (however dysfunctionally) some form of increased attention. However, a significant portion of resistant behaviors are actually far less obvious. They are quiet and concealed because they operate internally or play out subtly over longer periods. One crucial form of resistance in the classroom, disengagement, is not really an act per se or something we can pinpoint at all; it's a process, something that unfolds in the minds of learners who, like all of us, are doing their best to feel good and to keep from feeling bad.

Disengagement is a process because it comprises incremental decisions made over time in response to conditions and relationships. According to educational researcher Robert Balfanz and his colleagues, disengagement involves "detaching from school, disconnecting from its norms and expectations, reducing effort and involvement, and withdrawing from a commitment to [academic achievement]."[1] When disengagement leads to observable expressions and actions, those behaviors are prone to misinterpretation because the logic that propelled them remains hidden inside the student's mind. Educators misread such behaviors all the time, not because we don't care or have somehow lapsed professionally but because we have been trained to think of schools as meritocracies and our actions within them as promotions of that agenda (see chapters 2 and 3). We think we are being encouraging, engaging, and equitable when, as we will see, many of our "commonsense" approaches to disengaged students are the opposite. In the following pages, we will see how students disengage through self-handicapping, avoidance behaviors, and various forms of withdrawal.

Self-Handicapping

Why do students put off assignments until the last moment? Why do they stay up late talking and texting with friends the night before a big test? Why do students say they didn't put much time or effort into their work? Why do they take on too many extracurricular activities and allow their academic performance to suffer? Educators who ask these questions sometimes answer them by locating problems in the students' relationships or in the students themselves. "She's lazy." "That kid has no organizational skills." "He's hanging out with the wrong crowd." "They come from families that don't value education." "He only thinks about basketball." "She has checked out." Though seemingly obvious and seductively descriptive, such explanations are often rooted in profound misconceptions about when and where students choose to disengage. And if those explanations are accepted or allowed to persist, they can prevent an acknowledgment of how our practices influence students' decisions to select other activities over academics. By attributing drops in performance to innate characteristics or bad attitudes, such statements effectively turn the symptom into the problem. This strategy may absolve us of our complicity but it helps little in changing the dynamic of resistance.

What alternative explanations for disengagement might better capture students' underlying motivations and point us toward practices that will make a positive difference? To answer that, we need to look at the circumstances surrounding the students' behaviors and analyze the logic of their decision making. What we find there surprises many educators: *intentionally failing sometimes makes perfect sense.* Confronted daily with tasks and tests that put their abilities (or lack thereof) on public display, many students develop highly sophisticated strategies to manipulate others' perceptions and protect against the possibility that they will be seen as incapable or, worse, stupid. One diversionary strategy of disengagement that consistently undermines achievement is *self-handicapping.*

Self-handicapping occurs when students create impediments to successful performance to provide themselves with opportunities to avoid, excuse, or discount any resulting failure.[2] It is a strategy of deflection designed to redirect "the attributions of others away from low ability causes and toward circumstantial or situational causes of failure."[3] Students who frequently use self-handicapping strategies become masters of diversion, finding innumerable ways to tell adults and peers, "Look over *there,* not here. Right *there* is the reason I didn't do well (not that other thing you might be wondering about—my innate ability)." After they underperform at some task, students often explain that an earlier circumstance or event hurt their performance. But if the circumstance was unplanned or unintentional, it isn't technically self-handicapping. Self-handicapping is an attempt to influence others' perceptions about one's capabilities by deliberately choosing, *beforehand,* to do something that makes the individual underperform later. It is the strategic choice to do something else, not the explanation of what the student did, that makes a behavior self-handicapping.

For example, a student who says she failed her Algebra II test because she had to babysit her cousins until late the previous night is providing an explanation of her diminished performance, not self-handicapping. But if she purposely stayed up late talking on the phone with friends so that she could use her lack of sleep as an excuse for her failure the next day, then she would be employing a self-handicapping strategy. For students to choose this strategy, they must believe they can manipulate the perceptions of others and that their explanation will keep others from attributing their performance to low competence. Plus, they must be willing to sacrifice their own achievement to guard against any appearance that they lack ability. In essence, they are using intentional failure to resist the possibility that they might look dumb.

The thing is, students who adopt this strategy are anything but dumb. They are actually reading the social and academic landscape quite accurately and employing shrewd logic in response to it. Trained by schools and society to separate ability from effort (see the explanation of mind-sets in chapter 5), students as young as age ten learn to broadcast certain types of explanations to convince others around them that any failure is due to autonomous choices rather than inborn qualities. "There's nothing wrong with me," they explain, "because I *chose* this other thing over academics." Researchers have found that lower-performing students are more likely to explain their failure as a consequence of circumstances rather than a lack of ability. For this reason, those who most require the benefits of engagement are the same ones who are most likely to adopt strategies that hinder it. Surveying a wide variety of research on self-handicapping behaviors, educational psychologists Tim Urdan and Carol Midgley observe that "self-handicapping is part of a vicious cycle in which handicapping leads to lower achievement, thereby creating a greater need to handicap."[4] This suggests how important it is to interrupt the cycle early before it produces greater and greater levels of resistance and disengagement.

Low-performing students are not the only ones who disengage through self-handicapping—high-performing students do it too. Those in honors tracks, in AP classes, or even in GATE/TAG programs often consider themselves exceptional (and any system that labels them this way—while neglecting to give others such lofty labels—is surely complicit in this judgment). Therefore, when they confront situations in which they are expected to confirm their designation, they may fear that they will not measure up. Failure for them is understood to be anything less than an exceptional performance, an attitude that can lead directly to self-handicapping behaviors particularly when the pressure to compete is high.

Although self-handicapping is technically a motivational strategy, it presents as disengagement, as a form of resistance. It is a form of resistance because students are deflecting perceptions and manipulating circumstances to do less schoolwork or purposely underperform because they don't believe their educational situation is conducive to their reputation or well-being. The desire to draw attention to circumstances and choices rather than intelligence and competence leads to actions that decrease school engagement. By procrastinating, withholding effort, claiming shyness, declaring fatigue, feigning illness or pain, using drugs or alcohol, or staying overinvolved with friends or overcommitted to activities outside school, and then declaring such hindrances to others when failure is imminent, students avoid the implication that their intrinsic worth or capabilities were the reason for their diminished performance.

To the educator who hears students saying basically, "I could have succeeded, but I chose not to," it may look a lot like they do not care about their education or at least did not care about their performance on that particular day. We need to remember, however, that the inner drive compelling students to choose self-handicapping behaviors arises from the need to feel competent and autonomous. Self-handicapping students actually want to be successful and to be seen as such, but if the possibility exists that their failings will be attributed to their innate qualities over which they have no control, then they will create circumstances they *can* control to shift attention elsewhere. Ironically, their desire not to look dumb leads them to act in ways that virtually guarantee reduced outcomes. They deliberately *choose* to fail rather than risk the possibility that they would have no choice but to fail publicly.

What school and classroom environments would make a student do this? Put more directly, how might our practices make students want to resist in this manner? The truth is that a lot of what we do in schools contributes to the logic of self-handicapping. Midgley and Urdan frame those contributions in terms of schools' "evaluative demands," or the situations in which students are assessed, compared, and otherwise examined. The researchers conclude that "when students perceive that they are being evaluated on the basis of their ability relative to the ability of others, they may be more likely to use [self-handicapping] strategies than when they perceive they are being evaluated in terms of their effort, improvement, and mastery of the work."[5]

Study after study indicates that school practices that make ability differences salient actually encourage students to adopt self-handicapping strategies. Examples of ability-emphasizing practices include praising students for their intelligence, pointing out more successful students as a model for others, posting grades (even anonymously), grading on a curve, tracking or using any form of ability grouping, displaying the work of high achievers, repeatedly emphasizing grades and test scores, rewarding students for exemplary academic achievement (or punishing those who underperform by holding them in at lunch or withholding "privileges" like athletics or other extracurricular activities), and instituting high-stakes tests that determine whether a student will advance to the next grade or receive a diploma. We often use techniques like these because we think they both motivate students to do their best work and engage those who may be reluctant to try. But when we make ability differences a core feature of the learning environment, students rightfully become obsessed with how they are perceived. They are then apt to disengage from or resist classroom activities in which they feel insecure. In effect, schools that operate as ability contests force student to compare themselves with others, which essentially teaches them to prioritize their appearance over their learning.

Luckily, it's not difficult to reverse this trend. Simply shifting classroom and schoolwide orientations from performance- to mastery-based goals can drastically reduce self-handicapping behaviors (see chapter 5). When the focus of education moves from *demonstrating* competency to *developing* it, students will learn rather quickly that there is no need to engineer the perceptions of others because failure no longer functions as an indictment of their ability; instead, failure is understood as a necessary step in the learning process. In classrooms and schools where mastery-based goals (e.g., comprehension, improvement, collaboration, and proficiency) are made explicit and reinforced, the humiliation of the mistake is removed. Mistakes are framed as opportunities, effort and incremental progress are valued, and everyone is given work that challenges them to keep growing.

An environment like this produces no incentive for students to compensate for their insecurities with self-handicapping stories, because their peers are too busy trying to understand, improve, and help others succeed to worry about whether someone is "dumb" or "smart." Those categories don't even make sense anymore. With no social stigma attached to the inevitable failures that come with learning something new, students have little reason to resist and ample motivation to engage. This underscores how important it is for educators to monitor and positively shape the learning environment to make sure there are zero social consequences for struggling academically, to frame mistakes as normal and needed parts of learning, and to use assessments formatively until students are ready to demonstrate their proficiency summatively. In short, anything that makes ability less salient than learning will help to reduce self-handicapping.

Avoidance

Whereas self-handicapping occurs before an academic activity, avoidance behaviors occur during it. Motivated less by the desire to demonstrate ability and more by the desire to avoid demonstrating a lack of ability, avoidance behaviors are what psychologists call *maladaptive*. While avoidance behaviors possess a certain logic in that they are a strategic response to a situation perceived to be threatening, they remain maladaptive because they ultimately exacerbate rather than prevent negative outcomes. And like self-handicapping, avoidance behaviors are most likely to arise when school and classroom settings threaten students with the stigma of incompetence, thereby forcing them into a resistant stance. Avoidance behaviors are forms of resistance because they represent students' attempts to refuse a particular academic demand, even though that refusal may be done quietly and unobtrusively. Students use avoidance to disengage from learning opportunities in a variety of ways, but one of the most insidious—insidious because it is the least visible—is the practice of help avoidance.

All students need help. Learning is greatly enhanced when the learner is in the presence of more knowledgeable or more skilled people and can draw on their expertise to overcome challenges. Without help, learners would frequently get stuck in their own confusion and stagnate in their development. When perplexed, learners enter a state of momentary disorientation and uncertainty as new knowledge conflicts with previous understanding. Those moments are often ideal for the interventions that help provides. For example, students may calculate the molecular components of a solution, only to be told by the teacher that their list of ingredients is incorrect. Or, a student's explanation of the causes of the American Civil War might be very different from the one the teacher just provided. In each instance, the student probably experiences a moment of perplexity that would be ameliorated if he or she sought help. The help can take the form of further explanation, more-elaborate examples, better hints, more-probing questions, deeper engagement, and so forth. But whether the student actually asks for that help is another matter altogether.

Why might a student avoid seeking help? James Dillon, a philosopher of education, once estimated that "95 percent of the questions that we have in mind to ask we never go on to utter . . . [W]e may think the better of it and follow one of the numerous other paths available."[6] If Dillon is right, some help avoidance may have to do with the individual's use of other strategies to overcome confusion or challenge and therefore may not necessarily represent a form of resistance or disengagement. But in their survey of dozens of studies investigating help avoidance in the classroom, Allison Ryan and her colleagues report the following:

> Research has identified several reasons why students avoid asking for help in the classroom. First, it may not be practical or feasible to ask for help in a given situation. There may be explicit rules or norms against help seeking and, thus, students may refrain from asking for help because they do not want to get in trouble. Or students may judge that asking for help is not going to be effective because (a) there is not a competent, willing helper who can provide assistance or (b) it will take too long to get help. In addition to such practical and expedient concerns, research has identified two psychosocial concerns that underlie the avoidance of help seeking: desire for autonomy and threat to competence.[7]

Predictably, the greatest threats to autonomy and competence occur wherever performance-based orientations predominate. Ryan and her colleagues note that "when students adopt a goal to outperform others but receive information that they are not achieving that goal, they are particularly vulnerable to negative perceptions about help seeking and are more likely to avoid it."[8] And like self-handicapping, help avoidance is observed most prominently in lower-achieving students because they tend to feel more threatened more often. Consequently, the very students who need the help the most tend to seek it the least.

In addition, the perception that help seeking makes students dependent on the teacher conflicts with the adolescent desire for autonomy and in turn inhibits students' decisions to ask for help when they need it.[9] To respond to such students with questions like "Why don't you ask me for help? I'm here to help. Ask me for help!" is to miss the point—they don't want that help, because requesting it signals that they're struggling, and struggle is a sign of being incompetent and needy. Here the problem is not the help avoidance; the problem is the context and culture in which that behavior is occurring.

We know this because researchers have conducted both experimental and survey-based studies, all of which show that "students are less likely to seek help under performance goal conditions than under mastery goal conditions."[10] But in classrooms where understanding, improvement, and mastery were emphasized, students were significantly less likely to avoid seeking help when they needed it. Even students who professed an internal performance orientation ended up seeking more help when they were put into a mastery-learning context.[11]

The same outcome has been observed in the quality of teacher-student relationships. Familiarity and positive relationships are associated with greater help seeking. Moreover, teachers' concerns "about the social and emotional well-being of their students was related to less help avoidance, particularly for students who doubted their [own] ability to successfully do their academic work."[12] Findings such as these suggest that the social-emotional aspects of teaching can be just as critical as, if not more so than, the content being taught.

To that end, students have social goals that can encourage or discourage help seeking, depending on their orientation. Some students are oriented more toward intimacy, to be accepted by valued peers and to experience closer, more interpersonal relationships. Others are oriented more toward social status, to be granted a certain level of visibility, prestige, or rank among a larger peer group. Not surprisingly, a status orientation functions similarly to a performance orientation in that both involve the need to manipulate others' perspectives to maintain one's image or reputation. Ryan and her colleagues argue that "because help seeking is a public behavior that has the potential to garner attention and evaluation from one's peers, students who have a status-goal orientation perceive help seeking as threatening to their self-worth and are more likely to avoid seeking help when they need it."[13] Educators who try to convince students with status-goal orientations that help-seeking is benign if not beneficial (that it will benefit them, that it will help them succeed, that they should feel more comfortable asking more questions) will likely produce little change in these avoidance behaviors. Students are unlikely to change their avoidance behaviors in this case, because the root cause of the disengagement is being ignored. Even warm and genuine expressions of care, affection, and hope will probably have little impact until the social and academic context that prioritizes status and appearance is successfully altered.

Efforts to change performance- and status-goal orientations may take time, but they are not difficult. Any time educators can reinforce the idea that education is about *developing* competence, not about *demonstrating* it, we will be helping to reduce the forms of resistance and disengagement that arise from performance anxieties. (This point has clear implications for how we might protect our students from the many negative side effects of high-stakes, standardized accountability systems, which, for good or for ill, are deeply committed to performance-goal orientations.) Classic teaching techniques long known to yield high achievement are still pertinent here: cultivating the students' interest and curiosity, encouraging their persistence, minimizing frustration, balancing challenge with support, encouraging and monitoring collaboration, and enhancing students' confidence all are terrific ways to move classroom and school cultures toward mastery- and intimacy-goal orientations. Because avoidance behaviors are forms of resistance born of insecurity, the solution is not to attack the behavior but to attend to the underlying fears and the unsupportive contexts that are driving the retreat.

For example, simply replacing the ubiquitous query "Any questions?" with other options might be a good start. That age-old technique of checking for understanding is frequently translated in students' minds to read something like this: "Who would like to demonstrate that they are the dumb one by broadcasting their confusion or misunderstanding with their raised hand so everyone can see it?" It's no wonder so many classrooms are at their quietest immediately after the teacher asks, "Any questions?" To truly address the underlying causes of avoidance behaviors, we have to allow students to tell us what they know (not expose them when they're most perplexed). Then it's our job to look for areas of confusion and misunderstanding, around which we will shape our pedagogy.

When we can build up students' confidence as high as their curiosity, then we can check for understanding through invitation, like this: "Who would like to ask the first question?" or "Let's think together—what am I missing, forgetting, or making confusing?" In this last example, the responsibility for any confusion shifts onto the teacher. This makes it easier for students to express their need for help, because the question is delivered in the form of *giving* help to the teacher. Likewise, when we deemphasize grades and highlight learning, recognize understanding and minimize correctness, remain critical without being cruel or sarcastic, and portray errors as signs of effort not incompetence—when we do these things, we can greatly reduce the occurrence of maladaptive responses.

Forms of Withdrawal Easily Misunderstood and Dismissed

As we have seen, students sometimes disengage through evasion. Fearful of what learning activities may require of them, they dodge opportunities to try something on their own or they duck under chances to seek help. They stay in the game to some extent, but they manipulate it, their peers, us, or themselves to avoid appearing dumb. Other times, students move beyond disengagement into withdrawal. In these instances, they remove themselves in some way from academic activity. The extreme version of withdrawal is dropping out of school, but there are all sorts of ways students can withdraw right in front of our eyes. Let's look at a few examples of such behaviors and how educators often misread them.

Relativism and Nihilism

As adults, we easily forget how hard it can be for youth to make sense of themselves and their world when their new cognitive capacities reveal everything to be so utterly complex. We adults have been using our developed brains for years if not decades longer than kids have, and as a result, we sometimes think that because youth are capable of adult ways of thinking they will necessarily respond with adult ways of behaving. But we would be wrong. Adolescents' powerful new competencies that emerge with the advent of theoretical thinking, critical imagination, and executive functions are a tremendous resource (see chapter 4), but they do introduce teens to questions and concerns that can destabilize previously secure notions of right and wrong, truth and deceit, fact and opinion, beautiful and abhorrent. For them, this destabilization can yield occasional epiphanies, but it can also introduce profound confusion. Vacillating between such markedly different experiences can stimulate big mood swings during which excited engagement may be immediately followed by exhausted withdrawal, sometimes within the same class period. For us, these rapid changes can make it difficult to discern which version of a student we're dealing with from one day to the next, or from one moment to the next. The challenge of these emotional swings can lead us to become as snarky and dismissive about "adolescent angst" as youth are about adults who "just don't get it."

In those moments of destabilization, we need to remember that an adolescent's cognitive and emotional state is as precious as it is fragile. Underneath their brooding or their simmering hostility, many adolescents are posing some pretty big questions: What is the truth about something if everyone has such different opinions about it? What is the right belief to hold, the correct value to possess, the most ethical way to behave? Who is the real "me" when I have to change myself in each different setting to fit in? What is the point of it all?! Questions like these can lead to amazing discoveries of the self and the rest of the world—discoveries that inform if not energize a student's life trajectories. But they can also produce a sense of helplessness or devastation when the world's relativism grows beyond the adolescent's ability to make meaning of it. The result can be nihilism.

Nihilism, in this case, is a form of withdrawal, a type of resistance.[14] The belief in the essential meaninglessness of it all that youth sometimes adopt provides a temporary suspension of decision making about the ultimate questions of life. A relativistic swirl of religious, political, interpersonal, intrapersonal, aesthetic, and moral questions can conspire in the adolescent mind in a way that makes the individual look not for answers but for the off switch. Nihilism provides that off

switch (or at least a dimmer). By questioning the point of the questions themselves, youth effectively turn off the need for answers for a while. In doing so, the
adolescent may also turn away from or outright reject some inquiries and activities at school. Even though some of the best things we can do for adolescents in
school is to give them juicy topics and complex issues to wrestle with, debate, and
solve, many youth feel inundated by complexity and may feel the need to intellectually and existentially retreat.

For example, in a study conducted by the educational psychologists Deanna
Kuhn and Amanda Holman, students were given the following prompt: "Many
social issues, like the death penalty, gun control, or medical care, are pretty much
matters of personal opinion and there is no basis for saying that one person's
opinion is any better than another's. So there's not much point in people having discussions about these kinds of issues. Do you agree, somewhat agree, or
disagree?"

Although the participants' answers varied across cultures, many teens agreed
with the statement and provided such reasons as, "It's not worth it to discuss
because it's not something you can get a definite answer to," or "There's no point
because you're not going to get anywhere; everyone has a right to think what they
want to."[15] Youth with such opinions may choose to withdraw from or outright
resist academic activities that delve into the "gray" areas of our world, especially
activities explicitly designed to be open-ended. Students temporarily withdrawing into nihilism may withhold effort on assignments, challenge the purpose of
lessons, or question seemingly obvious givens in their quest to expose the futility
of educational pursuits. They may be indifferent, dismissive, careless, and even
scornful when it comes to academic activity and the educators who facilitate it.
They do this because, to them, "None of it matters anyway."

While such utterances and attitudes sometimes suggest forms of resignation
and despair that can accompany clinical depression (and it is important to speak
to parents or a mental health professional, or both, if suspicions of this nature
accumulate), often youth are merely testing the waters with this resistance. They
want to see if others can point a way out of the meaninglessness, if anyone can
challenge their thinking and break through the nihilism. Though we might be
put off by students' outward appearance of insolence or arrogance, we can best
help them move through their nihilism by maintaining a good relationship with
them, acknowledging the complexity of the world and their thinking, and gen-
tly challenging the (temporary) meaninglessness to which they seem attached.
Kuhn and Holman perhaps state it best: "If adolescents are to regard intellectual
discourse as worth the effort it entails, they must see the point of it. Otherwise,

they are not going to be disposed to involve themselves in it in any deep way. Doing so requires progressing beyond the relativists' stance that any opinion is as good as any other to the recognition that some opinions have more merit than others, to the extent they are judgments supported in a framework of argument and evidence."[16]

Though nihilism often presents itself as withdrawal, we should remember that it is also a technique of resistance, a way of providing the individual with intellectual and existential shelter to compensate for feeling overwhelmed. If educational settings and relationships encourage the individual to continue to stay engaged and curious, then nihilism is typically temporary too.

Narcissism

Like nihilism, adolescent narcissism is usually short-lived. The self-absorption and self-centeredness that can occur in adolescence is sometimes a response to the stressors of having to manage various self-representations across multiple social networks. School, family, religious community, close friends, more distant friends, romantic partners, sworn enemies, teammates, online connections, extended family, neighbors—each of these relationships or contexts demands different things of the individual. Feeling unsure about *how* to be or *who* to be in those various situations can lead an adolescent to an understandable preoccupation with self-care. Such self-care can become narcissistic when it begins to eclipse empathy, compassion, and relational vulnerability. In an effort to protect themselves from too much social volatility or too many competing relational demands, some adolescents withdraw into a self-obsessed hall of mirrors, in which every relationship and every context is expected to reflect back a positive version of their beauty, power, intelligence, and prestige. A grandiose sense of self-worth, an exaggerated characterization of achievements, and a sort of swashbuckling exterior is used to hide internal insecurities about being insignificant or helpless; this narcissism can lead to an overriding need to be validated if not admired.

Students having some of these tendencies may resist academic work because it can expose the myth of their grandiosity and force them to collaborate with peers who probably do not share their inflated self-appraisals. Even though success and acclaim are desired by adolescents with narcissistic tendencies, the fear of being unmasked or made to feel vulnerable can lead to various forms of withdrawal from school activities. Sharing work, doing group projects, being asked to put a problem on the board, or having to negotiate strained perspectives in disciplinary situations can force some students to choose between protecting their exaggerated sense of self and engaging in more authentic, growth-supporting relationships.

To help students choose the latter rather than the former, we must make schools and classrooms safe spaces for risk taking and vulnerability. By establishing behavioral norms, constantly monitoring student comments, and conducting targeted interventions that help adolescents better negotiate their relationships, we can help build confidence without encouraging superiority. Humor can help a lot here. When teachers and students are able to laugh at themselves and allow others to join in those gentle and often silly moments that reveal our common humanity, it can help break down assumptions that any of us are somehow greater than others.

The same goes for criticism. Students withdrawing into narcissism, however temporary it may be, need to be pushed to remain open to critiques of their work and behavior. Many will resist individual conferences, group activities, or peer feedback sessions because these activities involve evaluation and the potential to be identified as something short of "the greatest." Getting students to talk about their fears regarding such activities—and even discuss the swagger or arrogance that may cover such insecurities—can help break down narcissistic tendencies and open students to a deeper engagement with the material and the people in their midst. Similarly, using both content and disciplinary interactions to explore the necessity of empathy can also help narcissists move from self-obsessed to more other-aware ways of thinking and behaving. In doing so, we may need to show students that thinking about others' needs does not mean abandoning their own. If we can help students recognize that empathy and self-care often function best when integrated, we can enlist their support in cocreating learning communities where compassion and negotiation prevail over entitlement and vanity.

Multitasking

In our technology-saturated world, the temptation to turn away from difficult work seems to be ever present. Smartphones, televisions, computers, video games, tablets, multifunction watches, digital audio and video players, and whatever new gizmo our modern society generates this week are all competing for our students' attention. Through their various alerts, ringtones, dings, and vibrations, these devices pull our students' focus (and our own) away from academics and toward indulgence. When students become habituated to those distractions—when youth allow them more than ignore them—it can reinforce cognitive pathways that actually make focus more difficult. In this way, multitasking not only constitutes a form of disengagement, but may also contribute to diminished intellectual functioning.

Cognitively speaking, multitasking isn't really possible.[17] Our brains cannot maintain focus on multiple tasks at one time, particularly when those tasks require higher brain functions. Students may be able to walk and chew gum at the same time, but there is no way for their brains to handle the cognitive load of solving problems using integral calculus while also texting with friends. Cognitive psychologist Jeb Schenck calls multitasking "a neuromyth." He explains that "the brain cannot track multiple pieces of information with the same levels of attention. It can rapidly engage, disengage, shift, and reengage with different items, but the capacity of the attention systems is limited. Consequently, if too much information is coming in, portions of it will be missed."[18]

Students who are permitted to attempt schoolwork while also interacting with their smartphones (or updating their online status, or texting, or watching YouTube videos, etc.) are actually building neural networks that may make it more difficult to initiate and sustain focus over time. To "train the brain" to think with what some have called "continuous partial attention" forces it to divert mental processes from the slower but far more powerful brain system 2 to the far faster but much simpler and reactive brain system 1 (see chapter 4). And system 1 is most definitely *not* where poems are written, equations are solved, labs are conducted, and historical events are analyzed.

Accordingly, students who claim the ability to simul-engage need to be disabused of that notion and shown how multitasking is actually a form of minute-to-minute *dis*engagement. They will often resist this assertion, because of the many immediate, dopamine-generating rewards associated with a digitally diverted attention and their mistaken belief that they can do four things at once. When we ask them to put away their devices or when we push them to stay focused on just one thing at a time, they may express their resistance by claiming our restrictions are unfair limitations of their freedoms or are inaccurate assessments of their abilities. (A student actually once told me, "Just because *you* can't multitask doesn't mean *I* can't.") To counter such claims, we need to engage their resistance with explanation and demonstration rather than just rules and surveillance. That is, we need to *show them what their brains can do* when they devote the necessary time and protect the indispensable concentration that allows their brains to function optimally. Providing challenging activities, encouraging students to engage without distraction (despite their complaints), and then describing clear behavioral expectations—and maybe doing a bit of hovering and reminding once they get started—can help students experience the power of their intellect. When such experiences are emphasized and repeated, the desire to digitally withdraw is likely to decline because the rewards that come from sustained attention are just too good to pass up.

Poor Self-Regulation

Like intelligence, the ability to manage distraction is something students (and educators) develop over time. Trying something new, attempting something difficult, confronting a challenge—these things require focus, and focus requires self-restraint. For example, as adults we have learned what we need to do when we cook a new recipe. It's as simple as reading it and doing what it says, right? Wrong. We actually use a series of complex mental processes to make sure we get it right, processes we've either learned through trial and error or from watching more-experienced cooks. We prepare by clearing an area on the counter and directing our attention to the task at hand; we put the recipe in a place where it can be easily read and consulted; we gather ingredients and implements according to what's listed on the recipe; then, step by step, we read the recipe, check to see that we understand it, double-check things like "tablespoon" versus "teaspoon," or "bake at 325°F" versus "bake at 425°F," and slowly and deliberately follow the instructions. Often we have to go back to reread portions we found confusing or thought we may have misread, and we monitor our performance and the outcomes as we go along. At the end, with a finished dish, we assess the final product and determine if it could have been improved with modified processes, different ingredients, or better technique. And sometimes we do all of this amid music playing, the TV blaring in a nearby room, the phone ringing, and family members coming in and out to get a snack while we cook. Though proper ingredients and technique are important, it's our focus and self-restraint that make a dish successful.

Cognitive developmental psychologists have a term for this process of initiating, sustaining, and reflecting: *self-regulation*. To effectively self-regulate, learners need to manage their minds as much as, if not more than, they manage their learning environment. For adolescents in particular, this can be tough. The teen mind is sometimes a bit unruly with its social preoccupations, academic insecurities, emotional reactions, and theoretical deliberations all simultaneously interacting without fully developed executive functions to regulate them. Add to this the often slow maturation of impulse control and delayed gratification, and it's clear that learners are prone to distraction. As a result, students with poor self-regulation can appear to withdraw effort or reject the value of learning activities, further exacerbating behavioral, academic, and relational problems in the classroom if their behaviors are consistently misread. The problem may not be their attitude per se; rather, it may be that they simply haven't developed skills that allow them to self-regulate.

Researchers have demonstrated that self-regulation is best understood as a skill-set, that is, a combination of strategies we learn incrementally over time and can always improve. When learners self-regulate, they exercise control over their learning by using specific tactics to approach, complete, and contemplate the task at hand. Skilled self-regulators are able to engage flexibly and adaptively in multiple contexts on varied tasks. They know what they need to do to get and stay focused, and they have a host of strategies to choose from to successfully complete a task. Psychologists have different terms for the different components of self-regulation, but most descriptions adhere to a three-stage, sequential process.[19] When students are self-regulating, they are engaged in these three stages:

- *Planning learning*: initiating interest, setting goals, assessing the learning environment, preparing materials, clarifying expectations
- *Controlling learning*: sustaining focus, self-monitoring, adjusting, integrating feedback, managing distractions
- *Reflecting on learning*: self-evaluating, attributing success, identifying areas in need of improvement, projecting subsequent efforts

Many of these processes, though they seem natural, are actually learned through observation, practice, modification, and then more practice coupled with the help of more-skilled regulators with whom the learner has a good relationship. For students to become skilled self-regulators, they need time, practice, and assistance in generating strategies that allow them to meet task demands.

In the classroom, naive self-regulators sometimes appear resistant when they actually just need skill development. They may lose interest too quickly or succumb to distractions too readily (e.g., sharpening their pencil for the fourth time, getting up to throw something away every few minutes, turning to talk with friends rather than start the activity) because they have not prepared themselves to initiate and sustain focus. In the planning stage, they may set goals that are too distant and nonspecific to orient themselves to the task with sufficient motivation. They may articulate a genuine desire "to be successful" or even "to do well in this class," but such declared goals are too vague to direct their attention and elevate their interest in a particular activity. Students with such goals need help in creating more targeted, activity-specific objectives such as "to be able to chart what happens to carbon dioxide during photosynthesis" or "to accurately graph an exponential curve." Helping students to see the connections between immediate goals, subsequent actions, and incremental successes will help them develop the skill to self-regulate.

The same is true for the controlling stage. Naive self-regulators frequently have an unfocused plan for action, and they fail to self-monitor. After applying little effort to understand something, they often wait to be told precisely what to do or they ask to be spoon-fed the directions or even request to be told the answers. In such cases, students may seem lacking in academic content knowledge or unmotivated to learn, but it may be more accurate to say they are unskilled at controlling their attention. After they initiate an activity, they may fail to monitor their own focus and may avoid going back to previous steps or earlier texts when confusion arises. Students with poor self-regulation skills habitually raise their hands for help before even attempting to face a challenge on their own, copy their more proficient peers' work, or simply put their pencils down and do something else. Teachers who "help" such students in those moments by relenting to their requests or allowing their unfocused behavior (often accompanied by the statement, "as long as it doesn't disturb others") are actually reinforcing dependency and obstructing the development of the students' self-regulation. Likewise, simply telling students to get to work would not help poor self-regulators; nor would punishing or threatening them if they fail to do so. They need skill development, not reprimands.

We can assist students with underdeveloped self-regulation skills by explicitly teaching what to do when they get confused or lost or when they simply lose track of what they are thinking. "Stop and ask yourself as you go along," we might say, "do I understand this? How do I know?" A naive self-regulator might have the mistaken notion that his or her more successful peers are all "smart" because they seem to understand everything the very first time they encounter it. But it is far more likely that the peers are checking their understanding, observing their own attention as they go along, and then circling back when they need to.

These more-successful students are likely using a more sophisticated set of self-regulation skills that allow them to stay engaged and productive. It is important to explicitly name and demonstrate the strategies successful self-regulators employ to control their attention so that less skilled self-regulators can demystify what it takes to be academically successful. We might say, "Stop and give yourself mini quizzes in your head. Try looking away from the text every few minutes to see if you know what you're studying while you're studying it," and then model that behavior with an example that appeals to students. (Examples from our own lives in which we ourselves had to use specific skills to overcome difficulties are often quite revealing and they offer the added possibility of relational connection.) Educational psychologist Kenneth Kiewra argues that to effectively teach learning strategies, educators must "(a) *introduce* the strategy by modeling and describing it, (b) *sell* the strategy by telling why it works, (c) *generalize* the strategy by telling where else it is useful, and (d) *perfect* the strategy by providing practice opportunities."[20] Showing students how to "pay attention to their attention" and regularly reinforcing the development of new strategies will empower them to control their own learning (and generate a sense of autonomy and agency) rather than have it controlled for them.[21]

Finally, during the reflecting stage, naive self-regulators may behave in ways that make it seem as if they do not care about the task at all. They often rush to finish as if being done, rather than learning and growing, were the point; again, performance versus mastery goals are important here. And once released from the completed task, they may look for opportunities to do other things like socialize. These behaviors suggest that the students may be skipping the reflecting stage altogether, not because they are resistant per se but because they lack developed strategies to reflect. To move new knowledge and skills from short-term to long-term memory, learners need to *do* something with the information, to connect it to previous understanding, to make meaning of it. By reflecting on what is being learned and on how they learned it, students engage in rich cognitive activity that provides both knowledge and strategy development.

Skilled self-regulators pause at the end of an activity to consider what they learned and what implications it may have for them. They might also think about what made their learning successful, asking internal questions like, "How well did I do?" "What strategies helped me stay focused and successfully complete the task?" "How hard did I try?" "What might be improved?" "What should I do next time?" We can model the reflecting stage by asking such questions aloud, by doing quick pair-share activities in which students discuss the strategies they used to stay on task, or by having students complete exit tickets describing how they sustained their attention throughout the activity and what they might do next time to improve.

When students are given opportunities to observe, practice, and even invent solutions that help them stay focused, they will take ownership of their strategies. This move from emulation to regulation is likely to help reduce their level of resistance because they know they have what they need to manage their own minds when inevitable distractions arise.

Promising Practices: Engaging the Disengaged

Although students' disengagement can be shortsighted and self-harming, it is often a logical response to less-than-optimal educational situations we helped create. In this way, disengagement is a form of resistance, a way that students act out their dissatisfactions or fears. Learning to see the logic of the disengaged response, to recognize what drives it, and to identify what we can do to prevent or address it can help turn disengagement from obstruction to opportunity. Let's look at a few suggestions for practices that may help in this regard.

Encouraging Student-Led Parent-Teacher Conferences

Students often disengage or withdraw from academic activities because school feels like an obligation more than an opportunity. They attend adult-defined spaces with adult-set objectives and must adhere to adult-mandated expectations to prepare for adult roles. Some of the more engaging activities we can provide for youth are those that transfer the locus of control from us to them. Establishing student-led parent-teacher conferences is an excellent example of such a transfer.

Parent-teacher conferences are an amazing opportunity for families and educators to better understand one another, to collaborate, to make sense of past performances, and to chart future successes. Too often, however, especially with students who struggle in or resist their schooling, these meetings become exercises in shame, blame, and humiliation. Nobody likes sitting around while superiors detail your every fault, attitudinal problem, and error. Adolescent insecurities arising from academic or social problems, and the lapses in motivation and engagement that can accompany them, are rarely improved by being lectured and scolded in such a public manner.

Perhaps the best way to shift this dynamic is to put the student in the driver's seat. Rather than relegate students (and parents or guardians) to passive and receptive roles during parent-teacher conferences, we can activate their engagement by putting them in control. We can do this by having students prepare for and organize *their* conference, requiring them to select items that represent their best work, helping them to choose specific assessments they have completed to characterize their emerging knowledge and skills, and pushing them to describe the areas in which they need additional support in light of the evidence they collect and explain.

Weeks if not months ahead of the conference, each student can begin to develop a file (or a presentation, a performance, or any other authentic instrument that would work for your purposes) and then add to it and refine it as the meeting approaches. Students can use artifacts in that file to show their progress, identify their goals, and articulate their needs. Parents could be alerted and involved in the process, and teachers, counselors, school psychologists, social workers, administrators, and coaches could be enlisted where appropriate to provide feedback and support. Then, when the conferences approach, students can prepare an agenda for the meeting using their parents or guardians, their teachers, and other school-based professionals as consultants. As educators, we can help students with that agenda by suggesting various formats. For example, students could plan to start with introductions, move to goals, then describe areas where they have been most successful and why, then areas where they have struggled and why. Students then might talk about where they are headed next, and conclude with what they need from adults. Helping students beforehand to revise their agenda and prepare for the meeting is a terrific way to examine various forms of resistance that may be operative, and it's also a great technique to put the learner in a position of authority and control amid a context of support.

At the actual conference, both the educators and the parents or guardians attending may need to shift their expectations and behaviors at first to safeguard the student's role as the facilitator most responsible for the content and process of the meeting. The silent moment at the very beginning of the conference, when students say nothing, look expectantly to the adults in the room to tell them what to do, and "wait to see if this whole student led-conferences thing is for real" can powerfully reinforce their agency in their learning when the adults say to the student, "What do you have for us, and what can we do to support your learning?" As long as sufficient collaborative preparation was done before that meeting, students can be counted on to identify precisely what they are learning, how they are growing, and where they are stumbling, and they can do so in ways that are probably far more accurate and motivating than anything we might declare for them. Rather than something to dread, this student-led approach can help make parent-teacher conferences something to celebrate.

Providing Voice and Choice

As discussed before, self-determination, self-realization, autonomy, and agency are crucial to many adolescents, especially those from individualist cultures. Researchers Idit Katz and Avi Assor have found that choice can greatly enhance students' engagement—but just presenting options is not enough. Students need to feel that the choices offered are relevant to their goals and interests and that their actions will have a consequence in some meaningful way. In general, choices that provide opportunities for self-realization tend to support students' autonomy and are therefore intrinsically motivating (see chapter 5). More specifically, researchers have found that students' sense of autonomy tends to increase when teachers observe the following practices:

- Minimize coercion and interference.
- Show understanding for students' perspective and feelings.
- Provide a relevant rationale for the task.
- Avoid close surveillance and frequent intrusions.
- Allow criticism and some expression of negative feelings.
- Offer choice by allowing students to choose tasks and goals and to select their work methods and the ways their work will be evaluated.
- Conduct an initial assessment of students' knowledge and then set optimally challenging tasks.
- Match the complexity and difficulty of the task to students' abilities and perceived competence.
- Provide feedback that helps students judge their progress, correct mistakes, and redirect efforts while avoiding feedback that compares students' abilities with those of other students.
- Encourage peer acceptance and empathy while minimizing social comparisons and competition.
- Offer options that do not conflict with important values of the students' culture (e.g., individualist cultures and collectivist ones value autonomy differently).[22]

These research findings suggest that in the classroom, students will tend to be more engaged when they get to choose not just *how* they will do things, but how those things will *align* with their identities, aspirations, passions, and connections to others.

Similar to the way choice operates, students tend to invest more in academic activity and stay engaged despite distractions and negative experiences when they have a voice in their learning community. In fact, student voice has been shown to be a powerful motivator for students from all backgrounds. Broadly defined, student voice activities are those in which youth have the opportunity to influence decisions that will shape their lives and others either in or outside school. Whether adolescents express themselves through verbal criticisms (or statements of gratitude), essays, letters to the editor, art installations, spoken word, participatory action research, activism, or something else, the activity of mustering ideas and sharing them publicly is essential to the development of adult ways of engaging the world. To counter disengagement, voice gives students a reason to engage.

Much has been written about the importance of student voice and the many ways to facilitate it, but a common mistake many educators make in this work is thinking that solicitation of students' opinions is all it takes.[23] Asking students what they think about something or surveying them for their perspectives may be an effective technique for generating greater engagement and learning what might be influencing resistant behaviors, but it lies at the weaker, adult-driven end of a whole spectrum of student voice activities that can (and should) be much more student-driven. We want to encourage students to express their opinions, but we also need to engage them as consultants with ideas, participants in a community, partners who take responsibility, activists who organize, and even leaders who step out in front and direct the work.[24] The more agency we grant to youth and the more autonomy they experience when they choose the form of their expression and the role they want to play, the more we are teaching them how to exert influence, hold themselves and others accountable, and make decisions that positively affect others. To truly engage students' resistance and tap into the vision it often represents, we sometimes need to move beyond seeing youth only as pupils to direct; we also need to engage them as community stakeholders with whom to collaborate, as people whose desire for change we need to engage.

I'm Done

At lunch over pizza slices and sports drinks, Marisol and Vincent are talking about their experiences with Mr. Jenkins, their math teacher.

"It's like he only cares about you if you're nice and getting A's," declares Marisol. "If you get frustrated, he tells you to just calm down. Like that helps."

Vincent says, "I dunno, I kinda like him sometimes 'cause he doesn't play. I mean, Joey can't joke around in there like he does in other classes. He shuts Joey up." When Marisol looks at him funny, Vincent offer another perspective: "But the way Jenkins grades work is totally unfair, and if you try to talk with him about it, he just tells you, 'Life is unfair,' and then does what he does. I got all mad about my participation grade last week, but I knew I couldn't do anything about it. So I just tuned the dude out and did my own thing for a couple of days."

Marisol asks, "I know, right? Participation grades in a class where you don't want to participate?! STOO-pid, yo." Marisol pauses and then asks, "What did he do when you got all mad?"

Vincent replies, "He sorta ignored me and waited for me to chill. Then there was a test coming up, and he told everyone they'd fail unless they buckled down, so I started doing my work a little more. But now I basically just do the basics and wait for the period to be over."

Excitedly, Marisol replies, "That's what I mean! If you agree with him and get A's, he likes you, but if you disagree about anything or ever get pissed about something, he either ignores you or sends you out. There's a kid from Jenkins's class in the hallway or down in the office, like, every other day. And it's like he's proud of it."

"I know," says Vincent, "that whole 'my way or the highway' bullshit he says whenever there's friction just pisses me off. There are more of us than him—why's he always gotta be Mister Dictator?"

Looking ahead to next year, Marisol says, "There's no f—— way I'm taking AP with him senior year. No way. I'd lose my shit in there for another year."

Thinking that he actually wanted the AP credits but also wanted never to be in Mr. Jenkins's class again, Vincent decided to agree so Marisol wouldn't feel abandoned. "I feel you," Vincent replies. "I'm done with that dude."

CHAPTER 7

"That's Not Fair!"

Why Indignation Is Better Than Resignation

IMAGINE THAT YOU are about to add one of two students to your classroom or caseload. You have a choice between a withdrawn student and an angry one. Which one would you pick? If you're like most of us, you'd typically pick the withdrawn one. With class sizes and caseloads as large as they are and accountability measures as pressing as they can be, the prospect of a quieter, more reserved, and less disruptive student may be less threatening than a high-need, attention-stealing, resource-demanding, and potentially volatile one.

We aren't bad people if we chose the withdrawn student over the angry one, but that choice does suggest that we tend to prefer resignation over indignation. And even if we ourselves don't have such a preference, the institutions in which we work are often far more comfortable with student (and educator) withdrawal than with misunderstanding, resentment, neglect, and indignation. If we're all in the same boat together, we tend to prefer people who don't rock it. That makes sense as long as the boat is headed in the right direction and everyone in the boat is happy. But is that the case in our classrooms and schools?

This chapter argues that resignation is not something to favor and that indignation is not something to fear. To fully grasp what resistance is and what it can do to invigorate learning communities if it is productively engaged, we need to rethink what we've been taught to do with angry students and shy ones. Resigned and indignant behaviors are students' responses to learning environments that are not working for them. Seeing those behaviors as forms of resistance reveals, again, that engagement with students exhibiting these behaviors is a much better response than avoidance or punishment.

149

Why We Should Accept and Expect Indignation

Few of us ever prefer to get angry or willingly put ourselves in situations where we will be confronted by people who are mad at us. We don't like to do that because it's unpleasant. Experiencing anger (ours or someone else's) raises our brain's threat response, pumps stress hormones into our system, makes us feel afraid, and warns against investing in any relationship with those who might be irate. Trained to be nice, we often shy away from confrontation and do whatever we can to keep others from getting upset with us. Unfortunately, as educators, the avoidance of confrontation and indignation is essentially impossible. Because we are in the business of having to tell people what to do, where to go, what to say, and how to act, it shouldn't surprise us that we confront regular resistance against our directives and frequent rage at our impositions. Anger and conflict come with the territory.

The Role of Conflict

Student resistance frequently introduces conflict. The educator wants to do one thing, but the student wants to do another—and the difference between the two produces discord. Because progress and productivity are vital to a school's success, conflict is typically viewed as a destructive force. It is understood to disrupt advancement and diminish output; its tendency to produce emotional disturbances is believed to slow people down and cause greater academic mistakes. In short, we tend to think that conflict either breaks things or puts the brakes on them. Seen in this light, conflict is something to avoid or suppress at all costs. The trouble is, when conflict is presumed to be the antithesis of learning, any resistance that produces conflict is automatically labeled the problem.

But what if conflict isn't an impediment to learning but was actually its catalyst? What if conflict, like resistance, were understood as a *resource* for students and educators in a learning community? Such an orientation might help us to realize that we should expect conflict in all human relationships, that it is the norm, not a disruption. Conflict emerges from competing needs or competing explanations of what we've experienced. And it is almost always present, whether we choose to recognize it or not. Because it is impossible for a group of people (or even just two persons) to always want the same things at the same time and to see things in the same way, conflict is as fundamental to relationships as is connection. One of the reasons we often prefer our friends and family to others is that their similarity to us reduces the work of having to relate across differences. But in a diverse world with diverse ideas of purpose, truth, beauty, justice, and morality, conflict might be best viewed as an opportunity for deeper responsiveness. This opportunity is especially evident in classrooms and schools filled with so many different adolescents, each of whom needs to explore, invent, and challenge.

The point here is that we need to embrace conflict in our work with youth. When things appear to be going smoothly, the temptation is to suppress resistance and avoid conflict because we have forgotten the refusals, rejections and clashes that actually produced that progress. For relationships to flourish in and outside the classroom, both individuals and groups need conflict to discover who they are and who they might become. If we are brave enough to engage or even welcome resistance, students will learn to see that conflict is not the end of the relationship but the potential for its deepening.

Moral Awareness and the Need to Push Back

Conflict typically arises when change occurs, and few examples of change are more glaring than a growing adolescent. Chapters 4 through 6 have demonstrated the extent to which adolescence is a developmental period of significant biological, cognitive, social, emotional, and relational transition. The developmental tasks of adolescence—namely, the changes youth must experience if they are to move successfully into adult ways of thinking, feeling, behaving, and being—indicate the magnitude of these transitions. According to the Raising Teens Project, a collaboration of the Harvard Center for Health Communication and the Massachusetts Institute of Technology's Work-Life Center, there are ten major tasks of adolescent development:

- Adjust to sexually maturing bodies and feelings
- Develop and apply abstract thinking skills
- Develop and apply new perspective on human relationships
- Develop and apply new coping skills in areas such as decision making, problem solving, and conflict resolution
- Identify meaningful moral standards, values, and belief systems
- Understand and express more complex emotional experiences
- Form friendships that are mutually close and supportive
- Establish key aspects of identity
- Meet the demands of increasingly mature roles and responsibilities
- Renegotiate relationships with adults in parenting roles[1]

The task concerned with the identification of moral standards merits closer examination because it directly addresses a core reason for students' resistance.

Adolescents' greater capacity for theoretical thinking and critical imagination, combined with the ability to plumb deeper levels of introspection and reflection, creates a heightened awareness of ethical concerns. As a result, conceptions of fairness, and both subtle and glaring distinctions between right and wrong, tend to move to the forefront of many adolescents' consciousness. With the ability to discern not just the effects of actions but the emotion-driven purposes behind them, adolescents are able to apprehend the ethical landscape on which decisions play out. They also develop the ability to consider the perspectives of others and do so with levels of complexity and empathy that were largely impossible at a younger age. This capability allows youth to separate intent from impact in their interactions with peers and adults and to consider others' outlooks and experiences alongside their own. These new talents can lead to far more sophisticated interpersonal negotiations and political deliberations than were possible in childhood. The result for many youth is a penchant for moral inquiry that finds expression in unbridled excitement about "rightness" and uninhibited condemnations of "wrongness." This can make youth really fun to work with, and it can make them quite a challenge too!

Theorists and researchers have generated various stage-based models to describe the changes in belief structures and rationale that people undergo as they make moral decisions in childhood, adolescence, and adulthood. In general, these moral development models ascribe a movement from self-centered, self-protecting considerations to more abstract and often selfless principles supporting the common good. People are generally understood to move from individualistic concerns ("me"), to mutual or reciprocal interests ("you and me"), to more interdependent ways of thinking ("us") as individuals determine whether a particular action is either right or wrong.[2] Lawrence Kohlberg's original model of moral development focuses on an "ethic of justice" and was later expanded (and critiqued) by Carol Gilligan's model that is based on an "ethic of care."[3] Scholars in the principle-centered Kohlbergian tradition suggest that moral reasoning depends on detached, objective, and rule-bound codes of justice, whereas those following Gilligan advocate person-centered models in which individuals make moral decisions in an effort to sustain relationships, improve connectedness, and elevate compassion.

Similarly, Bob Selman's work investigating the development of "perspective taking" in the human life cycle suggests a blending of these justice- and care-based systems. According to Selman, a developmental psychologist, people demonstrate an incrementally evolving capacity to consider another person's viewpoint while holding their own.[4] And William Damon's research has extended theories of moral development into the ways people gradually change their self-understanding, sense of individuality, and character. His work suggests that adolescents and adults develop a "moral identity" that is eventually organized by a sense of purpose or an "ultimate concern." This identity shapes individuals' awareness of responsibility and drives their decision making when ethical challenges arise.[5]

Each of these theorists argues that for adolescents to develop morally, they must be provided with ample occasions in which moral issues are considered. The greater exposure youth have to diverse ways of thinking and deciding, the richer the conundrums they encounter, and the closer their relationships with trusted elders, the more likely the youth will be to grow a moral code that feels both authentically theirs and rooted in collective values. Educational researcher Joan Goodman perhaps states it best: "If children are to become critical thinkers, tolerant of competing interests and loyalties, and strong independent moral agents, they must be active participants in moral decisions, they must become proprietors of their own morality."[6]

Whose Purpose and for What Purpose?

In each of these models, the evaluation of right and wrong and the development of deeply held and personally constructed values undergo substantial change during adolescence. Though volumes could be written about the relationship between these theories and adolescents' occasional inclination to resist their schooling experiences, the notion of purpose is perhaps the most illuminating for our analysis here. To have a purpose, according to William Damon, is to feel "that there is meaning in one's present and past life." And if individuals feel their life has meaning, they tend to be mindful of "order, coherence and purpose in [their] existence, the pursuit and attainment of worthwhile goals, and an accompanying sense of fulfillment."[7] Studies have linked the phenomenon of purpose to psychological, social, and physical well-being in adolescence and adulthood. Purpose is associated with higher levels of social activity and political activism, elevated life satisfaction and happiness, and decreased instances of depression.

On the flip side, youth who report a lower sense of purpose tend to engage in antisocial behaviors and act aggressively more frequently than those who report a clearer and stronger sense of purpose.[8] An adolescent's sense of purpose therefore involves cognitive, emotional, moral, motivational, and religious elements and plays a big role in general well-being. Purpose integrates some of the deepest drives an individual can have, and when dismissed, ignored, ridiculed, or repressed, it can produce significant and often quite emotional forms of resistance.

When might an adolescent's sense of purpose foster resistance in the classroom? What purposeful intentions contribute to resistant actions? To answer these questions, it may be helpful first to think about the many things educators do that seem disconnected from a sense of purpose. A considerable portion of what we do most days is probably routine, going-through-the-motions sort of stuff. Get up; get something to eat; check the mobile device for email, texts, or news; shower, brush teeth, and get dressed; plan logistics with family; go to work or school; and so on. While seemingly mundane, the goals we set to get those things done on a moment-by-moment basis are actually anchored in deep, abiding, far-reaching objectives. These deep-seated goals allow us to tolerate the triviality of daily existence because we know at some level that the triviality is part of something bigger. We can deal with the minutiae because the larger point of our efforts has meaning for us, it fulfills some purpose we have for our lives, and it makes us feel like we are making a difference.

Our students, however, do not necessarily share that sentiment. Constrained by schooling experiences that may make them feel captive to other people's goals, indoctrinated with other people's meanings, and dictated by other people's morals, their sense of purpose can feel imposed instead of inspired. The larger, more fulfilling, and purposeful activities adolescents crave may elude them as they make their way through an average school day. To them, the minutiae often crowd out the meaningful so much that many youth begin to wonder, initially to themselves but later in increasingly defiant and audible tones, "What's the point?" And so, if we are to tap into the power of purpose, we first may need to recognize how often we stifle it.

What makes purpose personally influential and socially powerful is the way it activates the individual's intention to, as Damon puts it, "accomplish something that is at once meaningful to the self and of consequence to the world beyond the self."[9] This desire to make a difference, to contribute in some substantive way to something larger than ourselves, is the foundation of some of the bravest and most consequential achievements in human history. It is the stuff we often teach about in school to motivate students to become better people. We present stories and historical events that provide exemplary combinations of morality and action because we want our students to see what's possible with a well-developed sense of purpose. Often the protagonists we feature are revolutionaries, iconoclasts, breakthrough thinkers, and countercultural heroes, people whose senses of purpose were meaningfully informed by a need to resist. (This may explain part of students' frustrations with school in that we extol the value of a "Give me liberty or give me death" orientation but deliver it within a "Sit down and be quiet" context.) Sometimes our presentations of these purposeful heroes are inspiring and life changing for our students, but a lot of the time, they aren't. Our own sense of purpose and need for meaning might be fulfilled by presenting this content to students, but it may not mean squat to them.

If students' sense of purpose helps to explain why they do what they do, it may also help to explain why they refuse to do what they're supposed to do. Students resist even our most purposeful intentions not because we're wrong or because we don't care; indeed, we are often right and usually care immensely. They resist our most strident attempts to inculcate a sense of purpose in them, because for that purpose to be authentic, it has to be *theirs*, not ours.

If all we ever do to inspire a sense of purpose in youth is present morals and meanings we think they ought to adopt, they will resist. If we are lucky, they may resist by outright disagreeing with us or interrupting proceedings to register their discontent. In these cases, their feelings are made visible because they are taking the risk to raise them aloud and bring them to the relationship, however tense and contested that relationship may be. At least then we have something to work with. If we are not careful, however, students will take their disillusion and disappointment underground by finding subtle and often invisible ways to withdraw and disconnect.

To develop a sense of purpose, youth need opportunities to invent it; to express, test, risk, and reconstruct it; and to relate it to others. They need to weigh options, explore gray areas, delve into controversies, challenge conventions, and find the individual explanations and orientations that make them want to get out of bed in the morning and get to work on something. Test prep classes, for example, will rarely accomplish this. This is not to say that guiding and even telling students about the morals we want them to uphold is a bad thing. Indeed, we often need to do that and should, especially when their actions are harmful, oppressive, or indifferent to the needs of others. But if too much of what we do under the auspices of character education, citizenship instruction, service learning, and standards-based instruction is predicated on a "receive and believe" model, and if too many of the messages we send through our disciplinary interactions and classroom management systems position students as objects rather than agents, we are virtually guaranteeing they will push back against us or look elsewhere for inspiration.[10] Like a lot of motivational factors, a sense of purpose tends to be most powerful when it is generated internally and given a chance to grow relationally. Though the energy that comes from a burgeoning sense of purpose has an internal origin, it needs an external outlet, and our students are either going to find that outlet in relationships *with* us, or in other, less academic venues *in spite* of us.

The Value of Idealism

Related to students' sense of purpose is their belief in the possibility of perfection. We usually call that sentiment *idealism*, and in far too many educational settings, it is thought to be synonymous with naïveté. It isn't. Naïveté is a condition of ignorant expectation, a character flaw in which the individual's assertions or projections are based on too little information or too much confidence. Naïveté gets people in trouble when they don't know what they're getting into or when they completely underestimate what's required to make something happen.

Idealism is different. It involves a recognition of situational inadequacy, combined with a vision for something better, enhanced by a hope for its possibility, and powered by a drive to make it real. Idealism motivates; naïveté doesn't. Idealists think and act from their ideals. They hold on to hope, possibility, purpose, and faith because they see something they believe can be actualized and they want to participate in its creation. Idealists get in trouble too, but they do that more because they see what's troubling than because they don't know what they don't know. Naysayers may roll their eyes, and cynics might assume the worst, but idealists possess a certain courage to retain their vision despite the social circumstances or even the evidence.

Juxtaposing the real to the ideal, adolescents often prefer what they can imagine over what they see. Their expanded creativity, perspective taking, sense of purpose, relationships, and sometimes even their indignation allow what Michael Nakkula and I call "possibility development."[11] Idealism can be an important expression of this process. Why then does our society so often dismiss the idealist? Why are we sometimes quick to tell youth in a snarky tone that they're being idealistic, as if it's something to avoid? Are we so concerned about the dangers of naïveté that we must belittle idealism and discipline students to expect diminished hopes as they grow older? Is this the price of admission into adulthood—lowered aspirations for oneself and the world?

I'm convinced that much of our culture's pathologizing of youth stems from our desire to avoid reacquainting ourselves with those hopes and ideals we may have abandoned long ago. We also denigrate adolescent idealists because their visions may serve as a reminder of how much we have gotten wrong as adults, how we continue to allow—if not create—suffering, war, torture, environmental destruction, animal cruelty, poverty, indifference, and the like. We sometimes laugh at so-called idealists because if we truly engaged what they were envisioning, we'd have to consider changing what we think and do. In some ways, it's braver to be an idealist than to submit to whatever reality is being presented, but we don't welcome that kind of bravery as much as we maybe should. It's sometimes easier to dismiss, regulate, or ridicule our adolescent idealists so we can get back to the business of getting through our lesson, enduring an assembly, reading a textbook, and so on. This approach virtually guarantees their resistance.

Adolescents are often idealistic because their brains and their exuberance compel them to be. Their new cognitive and social abilities emerge with insufficient life experience or impulse control to temper them, but that doesn't mean their ideas aren't worth engaging. The distance between what is happening now and what could happen in the future can be maddening when you have so little power to realize your vision or when nobody will take your ideas seriously. And this is exactly what school feels like to many youth. Idealists need audiences and opportunities, and we rarely give them either. "Thanks for sharing, Johnny. You can tell me more about that some other time if you like, but right now we need to get through this chapter." Responses like this tell students that their deeply considered or even spontaneously generated ideals are tangential to the real work in school. It is a reasonable response for Johnny to slump down in his chair and tune out for the rest of the period (or look for ways to disrupt things) when the powerful connections he's making and the hopeful futures he's imagining are considered peripheral to whatever closed content he is being asked to learn. Many youth care deeply about the world they are inheriting and feel a mixture of excitement and fear about assuming responsibility for it. They need practice playing with ethical quandaries and probing moral meanings, and their expressions of idealism are perfect opportunities to do that precious work.

Students' Strong Sense of Fairness

When we fail to provide sufficient opportunities for youth to express their idealism and find their purpose, they may try to create such opportunities by announcing their discontent. They do this in their own vernacular, with their own style. In a staff or faculty meeting, adults might say, "I have a concern about that particular decision," but adolescents often just go with, "This sucks!" Or they complain about something—maybe everything—as being unfair. Often (not always) these are the cries of the idealist, the ethically critical contrarian who recognizes that how it is pales in comparison to how it *could be*. Disruptive though these comments may be, the way we respond to them can make or break our relationships with students.

The claim "That's not fair!" has a lot going on within it. It suggests that the speaker has a theory about what might be fairer, and it presents an ethical stance against the perceived injustice being allowed to occur. To declare one's critique in a public setting like a classroom can of course be the sly move of a bored student who seeks to bog down the class in specious claims about unimportant actions to avoid more taxing activities that may follow. But in some cases, students go public with their "unfair!" critique to request dialogue and negotiation. They want to take part in designing something different, something more just. That's the kind of resistant impulse we want to encourage if we can, because perspective taking, moral development, and purpose all depend on regular experimentation and interaction. And students' concern with making things fair is a sign of a developing ethical code if not the emergence of empathy—that's good stuff.

Our students' ideals will never have a chance to be engaged and subsequently developed if their criticism is dismissed or if the critics themselves are cast off as yet another in a long line of "whining" teens who think they know more than they actually do. Of course they don't know fully what they're talking about, and of course they don't have the years of experience or the institutional perch to survey the complex ethical landscape involved in making classroom management decisions, disciplinary calls, and curricular choices. They don't know what is involved in such decisions, partly because they are young, but also because they are so rarely afforded opportunities to see what we see, to actually weigh the intricacies and explore the ecologies of human systems. We deliver endless batteries of often irrelevant standardized assessments when the real, meaningful, organic tests are right in front of them—the ones that show whether they can discern right from wrong and act in purposeful, moral, and community-enhancing ways.

Despite what many educators may think, we don't have to surrender to students' critiques to engage them. Other than a little time, we don't lose anything by considering the merits of their complaints. Sometimes all we need to do is show them how we arrived at a situation or a decision and explain the various competing interests or concerns. Then we can ask them how they would decide things. If they demonstrate in their explanation that they're stuck in self-centered or retributive modes of thinking, it is a terrific opportunity to push them to consider other people or greater needs. By hearing "That's not fair" as a request for dialogue and deliberation, we can open up classroom interactions so that relationships can be strengthened and moral development can be enhanced. This can make education profoundly relevant if not reverent.

What to Do with Anger

The perception of unfairness sometimes produces anger, an emotion we often fear and therefore try to suppress in our relationships with adolescents. They may yell at us, say hurtful things, tell us to "f— off!" and otherwise act in ways that bring classroom functioning to a screeching halt. Those moments when students flare and everyone turns to watch are, in many ways, our final exams. At times like these, all of our democratic rhetoric, beliefs about what's possible in public education, and technical skill in working with diverse others are put to the test. How will we handle it? What will we do? Will we further escalate the situation, forcibly send students away, refer the problem to someone else, use raw "power over" moves to threaten students and coerce their behavior, or will we do something to calm it, relate to it, and redirect it?

In hot moments like these, it may be helpful to remember that indignation is a form of connection. It is not indifference. It is not resignation. It is not withdrawal. Angry students are still there, right in front of us, in school and in our classroom, mad and loud as they may be. The key is to use that presence to stay connected, to recognize that they're taking the risk to register their emotional reaction rather than sublimate it, to see that they're trying to be an agent in the situation instead of a victim. We need to find out what they're thinking and how they're making sense of the circumstances and their own decisions before making any disciplinary moves. How do they see the events and our roles in them? What do they want to achieve? What do they envision as the ethical thing to do? Whose needs are they prioritizing in their interactions? Who or what do they see as their impediments? How might we and our students work together to chart a different path? Questions like these "engage the rage" instead of suppressing it and thereby can help move resistance from a destructive to a productive force.

Individuals don't often make their best decisions when they are angry, because the far less sophisticated fight-or-flight response in the brain often takes over. Adrenaline and cortisol surge, the heart rate increases, eyes dilate, and we feel ready to pounce or sprint away much more than we are prepared to delve, deliberate, and discern. Some people get addicted to the rush of an angry response, but most of us—students included—feel uncomfortable with anger, so we try to avoid it. But avoiding anger will not make it go away. Something important is happening when strong emotional reactions occur. As with many other resistant responses, the trick is not to get fixated on the expression but instead to try to understand what stoked the anger in the first place. For all educators, from the classroom teacher initially confronting the anger to the counselor, administrator, school psychologist, or social worker who sometimes has to handle the fallout, it is usually better to say to the student, "Tell me what you are feeling and why," rather than, "What did you do?"

When working with angry students, we also need to remember that they often have good reason to be indignant. They may spend time in the opulent palaces of shopping malls or big-box stores with appealing sights, sounds, and smells. They watch media with rich images, powerful storylines, and exciting action. They listen to stirring music with beats, melodies, and lyrics that explain their experiences and present larger-than-life figures to worship. And then they enter our often bland, crumbling schools in which outdated technology, nonfunctioning drinking fountains and toilets, uninspired curricula, and relentless worksheets appear with more regularity than they should. Those juxtapositions make the fiscal priorities of our nation obvious, and they implicate us in an absurd system that students have every right to critique. If good education is supposed to excite the hearts and minds of students, we cannot simply recoil at students' anger, particularly when it is justifiable. Their anger deserves our attention and our respect.

"Hey You!" Doesn't Help

Often, students are reacting not to the immediate situation but to the cumulative effect of being labeled, dismissed, and ignored not just by their peers but also by the adults who are charged with their care and education. As discussed in chapter 2, educators often hail students in ways that broadcast to others how the students should be understood. This hailing influences not just how audiences are supposed to see hailed individuals but also how those individuals are supposed to see themselves. For example, the "class clown" tells jokes, makes wisecracks, or invents antics that expose hidden assumptions or unspoken principles operating in the learning environment. Through humor and buffoonery, these students are often quite skilled at revealing the arbitrariness, hypocrisy, or injustice of our systems and decisions. Indeed, satirists from Mark Twain to George Carlin, Dave Chappelle, and Tig Notaro are incredibly adept at laying bare the inconsistencies and idiosyncrasies of our everyday experiences and assumptions. When our students present such behaviors, however, we hail them as "class clowns" to demonstrate to others that their actions are neither critical nor contributory but are instead mere shenanigans we should all learn to ignore or subdue. This is why hailing can make students indignant.

Hailing resistant students as "whiners" or "rebels" (or worse) may temporarily stop their opposition if they consider those labels shameful, but it may also tell them that *we* are not worth engaging in the first place. Students want to be known, but they do not want to be labeled. Because teens are so invested in the processes of self-exploration and self-definition, any experiences that make them feel their identity is under someone else's control are likely to foment resistance. Such a reaction is less likely in collectivist cultures where deference to community norms is prioritized (if you are perceived to be a member of that collective; if not, then the same conclusions may still apply), but it may be exacerbated in individualist ones. Whether it occurs through curricula, conversation, discipline, greetings, nicknames, dress codes, test scores, or the labels and pseudo-diagnoses we supply at parent-teacher conferences, hailing effectively delimits the identity formation process. It's as if educators are saying, "Despite your autonomous efforts to self-identify, by hailing you, I am determining how you will be understood, received, and manipulated. By hailing you, I am foreclosing your options."

Research supports these conclusions. Sociologist Dia Sekayi investigated the roots of students' intellectual indignation and has found that a leading cause of conflict is adult misperceptions of students' motivations, academic preparedness, and identities. Sekayi traces these misperceptions to a pervasive lack of effective interpersonal communication.[12] In addition, educational philosopher and researcher Alice Pitt has analyzed dozens of theoretical and empirical studies of student opposition in school. She observes that resistance might be best understood as "a response to feelings of being misrecognized or unaddressed."[13] And developmental psychologist Susan Harter notes that by early adolescence, students' self-representations typically include social attributes ascribed by others (e.g., they self-describe using labels they've adopted, labels like "talkative," "rowdy," "shy," and "class clown"). They do the same with academic labels picked up from comparisons with others (e.g., "smart," "not good at math," a "hands-on learner"). Then as they mature, adolescents increasingly present different selves to different people in their lives (e.g., to their father, mother, close friends, teachers, coach, grandmother) and they ascribe a variety of roles specific to each relationship (e.g., student, teammate, brother, sister, son, daughter). These findings indicate that adolescents are very attentive to context, powerfully dependent on others' opinions of them, and incredibly receptive to the labels that are applied to their representations.[14] It is therefore no exaggeration to say that hailing *makes* students' identities. And when students are routinely reminded that they are not in control of how they are perceived, indignation is a logical response.

The Diagnostics of Indignation

Students are not just being disobedient or aggressive when they express indignation in the classroom. The anger they express in their disagreements with our policies or with the unfairness of our responses serves a diagnostic purpose. That is, their resistance alerts us to the areas of our learning communities most in need of attention and possible modification. To be receptive to these alerts, we may have to recognize the extent to which schools are predicated on unequal distributions of power and voice. Adult educators largely run the show and control the flow of bodies, conversations, and materials. Student resistance in the form of complaints or angry refusals often contains critiques of such domination and as a result provides opportunities for reflection and improvement. If we listen to student indignation, we will be able to form relationships with students and hence make our schools and classrooms feel less oppressive and more responsive.

The risk in this approach is that we may romanticize adolescents' oppositional behaviors. Students' resistance and indignation are not necessarily the result of political critique, pedagogical analysis, or interpersonal evaluation. Some students merely make inappropriate jokes and complain as a way of avoiding work; thus, their motivation is not always ethically driven or even helpful. Sometimes their reasons for being disruptive have more to do with spite, revenge, discrimination, or having a laugh at someone else's expense. This is why none of what has been detailed above should be taken as an argument to eliminate discipline. Some behaviors ought not to be encouraged. But as we make decisions about which behaviors to prefer, we need to ask the question we posed at the beginning of this chapter: When we discipline youth in schools, are we giving preferential treatment to resignation over indignation? To ask it more plainly: Do we prefer those who withdraw to those who rebel? It is to that question that we now turn.

Resignation: What We Need to Avoid

Chapter 6 explained several ways students resist school by withdrawing from it. These forms of opposition typically mark a retreat from relationship rather than an attempt to change its terms. Students who withdraw from classroom activity rather than disrupt it are often passed over if not forgotten. Those who resist more outwardly and loudly get the lion's share of our attention (negative though it may be), which is shared with the students we think of as our "good kids"—those whose behaviors and academic performances frequently receive our most public tributes. Too often, the quiet ones in the middle are sometimes all but invisible. And for some, their invisibility is intentional. They retreat and hide right in front of us, resisting anything that might require a more active engagement with the content or a more authentic relationship with others. What's more, we often help them do it.

Shyness

Some students resist not with outward displays of refusal but with passive forms of withdrawal. Sitting amid their more verbal and active peers, some take advantage of opportunities to pull back and disappear because engagement makes them anxious. We often refer to these kids as "shy" and do what we can to protect them from experiences that seem to scare them. At some level, such as response is understandable and compassionate, but the research on shyness indicates that common practices designed to help socially inhibited students are often driven by incorrect and problematic assumptions. To align our practices with what scholars have found, we need to recognize that shyness is a form of resistance and disengagement that endangers students' academic achievement as well as their social and cognitive development.

Nearly everyone experiences shyness on occasion. New circumstances, unknown social situations, and other unfamiliar contexts can temporarily elevate stress and lead us to be cautious, reserved, and even withdrawn at first. Most of these feelings subside as it becomes clear what role we are expected to play and with whom we can most easily associate. But for some, shyness is a persistent recurrence of stress and withdrawal regardless of the familiarity of the situation. Shyness is associated with negative self-worth, shame, embarrassment, and interpersonal inhibition. In social situations, shy people speak less than others, avoid eye contact, and experience an elevated heart rate and an increased release of stress hormones. Though researchers have used an array of terms to refer to the same basic phenomena (e.g., behavioral inhibition, social inhibition, social wariness, social reticence, social withdrawal, social anxiety, social phobia, timidity, low sociability), and though shyness is not the same thing as introversion or the desire for solitude (both of which frequently contribute to positive social and academic outcomes), the findings are clear: when shyness is allowed to persist unaddressed, it rarely leads to positive outcomes and may worsen students' tendencies to disengage and withdraw from academic activity.[15]

Without exception, developmental psychologists agree that humans need relationships to develop and to learn. It is in the process of engaging others that the learner sees how different people's minds work, and this expands what the learner can conceive as possible. Being able to express themselves provides individuals with a sense of mastery over what happens in their lives, and that expression helps to produce relationships characterized by reciprocity, communication, and growth. In the classroom, whenever students are able to verbally interact with a more knowledgeable or more skilled person, their "zone of proximal development" expands and they have the potential to learn more. But the key word there is *interact*. If shyness reduces or terminates interaction, then relationships—which are the primary catalyst of learning and development—are also restricted.

As evidence, research has demonstrated a series of negative outcomes associated with shyness:

- Restricted peer networks
- Social rejection
- Victimization
- Submissive if not avoidant problem-solving styles
- Elevated self-blame and shame
- Less sophisticated academic responses
- Less developed language skills
- Dependency on adults
- Diminished academic achievement
- Poor relational quality even with close friends
- A propensity to develop anxiety disorders, social isolation, and depression later in life[16]

Caught in a cyclical process in which repeated withdrawal, disengagement, and avoidance lead to impoverished social skills, shy students' continual retreat can lead them to be more anxious in social situations and more apt to apply negative self-appraisals when things do not go well. In turn, this can make it increasingly difficult for shy individuals to initiate contact and develop the skills typically learned in peer interactions, not to mention the negative effects such withdrawal can have on academic achievement. Undeniably, if shy students are not helped to develop better strategies of social interaction, they may prove to be their own worst enemies.

Research has demonstrated biological factors may predispose some students to an enhanced activation of their "fear circuitry" when they are in social situations. Such patterns may be further exacerbated by parenting styles that overprotect, enable, and control the child, which can further impede social success. In an effort to spare their child from negative or stressful experiences (or to preserve the parents' need to be needed), some parents shelter kids from situations in which relational skills might be developed. This protective reaction can promote dependency, hinder social-emotional development, contribute to submissiveness, and lead children to expect that adults will support their need for avoidance and withdrawal. In this way, a child's initial feelings of insecurity combined with overprotective parenting can result in a vicious cycle of helplessness, rescue, retreat, repeat, which can prevent the child from obtaining important social competencies. In fact, researchers have found strong correlations between overcontrolling, intrusive, and exceedingly protective parenting styles and children's and adolescents' socially withdrawn and reticent behaviors.[17] Furthermore, when it comes to bullying and other forms of victimization, overprotective interventions designed to protect shy children and adolescents can end up making them easy targets.[18]

A difficult thing to admit here is that *teaching* practices often mirror the over-protective parenting styles just described. We avoid calling on shy students, we refrain from putting them in roles in which they must speak for their group, we rush in to protect them when other students may be ignoring or picking on them, and we allow them to grow silent and virtually disappear in class debates or discussions. We do this because we want to help them, but what we are actually doing is encouraging their disengagement, lack of development, and resistance.

Sometimes we overprotect because we fear the angry phone call or visit from an overcontrolling parent. Other times, we may do it because we ourselves enjoy the feeling of protecting those we perceive to be helpless. Or maybe we overprotect the shy ones because doing so triggers our own memories of being victimized when we were young. Regardless of the reason, we need to take the long view and recognize that persistent and permitted disengagement leads not to safety but to isolation, rejection, and stunted development. In truth, we do the shy students no favors by allowing their shyness to persist unchallenged. The "Promising Practices" section at the end of this chapter offers specific suggestions for how we can help shy students reengage.

Dropout Versus Push-Out

A lot has been written about the tragic dropout rates in the United States over the past several decades, especially among low-income and minoritized youth.[19] The precursors, patterns, and outcomes of adolescents' premature departure from school are all abundantly clear at this point and far too extensive to recount here. But one finding that resounds across much of this research is that dropout is more accurately understood as "push-out." Students don't just suddenly decide one day to "drop out" of school. They go through a somewhat lengthy process of being alienated, misunderstood, rejected, mislabeled, underserved, discriminated against, and stressed in school from the elementary grades through middle school and into high school, if they even remain that long. Changing the term from *dropout* to *push-out* shifts the phenomenon from being a decision to being a pro-gression. Though various tipping points can send students over the edge (many of which pertain to factors outside the control of a school or its educators, such as family member illness, economic instability, crime, drug abuse, military ser-vice or return, gang activity, and family breakup), rarely is a single event the sole causal factor in a student's "decision" to withdraw from school. Push-out happens gradually, in countless accumulating experiences. Researchers have demonstrated that the same triggering events often pointed to as the cause of push-out can actually be ameliorated by school if the student's relationships with educators are supportive and if the learning community is highly committed to the student's development and well-being.[20]

If the signs of potential push-out become clear in early elementary school, the hard question to ask is, How do we educators sometimes inadvertently convince students over time that a complete withdrawal from school is a better option than staying enrolled? One way we err in this way is by treating their many expressions of resistance and their many forms of early and minor withdrawal as the problems themselves, rather than as symptoms of problems. If we can muster the courage to look at the relational aspects of the push-out phenomenon and our complicity in them, we will see that students are withdrawing and resisting in response to us and the environments we create. Their behavior may be problematic, but it isn't technically the problem—we are.

When students are argumentative, angry, rebellious, and abusive in school, they're actually still giving us a chance. They're still there, in classrooms, relating to us in whatever way they can, waiting and hoping for things to change in some substantive way. It may be difficult sometimes to see their resistant behaviors as anything other than the problem, but the alternative is to blame them for being the victim of our malpractice. If we respond to their pushbacks with more pushing away, we're basically telling them that their contrariness or alternativeness or defiance—or whatever we want to call it—isn't welcome here and that dropping out is their best bet. This is why it is so important to examine whether our reactions to, and relationships with, youth communicate a preference for resignation over indignation. When roughly *one million students every year* drop out of school before receiving a diploma, this prioritization may have momentous consequences.[21]

Promising Practices: Using Relation to Address Indignation and Resignation

Many if not most of the practices mentioned in previous chapters would have some positive effect on teacher-student relationships and may even diminish the conditions that produce students' indignation. To directly address issues of trust, agency, and the development of purpose in the classroom and to use conflict as an opportunity to deepen rather than sever relational connection, I am suggesting here how we might handle a flaring student and a shy one in the classroom.

Working with Shy Students: Engage Them

To meet shy students' needs, we may need to remind ourselves and our colleagues that being shy is a fear-based form of social resistance and relational disengagement. And educators should not allow students to cut themselves off from the interactive aspects of learning. After all, if engagement is essential to positive educational experiences, we need to make sure all of our students are connecting not only to the content but also to one another and to us.

So what should we do? First, we must recognize that shy students do indeed need our help. But just as a person learning to swim is not helped if he or she never gets wet or is thrown in the deep end of the pool before the learner is ready, we need to teach incremental skills in the shallow end and slowly move individuals toward deeper water where those skills most matter. This means being sensitive without being enabling. By establishing incremental risk-taking opportunities and building the necessary community so that embarrassment is minimized and mistakes are welcome, we can help shy students become more active in the social aspects of learning. Other ideas include the following:

- Providing structured exposure experiences in small-group activities in which each student has clearly defined roles and the roles rotate so that everyone has a chance to experience more up-front (versus backstage) behaviors
- Modeling and practicing the sort of listening and interacting skills needed to develop relationships with others, and providing pointers and reminders (not punishments) when students demonstrate they do not know how to behave
- Identifying which social risks a shy student wants to practice, and working with that student to identify the support he or she needs to achieve the stated goals, then tracking those accomplishments over time in consultation with parents
- Before class, giving shy students a list of preview questions we know we will ask during the period, and letting them pick which one (or two) they want to voluntarily answer in class; then debriefing one-on-one how it went afterward, moving toward more engagement over time on negotiated terms

- Establishing a classroom culture in which ridicule is disallowed and class-wide responses to it are practiced
- Encouraging involvement in sports and other extracurricular activities (research suggests these domains are often very helpful in getting shy kids to come out of their shells)[22]

Working with Angry Students: Don't Take the Bait—Relate

When a student suddenly responds with a level of indignation that, to you, seems to be of greater magnitude than the situation calls for, do whatever you can to de-escalate. The student's anger is real, and the situation is likely to be perceived by the student differently than you are perceiving it, so be as inquisitive and unthreatening as you can. Try to learn more and provoke less. Take a moment to remind yourself that conflict can be productive, that indignation is a reasonable response to perceived wrongs, that adolescents are not yet skilled in managing impulse control, and that they do not possess a well-developed range of potential responses to complex social situations. They're not yet mature, so they're likely to act in immature ways. Plus, some students may only have rage as their emotional go-to; it's your job to work with that limited skill-set just as you would if you were trying to teach them new content by building on what they already know. Don't just react to the situation—use it to teach something.

And before you respond to an angry student, remember that how you look is just as important as what you say, especially in those initial seconds when everyone is watching what you do. To make sure your nonverbal messages match your verbal ones, take a half-step backward away from the angry student, lower your arms, and assume a neutral and open stance with your hands at your sides or in your pockets (no crossed arms, no pointing fingers). Speak in gentle, measured tones, and try to make sure your facial expressions convey compassion more than condemnation. Know that everyone in class is watching every aspect of the interaction, so it's a teachable moment for you, for the angry student, and for the rest of the class.

Then acknowledge the student's feelings, tell the student what you plan to do, and give him or her a momentary break to calm down and gather his or her thoughts. Do not threaten the student with punishment. Do not respond with sarcasm. Do not embarrass the student with whatever snippy retort just popped into your head. (We were once teenagers too and probably learned a host of terrific comebacks in that era, but we need to be the adult in the room right now. The point is not to win the battle but to use the conflict to deepen the relationship.) Instead, say something like, "I can see that you're angry. Let's talk in a few minutes about why, then work together to develop a solution. How about you take a minute to go get a drink of water before we talk?" Sure, the student may have just said something inappropriate or hurtful, and yes, the student may be way out of line, but that doesn't matter right now. What matters is the student's perspective, your expression of care, and your collaborative learning from one another. Don't push the student away. Keep him or her close. *Stay in relationship.*

When you talk with the student a few moments later, after he or she has had a chance to get a drink, situate yourself outside of earshot and view of his or her peers (hallways are great for this). Begin the discussion by making it clear you want to work with the student to figure out what is wrong, and don't get caught up in disciplining the student for saying whatever he or she said in class when the anger became apparent. That's a dead end. Even if the student hurled an expletive at you, it doesn't matter. Students know they're not supposed to say such things, so it's pointless to focus on that fact first. If you pay more attention to the "bad words" than the emotional reactions and what precipitated them, you're getting derailed. Stay on target. Find out what happened that made the student so mad. Repeat back to the student what he or she has articulated until the student expresses confidence that you understand the situation. Say, "Tell me if I am getting this right," or "Is that how you understand it?" Don't try to correct the student's perception. Things may have occurred differently from your perspective, but "the facts" aren't as important as the student's interpretations right now. So just listen, paraphrase, and check to see if you're getting it right.

Once you do get it right (and the student tells you that you have), don't waste the connection you're building by presenting your version of the events. The student will be expecting that. Instead, catch the student off guard by taking his or her perspective seriously. This will build trust. Use the positive momentum to move forward by enlisting the student's help in developing a solution. "Okay, what should we do to make this right?" you might ask. Don't let the student get away with monosyllabic responses or an "I dunno." Push him or her to take responsibility for being part of something better rather than being satisfied with being only the victim. You can be firm here. "That's not good enough, [name]. I am working with you here, and I need you to work with me. Let's figure this out together. What should we do?" Discuss.

After codeveloping a solution with the student, if you still have the student's attention and the student still has the energy, then and only then (if at all) should you discuss the language he or she may have used in class. But don't blow the interaction by disciplining the student or accusing her or him of being "disrespectful." It's likely the student is mad because he or she felt disrespected in some way, so punishing the student for breaking some rule about using abusive language will only squander the progress you've just made when you were focused on feelings and experiences. Say something like, "So before you go back to your seat, let's talk for a minute about what you said in class. What do you think about that interaction? How would you like me to handle it in the future? How do you plan to handle it in the future?" And whatever you do, don't ask for or demand an apology, ever. If all goes well, students might actually apologize on their own, of their own volition, which is far more meaningful and authentic than being compelled to deliver someone else's script. Forced apologies are really only power plays. They tell students they are the puppets and you are the ventriloquist. Forced apologies generate feelings of powerlessness and therefore tend to incite further resistance and resentment. If the student wants to apologize at that moment, great; but if the student doesn't, don't push it. In that interaction, you'll get much more out of the discussion if you stay in relationship and learn from the conflict than if you coerce students to comply with your rules or take care of you. Besides, you're the adult—you don't need the apology from the kid to feel okay. It's not about you. You need the student to learn, to behave prosocially, and to achieve. That's your goal.

And when it's time to make the transition back into the classroom, give the student one more out. Students need to save face when they reintegrate with their peers. They don't want to look like they were played; nor do they want to appear weak. So ask the student, "How do you plan to reenter the classroom? What behaviors will I and your peers likely observe when you take your seat?" Have the student describe what he or she will do. Provide some suggestions and limits if needed, and maybe say, "And hey, it's okay with me if you roll your eyes or suck your teeth when you head back into class. It's also okay with me if you take a minute or two to get back to work, but only a minute or two. I know how it is and I know how friends can be, so I won't take offense if you play it that way. I can take it. Understand?" Then let the student go.

And finally, if you can, it's a good idea to check back with the student in a few days to see how he or she is doing and to comment on the student's behavior since that point. Find positive things to say about the student's work or contributions to the learning environment since the confrontation. Maybe even make a call home just to express those positive developments. Demonstrate that you are the student's ally, not an enemy, and build from the base of understanding you've already set. Show the student that you understand, that you care, and that you want to know what's going on for him or her, including the roots of the student's resistance. Then get ready for the next flaring student, and repeat the process!

PART III

UNDERSTANDING
RESISTANCE
POLITICALLY

Sick of It

With tears in his eyes, William looks at his counselor, Mr. Jackson, and asks, "Why are they calling me the bully? I'm the one getting bullied!"

As Mr. Jackson fills out the paperwork to suspend William for fighting, the sudden tears makes him pause, put down his pen, and listen.

Wiping his cheek, William continues. "They make fun of me all day. They diss my clothes, they laugh when I talk, and they make fun of where I live. They've been doing this since middle school. I'm sick of it and I'm sick of them! Bradley had it coming, and I'll punch him again tomorrow if he talks to me like that. I'm sick of them."

After thinking for a moment, Mr. Jackson asks, "Who's 'them'?"

William replies, "The kids from the hills. The preps."

Though Mr. Jackson has been working with William for the past two years, trying to help William to better manage his anger and stay in school, he has never been more concerned about William than he is now. Mr. Jackson starts to worry that this suspension could be William's tipping point. Despite testing very well in elementary and middle school, William was tracked into the lower "college prep" classes as a freshman as a result of his eighth-grade teachers' recommendations. Looking at his records, Mr. Jackson can see that William's academic achievement peaked in sixth grade, started to drop in seventh, and bottomed out in eighth, with two Ds and one F. And now, the boy is failing three of his core classes: English, world history, and biology. When asked, the teachers in those three classes all have characterized William as a "troublemaker" who is frequently disruptive and threatening. One teacher has said William rarely works well with his peers unless he is allowed to sit with one of his "redneck buddies." In fact, William has recently taken to calling himself a redneck and displays the Confederate flag on his backpack and notebooks (when he bothers to bring them). This has brought even more derision from his peers and some concern from Mr. Jackson, who wonders about the racial implications of these displays. Perplexed about how to approach William's conflict with the "preps" and how to talk with him about the Confederate flags, Mr. Jackson shifts the conversation away from the fighting and toward academics.

"Tell me about your grades," he says. "Why are you failing three of your classes?"

William responds that he doesn't care much for the teachers in those subjects. "They act like they know everything when they don't, and they look at me like I'm stupid, so sometimes I get pissed, especially when they always side with the preps. I mean, they even wear the same clothes and talk about the same things."

Remembering that William once said he liked Mr. Yoder, his math teacher, Mr. Jackson asks him why Mr. Yoder is the exception.

"Because Mr. Yoder is a regular guy," William says. "I mean, he lives on a farm down near our house and he's just a regular dude. No attitude. I think he even rides ATVs like me."

Sensing an opening here, Mr. Jackson asks William if he would be interested in staying in Mr. Yoder's math class but transferring out of the other three classes and into the vocational ed program instead.

"Um, I guess," mumbles William. "Is that my punishment? Does that mean I'm not getting suspended?"

Mr. Jackson thinks for a moment about what William's question suggests, but he doesn't know how to respond.[1]

CHAPTER 8

"I'm Not Skipping Class—You Are"

Socioeconomic Reasons for Resisting School

THE WAY ADOLESCENTS think about their socioeconomic status (SES) is shaped by messages received from home, school, and society. Some messages are affirming and help to strengthen relational bonds and self-worth. Other messages are discriminatory and can create resentment, hostility, and indignation. For example, Langston Hughes once wrote, "Misery is when you heard on the radio that the neighborhood you live in is a slum but you always thought it was home." If school operates like Hughes's radio—if it makes students feel as if their home, their family, their community, their *identity* is something to be ashamed of—then opposition to school is to be expected.

This chapter examines the way student resistance in school may be traced to experiences of classism. Informed by the theoretical and psychological perspectives from parts I and II, our attention is focused here on the sociopolitical and economic dimensions of student resistance. While there is significant overlap between this chapter and the racial and ethnic aspects of resistant behaviors highlighted in chapter 9, especially when it comes to the antecedents of opposition and the typical institutional responses to it, this chapter targets the role of SES. In other words, how might the distribution of economic resources, the conferment of socioeconomic status, and the allocation of class privilege and oppression shape student oppositional behaviors? Put simply, how might student resistance be "classed"?

The Data Are Clear: We Have a Problem

In chapters 2 and 3, the theory of social reproduction explained why many students resist and what happens to them when they do. Derived from Marxist interpretations of class struggle, social reproduction theory says that students with lower SES are theorized to reject school because of its middle-class conformism and the limited prospects for upward mobility that seem available to them even if they choose to comply. These students' repudiation of school actually cements their class status rather than forcing the institution to better address their concerns and needs. This, in turn, reproduces the socioeconomic stratifications that gave rise to the inequities and refusals in the first place. Though this analysis overstates the situation and overdetermines the outcomes, it's hard to argue against the fact that disparities do exist, that they are intentional and harmful, and that they are getting worse, particularly for children and adolescents.

The Importance of Socioeconomic Status as a Predictor

Just as students are participants in communities, schools are participants in economies, and the U.S. economy is increasingly characterized by its inequity. In fact, as a nation, the United States has a greater level of income inequality than any other wealthy nation in the world, and it is currently more socioeconomically (and racially) segregated than it was before the Great Depression.[1] Since the middle of the twentieth century, the strongest predictor of students' educational achievement has been their SES.[2] Though racial and ethnic differences can be used to explain many troubling trends in education, disparities in academic achievement track most closely to differences in income, so much so that the achievement gap between wealthy and poor students is now twice that of White and Black students.[3] More than race, gender, school quality, friendship networks, or motivational and aspirational measures, students' location in the social class hierarchy is still the best forecaster of their engagement and subsequent success in school.[4] This may not be the way we want it, but it is our current reality.

Because the rate of social class mobility is far lower in the United States than in other industrialized nations, many Americans are growing increasingly worried about the nation's ability to compete in a globalized economy when so many of our students are left behind.[5] But the U.S. educational system actually does a terrific job if you evaluate it solely on how well the highest-earning segment of the population performs. For example, if we investigate students' performance on an internationally recognized test (the Programme for International Student Assessment, or PISA) but restrict our sampling only to the public schools in the wealthiest neighborhoods in the United States, we find that the nation ranks fifth in math, first in reading, and first in science worldwide.[6] This means that upper-class U.S. students tend to post scores that beat most of the rest of the world. Though there are numerous other variables we might add to this analysis and no single test should be taken as a comprehensive characterization of a population's learning, these figures do suggest that the wealthiest American students seem to be well served by U.S. schools. However, if the data from U.S. schools include *all* students' PISA scores from *all* socioeconomic levels, the nation drops to twenty-fifth in reading, twenty-ninth in science, and thirty-seventh in math.[7] Clearly, if we want to understand what is and is not working in public schools and why so many nonwealthy U.S. students may resist their education in ways that lead to diminished academic performance, we simply cannot afford to "skip class."

The Extent of Poverty Among School-Aged Children and Adolescents

According to the U.S. Census, the poverty rate in 2012 for children under the age of eighteen was 21.8 percent.[8] This means that of the seventy-four million kids in this country, over sixteen million are living in poverty. As large as these numbers are, they only capture a fraction of those who struggle to survive on comparatively lower family incomes. These figures depend on where the federal government sets the poverty line—the level at which, if you earn less than that amount, the government considers you poor. For a family of four in 2012, the federal poverty line is $23,550 per year. This equates to earning $64.52 per day, or roughly $450 per week. But according to Columbia University's National Center for Children in Poverty (NCCP), families need an income about twice that amount to cover the cumulative cost of food, housing, transportation, utilities, health care, and clothing.[9] Anyone below that doubled amount is considered "low income." The scholars at the NCCP and elsewhere argue that a more accurate way to assess the number of students struggling with their socioeconomic situation would be to focus on all low-income families rather than just those in poverty. Using this standard, a full 45 percent of U.S. children—*that's nearly half of our nation's kids and more than thirty-three million people*—live in low-income families. This figure would be cause for great concern in any nation, especially the richest nation on the planet.

The Effects of Living with Low Income

While movies and television are full of rags-to-riches stories, and professional sports and lottery tickets offer low-probability rescues from chronic poverty, the actual challenges of low-income circumstances make it increasingly difficult for individuals to improve their status. With an ever dwindling social safety net, a largely regressive tax structure, and a minimum wage nowhere near what it takes to cover the basic costs of living, millions of families—even those with full-time wage earners—struggle to make ends meet. And it is the children and adolescents within those families who are most vulnerable. As of 2012, one in five adolescents lives below the poverty line and over 40 percent live in low-income families, and both of these figures are on the rise.[10]

Some of those injurious effects relate directly to school. Researchers have found that secondary schools in high-poverty areas are often marked by high degrees of bullying, fighting, teacher turnover, and even teacher vacancies, each of which is known to negatively affect academic achievement.[11] And according to the National Center for Education Statistics, the dropout or push-out rate of students living in low-income families is about 4½ times greater than the rate in higher-income families.[12] Because of the enormous stressors associated with living in low-income circumstances, the added pressures and additional work of school may be experienced by some students more as a burden than an opportunity.[13]

Many low-income students are right to resist their schooling experiences, given the stark disparities between themselves and their middle- or upper-class peers. Low-income students are far more likely to be taught by underprepared teachers; to attend underfunded schools; to inhabit decaying buildings; to receive outdated curricula; and to face metal detectors, security cameras, and roaming police officers in the hallways. Overall, schools in the United States are highly segregated by income, social class, and race or ethnicity. To explain this, some analysts point to the choices people make when they select neighborhoods to live in, while others point out the long history of redlining in real estate, exclusionary zoning laws that concentrate low-income housing in already blighted areas, and state and district policies that distribute funds to schools largely on the basis of property values. According to the education scholar David Berliner, policy makers "have allowed for apartheid-lite systems of schooling to develop in our country [in which] 48% of high poverty schools receive less money in their local school districts than do low poverty schools."[14]

Stark disparities like these have led the American Psychological Association to conclude that "the education that poor, urban students in public schools receive is demonstrably insufficient to make them competitive with their more advantaged, middle and upper income peers." The association points to glaring deficiencies in schools that serve largely low-income students: from poor physical plants, to inadequately credentialed STEM (science, technology, engineering, and mathematics) teachers, to a lack of college-preparatory or AP courses, to outdated and insufficient textbooks, equipment, and other supplies. The group concludes that "conditions in high-poverty schools too often render them sites of developmental risk rather than competent assets that would enhance student developmental outcomes."[15]

Claiming they are addressing such inequities, a variety of fast-track teacher certification programs have appeared across the nation led by the high-profile and well-funded Teach For America (TFA). But even these approaches disproportionately supply needy schools in low-income neighborhoods with a revolving door of underprepared, itinerant, "teach for a while" recruits—a practice that exacerbates a host of problems unique to under-resourced schools and would never be tolerated in middle- and upper-class neighborhoods.[16]

Neuroscientific Overreach

Rather than address the societal and structural factors that create and sustain poverty, new forms of research analyze students in low-income families to provide additional (and highly problematic) rationale for locating problems associated with poverty in the poor themselves. Using brain-imaging techniques along with surveys and ethnographic observations, these recent studies have concluded that the stress associated with poverty reduces students' ability to think well. Because of the students' upbringing and what researchers characterize as inadequate caregiving by parents or guardians, low-income students are theorized to lack sufficient impulse control, have reduced retention and recall of information, demonstrate diminished self-regulation, and even have smaller brains.[17] Researchers conclude that poor and working-class kids end up with what amounts to a reduced "cognitive bandwidth," which causes them to lag behind their middle- and upper-class peers.[18] This supposed deficit presumably makes learning harder for low-income students and makes teaching them a greater challenge too. Of course, concerns about economic inequality and the needs of the so-called 99 percent (the name for the vast majority of people who are not the in the wealthiest 1 percent of our population) have pervaded the news cycle since the economic collapse of 2008. But online, print, and broadcast media have taken up this cognitive-bandwidth story as another in a long line of neuro-narratives that essentially blame victims for their circumstances. The stories prevail, despite widespread credible criticism of the studies' methodologies and conclusions.[19]

It's important to remember that science has been used for over a century to identify "defects" in "nonnormative" populations. Through phrenology, eugenics, the bell curve, and other "scientific studies," researchers have supposedly shown how some groups are intrinsically better than others. The implications of these studies are that the sorting mechanisms we use to rank various populations ought to be strengthened rather than abandoned, that unchangeable biological or cognitive characteristics justifiably produce differences in status (instead of the other way around). To be fair, the researchers investigating the relationship between poverty and cognition are careful to point out that "being poor means coping not just with a shortfall of money, but also with a concurrent shortfall of cognitive resources. The poor, in this view, are less capable not because of inherent traits, but because the very context of poverty imposes load and impedes cognitive capacity."[20] However, the policy recommendations of these researchers suggest problematic implications for education. For example, researchers tell officials to "beware of imposing cognitive taxes on the poor just as they avoid monetary taxes on the poor. Filling out long forms, preparing for a lengthy interview, deciphering new rules, or responding to complex incentives all consume cognitive resources. Policy-makers rarely recognize these cognitive taxes; yet, our results suggest that they should focus on reducing them."[21]

How might we translate these recommendations for educational settings? Is the implication here that poor students should receive simplified content, less complex assessments, and activities that are more "dumbed down"? If low-income students are too stressed and distracted to learn optimally, is this rationale for segregating them into separate tracks so that their diminished achievement doesn't negatively impact learners who don't possess such deficits? In identifying the cognitive challenges low-income students face, are we contributing to perceptions that poverty is an intractable condition whose remedy will likely not include efforts to achieve socioeconomic justice? If it is far cheaper and easier to test, identify, sort, rank, and segregate students than it is to pursue equity and eradicate poverty, will studies like these be used in schools to help students in poverty or to abandon youth to their fate? For comparison, why aren't we investigating the neuroscientific stressors associated with different socioeconomic classes? Why not study wealthy kids under the chronic stress of overbearing parents obsessed with grades and getting into the "best" schools? What about the negative impact of affluence, consumerism, and the competition to always have the most and be the best? And why not investigate forms of parental neglect that occurs in middle- and upper-class homes?

Part of being an effective educator of low-income youth is being a critical consumer of the research that purports to characterize their experience. As the findings from neuroscience filter into schools and classrooms, we need to carefully consider how we will answer questions like these and which practices we would advocate when the time comes to reform.

Shamed and Strained: Adolescent Experiences of Low Socioeconomic Status

Adolescent social decision making takes place on an economic stage. That is, teens interact with peers and adults by playing roles that are at least partly defined by SES; furthermore, they form relationships and make meaning of situations according to settings and scripts shaped by socioeconomic forces. Carried into school, those roles, settings, and scripts influence adolescents' identities and drive many of the behaviors, academic and otherwise, that they will choose in an attempt to get their needs met. Class therefore matters, and it sometimes matters a lot.

The socioeconomic aspects of "doing school" and interacting with peers and adults on its various stages can direct a significant portion of adolescents' energy away from academics and toward concerns about status. This is not because students consider academic achievement unimportant but because its consequences are much further removed than more immediate discriminatory experiences that can arise between students, peers, and educators. Issues of identity, purpose, community, and possibility frequently surface as adolescents attempt to make meaning of classist messages received in and around the classroom.

For example, consider the following list of questions students might ask themselves as they prepare to enter school: Will I be liked by the right people? Will they think what I am wearing, how I look, and how I talk is cool? Will other people like the things I like? Will others do the things my family does? Will I be popular, and what will it take to gain that status? What kind of friends should I choose? What kind of people will want to befriend me? Who is an attainable romantic partner? What kinds of after-school or weekend activities should I be doing? Can I afford to go where my friends go and do the things they do? Do I have the cool things others have? What things don't I have that I wish I did? What can I buy for lunch, and how does that compare with my friends? How do my peers get their spending money? When I am asked, what will I say my folks do for work? How does my home and neighborhood compare with those of others? Can I talk about my family with pride?

Every one of these questions is influenced by a student's social class. When asked by wealthy or middle-class students, these questions may help secure and sometimes even flaunt privilege, but when asked by those in low-SES situations, the questions can produce exclusion and shame. How, when, and by whom they are answered and whether those answers are accepted or problematized has enormous implications for the way SES is revealed, reinforced, and resisted in school.

The stress of living with inadequate resources that strain day-to-day decisions, the seduction of consumerist lifestyles that can't be sustained, and the confrontation with assumptions about certain socioeconomic groups that are supposedly classier, more cultured, better mannered, or simply superior to others can combine to make poor and working-class students feel ashamed about their status. Embarrassed that they do not have what others have and cannot do what others do, some students from poor or working-class backgrounds may resist classroom activities that require social engagement with middle- or upper-class peers. In the same way that students want to avoid looking dumb, socioeconomically marginalized youth may be reluctant to get started on group work or refuse to engage in classwide academic exercises whenever those situations threaten to put their secondary status on display. Already at risk of being labeled or ridiculed because of what they wear, how they look, or where they live, some students will withdraw from academic work because they don't want any of their potential mistakes to confirm their lower status. The effects of these forms of avoidance are worsened when educators misinterpret the behaviors as disrespect or laziness. This is why it is important to remember that if classism-based shame lies at the root of students' classroom resistance, their "defiant" behaviors may be protective, not destructive. Therefore, student resistance to degrading contexts, injurious messages, and unsafe social circumstances—all situations that educators sometimes cocreate—can be read as a form of self-care.

To comfortably engage academic activities and willingly and productively collaborate in classroom settings with peers from a range of socioeconomic backgrounds, students need to feel confident, competent, and connected. This is easier to do when their SES is regularly affirmed and valued by others. With the right clothes, hair, shoes, friends, car, house, vocabulary, and attitude, students happily believe they will supply the right answers. Because school cultures typically convey a middle-class bias (see chapters 2 and 3) and most professional educators emerge from middle-class backgrounds, middle-class students tend to experience home and school cultures as seamless venues for these "right" expressions. Because the behavioral expectations and models of achievement in middle-class homes mirror those typically preferred at school, the transition from home to school is somewhat effortless. From middle-class students' perspectives, there is no discernible class bias at school, because the atmosphere there is consistent with what they know, seems natural, and feels "just right." And when school sounds and feels like home, the result is not just consistency but validation. Students who experience this kind of cultural support will tend to let their guard down, be more willing to take intellectual risks, and be more motivated to achieve and to please teachers. Moreover, their relationships with others at school will tend to flourish because the context says to them, "You belong here. This is yours."

But when classrooms make some students feel as though they don't have "the right stuff," school can feel unfriendly if not abusive. The same middle-class biases and backgrounds that allow middle-class students to feel "normal" and confirmed can make students from low-income families feel alienated and excluded (and, as we will see in subsequent chapters, this pattern also occurs with students who are marginalized because of their race, ethnicity, or linguistic heritage). Researchers have found that students from poor and working-class families commonly experience incongruence and separation when moving from home to school.[22] Sociologist Annette Lareau has found that poor and working-class families raise their children with a "sense of constraint," whereas middle-class families' tend to raise children with a "sense of entitlement."[23] Neither approach is intrinsically better for children than the other, but given the middle-class biases built into educational institutions, one group is certainly privileged and rewarded while the other is pathologized and punished.[24]

Poor and working-class adolescents have rich resources to draw from in their experiences outside school. Unfortunately, educators in school tend to draw from and accept the knowledge of middle-class students much more frequently. The disadvantages of being poor are magnified by the misalignment between low-income students' experiences and expectations and those of their teachers, counselors, and administrators. When students from poor and working-class homes confront different forms of valued knowledge, different expectations regarding how they are supposed to interact with authorities and institutions, different uses of language and time, and different ways of prioritizing self-advancement versus family deference, they often experience school culture as something quite separate from home. For these students, attending school can feel like visiting an alien and somewhat hostile land.

Ignoring the advantages this cultural gap confers on some at the expense of others, many well-intentioned educators try to motivate reluctant or resistant low-income learners by framing school as a chance to "better themselves," or by presenting learning as an opportunity to be successful. But many students interpret messages like these not as academic encouragement but as pressure to separate from their presumably less successful community of origin. The motivational message comes packaged with a classist judgment that compels students to choose between school and home. "You want me to better myself? To be better than *whom?*" students might wonder. "You want me to be successful? Compared to *whom?*" they might speculate. Many students interpret these signals to mean that they can either be successful at school, and therefore sever themselves from home, or they can remain connected to home but experience failure at school. These interpretations are, of course, not the intent of the message, but that is often the way they are perceived, and in this case, it is the student's perception—not the educator's intention—that will direct the student's actions.

Faced with such a difficult choice, some students may be resistant to these motivating messages (and the messengers who deliver them) and may not comply with directives that are perceived to require capitulation. Many students and their families implicitly recognize that if education-as-self-betterment messages are taken to their logical conclusion, any effort to be "bettered" through schooling effectively supports a ranking system they need to resist. In a sense, if one agrees to be "bettered," one also agrees to classify as "less" or "worse" those who haven't sufficiently accepted what school has to offer. These messages cannot feel good when the people implicated in its logic are a student's primary caregivers, closest relatives, and most prominent role models. Explaining this phenomenon, educational researchers Michelle Fine and April Burns state that "'opportunities to succeed' may tear at the fabric of biography, identity, loyalty, and belonging . . . [The offer to exit] one's class status . . . may double as cruel seduction. Every 'terrific opportunity' may be filled with the potential for abandonment and shame. Every 'offer' may be tainted with the weighty sense of those left behind."[25] A student doesn't necessarily want to be "better" than his or her loved ones, because the student knows that this type of posturing ruins relationships based on egalitarian or collective orientations. After all, relationships are usually at risk and fights are typically on the horizon whenever someone is compelled to say, "You think you're better than me?!"

Given this risk of alienation, it's not surprising that Lareau found in her research that some low-income and working-class parents teach their kids "to keep their distance from people in positions of authority, to be distrustful of institutions, and, at times, to resist."[26] From low-income students' perspective, if the price of school success is the dissolution of ties to their primary caregivers, then resistance to, and failure in, school may be a way to protect important relationships in their home community. This is why schooling experiences that communicate class-biased expectations are often interpreted by low-income youth to say,

"You belong somewhere else. This is not yours." And this is also why resistance to these messages makes perfect sense.

Resistant Behaviors with Socioeconomic Roots

Like all social categories, socioeconomic class produces implicit and explicit messages about what educators should expect from some students compared with others. Students pick up on the same messages. They too learn to read socioeconomic cues about which types of people can be trusted, which friends and teachers will most likely offer positive interactions, and who might best be avoided or resisted. Because identity is anchored in home and community experiences, and because so many of those experiences depend on the resources and opportunities tied to socioeconomic conditions, there is little exaggeration in students' use of the acronym CREAM to refer to the way "cash rules everything around me." When adolescents begin to discern the stark disparities in wealth, income, resources, and even the quality of schools, health care, day care, job training, transportation, housing, nutrition, libraries, and parks that are associated with class differences, outrage is a common if not justifiable response. Knowing that the deck is stacked, many students enter school recognizing that the institution tends to be better equipped to serve the well-served than it is to meet the needs of the needy. As a result, many low-income and working-class students may be skeptical, guarded, and angry at school.

Carrying emotions like these into the classroom, socioeconomically disadvantaged students sometimes confront teachers' meritocratic beliefs and practices that foster middle-class supremacy by making status seem like an earned category (see chapters 2 and 3). Students are also tracked according to "ability" as if the criteria for tracking were constructed outside of class advantage. Constraining how, where, and with whom students move during their school day, our schools' tracking regimes further stigmatize status by conflating it with intelligence or potential. Additionally, low-income students may encounter educators' erroneous assumptions about the causes and effects of poverty—assumptions that can blame the victim for circumstances beyond their control. All of this can exacerbate low-income students' propensity to rebel against those who misunderstand them, and it can make some youth prone to defy officials who are believed to demonstrate discriminatory behaviors.

The result is that many low-income students learn to choose resistance over compliance as a way of protecting their sense of self-worth, and they may do this even when they know their behaviors will be self-defeating. Their individual actions can produce adversarial rather than collaborative school environments which, in turn, only reinforce antischool attitudes that can pervade communities and persist across generations. To interrupt this cycle, educators need to recognize students' various outward and inward manifestations of resistance against classism in school.

Outward Manifestations

How does a low-income student construct and maintain a strong and positive sense of self in a classist school environment? Critical ethnographer Wendy Luttrell states that "students' attempts to assert a self (or at least an image of a self) and to have this self (image) be recognized and valued by others is what life is all about" in middle and high school. She explains that because of schools' tendency to convey discriminatory messages, marginalized students must often construct a "defensive self," one that can guard "against different forms of institutional 'lacks' and 'attacks.'"[27] Rather than passively accepting the injurious messages it receives, this defensive self is ready to push back, to repudiate, or to retreat. It may lower its guard when care, challenge, inclusion, and respect are abundant, but if negative experiences are sufficiently consistent it will remain on alert, prepared for the worst. To engage school on its terms while protecting against insult or exclusion, this defensive self will tend to resist.

Fierceness, Sensitivity, and Defensiveness

The outward manifestations of students' resistance against classism take numerous forms. (Students' responses to racism, sexism, heterosexism, ableism, and xenophobia have similar outward manifestations.) Visible resistant behaviors range from feats of strategic thinking that can expose and help change problematic trends, to reactive and impulsive behaviors that sometimes further estrange students from educators, school, and learning itself. Studies have found that adolescents who seek to oppose the classist components of their education will often cultivate an aggressive posture to compensate for the dissatisfaction that comes from being made to feel second class. Educational scholar and activist La Paperson calls this process "developing a fierceness."

In Paperson's research, fierceness functions as an external cover that allows students to remain "tough" while internally they "[deflate] aspirations enough to carry through hard realities" and learn "to contend with feelings of self-blame, defeat, [and] doubt."[28] Similar to Luttrell's "defensive self," Paperson's "fierceness" may cause some students to react swiftly against any perceived slights and to preempt any derision or exclusion by doing the deriding and excluding first. This preemption may seem like bullying, but we may more accurately call it *respond-ing* to being bullied. For example, researchers Duane Thomas and his colleagues understand these preemptive behaviors as examples of "rejection sensitivity." A form of reactive emotional coping, rejection sensitivity involves "expectations of rejection in situations involving others, a lowered threshold for perception of negativity, an increased propensity for personalizing negative cues, and intense affective reactions, all of which [can] lead to an anxious, hostile, and aggressive interpersonal style." Thomas and his coauthors found such behaviors to be prevalent in the adolescent students they researched, particularly those who were "vulnerable or sensitive to social rebuffs and interpersonal difficulties" because of experiences of marginalization.[29]

Both Paperson's and Thomas's explanations suggest that outward manifestations of resistance are only the surface representations of much deeper and often painful experiences. As educators, we may only witness the visible expressions of rejection sensitivity, developed fierceness, or the defensive self, which is why it is critical to approach those expressions, again, as symptoms of problems rather than as problems themselves. To successfully address the root causes of classism-based resistance in schools, we need to access and understand the meaning behind students' opposition and prepare ourselves to change the environment that spurs the opposition. And we need to do this before we move too quickly to punish the behaviors students may be inventing to cover their distress. The outrage, disruption, and intimidation that socioeconomically disadvantaged students sometimes display may be their attempts to reject the insinuation of their second-class status. In other words, they may be trying to stand up for themselves—a goal we ought to champion.

By resisting the environments and the people that make them feel like a no-body, students' outward expressions of resistance create opportunities for them to "be somebody." Calling other students names, acting aggressively in the hall-way, making sarcastic comments in class, refusing to complete academic tasks, and snubbing teachers' directives—all of these behaviors, bothersome though they may be, can provide low-income students with a sense of power, autonomy, and prestige that is otherwise under threat because of their SES. Unfortunately, these outward expressions of resistance frequently get students in trouble. Aggressive and disruptive behaviors typically attract the disciplinary attention of teachers, counselors, and school administrators who are charged with maintaining a safe and orderly learning environment, and for good reason. Students need learning communities that are free from abuse. But when educators respond to students who contravene behavioral norms, expediency may override a nuanced assessment of students' socioeconomic circumstances, their experiences of classism, and the institution's complicity in problematic trends. This oversight can further alienate and enrage already marginalized students.

For example, educators often respond to student transgressions by using stern directives, reprimands, threats of failure, referrals, detentions, and suspensions. Ostensibly, the goal is to add some level of discomfort or suffering to students' experiences in hopes that it will convince them to cease the troubling behavior. The assumption in this approach is that the circumstances before the disruption were preferable to the circumstances during or after it and that some form of punishment will persuade the student to return to the norm. But that may not be the student's perspective at all. Researchers Paul Corrigan and Simon Frith point out that "every use of formal, repressive power reinforces working-class experience of education as imposition . . . [E]very (regular) experience of failure confirms the reality that 'this place has nuthin' for me.'"[30] Consequently, if a student experiences *the norm as the problem*, it is logical for him or her to conclude that disrupting it might be part of a solution.

Troubling the School Game

The many "off-task" or "disorderly" behaviors of so-called troublemakers may be little more than students' attempts to avoid, delay, or halt work; thus there are good reasons why educators might act to restrict those behaviors. But not all student (mis)behavior has that intent. The very act of getting in trouble may be the student's strategy to interrupt the status quo and take a position within a troubling environment as an agent of change. Students may see the school game as rigged and therefore seek to undermine its injustices and humiliations. In such cases, the student's intent, as Paperson puts it, is not to get in trouble but "to trouble the school game."[31]

Unfortunately, when we punish student behaviors that represent their attempts to oppose classism (even when those behaviors are ill planned or poorly executed), we effectively silence their insights. Doing so may communicate to students that the institution is more invested in the preservation of oppressive norms than it is in the cultivation of equity. This is why it may be far more revealing to describe students' resistant behaviors as "troubling the school game" than it is to hail those students as "troublemakers." Labeling students "troublemakers" frames them in deficit terms because their (mis)behavior is believed to arise from a lack of deference to, or respect for, the norm. In contrast, understanding low-income students' resistant behaviors as "troubling the school game" begs an important question: What "school game" or norm is being troubled here? Asking a question like this orients us to cultural, systemic, political, and interpersonal antecedents of students' disruptive behaviors. It temporarily suspends blame so that fuller analyses of contextual factors can be undertaken with curiosity rather than retribution. Questions about troubling the school game might also help replace punitive responses with more restorative approaches (see chapter 11). After all, when students' disruptive behaviors are an attempt to destabilize and reform circumstances that impinge on their well-being, trouble may be a good thing.

Sometimes students "trouble the school game" by employing humor, mockery, satire, and the antics of the "class clown." For low-income students, these expressions may be as theatrical as they are political. With peers as their audience and the classroom as their stage, some students will engage in various forms of "mischief" to expose classist elements in the learning environment or to detract from the general success of a culture that marginalizes them. Sensing that their ways of communicating or the values they learned at home are being disparaged, students with low SES may make fun of the teacher's syntax, deride peers' usage of academic language, snicker or scoff at those who display acceptance of the institution's norms, or playfully enact parodies of the content being learned. At one level, socioeconomically disadvantaged students may do such things simply to broadcast their complaint that "this is stupid!" or to garner the attention of an audience that may seek (or merely tolerate) entertaining distraction. But at another level, low-income students may be using theatrics to reclaim whatever sense of identity may have been denigrated as a result of pervasive and alienating middle-class norms.[32] Looking to relax social rules that make them feel like they don't fit in, some students use the classroom stage to stand out.

In addition, some forms of classroom drama may function "as a pressure valve, releasing pent-up anger and frustration."[33] Students may become incensed by little things, like not being allowed to sharpen their pencil or get a drink at a particular moment as if that single issue is absolutely critical to their well-being. Teacher-student interactions regarding such issues may become inordinately heated and may befuddle educators who can't figure out why a student is choosing such an insignificant issue to vehemently oppose. A student's motivation for getting angry at that moment, however, may be to let off some steam built up by an accumulation of marginalizing experiences. It may not be the issue itself they are resisting but the general trend they feel forced to endure. In this way, students' initiation of these momentary dramas may have roots in classist experiences at school.

Everyday Behaviors as Critiques

Jonathan Silin and his colleagues at the Bank Street College of Education have noted how outward manifestations of classroom resistance do not always take the form of "dramatic, open acts of defiance." Resistance also appears as everyday behaviors like "displays of bad attitude," "alibis for work not done or done poorly," and "pretending to be busier, dumber, and in other ways less competent than one really is in order to withhold" labor from those who supervise them. These outward manifestations may be designed by students to retain some semblance of pride and self-respect amid a learning environment that is too often humiliating and disrespectful.[34] In addition, marginalized students often resist what we do in our classrooms because they do not want to have to do "our" work. The work doesn't feel like theirs because the school doesn't feel like theirs (and the faculty doesn't represent them, and the curriculum fails to inspire their curiosity, etc.). To some extent, their subtle subversions do weaken the institution's ability to carry on oblivious to their discontent and that in itself may be worth the risk for many students. But if we use our power only to label, discipline, and exclude (rather than to stop, inquire, and negotiate), these everyday acts of resistance will rarely produce much change.

To reverse the effects of class marginalization, we may have to look for and engage the critiques that sometimes undergird student behaviors. This can be difficult when those behaviors seem pointless, work avoidant, or simply annoying, or when all students seem to be engaging in them regardless of their SES. A teacher might ask, "If every one of my students is doing these things, how can it be resistance against classism?" Middle and high school teachers are likely to be quite familiar with an array of common student (mis)behavior, and because of its ubiquity, teachers may not consider how it contains subtle class critiques. Silin and his coauthors describe how students may pretend "to be incompetent when they are, in fact, unwilling; [pretend] to pay attention when they are daydreaming; [pretend] not to have heard instructions when they have chosen to ignore them; . . . [pretend] to need to go to the bathroom to avoid participating" in an academic activity; or pretend to be unable to complete their homework as a way of silently protesting having to do it.[35] Students may also feign confusion, claim "I don't understand," and appeal to the teacher's need to be needed just to avoid more work.

Because these actions lower productivity, slow pacing, and maximize time for leisure and socialization, they are not solely the behaviors of poor and working-class students. Nor do they always stem from experiences of classism. Indeed, they are tempting and effective diversions for many students for a multitude of reasons. But if these forms of resistance function to lower expectations and shift the intellectual work being done in the classroom from the student to the teacher, they may have a disproportionate effect on students already suffering from class-based discrimination. That is, just because resistant behaviors are evident in all socioeconomic groups doesn't mean that the ill effects of those actions are distributed among those groups equitably.

For comparison, consider this: the sociologist Daniel McFarland has observed that middle- and upper-class students also "resist authority and defy teachers." The difference is that the strategy of these students is typically not to undermine the system but "to carve out niches of even greater autonomy through negotiation," thereby consolidating their privileged status through manipulation.[36] Socioeconomically marginalized students, on the other hand, may react to their classist circumstances by choosing behaviors that garner educators' negative attention. Subsequently, low-income students' relationships with educators may become more disciplinary than academic. When teacher-student communications more often take the form of reprimands or punishments (as opposed to inquiries and acknowledgments), low-income students may become further marginalized and may face reduced opportunities for academic achievement at the same time that more-privileged peers obtain greater freedoms and resources. The momentum of this vicious classist cycle may be unstoppable unless educators recognize and engage student resistance as a tactical, political act.

Swapping One Form of Marginalization for Another

When educators fail to recognize marginalizing tendencies in the learning environment, those students whose status is least respected may take it upon themselves to invent alternative ranking systems that reverse mainstream norms. Having learned firsthand the power of cultural messages that make some people "better" than others, youth sometimes create their own symbols and subcultures to reclaim a more advantageous status, even when that status is only recognized within the subcultures they create. Education scholar Ellen Brantlinger recounts how low-income adolescents create this subculture: "[They] engage in various forms of resistance to being stigmatized and excluded. One form is inventing an alternative scale for gauging social value. They assert that, unlike wealthy people, they are not snobs, selfish, or full of themselves. Epithets such as good students, preppie, and respectable ones are imbued with derision and cynicism. Counter-culture and anti-intellectual sentiments result in high achievers being called nerds or geeks. Misbehaving youth and even low achievers may be seen as cool. Negative terms become semantically positive, [such as the] use of 'bad' for things they like and value."[37]

By reversing the value of specific terms, marginalized adolescents challenge the legitimacy of the social hierarchy. Using their insider knowledge about what those terms mean and how the terms are classified, they broadcast subculture membership. Similar to the way middle- and upper-class students use exclusion, language, clothing, hairstyles, and other displays of status to secure resources and privileges, low-income students often define social situations and symbols in countercultural terms as a way of resisting classist norms. The effect can be liberating and self-affirming even when it may undermine students' inclusion in mainstream forms of education that largely cater to the middle class.

But without opportunities to scrutinize these expressions in collaboration with peers and class-sensitive educators, the positive and affirming aspects of students' subcultural inventions can morph very quickly into problematic forms. When low-income students claim, for example, a "redneck" or "gangsta" identity as a way of venerating (rather than denigrating) their second-class status, they may exacerbate their marginalization at school due to the anti-academic postures of those cultural representations. If no one is asking students why they are choosing those expressions and no one is getting them to articulate the critiques of classism their expressions may represent, students may unthinkingly adopt the racist or violent ideologies presented to them by popular culture.

And youth don't just pick up these symbols because they're "cool." These alternative ideologies offer forms of power and prestige that compensate for the powerlessness and shame that often accompany class-based alienation. More specifically, when poor Whites claim to be a "redneck," it may be their way of expressing pride in working-class skills, communitarian values, and rural knowledge. On the other hand, the label may also be a way for adolescents to use White racial superiority and reactionary politics to elevate their status by swapping a racist hierarchy for a classist one. Likewise, when poor African American or Latino adolescents claim a gangsta identity, it may be their way of attaching themselves to the powerful forms of language, style, music, dance, and visual arts imbedded in hip-hop, expressions that provide deep meaning, critique, and even rescue for countless racially and socioeconomically marginalized youth. But if the violence, misogyny, hypermasculinity, and drugs of gangsta expressions lead to behaviors that conflate fear with respect, adolescents' subcultural inventions can worsen their exclusion and diminish their academic achievement. Again, if we neglect to inquire about adolescents' class-based choices in expression and never push students to name the critiques of classism their behaviors may represent, we may be abandoning them to the problematic whims of pop cultural representations that provide few if any tangible benefits for marginalized youth.

Outward manifestations of class-based resistance in school is not the sole province of the socioeconomically marginalized. Recent research on cheating suggests that the majority of students who resist school by copying one another's work, stealing test prompts, distributing answers to friends, or writing notes on wrists or hat brims are actually students from middle- and upper-class backgrounds.[38] For these students, cheating is a resistant strategy used not to dismantle class privilege but to bolster it. This highlights how resistance arises from different intentions and produces different consequences, depending on the individual's position in social hierarchies. Upper-class White girls resist differently than middle-class African American girls, and both groups resist differently than low-income Christian Latinos or Hmong lesbian sophomores. Inequities are therefore best addressed simultaneously at the contextual and the individual level.

Think of it this way: a person who has been exposed to toxic chemicals in his or her neighborhood requires both immediate medical intervention and an alteration to his or her environment. Doing only the treatment without also attending to the circumstances of the exposure will solve nothing. Likewise, convincing an individual student to stop resisting will be far less productive than learning from that student's resistance which social forces, institutional practices, and structural conditions we should reform. Students' outward manifestations of resistance against the toxicity of classism are clues we can use to pinpoint problems and start working toward solutions.

Inward Manifestations

When adolescents encounter classist messages (and racist, xenophobic, sexist, ableist, and heterosexist ones) early in their development, they can sometimes absorb the messages as concrete appraisals of their identities. Without an emerging capacity to handle multiple perspectives and with limited ability to approach reality as one of many possibilities, negative messages about the self are often received as descriptive rather than interpretive during childhood. Consequently, the younger the student, the more likely he or she will believe "I am what they say I am." These internalized messages can take years if not decades to realize and reform.

But as adolescents mature, they grow in their cognitive, emotional, and political capacity to respond to injurious messages in ways that preserve self-worth and self-efficacy. With increased capacity to see perspectives as constructed and to discern other people's agendas, older adolescents can sometimes rebound from negative messages more readily. Older teens are able to analyze issues of power, privilege, and oppression; to form theories about right and wrong; to distinguish between fact and opinion; and to express visions for what's possible. They begin to understand themselves as participants in systems. They begin to see how their environment shapes their actions and how their actions shape family systems, school systems, community systems, or larger cultural, racial, gender, and economic systems. When those systems oppress some and privilege others, adolescents become increasingly aware that resistance can produce change.

But these maturing analytical processes don't just develop naturally. Like any skill, they grow when opportunities are provided to examine events and practice responses. In learning environments where resistance is pathologized more than it is engaged, there is little chance that more nuanced forms of resistance will flourish. Students may get stuck in reactive forms of opposition and resort to simplistic forms of analysis because they haven't been able to exercise the cognitive and emotional muscle of their developing and increasingly politicized minds. The ability to read a marginalizing social context and respond productively to it is much more likely to be cultivated when resistance is considered an understandable response to negativity if not an essential component of how people bounce back after adversity.

For the past several decades, psychologists have investigated this ability to bounce back and have called it *resilience*. Resilient youth are able to cope with difficulties, recover quickly from trauma, and generally handle negative experiences without withdrawing, shutting down, or resorting to antisocial behaviors. All adolescents possess resilient traits to varying degrees, but some teens accumulate a more robust set than others because of a host of contextual and individual factors. Studies suggest that the primary factor in developing resilience is the existence of caring and supportive relationships with family and with adults and peers in contexts like school.[39] For students who come from marginalized backgrounds, those supportive relationships may involve explicit and implicit lessons about how to oppose negative messages received from mainstream society. Parents in low-income families, for example, may specifically teach their children how to respond to marginalizing experiences not by outwardly resisting but instead by enhancing their resilience. Strategies may include the following:

- Highlighting those things adolescents have control over and focusing their energies on making changes within those domains
- Practicing self-discipline, and emphasizing the value of hard work

- Recognizing who is trustworthy and supportive, and devoting time and effort to cultivating those relationships
- Honestly naming one's skills and weaknesses, and working to improve both
- Teaching good communication skills and how to relate to others in ways that feel authentic yet responsive to context
- Learning how to challenge authority respectfully and productively, and choosing when it is most prudent to do so
- Identifying where sources of support lie and who is best situated to provide help when it is needed
- Modeling the differences between assertiveness and aggressiveness
- Showing how to deal with strong emotions in ways that allow for reflection and thoughtful action
- Taking the long view, and thereby refraining from blowing things out of proportion and creating more drama and trauma than the circumstances require
- Demonstrating healthy ways to deal with stress, and distinguishing them from unhealthy responses
- Looking for ways to make positive contributions to the family, school, and community[40]

As powerful as these resilient strategies are, many parents in low-income (and in middle-class and wealthy families) may not be equipped to teach them. Some adults are too busy, some are too stressed, and some are simply unaware that these approaches exist. Educators are in an ideal position to fill that gap. Each of the listed strategies can be taught in school, especially when educator-student relationships are characterized by trust. In those moments when we observe self-destructive forms of resistance, particularly when those behaviors arise from students' experiences of marginalization, we can promote strategies of resilience as a way of transforming students' reactivity into proactivity. This neither ignores nor dismisses students' critiques but instead channels their reactions into behaviors that may be more productive and successful over time.

When we and our institutions label expressions of resistance as evidence of a bad attitude and respond with punishment or humiliation, it can force necessary self-protective processes underground. Absent relationships and spaces in which low-income students can process their discontent and pain, some adolescents will turn their resistance inward. As discussed in previous chapters, these students may self-handicap, avoid asking for help, withdraw from class activities and interactions, and generally look for ways to check out. This internalizing of resistance can have a ruinous effect on students' academic achievement and can intensify feelings of shame, disillusionment, and despair. Though outward manifestations of resistance may produce more conflict in the classroom, they may be easier to address than quieter but more insidious, inward forms that go undetected in the hustle and bustle of everyday school events. For this reason alone, we must understand that common ways of responding to student resistance may worsen rather than improve conditions for low-income students.

Promising Practices: What to Do, and What *Not* to Do

Part of the work in reforming how we address resistance against classism in school involves changing our own perspectives and practices, not students'. What follows are a few of the most glaring intellectual and institutional responses scholars have identified, along with several suggestions for what we might do to change them.

Avoiding the Blame Game and Bootstraps Rhetoric

Most of us are taught to equate poverty with disability, to attribute the problem to individual choices, and to blame families and communities for undermining their children's mobility. Put bluntly, we are trained to believe that people are poor because they are unprepared, dysfunctional, lazy, or stupid. This attitude deflects attention away from systemic and cultural forces that exploit and marginalize, and it allows us to divert resources away from people we believe don't deserve them. This *deficit orientation* places value judgments on communities that do not follow or do not have access to middle-class ways of knowing and behaving, as if middle-class norms are somehow better, rather than just dominant. Under a deficit orientation, the plight of marginalized people is blamed on character flaws more than on the distribution of resources that limit their potential and the cultural imperialism that marginalizes their perspectives and talents. In the classroom, this perspective yields *banking* forms of education in which educators seek to fill up the supposedly empty vessels of children's minds with the proper middle-class ways of thinking, acting, and relating. This approach further alienates already-marginalized students by forcing them to choose between academic achievement and their cultural identity.

In addition, well-intentioned educators cite upward class mobility (i.e., "Pull yourself up by your own bootstraps!") to try to motivate low-income students to perform better in school. But as Stephanie Jones and Mark Vagle point out, educators often do so "without doing the work it takes to better understand what is informing those discourses—and the economic policies shaping workers' realities—[which] may unwittingly alienate the very students they hope to inspire."[41] Claiming that students' success is entirely up to them or that they will undoubtedly achieve in direct proportion to their merits can indeed be motivating and empowering, but without concurrent acknowledgments of systemic forces that impinge on those efforts, many students will hear such encouragements as hollow promises that fail to reflect their reality.

One of the best ways to address the understandable resistance we observe in low-income youth is to examine the assumptions and practices that drive our impoverished view of "the problem." We can investigate these aspects of our practice in a variety of ways. For example, critical-friends groups could focus on the relationship between classism and school outcomes. Staff development sessions could use scholarship on SES to examine schoolwide practices and social climate. The school could facilitate community conversations that position families as the experts of their experiences. Another useful method is shadowing activities, in which educators follow low-income students through their day and then reflect on what was observed and learned. Throughout these approaches, it is crucial that educators use socioeconomic class as a lens to examine how our society functions, how status is decided and rewarded, and how institutions like schools sometimes reproduce as well as remedy problematic trends.

Following the Money

Because of the prevalence of socioeconomic bias in schools, educators who are committed to understanding and productively engaging low-income students' resistance may need to take an activist stance. Working well with marginalized students in the classroom is important, but advocating for equity and justice in the systems that surround those students may be just as critical. National, regional, and local organizations exist to raise awareness, combine efforts, and conduct campaigns to convince policy makers and school officials to reform the classist tendencies in the way we fund, staff, and allocate resources in education. Joining those efforts can produce meaningful change over time, and they can be a satisfying addition to a professional educator's career.

Discouraging the Policies That Demonstrate We "Don't Get It"

Schools too often give tacit approval of the marginalization of low-income students via school policies and procedures. These practices tell students that their socioeconomic status is either being ignored or being taken for granted. Consider some examples:

- Conducting fund-raising in which everyone is expected to pitch in, or where students sell candy, raffle tickets, coupon books, or discount cards in their neighborhoods despite families' vastly different capacities to solicit and to give.
- Trying to encourage more "parental involvement," but basing what good involvement looks like on middle-class norms and forms of discretionary time and money many families do not possess.
- Levying fees for class materials, athletic physicals, field trips, picture day, school dances, and the like.
- Saying to underperforming students something like, "You don't want to end up flipping burgers, do you?" within earshot of kids who have family members who work full-time doing such work.
- Allowing students to go off campus for lunch. This practice can stigmatize kids who get free or reduced-price lunches in the school cafeteria versus those who can afford to spend $5 to $15 per day at outside restaurants. In turn, the practice can further isolate class-based segregation, as groups in separate lunchtime arenas learn to socialize exclusively with each other.
- Establishing bring-your-own-device policies at school to enhance the use of technology, even though a significant portion of students do not own a smartphone, laptop, or tablet.
- Assigning homework with a frequency and difficulty that middle-class families interpret as an important extension of learning but that low-income families experience as an unnecessary burden, especially when no adults are home during the hours in which the homework would normally be completed and many students must work or babysit after school to support their family.
- Using cooperative grouping strategies, but doing so in a class-blind manner that may allow middle-class and wealthy students to use their status to control, ridicule, ignore, or humiliate others during the activity. This often angers if not enrages low-income students who may act out and get in trouble even though the genesis of the problem was the classism being perpetrated by their more privileged peers.
- Developing elaborate after-school sports programs but neglecting to provide safe and consistent transportation options for students whose parents or guardians work in the evenings when practices and games let out.
- Finally, but perhaps most importantly, tracking low-income students into lower "ability groups" ostensibly to tailor instruction, remediate skills, and enhance knowledge so that the students can one day attain levels

of achievement common to their upper-class and higher-tracked peers, despite the scant evidence that tracking accomplishes this objective (more on this in chapter 9).

These examples and more, if continued and not criticized, can convince low-income students that school is a place to resist more than a place to learn. Educators may therefore need to dismantle school policies and the assumptions that drive them if we are to recognize the needs of low-income students and build more equitable learning environments for them. If we set out to do this work, we need to realize that students from working-class and poor families do not need to be saved—they need our solidarity, advocacy, and activism. They are quite capable of rising to the highest levels of achievement as long as we remove the classist impediments in their way. Those impediments may be our policies and procedures, but they may also be our legislators, colleagues, parents, and students. Jones and Vagle observe that "a commitment to eliminating classism in schools will undoubtedly face some resistance from those who are happy with—and privileged by—the structures in place."[42] Consequently, our efforts to remove these impediments may require us to take a stand against pervasive but oppressive practices and stands up for justice-oriented solutions. In this way, it is the untapped reservoir of our own resistance that may offer the greatest opportunities for change.

It's Not About the Pencil

Ms. Atkins has a lot to do today. One of three school counselors at her high school, she is responsible for prepping the boxes of test materials for her faculty in advance of next week's testing. But when she rounds the corner to her office, she realizes she won't be doing that work for a while. Malik is sitting on the bench, holding a yellow referral slip and looking angry.

"What's up, Malik?" she asks.

He rises to hand her the referral. "This is so stupid," he replies. "Just ridiculous. I'm tired of this place and this racist bull——!"

Ignoring his language for the time being, Ms. Atkins reads the slip. On it, Ms. Carruthers, Malik's chemistry teacher, has checked the box for "defiance" and written at the bottom: "Malik is disrupting class and refusing to follow explicit directions."

"So tell me what happened," Ms. Atkins says.

"Ms. Carruthers was picking on me to pay attention all period long," Malik explains, "but was totally letting it slide when the White kids in class were texting under their desks or passing notes."

"So were you paying attention?" Ms. Atkins asks.

"Yes!" Malik nearly shouts. "I know exactly what we are doing in class, and I know all the things my group needs to get ready for tomorrow's lab. It's not hard. It's a list of steps and materials—no problem."

"So what happened to get you this referral?"

"Look," he says, "Ms. Carruthers is afraid of me and Chris. She looks for ways to pick on us, to get us thrown out. She doesn't see s—— when others mess around, but she always sees it when I even blink wrong. I mean, I got up to sharpen my pencil, and she told me to sit down. So I went to sharpen it anyway, and she got angry, then I got angry, and now I'm here."

Confused, Ms. Atkins asks, "So you are saying you're here because you sharpened your pencil when you were told not to, is that right?"

"Yeah, pretty much. That, and I told her she was racist for picking on me."

When Malik doesn't elaborate further, Ms. Atkins asks, "So, then what do you mean when you say she's afraid of you and Chris?"

Malik sighs, leans on his knees, and looks Ms. Atkins directly in the eye. In a softer and more measured tone, he explains: "Carruthers doesn't like Black people. Chris and I are Black. We're the only ones in that class. We are friends. We talk. We joke. But we do our work. She acts like we're like gonna rob the place sometimes. She never says anything positive to us and only calls on us when she thinks we're doing something wrong. And I'm not gonna lie, I do sometimes mess around in there, but I get my work done and I pay attention when I need to. Carruthers is racist. I called her that when she was writing the referral and her face got all red. But I know she won't talk about it. She'd rather kick me out."

"How do you know that?" Ms. Atkins asks.

"Because I've said it before and she just rolls her eyes, changes the topic, or starts writing referrals."

Unsure about how to address the situation, Ms. Atkins goes back to the issue of pencil sharpening. "So why did you have to sharpen your pencil right then?"

Getting more agitated, Malik replies, "It's not about the pencil! I got angry being told I couldn't do something I needed to do when the White dude who doesn't even *have* a pencil is next to me on his iPhone and the teacher doesn't care. It's not fair! It's racist. She's racist! This whole place is racist. And I'm tired of it."

Thinking for a second on what to say next, Ms. Atkins asks Malik, "So what should we do?"

"Just suspend me," he says. "It's what you do, right?"

CHAPTER 9

"You Don't Even Know Me"

Identity and Opposition in the Classroom

IT CAN BE tough working with students who resist. We want to move forward, and they only seem to push back. We work hard to try to understand their needs and respond appropriately, but they ignore our agendas and present contrary ones of their own. And often, to make matters more challenging, we try to make things fair and equitable for each of our students, but some still raise accusations of discrimination—accusations that may confuse or frighten us. How should we make sense of such behaviors and respond productively to them?

This chapter examines how racial and ethnic identity development processes often produce resistant behaviors in students and how those forms of resistance often play out in classrooms and schools. Using the widely accepted but deeply problematic theory of *oppositional identities* as a starting point, the chapter illustrates the extent to which marginalized students need to resist to form a healthy sense of self. In this chapter, I argue that resistance against perceived racism should be expected and engaged rather than maligned and punished. I also highlight how educators are prone to misunderstand the resistant behaviors of students of color and why we might actually welcome some of those behaviors as a healthy response to forms of racial and ethnic exclusion we all should oppose.

Disproportionality: The Color of School Discipline

Schools are neither ethnically nor racially neutral spaces. They pick favorites. They do this not necessarily because they're immoral or negligent but because they naturally represent the prevailing values of mainstream society, values that privilege certain forms of cultural expression while oppressing others. From pre-school to high school, we ask students to make sense of an array of racial and ethnic expectations that mark their appearances, attire, language, and modes of interacting as being either in or out. Those whose behaviors lie closest to the mainstream receive messages that mostly affirm their normativity, while those outside of it tend to receive messages that reinforce their marginal status. If and when those marginalizing messages are received with enough frequency at school, it's predictable if not understandable that classroom resistance will soon follow.

When it comes to education, student resistance often results in disciplinary intervention because student (mis)behavior, by definition, is understood by authorities to be destructive to the norm. Though nearly all students engage in classroom resistance in one form or another, decades of data from public schools show that some groups of students are disproportionately disciplined more than others. We call these trends "disproportional" because the instances of discipline in a particular group do not correspond to the size of that group. Some smaller populations tend to garner a much larger share of disciplinary attention in schools, whereas other larger populations post smaller instances of disciplinary interventions relative to their size. Before we turn to explanations for this phenomenon, let's look at the extent of the disproportionality.

Since the 1970s, researchers have repeatedly identified the overrepresentation of minority students in school disciplinary interactions. Again and again, studies find that the typical suspended or expelled student is more likely to be male, from a lower socioeconomic group, in special education, lower achieving, and non-White.[1] In particular, "national and state data show consistent patterns of Black disproportionality in school discipline over the past 30 years, specifically in suspension, expulsion, and office discipline referrals."[2] Though the findings are not as consistent, similar patterns of disproportionality in school discipline have been documented for Latino and American Indian students as well.[3] According to data gathered by the federal government in 2011–2012, African American students represent 15 percent of those in its sample, but they make up "35% of students suspended once, 44% of those suspended more than once, and 36% of students expelled. Further, over 50% of students who are involved in school-related arrests or referred to law enforcement are Hispanic or African-American."[4] And when it comes to corporal punishment, the Center for Effective Discipline found that African Americans are physically hit by educators at twice the rate of White students across the nineteen states that still legally use that form of punishment.[5] The problem of disproportionality in school discipline has become so pernicious that in January 2014, the U.S. Department of Justice and the U.S. Department of Education issued a joint report with policy recommendations, webinars, guidelines, and a host of resources "to assist public elementary and secondary schools in meeting their obligations under Federal law to administer student discipline without discriminating on the basis of race, color, or national origin."[6]

The question is, what explains this disproportionality? Might it be the result of socioeconomic factors more than race? To answer this, researchers have investigated whether socioeconomic status accounts for the disproportionality more than racial and ethnic differences. In most peer-reviewed research, it doesn't. For example, in a study analyzing national-level data, a team of researchers determined that race contributed to disciplinary outcomes independent of socioeconomic status.[7] In another study that corroborates this finding, researchers discovered that "disproportionate ethnic representation in discipline remains, even after controlling for SES."[8] So if socioeconomic factors can't explain the disproportionality, what does?

One common supposition is that students of color are disproportionately represented in referrals, detentions, suspensions, and expulsions (collectively referred to as *exclusionary discipline*) simply because they tend to misbehave more than others. As it turns out, they don't. In their study of a year's worth of disciplinary data from an urban school district, Russell Skiba and his colleagues compared disciplinary interventions involving White and Black students. The researchers found "no evidence that racial disparities in school punishment could be explained by higher rates of African American misbehavior," a conclusion corroborated in a comprehensive analysis of nationwide data published by the Civil Rights Project at University of California at Los Angeles.[9] Instead, Skiba and his colleagues found that Black students were more likely to be referred to the office for more "subjective reasons" such as "disrespect," "threat," "excessive noise," or "loitering," and that once there, they received harsher punishments than their White peers.[10]

Similarly, in their study of a large comprehensive urban high school, Anne Gregory and Rhona Weinstein found that a full two-thirds of disciplinary referrals were for vague and wholly subjective offenses. In fact, for racial and ethnic minorities at the school the researchers studied, "defiance of adult authority" was the most common reason for the referrals. The resulting disproportionality was striking: "African American students comprised 30% of the school enrollment, but they were 58% of the defiance referred. In contrast, White students were 37% of the school enrollment, but only comprised 5% of those referred for defiance."[11] Surveying scores of studies like this one and analyzing its own data from the Civil Rights Data Collection (CRDC) conducted by the Office of Civil Rights, the Department of Education concluded the following:

> The substantial racial disparities of the kind reflected in the CRDC data are not explained by more frequent or more serious misbehavior by students of color . . . [S]ignificant and unexplained racial disparities in student discipline give rise to concerns that schools may be engaging in racial discrimination that violates the Federal civil rights laws. For instance, statistical evidence may indicate that groups of students have been subjected to different treatment or that a school policy or practice may have an adverse discriminatory impact. Indeed, the Department's investigations . . . have revealed racial discrimination in the administration of student discipline. For example, in our investigations we have found cases where African-American students were disciplined more harshly and more frequently because of their race than similarly situated white students. In short, racial discrimination in school discipline is a real problem.[12]

Consequently, if we want authentic and accurate explanations for racial disproportionality in school discipline and we want to understand those educator responses and forms of resistance that may produce various (mis)behaviors, we need to look elsewhere. Unfortunately, the theory of oppositional cultures is where far too many educators land.

A Dangerous Explanation: The Myth of Oppositional Cultures

The causes and consequences of racialized differences in behavior, achievement, and discipline continue to be the source of much debate. Some analysts point to environmental and structural issues that can prevent minoritized students from fully realizing their potential in school. Theorists, researchers, and practitioners with this outlook tend to locate problems in the context surrounding students before identifying difficulties within individuals. Conversely, other theorists attempt to explain racial differences in achievement and behavior by analyzing personal, familial, and cultural qualities that are believed to create advantages for some and disadvantages for others. In this approach, problems are typically attributed to individual characteristics such as personality, beliefs, and habits, or family or community features such as values, child-rearing practices, and household stability. Here the assumption is that racial or ethnic minorities will succeed to the extent that they rise above *their* problematic origins. Often these theories directly or indirectly suggest that it is not the environment holding back students of color so much as it is their own dysfunction. Therefore, societal, institutional, and political inequities take a backseat to the "bad decisions" of individuals or to their personal shortcomings derived from what is perceived to be ignorance or deviance. There is no point in a strong social safety net if individuals are entirely at fault for their situation, or so the logic goes. The conclusion often reached by those who maintain this logic is that if we can convince individuals, families, and communities to change the way they conduct themselves, the barriers to success—barriers they supposedly created for themselves—will naturally fall away.

Despite ample empirical research that consistently challenges the latter explanation, it tends to dominate educational rhetoric and practices that target minoritized youth. These approaches have become embedded in academic and popular explanations regarding the disproportionate representation of racial and ethnic minorities in school push-out, failure, and disciplinary statistics. People who prefer this explanation tend to view marginalized students' resistance as a sign of personal or cultural deficits, as evidence that the students lack sufficient appreciation for what education offers, and will tend to squander rather than seize afforded opportunities. By extension, the role of the educator is to save students from themselves. This is why many refer to this explanation as the "blame the victim" or "save the savage" approach.

Consistent with this orientation is the theory of oppositional cultures, perhaps the most dominant explanation of racial differences in discipline rates and academic achievement. It was first promulgated in 1978 by the late Nigerian American cultural anthropologist John Ogbu in his book, *Minority Education and Caste: The American System in Cross-Cultural Perspective*, and has since been expanded and clarified over the last three decades in a series of publications by Ogbu and his associates.[13] The theory attempts to explain the diminished level of achievement and the greater occurrence of disciplinary interventions among ethnic and racial minorities by analyzing those groups' propensity to develop what Ogbu understood to be an oppositional orientation toward education.

Ogbu's theory rests on several assumptions about the differences between various minoritized groups. Some groups, he argued, should be characterized as "voluntary minorities" because they willingly emigrated to the United States in search of better employment opportunities or greater political or religious freedom. These voluntary minorities (largely from Asian and West Indian nations) were believed to collectively possess a nonoppositional orientation toward mainstream society and its institutions.[14] The logic goes that they *chose* to be here so an oppositional stance would effectively undermine their own agenda. "Involuntary minorities," on the other hand, were theorized to develop "oppositional cultures" due to the fact that they or their ancestors had been enslaved, colonized, or conquered. Native Americans, African Americans, Mexicans, Puerto Ricans, and Hawaiians all were understood by Ogbu to be involuntary minorities. As a result, he theorized, these groups possess what he called "oppositional cultures." Their opposition arises from their original circumstances in this country and the legacy of their oppression since that time, none of which was their choice.

When involuntary minorities enter school, the oppositional-cultures theory predicts that they will be initially motivated to achieve because they believe that more education will lead to better employment, higher wages, and greater social status. The theory predicts, however, that when these groups encounter social barriers, racism, exclusion, and other forms of discrimination, they perceive that the opportunities for acquiring the resources they need to safeguard their social mobility are being systematically withheld or that they are receiving lesser rewards for educational achievement than those in the dominant group. Confronting their marginalization, these groups are forced to reconsider whether mainstream institutions are designed to meet their needs. As a result, Ogbu theorized, involuntary minorities develop an oppositional culture that resists education as a viable means of social mobility. Ogbu theorized this reaction as a "cultural inversion," wherein some groups reject certain values of mainstream culture, including academic achievement, because those values represent the agenda of the oppressors. In this cultural inversion, involuntary minorities are understood to carve out a distinct culture within but against the mainstream as a way of preserving integrity and defending against their oppression. As the theory goes, student resistance to school in the form of tardiness, truancy, the withholding of effort, disruption, defiance of authority, and the destruction of property all are believed to stem from this inverted and oppositional culture.

Within the oppositional-cultures theory, Ogbu developed his "acting-White" hypothesis, which would eventually receive the most attention—positive and negative—from researchers and practitioners. Ogbu theorized that youth from involuntary minorities equate academic achievement with White mainstream oppression. He observed that obeying directives from school officials, complying with classroom behavioral expectations, applying effort and concentration in academic work, and generally engaging school in a way that leads to successful achievement exposes individuals from involuntary minorities to the appearance of complicity in their and others' oppression. To these marginalized groups, being successful in school is akin to acting White. Therefore, according to the theory, resisting if not rejecting school is a visible way to oppose one's subjugation and maintain forms of cultural inversion that prevent collusion with one's White oppressors.

Since the 1980s, school educators, academic researchers, and many in the popular media have adopted oppositional-cultures theory and the acting-White hypothesis as the preferred explanation for the persistent gap in achievement between Whites and racially or ethnically minoritized groups. Though his original theory of oppositional cultures was designed to characterize the experiences and behaviors of Native Americans, African Americans, Mexicans, Puerto Ricans, and Hawaiians, Ogbu's acting-White hypothesis has been used largely to cast Black students' resistant behaviors as self-destructive. In grocery store aisles, living rooms, faculty lounges, educational think tanks, and state legislatures and even at major political party conventions, the theory has become the dominant rationalization for Black resistance to school. (For example, then-senator Barack Obama alluded to this line of thinking in 2004 during his keynote speech to the Democratic National Convention: "Children can't achieve unless we . . . eradicate the slander that says a black youth with a book is acting white.") And it has been used to identify (and blame) African Americans who have adopted supposedly counterproductive behaviors in school and to ascertain why other, evidently less resistant minorities differ in their response to education.

This line of thinking might be okay were it not for one big problem: Ogbu's theory suffers from a series of erroneous assumptions and glaring omissions and has failed to stand up to repeated scientific scrutiny. Not only is the theory wrong, but it has also become an obstacle for those who seek to understand the origins and effects of racialized forms of resistance in the classroom. Consequently, to truly apprehend how and why many students of color resist in school, we must understand why the dominant acting-White hypothesis should itself be resisted.

How the Acting-White Theory Completely Misunderstands Student Resistance

Educators rightly recognize that some schooling experiences do exclude and alienate students from racial or ethnical minorities. These experiences cause some individuals, families, and even communities to hesitate to accept uncritically schools' intentions with youth of color. When a school asks (or demands) that students who are racially or ethnically categorized as "other" assimilate into the mainstream if they are to be accepted and successful, that request is often perceived less as an opportunity and more as a threat. This is especially true when assimilation requires the suppression of students' unique ways of thinking, relating, and expressing themselves—ways that are derived from the rich experiences of their racial and ethnic backgrounds. Adolescents need these cultural resources if they are to feel authentic, connected, and supported in school, and their resistance in the classroom makes sense when they are asked to abandon those cultural assets. Although Ogbu correctly identified students' occasional reluctance to accept school when it is presented to them in this assimilative manner, he erroneously identified what he thought students were resisting.

It's Not Academic Achievement They're Resisting—It's Their Marginalization

In his article "The Myths of Oppositional Culture," sociologist Garvey F. Lundy writes that the "fundamental error" in Ogbu's theory is "his inability to view Black students' behavior (which [Ogbu] calls oppositional) as a genuine desire to express their Africanness." To explain this point, Lundy asks, "In a society where Black people and their culture are relegated to the margins of power, are Black students rejecting educational success or are they rejecting the marginalization of their group and their culture?"[15] This question illuminates the vast difference between resisting the cultural expectations of the White mainstream and resisting educational achievement itself. Ogbu makes a crude and problematic categorical mistake by collapsing the two. In short, it's not that African American students are attempting to avoid being White; it's that they are rejecting a school culture that does not allow them to be Black. (The same goes for other racially or ethnically marginalized students.)

The acting-White hypothesis confuses students' resistance against assimilation with rejection of education. Researchers responding to Ogbu have shown that those two reactions are not the same. Sociologist Antwi A. Akom describes how in his African American research participants, "these cultures of opposition constituted a partial refuge from the humiliation of racism . . . and allowed [students] to nurture collectivist values that were markedly different from the prevailing individualistic ideology of the white ruling class."[16] When students resist those aspects of school that they experience as unwelcoming to their nonmainstream forms of expression, that resistance is a way of preventing the internalization of injurious messages about their self-worth. Their opposition to exclusion doesn't typically cause them to abandon the goals of academic learning and achievement. Scores of studies have amply demonstrated that African Americans and other "involuntary minorities" deeply value education, learning, and the opportunities that come with academic achievement.[17] In fact, some studies have shown that racially minoritized students such as African Americans and Latinos value education at a greater level than many middle-class White students do.[18]

Thus, Black and Brown students do indeed want to learn and succeed in school, but they don't want to have to surrender their Blackness or Brownness as a condition of that success. In classrooms and schools where authentic inclusion prevails—where students from a variety of cultural backgrounds are allowed if not encouraged to bring their "otherness" into the classroom and where diversity is celebrated and integrated into the life of the learning community—so-called involuntary minorities have little reason to resist because academic success and cultural preservation go hand-in-hand.

Resisting Convention Is Not the Same as Devaluing Education

In Prudence Carter's influential book, *Keepin' It Real: School Success Beyond Black and White*, the author reveals a crucial misinterpretation in the acting-White hypothesis, and many other scholars before and since have echoed this point. In her extensive interviews and surveys of urban students of color, she found that the accusation of acting White was not invoked when students performed well in school, but rather when they adopted the language, clothing styles, and music of the dominant group. Academic success was prized and even encouraged by her African American and Latino student participants, but if they were to maintain their street credibility and sustain their peer networks in the neighborhoods they call home—to "keep it real," as they put it—they were pressured to retain the styles, tastes, and preferences associated with their racial or ethnic group. One way of thinking about this is that the students wanted to avoid failing in school as much as they wanted to avoid failing their friends and family.

Carter demonstrates how the acting-White theory mischaracterizes marginalized students' ridicule of their peers' White-like styles and behaviors as if the derision also included a rejection of education. It didn't. Instead, Carter shows how highly proficient many students are at switching their verbal style, sometimes midsentence, from mainstream conventions of speech largely expected by their teachers and school officials to African American or Latino vernacular ways with words and sentences (i.e., "Ebonics" or "Spanglish"). These students know well to use the neighborhood styles of communication when they are with friends and family and to code-switch when school contexts require mainstream tones, registers, vocabulary, and accents. A reticence to make that switch readily or an inability to do it skillfully in the classroom does not indicate an opposition to school so much as it suggests a deference to an audience of valued cultural compatriots. Though verbal expressions, clothing preferences, and musical tastes are often viewed by educators as deficits to overcome (or worse, as subcultural rebellions that must be policed), for many racially and ethnically marginalized youth, those styles are primary sources of cultural affirmation, vitality, and inspiration. Therefore, teachers who expect all students to sound, look, or act "normal" may be fomenting resistance against school where none existed before.

They're Not Opposing Learning—They're Opposing Racism and Their Humiliation in School

While students who (over)commit to their peer group may disengage from school if the peer group demonstrates suspicion about or resistance toward schooling experiences (a phenomenon that, in my experience, occurs with White middle-class girls as often as it does with low-income boys of color), we have to be careful not to assume that such resistance indicates a lack of appreciation for education itself. Student expressions of resistance are frequently not indictments of learning and academic achievement so much as they are recognitions of and responses to the alienating experiences to which they may be regularly subjected at school. Through behavioral expectations, classroom rules, dress codes, language restrictions, designated holidays, a lack of staff and faculty diversity, culturally skewed assessment regimes, exclusionary disciplinary procedures, zero-tolerance policies, curricula that fail to reflect multicultural backgrounds, and a whole range of other subtle but powerful messages about the "right" or "normal" ways to conduct oneself, students from racial and ethnic minorities are forever confronting their marginalized status at school. Recognizing this, Lundy writes: "What the proponents of oppositional culture theory and acting White fail to perceive is that Black students, in their rejection of White cultural references, are embracing their own culture and asserting African agency. It is not a rejection of academic success but rather a rejection of White cultural hegemony."[19] In other words, when Black and Brown students resist in school they may be seeking to disrupt their subjugation more than interrupt their education.

There is a strong research base to support this contention. For example, the sociologist Karolyn Tyson has shown how African American elementary students begin school very much engaged and enthusiastic about their education. She observes that "not only did students not disparage achievement, but most of them readily owned up to their feelings of pride" when they did well in school.[20] The students in her study "openly expressed their enthusiasm and excitement toward learning and schoolwork" and acted in ways that "conveyed their strong desire for [academic success] as well as a lack of fear (of social ostracism) or self-consciousness about high achievement."[21] Tyson found that students did tease one another about their performances in school but they did so not for high achievement, but for *low* achievement: "Students felt stigmatized by failure . . .

[and] were solidly identified with academics [such that] good performance was rewarding to them and bad performance was punishing."[22] Among other things, the children's early enthusiasm suggests that there was no preexisting rejection of education that arose from their families, communities, or peer networks. To put it plainly, there was no oppositional culture to be found.

This begs an important question: from where did these students' eventual resistance to school originate? As Tyson's research participants progressed through the elementary grades, they encountered school cultures that emphasized the need to conform to dominant ways of acting and communicating. These cultures (either purposely or inadvertently) cast the students' racial otherness as deficient. She observed how educators undermined Black students' school engagement and achievement motivation "by suppressing what were deemed inappropriate behaviors and conveying messages of black cultural deviance to students in the interest of discipline and conformity to particular 'mainstream' cultural norms."[23] At the same time, Tyson discovered that children's increasing negativity toward school emerged from a desire to avoid *humiliation*, not learning. The students who were expressing negativity about school were the same ones who were struggling academically. Accordingly, students' dissatisfaction with school "reflected a desire to avoid further experiences of failure," which Tyson identifies as a "developmental process rather than a specifically cultural one."[24] In other words, these students' resistant behaviors were designed not to avoid acting White but to avoid looking stupid.

Referring specifically to Ogbu's theory, Tyson acknowledges that "some researchers imply that school failure is a result of negative dispositions toward school." Her research, however, indicates that "the relationship is reversed: failure seems to bring about the negative school-related behaviors and attitudes."[25] The fear of public failure, coupled with dominant behavioral expectations that frame Black cultural expressions as deviant, effectively teaches racially marginalized students to be suspicious of, if not oppositional toward, school. In this way, the acting-White theory functions as an erroneous blame-the-victim explanation for student resistance.

How the Acting-White Theory Ignores Systemic Racism

The theory of oppositional cultures rightfully recognizes the systematic oppression of "involuntary minorities," whose experiences in the United States are markedly different from other racial and ethnic groups. But the theory's focus on seventeenth-, eighteenth-, and nineteenth-century events obscures forms of institutional racism and structural inequality that persist in the present. This backward-looking focus contributes to the sentiment that racial oppression is an artifact of historical eras long since passed and that today's descendants of those oppressed groups who remain resentful, angry, or oppositional ought to "get over it already."

Unfortunately, a preponderance of evidence makes clear that full and equitable access to high-quality public education for racial and ethnic minorities has yet to be achieved. Consider the following: the inequitable way schools are funded (e.g., property-value formulas exacerbate the resource disparities between high- and low-income districts); the unfair distribution of high-quality educators (e.g., poor and ethnically isolated communities have a greater share of underprepared teachers, many of whom teach outside the subject area of their credential if they possess a credential at all); the disparities in class sizes between wealthy and under-resourced schools and districts; racially biased disciplinary procedures; school-to-prison pipeline trends; and either gentrification or real estate redlining that often pervades the neighborhood schools that serve minoritized populations. Factors like these make it hard to argue that the playing field is even.

Many observers point to the watershed 1954 Supreme Court ruling of *Brown v. Board of Education* as a symbol of our nation's commitment to desegregating schools. More illuminating, however, is the observation that today's African American and Latino students are actually more isolated than they were forty years ago. Moreover, district and state policy makers have all but abandoned racial and ethnic integration as a viable goal.[26] The *Brown v. Board of Education* decision did desegregate supposedly "separate but equal" public education, but it also dismantled a rich and powerful network of Black-run schools staffed by culturally responsive and community-accountable Black educators. In addition, the *Brown v. Board* ruling influenced waves of "White flight" migrations away from newly integrated schools and contributed to an era of neosegregation that now operates through zoning laws, real estate practices, legislative priorities, housing regulations, school choice, school funding, and school closings.[27]

Trends like these extend far beyond African American populations. For example, Japanese American children and their families were forced into internment camps and severely under-resourced schools during World War II solely because of their perceived ethnic affiliation. In the early twentieth century, Native American children were removed from their families so that they could be acculturated in federal boarding schools that possessed glaring deficiencies, including poor nutrition, overcrowding, below-standard medical services, and substandard teaching. And Mexican American students have long suffered from governmental, institutional, and societal repression through racist and xenophobic language policies, forced deportations, and worker exploitation.

If history is to be a guide in understanding the resistance of students of color, we must remember these trends (and the fact that it was Whites who originally accused "uppity," educated African Americans of trying to act White).[28] Unfortunately, the acting-White hypothesis effectively ignores these observations, which permits ostensibly well-meaning people to assign blame where it does not belong. The theory does this by attributing Black and Brown students' failure to *their* supposed self-oppression while absolving those with racial privilege of any complicity in the perpetuation of an exclusionary system. By ignoring historical, contemporary, and systemic racism, the accusation of acting White, as the scholar of education David E. Kirkland puts it, "helps Black schoolchildren hurt themselves."[29]

Furthermore, it is dangerous to apply the oppositional-cultures theory to instances of classroom resistance that are enacted by racially or ethnically marginalized students because the theory depends on unquestioned notions of White superiority. According to Ogbu's theory, the primary barrier to Black and Brown students is believed to be their inability to adopt White norms. The problem, in other words, is that they won't assimilate. Lundy writes that this deference to White customs and behaviors "reassures Whites of the superiority of their culture and the legitimacy of their agenda to impose it on others so that the Other can be enlightened and made in their image."[30] Though the real problem here is that whiteness has been given normative status, the acting-White theory inverts the accountability so that the problem is perceived to be marginalized groups' refusal to take the offer of salvation, a salvation that can only be achieved when they agree to be more White.

This inversion of accountability that is built into the acting-White hypothesis (as opposed to the "cultural inversion" in Ogbu's original theory) can be observed in schools all the time. When behavioral norms are set according to mainstream expectations about what looks and sounds "respectful," "civilized," "nice," "neighborly," or "normal," and when nonmainstream modes of interacting are suppressed, a de facto acting-White theory is probably at play. Sociologist Angela Valenzuela calls this assimilative tendency in public education "subtractive schooling."[31] This term highlights how schools often force marginalized youth to check the ethnic portions of their identity at the door in order to be taken seriously as motivated learners and well-behaved members of a classroom community. This requirement subtracts the cultural resources that most inform who these students are and how they think, communicate, and behave.[32] To be included and encouraged, students learn that they must sever their identities from their education. Schooling thus becomes subtractive rather than additive—and resistance against that schooling becomes a rational decision.

When we expect racially and ethnically marginalized students to adapt to mainstream norms—essentially, to assimilate—we shift the focus of change from the situation that oppresses them to the consciousness of the oppressed.[33] As an illustration, consider this question: Who is most often told that their racial allegiance or ethnicity is an obstacle to their academic success? Is it Irish Americans? Jews? Immigrants from Finland? Not likely, or at least not as often. For this reason, educators need to welcome and integrate multiple ways of knowing, talking, moving, and relating in the classroom—even behaviors that seem weird or countercultural to those in the mainstream—because doing so will help alleviate the persistent and insidious effects of the acting-White ethic in schools.

How the Acting-White Theory Fails to Stand Up to Science

Even though the oppositional-cultures and acting-White theories are widely believed, reiterated, and applied in schools, they have been consistently refuted by subsequent and rigorous scientific scrutiny. Dozens of scholars have carried out studies attempting to repeat Ogbu's findings; by and large, they have been unsuccessful.[34] One study from 2002 by David Bergin and Helen Cooks found that students "did not report avoiding academic achievement in order to avoid accusations of acting white" and "reported no loss of ethnic identity" when they performed well in school.[35] In 2008, Anthony Graham and Kenneth Anderson discovered that students "gave no credence to peer pressure or factors that could inhibit their academic progress such as potential social strife nor did they identify 'acting White' as a source of tension between their ethnic and academic identities."[36] And another study from 2011 broke down the oppositional-cultures theory into five major tenets but found no evidence of any of them. The researcher, Angel Harris, thus concluded that his investigation "challenges the existence of a pervasive oppositional culture among blacks."[37]

Researchers Erin Horvat and Kristine Lewis determined that monolithic characterizations of Black students like those found in the oppositional-cultures theory essentially misrepresented the heterogeneity within Black peer groups. Horvat and Lewis found that students "were not uniformly ostracized because of their academic prowess" but were in fact "embraced and celebrated." On those occasions when students were observed to downplay or camouflage their successes in school, it was only "during interactions with peers from whom they fear sanctions." Such downplaying is precisely what students from all racial and ethnic backgrounds sometimes do when they move within and between various peer groups. Regardless of identity, students learn to "discern and discriminate among friends when they decide to disclose information about their academic achievements and aspirations or to disavow claims to academic excellence."[38] This may be an effort by more academically successful students to maintain reciprocity in relationships with friends who may be struggling in school. Overall, studies like these provide an abundance of evidence that the oppositional-cultures and acting-White theories should be rejected as plausible explanations of student resistance in school. Simply put, it's time to move on.

Promising Practices: Learning to Read Student Resistance Authentically and Respond Productively

In the end, if we work with racially and ethnically diverse students, no matter what we do, we cannot entirely avoid racialized resistance. It *will* happen. The suggested practices briefly explained below are not designed to quell resistance but are meant to engage it, learn from it, and channel it into outcomes that enhance possibilities for students and educators alike.

Developing Culturally Responsive Pedagogies and Welcoming School Climates

Numerous books and articles have been written about the need for, benefits of, and techniques in culturally responsive pedagogy. It has a proven track record of successfully building ethnically and racially affirming learning environments in which the knowledge, skills, and dispositions of both marginalized and mainstream students are developed in an anti-oppressive context.[39] Rather than recount the extensive literature, curricula, and websites dedicated to culturally responsive practices, I will briefly describe here how the approach directly addresses the resistance of racially and ethnically marginalized youth.

Culturally responsive pedagogy, when done well, exposes students to political and historical content that directly addresses discrimination, stereotypes, institutional racism, and interpersonal prejudice. It gives students the context they need to understand what they are experiencing (or perpetuating), and it provides a venue for safer explorations of how oppression might be productively resisted. Research has made it clear that students will be less likely to resist their educators and schooling experiences when youth are given ample opportunities to learn more about their "othered" cultural heritage. This observation directly challenges the highly problematic conclusions and restrictions that Tucson Unified School District and the state of Arizona reached in 2011, when officials made it illegal to teach a culturally responsive ethnic-studies curriculum there. The more access that marginalized students have to their histories, and the more that access is provided at the schools in which they are expected to achieve, the more students will invest in prosocial behaviors and academic work at that school.

When ethnic and racial pride is viewed as something to enhance, not suppress, good things happen for marginalized students. They may begin to think, "I will represent my school because my school represents me." Rather than subtract cultural resources from students by making them conform to White middle class normativity, culturally responsive pedagogy is designed to close the gap between minoritized students' cultures and that of the school. Schools have achieved this through practices such as oral history projects, visits by ethnic minority community members, participatory-action research, and visible celebration of marginalized groups' achievements and contributions. In addition, educators committed to culturally responsive learning environments have provided opportunities for students and school officials to hold public forums on intercultural communication that can help channel student resistance into constructive conversations. At these forums, well-prepared facilitators (sometimes led by the students themselves) provide sufficient scaffolding to ensure that all participants can enter the dialogue no matter what their background and level of ethnic and racial identity (ERI) development may be.

These conversations can be terrific venues for drawing attention to problematic trends in the learning community because rather than creating divisions and spreading discord, they tend to build coalitions and solve problems. Though intercultural communication can indeed be difficult and emotional, focused and sustained efforts to reduce cultural misunderstanding, to educate those with racial privilege about their role in oppression, and to support racially and ethnically marginalized students who seek remedies in their learning environment can yield powerful and positive academic and behavioral outcomes. If the commitment is there, the possibilities are endless.

Interrogate Whiteness

Whiteness is perhaps the biggest obstacle to realizing racial and ethnic equity in our disciplinary responses to students of color who resist in school. Definitions of whiteness are as varied and as numerous as the interdisciplinary fields in which it is studied, but for the purposes of this chapter, I will define it as *the set of unearned privileges and cultural norms that are used to sustain White racial superiority and advantage.* Similarly, the critical ethnographer and philosopher Peter McLaren defines whiteness as "the invisible norm for how the dominant culture measures its own civility."[40] Using these definitions, it is clear we must interrogate whiteness—that is, learn to see its traces and scrutinize how it functions in conversations, shapes decision making, and creates and dismisses knowledge—if we are to overcome endemic and malevolent expectations about how "others" should behave.

How should educators interrogate whiteness? What would the process look like? To begin with, school-based professionals may have to overcome powerful fears and interpersonal tensions that impede a critical appraisal of whiteness as it operates in school practices. Psychologist Howard Stevenson identifies three main fears that White educators often possess as they move toward engaging students and colleagues of color on issues of race and ethnicity: (1) that they will be revealed to be ignorant of the behaviors of students of color; (2) that they will be humiliated and called racist when conflicts arise; and (3) that they will be devastated if and when their supposedly egalitarian ways of teaching in fact reveal inequities.[41] When these fears dominate their consciousness, White educators will be reticent to do the hard work of interrogating their assumptions about and complicity in structural racism, because doing so threatens their sense of self as a good person. It's not fun to admit to possessing racist attitudes; nor is it pleasurable to realize that we may be conducting ourselves in ways that are discriminatory if not oppressive. This is why interrogations of whiteness often have to begin with some consciousness raising. Unless there are experts of color who are willing and available to lead these discussions, the sessions are probably best facilitated by Whites for Whites. Experienced antiracist educators who are well versed in the many ways White educators come prepared by their culture to impede, deny, and escape interrogations of whiteness are essential in this effort.

Likewise, interrogations of whiteness may seem self-evident, boring, or a waste of time for many educators of color, especially when discussions are carried out in White-dominated contexts (these conversations may also be rage-inducing and alienating). Educators of color may be reluctant to collaborate with Whites who are either unwilling or incapable of unpacking White privilege, analyzing dominant cultural expectations, and questioning mainstream ways of framing "proper," "civilized," and "polite" behaviors that often pathologize students of color. Ethnically and racially marginalized educators may have tried to engage Whites on these issues before, only to have their experiences, feelings, and insights denied and denigrated, further confirming both their marginalization and the apparent futility of cross-cultural dialogue. It can be infuriating for educators of color to share their experiences of racism and exclusion only to watch as Whites shift everyone's attention to occasions in which they felt excluded or victimized by "reverse racism." For all these reasons, it is sometimes necessary to conduct interrogations of whiteness in separate affinity groups: Whites with other Whites, and educators of color with their ethnic and racial groups. This is not segregation but instead is a form of temporary, disaggregated support.

When groups are ready to reintegrate, it often makes sense to discuss an agreed-upon common topic such as a reading on whiteness, an analysis of school disciplinary data, or an examination of a school or community event.[42] Regardless of the format of these interrogations, it is paramount that naming discriminatory, racist, ethnocentric, and xenophobic ideologies and practices be part of the work, especially when such practices are operating in the room, not just "out there." Whiteness often dictates that we refrain from identifying these problems to preserve the veneer of polite or professional working environments. We need to move beyond that. Those normative environments are stifling if not oppressive for so many students (and educators) whose ethnic and racial identities are marginalized simply because they do not conform to the mainstream.

Students resist these normative learning environments partly to create openings in which their dissatisfaction with relationships and events can be expressed. When ethnically and racially marginalized students trouble our carefully constructed (or uncritically adopted) norms, it is a sign that our expectations may be exclusionary or that our schools may be subtractive. If that is the case, students in our midst are probably already undertaking important interrogations of whiteness. Their bravery and their resistance need to become ours.

Be Respectful

Sitting with his mom on one side and the school psychologist on the other, Gabriel stares at his grades in front of him while his history teacher, Mr. Grier, continues to explain things.

"You are so well-spoken, Gabriel," Mr. Grier says. "You have tremendous potential. You're a leader among your peers. But you need to check your attitude at the door. You need to be more attentive in the classroom and less concerned with being the big man on campus. We're all equal in here, and that means I have the same expectations for your behavior as I have for everyone else, and you're not living up to our standards. That's why you're in here today—you act out a lot, and it's getting you in more and more trouble."

Concerned that Gabriel's perspective wasn't being heard, Gabriel's mother encourages him to explain himself. "Tell Mr. Grier what you were telling me this morning."

Sitting up in his chair but still staring at the paper, Gabriel says, "You say we're all equal, but that isn't what it looks like."

His mother prods him to continue: "Go on."

"I mean . . ." Gabriel starts. "It doesn't matter. Whatever."

Sensing hesitation, Mr. Petersen, the school psychologist, intervenes. "Gabriel, this is an opportunity for you to say what you think and for us to work on meeting your needs. How do you see the situation?"

Gabriel turns to face Mr. Petersen and unloads. "Mr. Grier thinks he's being fair, but me and my friends are the only ones that ever get singled out in his class. We're not giving attitude. We're just being ourselves. This is how we act."

Mr. Peterson asks, "What do you mean?"

Gabriel answers, "You know, like, we don't have any problems in Mrs. Garcia's class. And I have an A in physics. But in Mr. Grier's class, we always get docked on our participation grade because of not raising hands and group work and stuff.

And we're always split up whenever we're in groups so we end up talking to each other. Then we get yelled at, and that's when things get stupid." Turning to look at Mr. Grier, Gabriel adds, "You act like it's just us with bad attitudes, but you don't even know the things people say to me in those groups. You don't hear any of that. This place is crazy, and then I get in trouble for acting out. But whatever, it doesn't matter."

Just as Mr. Grier is about to speak, Gabriel's mom tries to lighten the mood by explaining with a smile, "We raised Gabriel to be strong and critical—and also respectful—so I guess this is what you get!"

"Can you say more about that?" asks Mr. Peterson.

"Well, we are active in our community," she says. "And have always pushed Gabriel to be a self-advocate and to be proud of his heritage. Maybe that has something to do with how he's acting. I'll talk with him about this when we get home."

Mr. Grier takes the opportunity to try to provide some closure and replies, "I'm sorry if things have been difficult in group work, Gabriel, but again, it might be your attitude. You will get respect if you give respect, and I am guessing many of your peers feel you don't respect them."

Visibly frustrated by this suggestion, Gabriel turns to his mother and says, "See? See what I'm talking about? Nobody gets it. Forget it."

As Gabriel rises out of his seat and walks toward the door, his mother thanks Mr. Petersen and Mr. Grier for their time and assures them she will talk with Gabriel more at home.

CHAPTER 10

"Don't Make Me Assimilate"

Authenticity, Resistance, and Racism

CHAPTER 9 ESTABLISHED that at least one dominant explanation for marginalized youth's resistance in school got the phenomenon all wrong. Now that we are prepared to resist the acting-White explanation in our work with colleagues and youth, we need better explanations that can point to more effective responses. In this chapter, multiple alternatives to the oppositional-cultures theory are provided, each of which are supported by rigorous scholarship. Here, findings from developmental psychology are blended with political analyses of cultural, interpersonal, and institutional features that tend to grant privileges and advantages to some while subtracting them from others. (The misunderstandings and pedagogical mistakes often made as a result of these inequities and dispositions are explored in more detail in chapter 11.) Whether resistance emerges from identity formation, racial microaggressions, strategic parenting, or self-actualizing priorities within the individual, marginalized youth often resist because they need to. Our responses to that resistance therefore carry enormous consequences for our students' academic achievement, school engagement, and mental health.

Better Explanations for Students' Resistance Against Racism

Most developmental psychologists in the Eriksonian tradition agree that in the modern West, a person's identity is initially if not largely formed during adolescence. Identity is understood in a variety of ways by researchers and theorists, and there are some intriguing and often contentious arguments about what is meant by the concept in contemporary scholarship. (For example, is identity a performance? Is it internally held or socially constructed? Is it durable and consistent across different contexts and relationships, or is it wholly dependent on environmental contingencies?) But one thing widely agreed upon is the balancing act that identity formation typically requires: youth must learn to integrate their need for individuality with their need to belong. To be unique but not alone and to be included but not enmeshed are important developmental achievements in the adolescent years.

Often, however, this balancing act plays out in settings that transmit racist or otherwise discriminatory messages. Schools often send out such messages despite our efforts to the contrary. Depending on how a student receives those messages and is positioned within racial and ethnic hierarchies, her or his uniqueness can feel like an asset in one context and a liability in another. Likewise, inclusion can seem like a lifesaver in one arena and be experienced as anathema somewhere else. Ethnic and racial identity (ERI) development therefore involves both assimilation *and* rejection, immersion *and* withdrawal, acceptance *and* opposition—all in an attempt to safeguard experiences of membership and distinctiveness. Resistance, it turns out, is a crucial component in these processes.

Ethnic and Racial Identity Formation and the Need to Resist

ERI development models can be a powerful resource for educators who seek to understand the classroom resistance of ethnically and racially marginalized students. Identity, a meaning-making system that shapes thinking, feeling, and acting, is as political as it is psychological because identities are formed in (and in spite of) groups. This is why ERI developmental models generally trace the social, personal, and political metamorphosis of people's self-understanding as they try to make sense of both affirming and alienating messages about their ethnic or racial group.[1] Most models assume that an individual's ERI formation can be a liberating process that, if circumstances support it, gradually moves toward a psychologically healthier state. Research in the United States suggests that when individuals are able to reconcile discrepancies between their ethnic or racial self and their American self, they tend to perform better in school, engage in more prosocial interactions with peers and adults, attend and succeed in college, locate and sustain satisfactory employment, and report greater life satisfaction.[2] However, because "being a member of a seemingly permanent out-group subjects [individuals] to intentional and unintentional acts of discrimination, hostility, and marginalization," ERI formation also typically involves anguish, anger, and resistance.[3] Therefore, the ability to see how some adolescents make sense of their ERI amid contexts that both devalue and revere their identity is crucial for those who work with youth in educational settings.[4]

Over the past several decades, researchers have constructed numerous models to explain the phases that children, adolescents, and adults progress through as they form their ERI. White identity development models generally portray the evolution of a person's awareness of racism from a conflicted acknowledgment of one's privilege and complicity in oppression, to a retreat into White superiority, and then (if contexts and relationships support it) into a gradual unfolding of an antiracist ideology.[5] African American, Chicano, Japanese American, Chinese American, Southeast Asian American, Pacific Islander, and Native American identity development models have all been constructed to explain the particular phases and stages that occur as individuals confront their marginalization in mainstream society.[6] And biracial, bicultural, or multicultural models have been developed to expand simplistic either-or constructions of ERI and better capture the rich experiences of those who grow up in families with multiple races, ethnicities, or cultures.[7] Due to the normalizing symbols and forces of mainstream culture, each of these models involve aspects of resistance.

Because a full accounting of these models is beyond the scope of this volume, I will summarize in this chapter the political and psychological transitions that often occur in adolescents as they make meaning of racialized circumstances. I will do so by explaining the necessary and healthy role that resistance plays in two generalized phases: encounter and immersion. Though theories and models are built to generalize patterns across populations, it is important to remember that individual students will often react to the same circumstances in very different ways. Depending on the salience of ERI to their self-concept, the nature of the symbols and forces they are experiencing, the quality of their membership in one or more groups, and the expectations they have for how they should behave in light of cultural messages received up until that point, students may make very different decisions about how to act from one situation to the next. Figure 10.1 depicts the decision-making process that individuals often undergo when they decide how to respond to a situation. Each cloud represents a question that draws on the individual's intellectual, emotional, and political understanding of their ERI as well as an assessment of situational cues. The decision to act, and possibly to resist, is rooted in those understandings and the idiosyncrasies of each different situation.

FIGURE 10.1   The influence of ethnic and racial identity (ERI) on situational decision-making

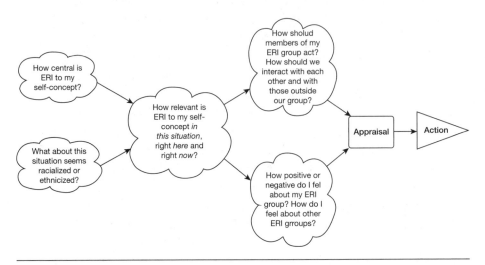

Source: Adapted from Robert M. Sellers, Mia A. Smith, Nicole J. Shelton, Stephanie A. J. Rowley, and Tabbye M. Chavous, "Multidimensional Model of Racial Identity: A Reconceptualization of African American Racial Identity," *Personality & Social Psychology Review* 2, no. 1 (1998): 18–39.

The Encounter

In the early stages of ERI development, a person's ERI is not salient. The individual "just is" and feels little need to consider the way her or she is perceived outside the family or community. But an encounter with discrimination or oppression changes everything. When the student faces what he or she considers a prejudiced or racist situation (or is facing it in an arena previously understood to be safe, such as a classroom), the confrontation with that oppression triggers psychological trauma but also profound growth. In what some psychologists have termed the *encounter* stage, the ethnically or racially marginalized individuals have to consider and potentially rethink their identity as well as the nature of their group membership. The encounter forces individuals to reorganize their ERI to make sense of the new information. They may ask, "How am I being perceived here? What aspects of my identity are being singled out? What implications does this have for my relationships with others? How do I feel? How should I behave?"

In school, the energy required to make sense of the encounter can hijack psychological resources that are usually available for things like socializing, studying, focusing on academic activities, and controlling impulses. As a consequence, the student may seem distracted, confused, or frustrated, if not hurt or angry in the classroom. Students in the midst of this encountering process may be resistant to directives from educators or may be oppositional toward peers, especially if those educators or peers are associated with the group responsible for the oppression. Ignoring or misdiagnosing marginalized students' responses (e.g., labeling their behavior as the fear of acting White) can aggravate their emotional turmoil and lead very quickly to flared reactions and rash decision-making. In those moments, it may be easy to blame these students for overreacting, but that would be a mistake. Their reactions are big clues that something is not right in the learning environment. Students in the encounter stage therefore need engagement, patience, empathy, and even our deference. They do not need labels or reprimands.

When our responses to students of color in the encounter phase fail to demonstrate an awareness of their struggle, the students may consciously or unconsciously seek exit strategies either through requests to excuse themselves (sharpening a pencil, getting a drink, using the bathroom, asking to see their counselor, texting a friend, etc.) or through (mis)behavior. Getting in trouble offers a way out—out of the situation, out of the room, out of the relationship, and out of the school. Students who invent these escapes may be attempting to simplify a complex situation by reducing it to an obvious disciplinary infraction. Doing something "wrong" may be easier than analyzing something complex, especially when the audience or authorities cannot be trusted to understand the racialized issues at play. Put differently, "I'm outta here" may be simpler to explain and less emotionally taxing than trying to figure out "What is happening here?" Getting in trouble therefore provides a triple benefit: an escape, a release of negative energy, plus a confirmation that they are indeed experiencing oppression. In addition, an amplified resistant response like "F—— you!" may momentarily raise students' internal and social esteem because they are rising up against forces that are perceived to oppress them. In this way, getting in trouble can feel heroic.

This is true for White students too. Adolescents with racial privilege are typically not accustomed to having their behaviors, beliefs, and taken-for-granted assumptions challenged. Much of their experience in the mainstream is affirming. But when peers of color confront them with critiques, accusations, and even rage, White students too will often seek escape. When they are confronted with their own privilege and their complicity in racism, White students may first reject the accusations and seek refuge in relationships that will provide comfort and reassurance that they are not a racist or that they are a good person. When educators provide this comfort, rifts between the privileged and the marginalized are often widened rather than bridged. If we're not careful, our differential responses to White students versus students of color can make it look like the students who confront racism are being disciplined while those who perpetuate it are being consoled. Whereas students of color who encounter racism may need some time to regroup and rebuild, White students may often need to remain in the situation and be helped to analyze it so that they can learn from it. Though this level of scrutiny may not feel good for the White students, it's a crucial part of their encountering phase if they are ever to adopt an antiracist ideology.

In the encounter phase, the resistance of students of color can be a pedagogical resource. When victims of racism and discrimination muster their skills and experiences to oppose and sometimes change the conditions of their education, other less resistant (and possibly more complicit) students are watching and learning. If inequity and injustice are to be made visible and if they are to be overcome, the reluctant and the ignorant need to see examples of its dismantling. Resistance provides the potential for such examples. How we handle that resistance teaches White students either how to retain their privileged inheritance or how to act against oppression. It's like a form of peer mentoring. By watching our reactions to marginalized students' resistance, White students tacitly learn how to control the "other" by ignoring, dismissing, pathologizing, or quashing opposition. Alternatively, White students may learn how to *engage* resistance, establish cross-cultural alliances, surrender privilege, and open democratic spaces in which resources are shared equitably and talents are nurtured fairly.

Absent these teachable moments, many White students will achieve adult identities that are personally positive but culturally limited and possibly corrupted with stereotypes and ignorance. Such identities limit their capacity to engage cultural difference and interact productively in diverse environments which, in turn, can diminish their own and others' academic and vocational success. In this way, engaging resistance isn't just about helping marginalized students—it's about helping the privileged ones too. Using student resistance as a resource is one way out of this vicious cycle.

Immersion

When sufficient encounters with racial oppression have occurred in minoritized students' lives to suggest that the patterns they are perceiving are not anomalies but in fact are systemic, they will often move into what is variously understood to be an *immersion* phase.[8] Geneva Gay, a scholar of race relations and multicultural education, describes the typical immersion phase in African Americans:

[The phase involves] the struggle to destroy all vestiges of the "old" perspective [which] occurs simultaneously with an equally intense concern to clarify the personal implications of the "new" frame of reference. It is characterized by high levels of egocentric and ethnocentric ethnic affiliation, ideology, and associational preferences. High levels of ambivalence may be present, too. The person may vacillate between feelings of rage and depression, power and help-lessness, anger and joy, pride and shame. Even toward other Blacks, the person may be alternately embracing and rejecting, and prone to apply "Blacker than thou" standards of being to fellow ethnic group members. Toward ethnic oth-ers, particularly [Whites], the predominant feelings are anger, hostility, and de-nial. In the search for different bases on which to fashion a new sense of ethnic identity, the individual withdraws from everything that represents the white world and Euro-American ideology, turns inward, and immerses himself or herself into the [ethnic, racial,] historical and cultural heritage. This immersion is evident in speech, dress, reading preferences, ideologies, and interpersonal associations.[9]

This immersion into one's ethnicity is often coupled with a resistance against the mainstream. When minoritized students become occupied with various forms of cultural affirmation, they often respond to exclusion and discrimina-tion by presenting themselves as distinct from what they perceive to be their opposite.

Likewise, White students may seek the safety, homogeneity, and support of whiteness and rationalize their seclusion and exclusion by pathologizing "others." In these cases, complex social relationships are often simplified into us-them po-larities. To claim who they are, students often reject "who I am not." This process of choosing and rejecting can be pronounced within school cultures pervaded by dominant messages that frame "appropriate" behavior, dress, and language in a culturally restrictive manner. Resistance in such contexts not only is inevitable, but may also be psychologically and politically desirable.

Ethnically and racially marginalized students in the immersion phase will tend to be extra sensitive to the nuances of covert or overt inequities that are often perpetuated through differing expectations of ability; varying responses to (mis)behavior; grading discrepancies; and inconsistencies in the communication of warmth, regard, or care. According to Gay, students who are ethnically im-mersed may not tolerate such variance, nor will they be "very interested in or receptive toward ethnic others. They are too preoccupied with discovering their own ethnicity and with trying to reconstruct a shattered ethnic reality. Develop-ing genuine respect for and appreciation of ethnic diversity is more appropriate for those youths" who have moved beyond immersion toward more integrated phases of racial identity development.[10] Therefore, to be culturally responsive to students in the immersion phase, we may need to recognize their occasional intolerance not as "reverse racism" but as a psychologically and politically driven reaction to their own marginalization.

Of course, abusive behaviors should never be tolerated in school settings, regardless of the student's background. But how we engage students about those behaviors and how we label them convey crucial messages about our own tolerance for racialized situations. Can we see the racial and ethnic aspects of student resistance? Do we *want* to see them? Will we allow if not encourage students who may be in the encounter or immersion phase of their ERI development to voice their concerns? Racially and ethnically marginalized students frequently want to know whether we can "go there." They test us with their resistance and then closely observe how we name their actions and respond to their behaviors. For students in the immersion phase in particular, these tests of resistance can make or break their relationships with educators.

This is why it is helpful to remember that student resistance against perceived racism and mainstream norms can greatly assist healthy ERI development. In a society in which racism and other forms of identity-based oppressions persist, resistance is a valuable tool. It can affirm social bonds, reinforce autonomy, confer status, detect boundaries, identify allies, and discern where oppressive systems may be vulnerable to change. When we engage rather than discipline student resistance, we can facilitate rather than frustrate ERI development. As table 10.1 illustrates and many other studies confirm, the development of healthy ERI is associated with some very important and positive psychosocial and academic outcomes.[11] When an educator reads adolescents' resistant behaviors only in terms of their presumed disrespect toward mainstream expectations—in other words, when students' resistance is suppressed rather than engaged—the profound opportunities for growth, connection, and learning depicted in table 10.1 can be lost. Preventing that loss should be an academic, cultural, and political priority in schools.

How Racial Microaggressions Can Add Up

Try as we might to eliminate the lingering effects of racism in our thoughts and actions, decades of cultural training are hard to erase. White educators sometimes say and do things that communicate racial and ethnic bias, or they occasionally default to dominant modes of appraising "others" and exclusionary ways of interacting with them. Educators of color sometimes also hold stereotypes and misconceptions about other ethnic minorities. These types of bias can infect relationships and produce intergroup forms of racialized resistance. We should know better and we should do better, but sometimes we don't. For White educa-

TABLE 10.1 Ethnic and racial identity development and associated outcomes

Racial or ethnic circumstances		Academic and psychosocial outcomes
When youth think more about and spend more time and energy exploring the meaning of their group membership . . .	it is correlated with . . .	more interest in learning; fewer depressive symptoms.
When youth resolve what group membership means to them . . .	it is correlated with . . .	more interest in learning.
When the importance of group membership to the students' self-concept or self-definition rises . . .	it is correlated with . . .	higher academic motivation; greater prosocial tendencies; greater peer acceptance and popularity.
When students' own evaluations of and positive feelings about their group grow . . .	it is correlated with . . .	greater academic efficacy, engagement, achievement, and school connectedness; elevated positive self-concept, prosocial tendencies, peer acceptance, interpersonal functioning; fewer depressive symptoms.
When students perceive others to evaluate their group positively . . .	it is correlated with . . .	greater school belonging; academic competence; higher grades.

Source: Adapted from Debora Rivas-Drake, Eleanor K. Seaton, Carol Markstrom, Stephen Quintana, Moin Syed, Richard M. Lee, Seth J. Schwartz, Adriana J. Umaña-Taylor, Sabine French, and Tiffany Yip, "Ethnic and Racial Identity in Adolescence: Implications for Psychosocial, Academic, and Health Outcomes," *Child Development* 85, no. 1 (2014): 43.

tors, the belief that we are caring, compassionate, just, unbiased, and nonracist people who work in a service-oriented if not selfless profession often helps us to feel good about ourselves, but it may blind us to the racial microaggressions we sometimes commit in the course of our work. And for many educators of color, such blindness is old news.

What exactly are racial microaggressions? According to psychologist Derald Sue and his associates, "racial microaggressions are brief and commonplace daily verbal, behavioral, and environmental indignities, whether intentional or unintentional, that communicate hostile, derogatory, or negative racial slights and insults to the target person or group."[12] Research suggests that these micro-aggressions may present some of the biggest challenges to our relationships with students who are ethnically and racially different from us and may contribute greatly to their resistance in school. The ways we ascribe intelligence, ask about a person's origins, praise someone's speech, claim not to see racial differences, deny the role that race plays in life success, or rebuff any observations about our participation in racism's perpetuation can be experienced as low-grade forms of hostility. Table 10.2 highlights many common versions of racial microaggressions experienced by marginalized students in school, how they are sometimes delivered, and how they are often received.

Though racial microaggressions are most frequently expressed by Whites, they can also be communicated by ethnically and racially marginalized people when they are interacting with other minoritized individuals. If confronted, the perpetrator may claim the purest of intentions and have at his or her disposal a host of explanations to excuse the behavior, but the target of the microaggression will likely experience such pleas as a nullification of the recipient's experience and expertise. In their paper "Racial Microaggressions in Everyday Life," Sue and his colleagues explore this tendency for the confrontation to degrade if not destroy the relationship.[13] For example, students may seek help from educators after experiencing frustrating or confusing racialized situations, or they may choose to confront adults who may have participated in events that students understood as racially problematic. When students recount these events and the teacher or counselor replies with statements like, "All of us are individuals," or "We are all human beings," or "We're all the same under the skin," students might feel misunderstood, invalidated, or erased. Statements like these were likely intended to be sympathetic and supportive, but they achieve the exact opposite.

Likewise, when Asian American or Latino students describe feeling overwhelmed with obligations and stress caused by family responsibilities, educators may encourage those students to take up more space in the family unit and make decisions for themselves regardless of family expectations. In doing so, the educator may be invalidating these students' deeply ingrained collectivist orientations and imposing an individualist worldview. This lack of sensitivity is also a racial microaggression, as well as a form of subtractive schooling.[14]

Students will often react to these situations by employing a wide variety of resistant strategies. They may indicate their displeasure with a scowl or roll of their eyes. They may grumble, "Whatever," and move on. Other responses include

TABLE 10.2 Examples of racial microaggressions common in school

Theme	Microaggression	Message
Alien in own land: When Asian Americans and Latino Americans are assumed to be foreign born	• "Where are you from?" • "Where were you born?" • "You speak good English."	• You are not American. • I read you as a foreigner.
Ascription of intelligence: Assigning intelligence to a person of color on the basis of his or her race	• "You are so articulate." • "You are a credit to your race."	• People of color are generally not as smart as Whites. • It is unusual for someone of your race to be intelligent.
Color blindness: Statements that indicate a White person does not want to acknowledge race	• "When I look at you, I don't see color." • "America is a melting pot." • "There is only one race: the human race."	• Your racial or ethnic experience is neither valid nor welcome. • You should assimilate. • I do not want to know or understand the nonnormative parts of you.
Denial of individual racism: A statement made when Whites deny their racial biases	• "I'm not a racist. I have Black friends." • "As a woman, I know what you go through as a racial minority."	• I am immune to racism because a person of color has befriended me. • Your racial oppression is no different than my gender oppression. • I can't be a racist, because I am just like you.

(continued)

TABLE 10.2 *(continued)*

Theme	Microaggression	Message
Systemic myopia: Statements that deny structural racism by appealing to progress and grand narratives of equality	· "That was then, this is now. Racism is a thing of the past." · "We've come so far compared to where we were." · "But look at the progress we've made." · "We all have the same freedoms now." · "We have a Black president."	· You should not complain, because things are better than they used to be. · Your current circumstances aren't bad. · Contemporary society is more or less devoid of serious racism. · I don't benefit from any racial privilege. · Racism is not systemic; rather, it was bad people doing bad things back then.
Pathologizing cultural values and communication styles: The notion that the modes of behavior and beliefs of the dominant White culture are ideal	· To a Black person: "Why do you have to be so loud/animated?" · To an Asian or a Latino: "Why are you so quiet? We want to know what you think. Speak up!"	· Leave your culture outside. · There is only one right way to communicate and act. · Be someone else when you come here; basically, be White.

Source: Adapted from Derald W. Sue, Christina M. Capodilupo, Gina C. Torino, Jennifer M. Bucceri, Aisha M. B. Holder, Kevin L. Nadal and Marta Esquilin, "Racial Microaggressions in Everyday Life: Implications for Clinical Practice," *American Psychologist,* 62, no. 4 (2007): 276. Copyright © 2007 by the American Psychological Association.

changing the topic and exiting the conversation, calling the perpetrator a racist, or withdrawing from the relationship altogether and recommending that peers do the same. How students resist depends on their circumstances (see figure 10.1), but a lack of immediate response should not be interpreted as acceptance. According to Sue and his colleagues, "when a microaggression occurs, the victim is usually placed in a catch-22. The immediate reaction might be a series of [internal] questions: Did what I think happened, really happen? Was this a deliberate act or an unintentional slight? How should I respond? Sit and stew on it or confront the person? If I bring the topic up, how do I prove it? Is it really worth the effort? Should I just drop the matter?"[15]

These questions require concentration and energy. To try to answer them, the student must divert vital cognitive functions away from academics and toward analyses of the microaggression. As a result, the student may have greater difficulty learning new concepts, mastering academic skills, following directions, and maintaining focus compared to those who do not face these microaggressions. Emotionally, the student who just encountered racial microaggression may seem preoccupied and on edge. Because adolescents rarely have well-developed impulse control to allow a full weighing of pros and cons before reacting, some teens may simply act out in ways that only befuddle less race-sensitive observers. In these moments, students are not resistant to learning; they are distracted by and concerned about racism in their learning environment.

As if microaggressions weren't confounding enough, the context can be tough too. Victims of microaggression have to determine how to respond not in racially neutral environments but in school settings where White, middle-class ways of thinking and behaving are often normative. Victims of racial microaggression therefore have to consider the extent to which they will be accused of oversensitivity or paranoia when they resist the implications of these supposedly well-meaning microaggressive statements. Victims may also have to ponder whether their reactions, especially their louder or more "emotional" ones, will confirm stereotypes about their racial or ethnic group. Furthermore, victims' desire to release pent-up frustrations in their response may have to be tempered by the realization that certain reactions will only increase the likelihood of greater hostility. Facing this damned-if-I-do/damned-if-I-don't conundrum, many victims of microaggression choose to do nothing, to remain silent. They don't resist and they don't respond, even though they may want to, because they "may be (a) unable to determine whether a microaggression has occurred, (b) at a loss for how to respond, (c) fearful of the consequences, (d) rationalizing that 'it won't do any good anyway,' or (e) engaging in self-deception through denial ('It didn't happen.').''[16]

Unfortunately, not doing anything occasions its own forms of damage. For one thing, when too many microaggressions go unchallenged, the perpetrators effectively learn that their actions are acceptable. Then when someone does stand up and resist, those instances can seem extraordinary, making it easier to dismiss victims for their seeming oversensitivity. And if students stay silent in the face of microaggressions, regularly deny their experiences of reality, habitually undermine their own integrity, and consistently bottle up their anger and frustration, those actions can take quite a toll on individuals' psychological and physical health. Adolescents' attempts to make sense of racial microaggressions in school can make it nearly impossible to focus on schoolwork and control impulses and hence can jeopardize academic achievement and relationships with others. Researchers have suggested that the accumulated experience of racial microaggressions on already-marginalized youth may influence racial frustration and anger even more than overt forms of racism.[17] And studies have shown that repeated experiences of racial or ethnic discrimination can intensify stress responses, increase depressive symptoms, and elevate participation in unhealthy activities (e.g., smoking, alcohol, drug abuse, violence) and nonparticipation in healthy behaviors (e.g., diabetes management, condom use).[18] In environments that allow racial microaggressions, victims will often find it difficult to prioritize academics or act with respect or compassion toward others. In such circumstances, resistance isn't impudence—it's survival.

Powerful Parenting and the Raising of Resisters

One explanation for racialized student resistance in school is as simple as it is powerful: youth are raised that way. Cultures, communities, schools, media, and peers are all highly influential socializing forces, but it is the family that plays the initial and primary role in the development of ERI. Countless families of color specifically and strategically teach their children to cope with microaggressions, stereotypes, institutional discrimination, and racism. The families know that schools are decisive arenas for these experiences, fraught as schools are with culturally lopsided curricula and skewed behavioral expectations that tend to privilege the mainstream and alienate "others." In response, parents and caregivers of color regularly instill in their children a sense of pride in their heritage at the same time that they prepare their kids for the inevitable experiences of marginalization. These pride and preparation messages go hand-in-hand. For children to love themselves amid relentless disparaging messages and contexts, it helps a great deal to have parental guides who reinforce children's essential worth and strengthen their capacity to defend. For this reason, many students of color enter school ready to learn and also equipped to resist.

Psychologists, sociologists, anthropologists, and ethnographers have long studied parenting strategies in ethnically and racially marginalized families. These scholars' findings indicate that parents who explicitly teach their cultural heritage and actively explore issues relevant to racial or ethnic exclusion, "including the dual messages of pride in group membership and preparation for bias," help to promote forms of ERI development that provide innumerable social and academic benefits.[19] As noted earlier, more robust forms of ERI are associated with greater academic achievement and more prosocial behaviors at school; therefore parenting that facilitates ERI development is likely to promote—not prevent—school success. In addition, politically conscious and race-critical forms of parenting can buffer the psychological damage that can occur when youth experience discriminatory or exclusionary interactions. These parenting approaches can also help establish the sort of home-base safety zones where children can let down their guard, analyze issues, share their feelings, and formulate responses.[20]

The work of psychologist Janie V. Ward reinforces these conclusions. Her explorations of the parenting and identity development of African American girls and boys have demonstrated the social, psychological, and political necessity of resistance. Ward observes parents worrying about what can happen to children of color if they naively accept White normativity and superiority. To guard against this, parents often act proactively by warning their children not to internalize injurious messages or adopt assimilative agendas. Ward documents how some African American parents intentionally "raise resisters" who refuse to allow themselves to become "stifled by victimization" or to be captured by "an ideology of victim blame." Her research shows how the knowledge taught in these "truth-telling" parenting strategies "mitigates self-abnegation, fosters self-esteem, and enables African Americans' resistance to oppression."[21]

Though it may be tempting to make the comparison, these parenting strategies are not the same as Ogbu's oppositional cultures. Nor should they be read as an inculcation of the acting-White orientation. The forms of parenting Ward and others have discovered concern the cultivation "of a critical consciousness that is invoked to counter the myriad distortions, mistruths, and misinformation perpetrated" about the lives and identities of people of color.[22] These parental practices are designed to compensate for and eventually overcome oppression and inequity, not reproduce it. Nowhere in the research is there evidence that

parents teach their kids to reject school, to refuse learning, or to devalue education. Studies actually demonstrate the opposite. Many Black youth are taught to
do their best in school, to listen to their teachers, and to demonstrate "respect
for authority (especially White), yet they also learn that they cannot afford to be
submissive."[23] Similar dual messaging has been observed in Latina mothers who
teach their daughters to be simultaneously rebellious and conforming as they
navigate racism and sexism both in and outside school.[24] Parents therefore use
resistance to convey a strategic "body of knowledge and requisite skills that can
help Black [and Brown] children and youth read, interpret, and oppose racial
bias and animosity, as well as affirm the self and one's cultural group."[25]

The intention in these racially and ethnically marginalized families is to raise
strong kids who can rise above discriminatory circumstances to achieve important academic, vocational, and familial goals. When parents raise resisters, the
impetus is to safeguard success, not protect or rationalize failure. In fact, a prevailing conclusion across the research is that parents of color tend to pay an
enormous amount of attention in their child-rearing practices to issues of racial
and ethnic marginalization precisely because schools too often ignore it. In this
way, resistance is a method of making visible what too many educators may try
to conceal.

Some educators may worry that parenting approaches seeking to, in Ward's
phrasing, "replenish the warrior spirit" will predispose students to hostility or
aggression. But researchers have found that this type of parenting actually "*de-
creases* the chances that discrimination will lead to anger . . . [and] *lowers* the risk
that anger or a hostile view of relationships, when they develop, will result in
violence."[26] Researchers have also concluded that "features of healthy racial socialization, including strong cultural identity formation and preparation for bias
experiences, are essential and distinctly influential in keeping African American
male youth from engaging in overactive, aggressive behaviors in the classroom."[27]
In other words, parents who prepare youth of color to resist may actually *diminish* the possibility that their kids will engage in aggressive behaviors at school.

The styles of truth-telling that strengthen Black and Brown students' identities and prepare them to deal with racism can sometimes shock and shut down
White students. Middle- and upper-class White adolescents may be more accustomed to parenting and teaching styles that prioritize comfort, encouragement,
praise, and entitlement, especially when it comes to racial socialization. Many
Whites are taught not to discuss race and to maintain "color-blind" dispositions
whenever such issues arise (see the treatment of color blindness in table 10.2).

But when White students encounter circumstances that are not tailored to these expectations, they may recoil. Often, White students perceive relationships with race-conscious educators and interactions in justice-oriented classrooms to be lacking in warmth, welcoming attitudes, and responsiveness to White middle-class norms of behavior and communication. As a result, White students too may resist.

One (Black or Brown) person's invaluable truth telling can be another (White) person's angry, abrupt, overly sensitive, confrontational, or rude style of engagement. The same spaces and relationships that students of color may perceive as a home-space can make White students feel uncomfortable, oppressed, or wrongly blamed. This often happens when students of color seek cross-cultural exchanges and forms of accountability in tones and registers that fall outside White mainstream conventions. Appealing to a supposedly universal need for folks to be "nice," to avoid being "attacked," and to "not make everything about race," many White students will resist these types of schooling experiences and the educators who facilitate them. In doing so, these White students may not be actively invested in oppression (though that may be part of their motivation), but they are interested in preserving privilege. Keeping these students in the conversation and holding them accountable for the effects of their actions is therefore necessary if schools are to become equitable and culturally sustaining venues for learning.

The different levels of awareness and preparation between White students and those of color suggest that we should apply differentiated approaches when working with ethnically and racially marginalized students versus those with racial privilege. Students of color may need to be heard, seen, and held accountable in terms that match their expectations, while White students may need to be heard, seen, and held accountable in ways that trouble theirs. This isn't being unfair; it's being culturally responsive, racially attentive, and anti-oppressive. To conduct all conversations with the expectation "Let's not get angry or raise our voices" will suppress victims' expressions of their experiences with racism and it will foreclose opportunities for all parties to learn from the conflict. If racism and discrimination are to be challenged, educators need to recognize the way resistance works differently for different groups. The parents of marginalized youth who are raising their kids to resist oppression have much to offer racially privileged families and communities that surround the school in which that oppression may operate. When it comes to analyzing racial and ethnic oppression, marginalized individuals possess a crucial asset: their position on the margins affords an invaluable and critical perspective on the practices and assumptions of the mainstream. Literally, those on the outside can see what many on the inside take for granted, and it's in moments of outsiders' resistance that normative practices and assumptions become visible to everyone. Their resistance is (or can be) everyone's insight.

Likewise, the strategies that families of color employ to prepare their kids for success in White-normative environments may help illuminate patterns that everyone, not just the victimized, ought to resist. After all, parenting strategies, pedagogical techniques, and disciplinary approaches that permit privilege to operate unchallenged and allow dominant expectations about behaviors, language, interaction styles, and concepts like respect to go undisputed should themselves be contested. In short, if we seek to dismantle racial and ethnic oppression and if we want to collaborate with marginalized parents in culturally responsive ways, we ought to try to raise a resister in each of our students *and* in each of our educators.

When Resistance Is Good for Students

Not all student resistance is emancipatory. Some forms of resistance are indeed destructive to the learning environment and to individual resisters' potential for academic success. But by engaging it, we can help youth to distinguish between productive and unproductive forms.

When students react to their circumstances by disparaging others, destroying property, using abusive language, or fighting, it may be what K. Wayne Yang terms an expression of "dangerous dignity" (see chapter 11) or what Janie V. Ward calls "resistance for survival." These ego-saving but ultimately self-defeating forms of resistance may emerge from compelling critiques of schooling experiences, but their actual expression does little to reform or improve those conditions. It may even make them worse. The individual student's desire just to survive with some shred of dignity in a situation that threatens his or her self-worth can lead that student to lash out, to do anything for a moment of control. Frequently, a cascade of events has already transpired before a student concludes that rebellion is the only way to protect himself or herself, but if we only spring to action when the rebellion appears, this may be evidence of *our* failure to see critically more than *their* failure to act "appropriately."

When we engage rather than suppress students' opposition, we can guide youth from what Ward calls a "resistance for survival" to a "resistance for liberation." Approaching resistance pedagogically rather than punitively can provide both students and educators with "an oppositional lesson in self-determination."[28] To make student resistance something good for students, we need to recognize that adolescents require time and guidance to develop the kinds of coping skills that both preserve personal integrity and challenge oppression. Student resistance presents opportunities to accompany youth as they make meaning of their experiences, as they imagine things differently, and as they make plans to achieve their goals. This kind of engagement acknowledges students' agency and the sentiment of their opposition while it advocates for critical analyses into what might promote change.

All students need help to determine the best course of action that will balance political critiques and personal desires with social expectations. This help is particularly valuable for students who are marginalized because of their race, ethnicity, socioeconomic class, gender expression, sexuality, disability, immigration status, or linguistic heritage. Students like these need our help to develop their resilience and practice their critical navigational skills that will allow them to maneuver through situations and institutions in which mainstream norms make some individuals feel like "others."[29] But the goal here should not be to show students how to assimilate. Rather, we want them to learn how to use resistance in ways that contribute to meaningful change. They already know how to transgress; what they need help in determining is how to transform.

Immigrant Status and Linguistic Heritage

The choice to focus on race and ethnicity in this chapter was strategic. The so-called achievement gap, the disproportionality in school discipline, the push-out rates, and the school-to-prison pipeline all suggest that an attention to race and ethnicity is warranted especially when school resistance is the subject of investigation. Given that this chapter cannot exhaustively treat all things relevant to race and resistance in education, some level of simplification has been necessary. For example, the discussion thus far mostly collapses ethnicity and race, which is a move supported by many researchers but still contested by some.[30] The term *student* or *educator of color* was used multiple times even though it suggests the reductive binary of White versus non-White (as if families aren't and haven't always been racially and ethnically mixed, and as if the criteria by which White or non-White designations aren't being manipulated and reconstituted all the time).[31] Furthermore, the chapter has paid little attention to, or completely ignored, the way gender, sexuality, SES, nationality, immigration status, and linguistic heritage intersect with ethnicity and race. So before moving on, and because this chapter's main focus is on race and ethnicity, we need to understand how at least two of those factors—students' immigration status and linguistic heritage—may contribute to many of the same forms of resistance detailed above.

The numbers of nonnaturalized residents in this country are impressive: nearly 3 million refugees entered the United States between 1980 and 2011, almost 2 million temporary workers and students live in the United States, and 11.5 million undocumented immigrants currently reside here.[32] Immigration status matters greatly for the vast majority of individuals within these groups, but unfortunately, many undocumented residents have good reason to worry. Amid the constantly shifting landscape of immigration reform and the rancor about "illegal aliens" that seems to dominate so much of what our media and political representatives say and do, immigrant adolescents attending public school have good reason to feel guarded.

Public education has become a central battleground for conservatives, moderates, and progressives to hammer out their differences with regard to undocumented residents. Many of these debates expose deep divisions in the American electorate regarding what and who school is for. Should public education welcome all students whether they are documented or not? Should instruction and curricula be provided in all languages, or solely in the "official" language of English? Should schools be multilingual and multicultural, or should educators expect immigrants to assimilate? Should classes be offered in which the histories, cultures, literatures, struggles, and achievements of specific immigrant groups are featured? Questions like these are asked in legislatures, school board agendas, and faculty meetings throughout the nation, and the fights over how to answer them have sometimes grown ugly. For those who already experience the pressure to "just be American" as a result of their accent, appearance, clothing, or culture, the effect can be chilling.

Outside school, immigrant adolescents sometimes confront even more alarming trends: stop-and-frisk policing techniques, "self-deportation incentives," restricted access to health care, worker exploitation, housing discrimination, purposeful barriers to education, and anti-immigrant violence. Laws have been passed in at least ten states restricting undocumented immigrants' access to social services like health care and education. Meanwhile, the DREAM Act (giving permanent residency to immigrants of "good moral character" who have arrived in the United States as minors, lived here for at least five consecutive years, and graduated from high school) has yet to pass Congress and be made federal law. These forms of oppression make clear that the United States—a nation that is almost entirely composed of immigrants or the descendants of immigrants— possesses strong currents of xenophobia. As a result, whether we admit it or not, the message immigrants often receive is, "You're not welcome here."

Immigrant students who enter school under these circumstances may be rightfully suspicious of the institution and its educators. They may underperform, withdraw, and resist to protect their threatened sense of self-worth. Some educators and policymakers will draw attention to those tendencies to argue that immigrants "don't value education like we do" or that "some cultures just aren't as academically motivated." *Research does not support these conclusions.* The explanations of students' resistant behaviors (and our misinterpretations of them) provided in this chapter largely apply to immigrant populations as well. Like all students, immigrant students do not want to look stupid; they do not want to have to check their culture at the door to be taken seriously as a learner; they do not want to be labeled and sent away to lower-tracked classes or alternative schools; they don't want to be laughed at; and they don't want to be labeled "gang bangers" when their occasionally tough exteriors are designed simply to get to and from school safely. Immigrant students want to be intellectually challenged and socially connected, and they want to be successful in school. Because of the xenophobic and racist tendencies within mainstream culture, immigrant students and their families are rightfully concerned about whether schools are committed to educating all students to reach their potential. The problem is the mainstream, not the margins.

Linguistic heritage also matters a great deal to many of these groups. According to the U.S. Department of Education, there are 4.7 million English language learners (ELLs) enrolled in our public schools.[33] We have decades of research overflowing with findings that support bilingual classrooms and dual-immersion pedagogies, yet these approaches are frequently ignored or maligned by legislators and district officials who are not accountable to populations that cannot vote. The home-court advantage that English speakers enjoy in school makes native English speakers look like they "earned" their success while it deprives ELLs equal access to education that is guaranteed by law and makes ELLs feel like unwanted visitors. To expect immigrant students to always be friendly, open, focused, appreciative, and compliant when the prevailing message we send them is "get out of here" is either cruel or irresponsible, or both.

Promising Practices: Engaging and Supporting Student Resistance Against Racial and Ethnic Oppression

The above analyses indicate that our work as educators occurs within an institution that has momentum and a heading. Our schools are going somewhere, with us inside them. To be a passive passenger in schools when their momentum is exclusionary and their heading leads to inequitable outcomes is tantamount to willingly participating in systemic oppression. To avoid this complicity, we need to develop skill-sets, policies, and dispositions that can change the momentum of our schools and reverse their heading. The practices below are intended to assist that effort.

Addressing the Politics of Ethnic and Racial Identity Development in the Classroom

The resistant, resentful, or angry student who is quick to complain about racial or ethnic issues or who may be prone to accuse peers and adults of racism should not be silenced. That student may be attempting to dismantle what he or she perceives to be injustice, and that's a good thing. (Admittedly, this may be hard to remember when you are the one that the student is targeting with the accusation.) At some level, the student's critique is an attempt to address inequity and to contribute to the community, not to destroy it, even though the behavior may be momentarily "counterproductive" from our point of view. The key in responding to forms of student resistance like this is to resist the temptation to determine whether an action was in fact discriminatory or not (i.e., getting bogged down in proving the purity of our intentions is frequently futile and may only contribute to students' perceptions that we don't get it). Instead, we can gain much more by drawing our attention to *the way behaviors are being received and perceived* by the resistant student. To do this, we can ask questions like, "How do you understand what's happening here?" "How do you understand my role in this situation?" "What's your role?" "What should I do to make this right?" "What might we do together?" Questions like these invite inquiry and collaboration and may help to break down us-versus-them ways of thinking that can polarize interactions and exacerbate misunderstanding.

Here are two things *not* to do when we are faced with angry students from ethnically and racially marginalized backgrounds who may be in the encounter or immersion phases of their ERI development. First, we shouldn't say, "Calm down." Few of us ever feel helped much in the moment when someone says "calm down" in response to our anger. Students are no different. What typically helps is the provision of a momentary escape (getting a drink at the water fountain, heading into the hallway for a minute, going to the bathroom to "wash up," etc.) followed by a conversation with someone who is willing and able to listen to the student's perspective and experiences and also help devise a productive, negotiated response. If we can be that person, terrific. If we're not up for the task because of our emotional state or because our own ERI development is not as sophisticated as the conversation will likely require, then we should refer the student to someone who can help. Ideally, the person should be some other adult professional at the school and should be nearby, trustworthy, capable, and available. (Then we need to get to work on our own ERI development so we can be more effective the next time!)

Second, if we do engage in conversation with the angry student, we must not try to regale him or her with what we had intended. One of the worst ways we can add insult to injury is when we force students to listen to what we had *hoped* to achieve, precisely when what they most need is for us to listen to what our actions actually *did*. Despite our greatest efforts to establish and maintain fair processes, students will sometimes assess everything we do for its racial or ethnic valences, and this interpretation can make it feel as though we can never win. Educators of color may be perceived by White students to make everything all about race, when such educators are merely using their expertise to identify patterns and assert themselves when situations do indeed carry racialized messages or implications. And White educators may be perceived by racially and ethnically marginalized students to be racist and ethnocentric simply because they are White and may therefore have to prove their status as allies before acceptance is granted.

It may be helpful to remind ourselves in these situations that the point is not to win; the point is to stay connected, to meet students where they're at, and to protect their academic achievement. An educator who expects the benefit of the doubt or who spends too much time explaining his or her intentions rather than examining perceived impacts is likely to contribute to marginalized students' alienation more than assuage their indignation. If students are angry at something we did, we should try to understand why that is. When in doubt, we need to focus on impact, not intention. Ask, then listen; don't lecture.

Likewise, we shouldn't interpret calmer and more accommodating student behaviors as acceptance. The quiet and compliant student in the immersion phase may have already written us off as a potential ally if we have ignored or suppressed opportunities to engage that student's resistance in the past. Some students may take their resistance underground and express it as withdrawal. Educators who seek to address racial and ethnic inequities in their classroom, school, and community must prepare for the political possibilities of all forms of resistance, even inward forms, rather than plan (and hope) for its placation. As a comparison, we often devote significant attention to helping those students who may be *socially* sensitive or shy, and we can generate a lot of rationale about why that attention is necessary (see chapter 6). But to what extent are we willing to direct similar energies, attention, and rationale toward meeting the needs of students who may be *racially* or *ethnically* sensitive? The ERI development that typically occurs in adolescence—and the classroom resistance that often accompanies it—is not just a psychological or political process that we can take or leave according to our interests. Because students' ERIs are inseparable from academics, a concerted attention to ERI development is part and parcel of good teaching.

Stopping Suspensions

According to a report by UCLA's Civil Rights Project, "over two million students were suspended during the 2009–2010 academic year . . . [O]ne out of every nine secondary school students was suspended at least once during that year . . . [T]he vast majority of suspensions are for minor infractions of school rules, such as disrupting class, tardiness, and dress code violations."[34] A common myth is that banishing students for a day or two (or three or five) will provide them with an extended opportunity to consider the consequences of their actions. The belief is that a mandatory suspension in students' attendance will become the turning point in their development so that deviant troublemakers will be scared straight, reevaluate their decision-making, and emerge as model students.

"If this were true," writes educational researcher K. Wayne Yang, "then more suspensions should lead to fewer pushouts and higher academic achievement—an outcome not reflected in the data at all."[35] On the contrary, multiple studies have shown that suspensions rarely if ever lead to productive changes in behavior and often exacerbate the same academic, social, and psychological difficulties that influenced the suspension-inducing behaviors in the first place.[36] Wang writes that students frequently return from suspensions "with the conviction that they were wrongfully punished and that the teacher is going to fail them. Aside from returning to the classroom resentful and unmotivated, they are, at best, momentarily threatened into submission or, at worst, destined to become push-outs . . . [S]uch an incident forces their peers to live with the violence of their erasure from the school community, perhaps affecting their attitude toward school permanently."[37] And for students who have consistently negative academic experiences, being required to leave school may feel like being rewarded with an "officially sanctioned school holiday."[38]

Worse still, the racial, ethnic, and gender disproportionality in school suspensions has been widely documented.[39] Therefore, whatever arguments we may be able to muster regarding the value of suspensions will all fail when compared to the practice's liabilities. Suspensions inconvenience working families, expose students to considerable unsupervised time, force students to miss entire days of academic instruction, create "troublemaker" labels that more often reinforce rather than reverse negative behaviors, and separate adolescents from the primary relationships and environments that offer the most support and growth during the day. And in many schools, the majority of suspensions tend to be given by a small cluster of teachers. In these cases, asking who is doing the disciplining may be just as important as asking who is being disciplined. When we analyze the racial and ethnic nuances of school discipline like this, we may find that the individuals needing the most support in learning how to behave properly are the *adults* in schools rather than the kids.

All told, banishment as retribution for wrongdoing rarely works. Luckily, alternatives to suspensions are myriad. Restorative-justice approaches (see chapter 11), community service, counseling, mentoring, behavioral contracts, skills-based and academic remediation mini-classes delivered during "in-school suspension," and eliminating "defiance" as a category for suspension—these approaches and many more demonstrate how stakeholders have resisted the status quo and invented ingenious substitutes. Simply typing "alternatives to school suspension" in an Internet search engine will yield scores of articles, Web sites, organizations, and other resources that will be helpful to anyone interested in replacing suspensions with more-productive institutional responses.[40] Educators, parents, community leaders, and students concerned about the racial and ethnic patterns in exclusionary disciplinary procedures are often those most responsible for leading the charge against suspensions in schools and districts. Seeing firsthand the effects that exclusion can have on marginalized populations, these individuals can help push schools to realize a crucial insight: the best alternative to suspending students may be to *suspend our assumptions* about what constitutes bad behavior and good responses to it.

Critically Examining School Discipline Policies and Outcomes

Researchers Pamela Fenning and Jennifer Rose suggest a four-step process schools should undertake "to create more proactive and fair discipline policies and practices for all":

> (a) Review of discipline data to determine what infractions result in suspension (e.g., whether minor nonviolent offenses result in suspension) and if certain groups are overrepresented in the most exclusionary discipline consequences, (b) the creation of a collaborative discipline team to create proactive discipline consequences that are fair to all, (c) the provision of schoolwide professional development to help promote cultural [responsiveness], particularly around issues of classroom management and teacher-to-student interchanges, and

(d) the development of more proactive school discipline policies for all students, based on models of positive behavior support.[41]

Given the disproportionality, misunderstanding, and discrimination noted in this chapter, Fenning and Rose's recommendations are worth considering if not adopting. But the composition of the discipline team is as crucial as the activities it undertakes. Because the inequities in in school exclusionary discipline can be partly attributed to mainstream expectations of what constitutes appropriate behavior, and because those expectations are largely constructed and communicated by educators who may have little experience in recognizing forms of oppression enacted through "commonsense" messages and practices, the members of whatever discipline team is formed must represent the diversity in the larger school community. The people at the table need to be able to advocate for those least served by the status quo. Fenning and Rose therefore recommend expanding the usual assortment of teachers, counselors, and administrators to include "mental health professionals, general and special educators, related service staff (e.g., security guards, office personnel), those living in the community, parents, and the students themselves."[42] A team like this may need sensitivity training so that it can rise above the very patterns of racial and ethnic exclusion it has been tasked to examine. Overall, these approaches offer clear pathways for educators and their collaborators to create discipline policies and procedures that are more proactive, more inclusive, less punitive, and less discriminatory.

PART IV

UNDERSTANDING RESISTANCE PEDAGOGICALLY

Back Off!

Damon's pathway to school most mornings is a tough one. Today is no different. Because his bus stop is the last one before school, the bus is always full when he steps aboard. And because of recent neighborhood rivalries, Damon has to fend off possible fights just to get a seat.

"What are you lookin' at?" says one student as Damon approaches his seat.

"Don't even think about it," says another.

After Damon throws a menacing look at a freshman girl sitting alone with her iPod, she moves over so he can sit down. The bus starts moving again, and he rides silently to school.

When the bus arrives, Damon's stomach is as tight as his fists. He steps off and wades through the crowds to get to his locker, talking loudly and using profanity with some of his peers, slapping and playfully squaring off against others, and staring down or averting his eyes when he sees a few he's doing his best to avoid. All the while, Damon is just hoping he can make it to class without having to confront a rival or duck a punch. Stopping at his locker, he surveys the hallway, waiting for the best time to make his move to class with the least amount of drama.

By the time he gets to his first-period English class, his mind is racing. He's scared, tired, stressed, and distracted, but doesn't want to be tardy and make things worse, so he hustles through the classroom door just before the bell. Bringing back the menacing look he used on the bus, Damon scans the room, again looking for a seat. He needs a desk that will put him near his friends so they're pleased, but not too close to what his mom calls his "trouble-buddies" that he gets distracted. And he definitely needs to sit far away from that kid who doesn't like him.

The teacher, Ms. Crocker, sees Damon shuffling slowly after the bell has rung and says to him, "Let's go, Damon. Take a seat so we can get started."

Damon finds an open desk, right next to one of his longtime, but distracting friends.

Eager to get the class focused and started, Ms. Crocker asks students to take out their homework. "Everyone please turn and face the front," she says.

Just then, Damon realizes he has left his book and homework in his locker. He tells his friend this, and some giggling ensues, along with a few playful insults they're used to trading when they hang out at home.

Ms. Crocker notices the interaction and says firmly, "Damon, I need your eyes up front and that homework out. Now, please."

Still holding the stress of his morning and wishing he had a few more minutes to relax with his friends before jumping right into academics, Damon sucks his teeth and turns around, again with that look he has already used twice this morning.

Ms. Crocker sees that Damon has no homework, no book, and is "giving attitude," so she walks toward him. "Damon, where's your worksheet and novel?" she asks.

Knowing his friends (and enemies) are watching but also knowing he doesn't want to start his day with a referral, Damon tries to switch his tone from how he talks with his friends to how he knows Ms. Crocker expects him to talk to her. In that split second, as he calculates what to say and how to say it, the stress gets the best of him. Damon looks Ms. Crocker in the eye and says, "Why don't you back off for a minute. It's in my locker. Chill!"

Surprised by, if not afraid of, his response, Ms. Crocker escalates. "Watch your language, Damon," she says. "See me after class."

With no novel to reference, his completed worksheet sitting in his locker, and a mixture of fear, rage, and disappointment in his gut, Damon slumps in his chair as his friends (and enemies) look on, laughing.

CHAPTER 11

"How Was I Supposed to Know?"
Misreading Students' Relational Needs

THE PRECEDING CHAPTERS have prepared us to avoid traps in logic that offer easy explanations but end up creating difficult problems, problems that typically leave us with few solutions beyond simply blaming students. For example, we have explored the liabilities of meritocratic claims, the dangers of performance-based orientations, the perils of praise, the myth of "oppositional cultures," the misplaced fear of indignation, and the problems with understanding classroom power as a zero-sum game. We have investigated the harm in avoiding conflict, the hazards of suppressing imagination, the threats posed by self-handicapping behaviors, the classism and racism of some of our assumptions, and the oppression built in to many of our "commonsense" responses. We have also analyzed a host of approaches, programs, and practices that directly reduce the propensity for students to resist or that capitalize on the positive outcomes that can emerge from students' opposition. Maybe we avoided these analyses before because we were trained to think about them using other explanations. Perhaps we haven't had time to analyze these issues sufficiently, given the demands of our work. Or maybe we just weren't motivated to investigate these matters because it didn't occur to us that we could do anything about them.

But now we know that our thinking, words, actions, practices, and policies—our pedagogy—sometimes make student resistance a foregone conclusion. The hard work left to do is to disentangle ourselves from interpretations and approaches that pollute our relationships with students and make them want to work against more than with us. This chapter is designed to do just that, to shift thinking so that better pedagogical practices will follow.

The Importance of Personal Connections

In their graduate preparation programs and during their induction into the profession, many teachers, administrators, coaches, and counselors are taught to be "objective." They are urged to distance themselves from their students, to create respect and maintain discipline by remaining emotionally detached and procedurally consistent. Some of these educators are told to "Show 'em who's boss" or "Never let 'em see you sweat" or "Don't smile until after Thanksgiving." These maxims apparently explain the necessity of curbing personal connections so that interpersonal relationships don't cloud professional judgment or complicate decision-making. The logic goes something like this: to be objective, the professional must remain unbiased; bias comes from the closeness of relationships; as a result, closeness must be avoided.

The trouble is, these forms of objective composure are precisely why so many students resist us. Students want enthusiasm and connection, but we often give them dispassionate distance. Students want to relate and emote, but we try to stay removed and indifferent. And to guard against relational transgressions we issue threats (detention!), withhold rewards (no candy for you!), or mobilize their fear of ostracism (suspension!). Essentially, to get students to do what we want, we make them feel either bad or afraid, which is a recipe for dependence, resentment, and outrage. These methods encourage youth to believe that adults will support them only if they are compliant and predictable. This, in turn, broadcasts a form of conditional acceptance that produces insecurities and generates resistance. (And as we have seen in previous chapters, anything we do in school that stimulates insecurities will typically reduce achievement.) Consequently, if we want our students to be educated more than manipulated, convinced more than coerced, and even indignant more than indifferent, we have to approach our work in classrooms and schools with a relational orientation.

You've Got to Connect to Correct

Educational philosopher Gert Biesta describes the importance of our connection with students: "Education is located not in the activities of the teacher, nor in the activities of the learner, but in the interaction between the two. Education, in other words, takes place in the gap between the teacher and the learner. If this is the location of education, if this is where education literally 'takes place,' then a theory of education should be a theory about the interaction between the teacher and the student. A theory of education is, in other words, a theory about the educational relationship."[1]

Indeed, the cognitive, affective, and social aspects of learning all convene in the teacher-student relationship. Though we forget it and may even be urged to ignore it, students' academic achievement is as much an outcome of relational health as it is the result of pedagogical technique. Our own experiences likely confirm this. The classes whose content we most enjoyed and in which we received the best marks were probably taught by the teachers with whom we felt the most connected. Sure, there are some students whose life circumstances make them more or less immune to the quality of their relationship with educators (e.g., those who go for the A regardless of how well they connect with their teachers, counselors, and administrators). But for every student like that, there are scores of others who won't do a thing for a teacher until the relationship is beneficial. For them, "you've got to connect to correct." This is why relationship and resistance are intertwined.

Agency with Connection (Not Separation)

A common misperception about adolescence is that it is a time of separation from adults. The adolescent's need to differentiate and to become a separate individual from primary caretakers, which is typically accompanied by a movement toward greater autonomy and independence, is often interpreted as a desire to sever connections with elders. As youth stay out more and come home less, and as allegiance to the peer group sometimes trumps deference to the family, parents and guardians may believe that their teens are cutting off relational ties. But this belief probably overstates the situation. Assuming home relationships are relatively fulfilling and healthy, it is more accurate to say that adolescents are *renegotiating* the terms of the relationship more than severing it. In short, they're not asking for agency *over* connection; they're asking for agency *and* connection.

Adolescents want the same agency-connection combination at school too. Unfortunately, research indicates that as students make the transition from elementary to middle school and from middle to high school, there is a steady increase in teacher-student conflict and a decrease in teacher-student closeness.[2] These changes may arise because secondary learning environments are often incompatible with the developmental needs of adolescents. The rigid bell schedules, rapid shuffling from teacher to teacher, and fragmented subject areas common in middle and high schools can make it difficult for educators to follow students' interests or make time to connect with youth more personally. Studies have shown how the cooperative and caring culture of elementary school stands in stark contrast to the more academically oriented and competitive climate often evident at the secondary level even though, developmentally speaking, adolescents require on-going, responsive, and close relationships with adults throughout the teen years. The relationally challenged learning environments found in many of our secondary schools may be further degraded by test-driven accountability mandates that accentuate the teacher-centered, content-driven pedagogies. These didactic environments can sometimes supersede opportunities for relationship formation, interpersonal learning, and social development—activities that we know are just as important at the secondary level as they are in elementary school.[3]

Scholars have observed that positive relationships with educators are particularly important during adolescence because youth are developing an identity and looking for adult models outside the family group to affirm it. Developmental psychologist Erik Erikson theorized that adolescent identity development actually begins as imitation and identification. Adolescents watch us and connect with us because we (sometimes) represent attributes they want to reproduce in themselves. Youth are therefore highly invested in relationships with trusted adults because those relationships offer occasions to confirm (or refute) their experiments in self-representation.[4]

But the adolescent's concurrent need for agency can introduce conflict between youth and those who are responsible for defining the boundaries of permissible activity and expression. Negotiations regarding control, privacy, obligations, rights, language use, behavioral expectations, and health and safety can become contentious as adolescents test the limits of their environment. When students' desire for autonomy leads them to the edges of what is allowed in their relationships with adults, youth may walk right through the boundaries we set to protect them (or at least the boundaries we believe are designed to provide such protection). If those crossed boundaries ignite educators' disciplinary reactions more than they mobilize efforts to understand and connect, then adolescents may feel forced to choose between autonomy and relatedness—an unhealthy choice to have to make. As we have seen, youth need both autonomy and relatedness to feel confident, secure, and motivated to learn. When agency and connection are out of balance, the inevitable resistance that surfaces is a sign not that the relationship is over but that it needs renegotiation and reinvention. A good first step is to establish trust.

Trust: Earning It, Not Expecting It

In many ways, trust is where agency and relation merge. Trust occurs when individuals attempt to identify the intentions of someone else and then decide whether that person is worth the risk of interpersonal engagement. The process of trusting involves research, assessment, and, if the other person's actions merit it, the willingness to be vulnerable to another person's actions.[5] In other words, trust is an observation paired with a decision that results in a relation.

The student's decision to trust the teacher (or the counselor, school psychologist, social worker, or administrator) is typically carried out in a compulsory setting. Students don't usually get to pick to whose class they are assigned or with which counselor they will work. This is why their decision whether to trust their educators is so momentous—it's often the only aspect of the relationship that is under their control. "You can put me in this teacher's classroom," they may think, "but I get to decide whether to trust that person or not."

Many of us proceed in our relationships with students as if trust has been given and deserved. We believe that because of our academic degrees, institutional position, years of experience, social rank, good intentions, and so forth, students ought to trust us from the moment the bell rings on the first day of school. But students often reject the presumption of trust, and they resist attempts to connect until we teachers have proven our legitimacy and trustworthiness. Research suggests that the decision to learn from a teacher and to engage in teacher-directed activity in the classroom typically comes *after* trust has been established, not before.[6] This observation is particularly true for students from marginalized backgrounds who may arrive at school justifiably leery of educators' intentions and suspicious of educators' capacity to understand and appropriately respond to students' unique talents and needs.

These observations underscore that academic achievement is rooted in relational dynamics. We must show youth that we are capable of mutual, reciprocal, volitional connections while using a relational pace that is neither too quick nor too slow.[7] If students are satisfied they won't be mistreated or misunderstood, then and only then will they become receptive to the new knowledge, advice, evaluations, and disciplinary interventions we provide, and only after that point will students demonstrate a willingness to share personal issues or take the risk to try something new in front of their peers. Students need to know, basically, that we "got their backs." In this way, trust is earned.

How can we reduce forms of resistance that arise from student distrust? How do we earn adolescent students' confidence? Educational researcher Kate Phillippo investigated questions like these in her study of marginalized students' relationships with teachers in urban high schools.[8] She found that students routinely examined teacher behaviors to determine whether a particular teacher merited trust. More specifically, students looked to see whether teacher behaviors demonstrated four characteristics: regard, respect, integrity, and competence.

Regard was evident when teachers gave caring responses to students' needs and demonstrated a willingness to extend themselves beyond required duties. Teachers who engaged students during passing periods or at nonacademic, school-related events or who provided direct academic support outside regular classwide instruction communicated to students that a relationship with the teacher was viable because the students could see that the teacher cared enough to go the extra mile. Students who observed these behaviors in their teachers felt "well regarded." On the flip side, teachers who demonstrated a lack of regard by arriving late to class, returning papers long after they were submitted, or expressing zero interest in students' personal well-being or academic success undermined students' willingness to trust them.[9]

Phillippo found that *respect* was also critical to students' decisions to trust. Students typically expect to be helped and guided toward success and are even open to being shown where they are making a mistake—provided they are treated as unique people with nuance and agency, not as representations of whatever stereotype the teacher may possess. In addition, the students in Phillippo's study reported that they experienced a lack of respect when teachers intruded too quickly or too deeply into their personal lives. Though the youth expressed a consistent desire to connect with their teachers, the students also expressed a need for privacy. They expected the teachers to understand the difference between functioning as a school official and trying to act like a friend or family member. These findings suggest that trust depends on specific types of respectful connection that recognize the functional limits of school-based roles and the necessity not to intrude.

The net result is that students want to be known by their educators and to feel meaningfully connected to them. But a tension remains. Students also don't want to be *too* close. This reticence to be too friendly with teachers or to move at a relational pace too fast for students' comfort may stem from a street culture that prohibits "snitching" to someone understood as a government official. Given at least a century's worth of disproportional adjudication of people of color, widespread racial profiling, deportation threats, and countless stories of police misconduct in interactions with minoritized populations, it is not uncommon for youth to take a cautious stance on relationships with educators. The caution stems from some students' belief that they shouldn't disclose anything personal or important to prying government officials—including educators—just as they shouldn't tell the police anything that might incriminate themselves or their family or friends.

Like police, educators are sometimes viewed as operatives in a state disciplinary apparatus whose agendas are considered suspect. This orientation may be exacerbated by some students' immigration status. Undocumented students (or those with undocumented family members) may rightfully fear closer relationships with teachers because of the possibility that conversations about home and family could disclose various relatives' immigration status. The students might fear that sharing such knowledge could result in deportation or arrest. Though academic pressure to achieve is typically experienced as a sign that the teacher believes in the student's capabilities, relational pressure can feel like a governmental investigation.

For students to trust their teachers, *integrity* also needs to be part of the dynamic. The participants in Phillippo's study identified the importance of teachers' visible adherence to a moral code that is expressed either through a commitment to fairness or through dependable actions that support and celebrate rather than denigrate and damage students' identities. Other studies have found that students tend to trust teachers who can reliably respond to classroom situations with a sense of justice, who remain consistent but not robotic in their disciplinary interactions, and who recognize students' need to save face and feel smart without being a pushover.[10]

Likewise, students will tend to trust teachers who prove they are instructionally *competent*. Phillippo found that the teachers who were organized and well prepared and possessed strong communication skills tended to be trusted more than those who didn't have these skills. Being good at what we do draws students in and makes them trust our leadership.

Taken together, these four qualities—regard, respect, integrity, and competence—suggest a pattern of shrewd and strategic observations that students use to evaluate teachers' behaviors and choose whom they will trust. Educators' efforts to prove their worthiness and cultivate real relationships without prying will undoubtedly increase students' willingness to engage and reduce the propensity to resist.

Misunderstanding Tough Fronts

The quality of the teacher-student relationship can have a profound influence on students' behavioral and academic outcomes, especially for students who are marginalized by assimilative or subtractive forms of schooling. Those who arrive with abundant racial, ethnic, linguistic, and class privileges are typically less vulnerable to the quality of their relationships with educators because these students enter school predisposed to accept its goals, its preferred styles of interaction, and its cultural assumptions. Students who conform to the mainstream receive affirmations of their worth with regularity and tend to "go along to get along" because the wind is at their back. Marginalized students, on the other hand, often face a sociocultural headwind. Having to push against consistent messages that confirm their "otherness," racially, ethnically, and socioeconomically disadvantaged students may be weary of normative approaches that make them feel both unwelcome and leery of teachers' capacity to understand them. These students are more susceptible to the quality of their relationships with teachers and may react with more resistance when those relationships are not optimal.

Whether student resistance leads to escalation or mitigation can often depend on how well teachers and students connect, communicate, and understand one another. Surveying the research on this matter, a group of educational psychologists led by Duane Thomas observe that a determining factor in the quality of teacher-student relationships is "teachers' personal views of their students": "Teachers with negative perceptions of the behaviors of their students adversely affect the degree of support they offer in classrooms, create an ambience that fosters more strained teacher–student relationships, and may increase student conduct problems."[11] When students pick up on these perceptions and the way they themselves are hailed in their interactions with teachers (see chapter 2), they may develop an awareness that they are always punishable, forever at risk of getting in trouble simply by being who they are.[12] When this happens, a student's hailed identity may displace self-perceptions that they are always available for intellectual challenge and academic success. Put simply, the student's feeling of "I'm punishable" can trump the feeling of "I'm a good student." Students who know that they are being labeled as "trouble" will therefore be inclined to enter relationships with teachers already politically unsettled, emotionally on edge, and ready to resist.

In her book, *Tough Fronts: The Impact of Street Culture on Schooling*, sociologist Janelle Dance illuminates a common set of teacher-student misunderstandings that can warp relationships, lead to unnecessary disciplinary escalation, and threaten academic achievement. She examines the production and reception of typically urban and, in this case, African American styles of dress, behavior, and language. In so doing, she highlights the different social and psychological requirements students face as they navigate between the streets and school (her observations are, of course, useful for populations beyond African Americans). The "tough fronts" she identifies are the hip-hop clothing styles, "aggressive" gestures, "irreverent" dialects, and threats of violence (which may or may not be actual) that are most closely associated with "the streets." Dance shows how these "gangsterlike" mannerisms reflect students' stylistic expressions and strategic choices far more than they signal actual gang affiliation. The problem she reveals is not that students adopt these expressions but that these behaviors are chronically misunderstood by educators.

To underscore this point, Dance describes three types of students who present tough fronts at school: the "hard," the "hard-core wannabe," and the "hard enough." Hard students represent a very small minority of typical middle and high school populations. These adolescents are actually involved in the illegal activities and violence typically associated with gangs. Hard students are very street-savvy, may have committed criminal acts, and are often truant. And when they do attend school, they are prone to resist their educators, disrupt classrooms, get in fights, and act abusively toward school officials. Hard students are caught up in a system that is largely beyond their control and have adopted gang-based codes of conduct to secure resources and protect themselves. It is worth underscoring that very few students who attend school match this profile.

According to Dance, "for the vast majority of students, assuming a hard or gangsterlike posture was merely a means to impress their peers . . . [S]triking a 'hard' pose was a means of conveying (or reiterating) the sentiment that 'I do not want to be a gangster, but I can behave like one if the situation demands.'"[13] Dance's second group, the hard-core wannabes, personify this approach. These youth typically do not live in the same neighborhoods as the hard students and thus have not learned firsthand the gestures and interactional styles required of a true gangsta lifestyle. But to garner respect from their peers, hard-core wannabes adopt a tough front that will ensure their inclusion even though their "hard" expressions are more a fashion statement than an indicator of an actual desire to be in a gang. The wannabe is essentially wearing a facade, "putting on a gangsterlike poker face and praying no one will call his bluff."[14] Hard-core wannabes may present the same mannerisms and postures as their hard peers but will try to avoid violence if for no other reason than they lack actual experience in "fronting" and fighting. However, the hard-core wannabe remains highly susceptible to peer influence when it comes to resistant behaviors in school and can be goaded into disruptive or violent situations when they are unable to prevent them.

Dance's third group is the "hard enough." These kids avoid the violence and posturing but may still don the same clothing and linguistic styles that distinguish their wannabe and hard-core friends. They live in the same neighborhoods and use the same mannerisms as their hard-core peers. Hard-enough students will defend themselves if needed but largely prefer to use tough fronts to stay under the radar and out of trouble. Looking and acting like they do is a way to broadcast affiliation with a subculture and signal membership with a peer group. But their behavior and appearance are precisely *not* a symbol of their affiliation with a gang; they are a means to survive the streets.

They may look and sound the same as their hard and hard-core wannabe friends, but hard-enough kids are simply trying to get through their day in a way that preserves their coolness and provides the fewest chances of violence. Hard-enough students still view school as the proper and probable means by which they will join the American mainstream, but they face daily dilemmas in how to balance what is required by school with what is demanded in the street. Hard-enough students are the ones who are likely to bring their homework to class somewhat regularly, but keep it folded up in their pocket rather than stored in an organized binder in their backpack, and they might not submit it unless the teacher provides surreptitious conduits for its delivery. These students' intention to be successful in school may be strongly felt and consistently supported at home but must be kept somewhat on the down-low to preserve their relationships with friends who may present a more resistant front while at school.

Contrary to what some students' swagger may suggest, the vast majority of students do not want to live a gangsta lifestyle. However, they may crave the attention and respect that gangster-like postures and mannerisms afford—even if that attention comes at the expense of their teachers' disapproval and even when students' hard expressions result in increased surveillance, discipline, and exclusion in school. The tough fronts that hard-core wannabe and hard-enough students present to allow them to travel safely to and from school can be difficult to simply switch off when they enter the classroom. And the stresses of figuring out which way to behave in one classroom versus the next (to make this teacher happy versus that teacher) are compounded by the diverse behavioral requirements at the neighborhood bus stop, in school hallways, at the cafeteria, and in locker rooms. Each situation is a complex social arena that demands a constantly varying fusion of school-appropriate behaviors and tough fronts. Navigating those spaces deftly is a challenge even for the most socially savvy students.

Unfortunately, Dance's research suggests that teachers who are capable of acknowledging these navigational challenges are rare. If teachers repeatedly misread hard-enough and hard-core wannabe students' behaviors, then the tough fronts that were an asset on the streets can suddenly turn into a liability in the classroom. This inversion occurs not because hard postures and mannerisms fail to keep the student safe and accepted but because educators fail to understand the nuances in such behaviors and how innocuous they typically are. The teachers in Dance's study far too often misinterpreted student fronts as threats even though such behaviors were often designed to *defuse* situations rather than escalate them (much like missile defense systems at international borders are there to preempt an enemy from ever launching a strike). Dance observes few teachers engaging students in a way that demonstrates an understanding of the streets. Teachers and other school-based professionals expected students to handle conflicts and offenses in the classroom in ways that were dramatically different from what the students had learned in their neighborhoods. This expectation persisted even though the students might not have shared the need for this differentiation or might have lacked the skills to switch things up when circumstances required it. Rather than teach those differences and allow some transition time as students switched from one set of behaviors to another, the teachers tended to respond with judgments, reprimands, referrals, and suspensions.

The students in Dance's study routinely complained that most of their teachers saw no differences between the hard, the hard-core wannabe, and the hard-enough kids and therefore treated them the same. Lumped together as a monolithic group, all three groups of students were presumed to be disinvested in school, prone to violence, and resistant toward, if not disruptive of, classroom learning activities. This blanket assumption ignored the subtle but considerable differences between the three groups of students and alienated those who were trying to succeed in school. Observing this, Dance concludes that "becoming hard" is not a process restricted to the streets but is actually facilitated by how students are received at school. Because they were misunderstood, alienated, and frequently punished, their connections to teachers were strained and their motivation to achieve in school was reduced. Desiring experiences where they could feel strong, competent, autonomous, and connected, tough-fronting students who were chronically misunderstood by educators were essentially provoked to resist school and to prioritize the streets over academics.

Unsympathetic teachers consistently alienate students who present tough fronts by responding with exclusionary discipline (referrals, detentions, suspensions) and academic threats ("You're going to fail this class!"). Such actions only confirm some students' suspicions that teachers are clueless and the school neither understands nor cares about them. More effective teachers, on the other hand, understand the code of the streets and the performances it requires. They don't sweat it when a student is unable to immediately shed those fronts when he or she walks through the classroom door. Dance's work therefore demonstrates the importance of learning to read student resistance as an expression of the larger ecologies from which youth emerge and giving students the benefit of the doubt when their behaviors don't conform to mainstream expectations. Her research shows that teacher misunderstanding may be more than just an error in interpretation; for many hard students, it can function as an act of provocation.

Misconstruing Anger

Anger is not a threat. It is an emotion. Apathy, disengagement, indifference, cruelty, violence, neglect—these are threats. But we are often afraid of anger and deem it a hazard because dominant constructions of "polite conversation" don't include it, and because we have been trained by our culture to avoid it so that we can seek and sustain an anger-free happiness. When we confront anger, we have to deal with the possibility that something is not going well, that we may be implicated in some sort of dysfunction or injustice. That's not fun for us, so we tend to steer away from situations in which anger may arise. But anger tells us valuable information, and people who are angry—students in particular—often have very good reasons for feeling that way. Anger, therefore, is a sort of relational thermometer, measuring the heat that may be rising or falling in the connection. To punish anger would be like smashing the thermometer because it's hotter outside than we wish it were. It's far better to preserve the thermometer and deal with the heat.

When we approach anger as a threat, we basically tell students that their emotional response is the problem. This ignores the messages that their anger may be trying to convey. Social psychologist Carol Tavris frames anger as "a political matter as [much] as a biological one. The decision to get angry has powerful consequences . . . [A]nger is ultimately an emphatic message. *Pay attention to me. I don't like what you are doing. Restore my pride. You're in my way . . . Give me justice.*"[15] We should consider ourselves lucky to be trusted with a student's anger. After all, we sometimes say we're lucky when students trust us enough to disclose their sadness, despair, or disappointment, but we rarely feel that way when they trust us with their rage—a double standard of which many students are acutely aware. But when students do trust us with their anger, we can very quickly squander that connection by attempting to control their expression. "Okay, okay," we say. "Lower your voice." "Take it easy." When we treat the anger and not the cause, we lose the opportunity to respond as an ally and instead position ourselves as an adversary. We effectively make the situation worse.

To move beyond an anger-as-threat response, we need do two things. First, we must recognize that the real threats are not the expressions of anger or even the feelings connected to it, but are instead the contexts, forces, and actions that *caused* the anger in the first place. Like so much of what we need to do in understanding and engaging student resistance in school, the key here is to analyze circumstances and antecedents, not just the behavior itself.

Writer, educator, and activist Michael Newman describes the "the energizing ecstasy of rage" that can take on a life of its own in both productive and destructive ways depending on how anger is engaged and channeled: "To make such experiences constructive, educators must help people manage this encounter between emotion and intellect. They can help people explore the causes of their anger, review the judgments upon which they have constructed their anger, and choose the level and kind of anger which will serve their rebelliousness. This process will be a delicate one in which educators seek to release and at the same time focus the passion and creativity of a potentially wayward emotion."[16]

We therefore might say to the angry student, "Tell me why you are upset right now. I want to know what happened that made you feel this way." Or we might ask, "What are you feeling, and what I can do to help?" Responses like these communicate care, empathy, interest, and a willingness to make changes, all core messages indicative of healthy relationships.

Second, we need to work harder to see the nuances in students' expressions of anger. When we misconstrue frustration, dismay, exasperation, exhaustion, despair, fear, stress, resentment, and pain as simple anger, we communicate to students that they are being neither seen nor heard accurately. While these emotions may all look alike when the student refuses to comply or appears to shut down, they are very different emotional states that require very different approaches. Misconstruing these feelings can frustrate rather than ameliorate students' negative emotions. When we find out precisely what the student is experiencing and we simultaneously bracket our own apprehensions about anger, we can help reveal underlying emotional distinctions that greatly matter in the student's decision making. This sort of touchy-feely stuff isn't a reprehensible side effect of the job but, in many ways, *is the work* of an effective educator.

Misreading Black and Brown "Aggression"

In chapter 2 we revealed how hailing students can constrain their agency and identity development and can lead to resistant behaviors in school. In chapter 7, we explored how student indignation can be misinterpreted and how it can play a positive role in efforts to achieve equity in the classroom. Chapter 8 analyzed how low-income students are sometimes misunderstood and how their resistance in school is often a response to that misunderstanding. In chapter 9, we examined racism, ethnic discrimination, and problematic theories of opposition and how they can cause some educators to erroneously conflate students' developmental and political processes with a rejection of education. And in this chapter, we have looked at how students' tough fronts can be chronically misunderstood by educators to the detriment of students' achievement motivation and willingness to cooperate. In each of these cases, student resistance is misconstrued, often be-cause of racist and classist assumptions about what constitutes proper behavior. One subtext in these analyses is that anger is an inappropriate emotion in school and that anger from Black, Brown, or low-income students is particularly danger-ous. This too is largely a misunderstanding.

If we combine these insights about anger with those about tough fronts, we end up having to confront the way anger and aggression are sometimes treated differently, in light of a student's race or gender in our schools. Researchers in-vestigating racial and gender disproportionality in school discipline have revealed how our misinterpretations of certain expressions can provoke the very forms of student resistance we may seek to avoid. For example, studies have yielded the following conclusions:

- "[The] cultural discontinuity between black families and the institution-alized structure of schools, which value cultural norms and standards of 'mainstream' white middle-class society, results in school personnel plac-ing greater emphasis on black children's behavior."[17]
- "Many teachers, especially those of European-American background, may be unfamiliar and even uncomfortable with the more active and physical style of communication that characterizes African-American adolescents. The impassioned and emotive manner popular among young African-Americans may be interpreted as combative or argumentative by unfamiliar listeners . . . Teachers who are prone to accepting stereotypes of adolescent African-American males as threatening or dangerous may over-react to relatively minor threats to authority, especially if their anxiety is paired with a misunderstanding of cultural norms of social interaction."[18]
- "White teachers perceived African American male students with move-ment styles and cultural expressions illustrative of aspects of popular Black culture (e.g., stroll walk, neighborhood jargon) to be higher in aggression, lower in academic achievement, and more in need of special education services. Irrespective of the race of the teacher, culturally relevant move-ment and language styles are often misinterpreted by teachers as aggressive and disrespectful."[19]
- "School personnel [tend to] view the dress and behavior of black males as recalcitrant and oppositional and exert strict control over them . . . [and] culturally based assumptions about black males lead them to face constant regulation of their dress, behavior, and speech."[20]

- "[Black and Latino students] are considered dangerous and therefore face constant surveillance and greater discipline for behavioral infractions."[21]
- "These responses may inadvertently communicate to African American students that their cultural style is not valued. Racial stereotypes of wrongdoing and consequent maltreatment by teachers have been associated with high levels of tension between African American male adolescents and their teachers in urban secondary schools as well as their strategic, yet maladaptive, use of aggression."[22]

These findings and many more suggest that educators' tendency to misread Black and Brown boys' behaviors can create what Russel Skiba and his colleagues call a "cycle of miscommunication and confrontation" that provokes continuous resistance and aggression in ethnically and racially minoritized students.[23] Echoing this observation, Thomas and his co-researchers note that in "a tragic set of reciprocal reactions," certain forms of aggression and resistance "can reinforce stereotypic images of young African American [and Latino] males, lower teacher expectations of their academic abilities and behavioral functioning, and prompt disciplinary referrals and special education recommendations."[24] In fact, researchers have drawn connections between teachers' perceptions of student anger and aggression and subsequent increases in coercive strategies that attempt to control or quash such expressions or remove the student altogether.[25] Thus, students may be "in trouble" or "at risk" more because they are targets than because anything they are doing is essentially wrong.

When we communicate to African American and Latino students that their culturally derived (not culturally deprived) and peer responsive (not peer pressured) manners of behaving are not valued, we provoke their disappointment, dissatisfaction, withdrawal, anger, and resistance. Their anger, to put it bluntly, is our fault. A seemingly harmless request for students to "watch your language" or simply "relax" when they are demonstrating these emotions sends the message that we expect them to be hypervigilant about their speech, behavior, and appearance and to curtail any expressions that don't fit mainstream norms. Such an approach forces marginalized students to devote cognitive and emotional resources toward assimilation, which means they have less to allocate toward academics. Whether intentional or not, messages like these create an unjust context for learning—a context that advantages some while it disadvantages others. To be specific, Black and Brown students are expected to suppress their authentic selves at the same time that White students arbitrarily earn the "normal" label.

This disparity is a recipe for White entitlement, and for resentment, resistance, and rage in everyone else.

When students of color get angry at us because of these injustices and we respond by asking them to "tone it down," we are suppressing both their expression and their emotion. Such suppression is not good for any learner and is particularly bad for those who enter school already marginalized by virtue of their race, ethnicity, culture, linguistic heritage, immigration status, class, sexuality, gender expression, or disability. Predictably, the suppression of anger is associated with several negative outcomes, including emotional distress, low self-esteem, behavioral overactivity, and poor social relationships.[26] Though it is our incapacity to welcome and draw upon students' cultural assets that provokes their anger, we further degrade our relationship with students when we label their resistance as the problem and compel them to turn their feelings inward. In this way, our misreading of Black and Brown students' "aggression" may contribute to the inequitable outcomes in achievement and discipline that are so prevalent in education.

Misjudging Dangerous Dignity

Individuals with suppressed emotions will typically seek outlets to express them, but White normativity in schools leads many youth of color to act with what researcher and activist K. Wayne Yang calls "dangerous dignity." Dangerous dignity is a position of self-respect that students take up in response to the exclusion, humiliation, and degradation they experience in school. Quick to anger and ready to resist, students expressing dangerous dignity are capable of pushing back against dominance and racist misunderstandings, but because of emotional suppression their reactions are often more cathartic than liberating. Their behavior may indeed threaten the efficiency of the classroom and the quiet of the hallways, but because of Black and Brown students' heightened visibility and many educators' fears about these youth, the only real danger their actions pose is to the students' own academic careers. When dangerous dignity is feared and punished, youth will be more likely to resist their educators and choose paths out of school if only because nonschool arenas offer more opportunities for self-determination and respect. To be clear, dangerous dignity is not an essential quality of Black and Brown youth, but is instead a form of provoked resistance contingent upon chronic marginalizing circumstances that are largely directed by educators.

The racial and ethnic components of dangerous dignities are often layered with gender too. Black and Brown males' occasional tendency to display bravado or macho attitudes can be read, in part, as a type of dangerous dignity that attempts to compensate for the disrespect and rejection they experience at school. Whatever we call it—"hypermasculinity," "cool poses," "tough fronts," or "machismo"—the swagger of male students of color is often presented as the epitome of villainous behavior in movies and television. Unless they are critiqued and replaced, those simplistic and skewed depictions can obscure the fact that dangerous dignities are a way to broadcast a psychological adjustment that preserves the integrity and worth of the self amid cultural cues that frequently malign it. Dangerous dignities are a way to exclaim "I'm large and in charge" to compensate for being made to feel small and controlled. Student resistance in the form of insubordination and disruption may be purposefully designed to communicate to others and to the self that "this environment will not define me," that "the way I am seen here is not the way I am understood among my friends and in my family," and that "if this place tells me I am considered 'other' here, then it will get an 'other' response from me." This is not to say that the individual student will reject the value of learning or the utility of education writ large. Rather, the student's bravado functions as a critique and provides a set of dispositions that protect against the othering experiences that come with being habitually marginalized and made to feel persistently unwelcome. In essence, students have been provoked, and they are provoking back, but with style.

Chronic humiliation, disrespect, and exclusion inevitably produce rage. When the presumed danger of that rage is amplified because of students' race or gender, sociocultural norms can place already-minoritized students at further disadvantage, simply because their emotions are read as more dangerous than those of more "normal" students. That there is a clear possibility Black and Brown students' resistant behaviors will further marginalize them in institutions in which compliance is valued more than critique is an indication of how insidious these patterns can be if left unaddressed, uninterrogated, and unchanged.

Misinterpreting Student Messages

Male students of color are by no means the only ones whose expressions and behaviors are misunderstood in school. The costs of those misunderstandings may be greater for these students than for others, but the experience of being misunderstood can provoke resistance in *all* students, regardless of identity or background.

After nearly two decades of mentoring, supervising, researching, and teaching classroom management and adolescent development courses, I have assembled a list of common misinterpretations I have observed among educators and students (table 11.1). Though the items in the table mostly pertain to teachers, it is likely

TABLE 11.1   The interpretive gap: Educator and student differences often revealed in disciplinary interactions

Educators' point of view	Students' point of view
Learning comes before relationship.	Relationship comes before learning.
(Mis)behavior results from a lack of control.	I (mis)behave because I'm powerless.
(Mis)behavior causes a lack of learning.	Lack of learning causes (mis)behavior.
(Mis)behavior gets you the attention you don't want.	(Mis)behavior often gets me the attention I do want.
Students come to school to learn.	I come to school to learn and socialize.
Relationships should not displace work.	Work should not displace relationships.
Unilateral power is a response to student resistance.	Resistance is a response to unilateral power.
The students are tired.	I'm bored.
Schoolwork and homework are for assessing and expanding learning.	Schoolwork and homework are for pleasing my teacher, getting points, and avoiding failure.
Some students have no ability to stay focused.	Some teachers have no ability to teach me things that are interesting or relevant to my life.
Being a young teacher makes it hard to establish authority.	It's often easier to connect with young(er) teachers because they tend to be more familiar with youth culture.
If I don't trust you, I can't give you agency.	If you don't give me agency, I can't trust you.
The meaning I make of our interaction is ours.	The meaning you make of our interaction is yours.
Care = the expression of concern and the efforts to help.	Care = knowing me and my needs, protecting me, giving me options, guiding me, and pushing me to do my best.

Students want neither structure nor accountability.	I want structure and expect accountability, especially when there is reciprocity.
I want to know what my students think.	Teachers may want to hear what I think, but they won't let what I say change what they do.
Students are disrespectful and rude.	Teachers are disrespectful and rude.
Students often can't "do school" because of their (deficient) backgrounds.	Teachers often can't teach me, because of their (privileged) backgrounds.
Students need to learn to accept responsibility for their actions.	Teachers need to learn to accept responsibility for their actions.
If you can't listen, you can't learn.	If you can't listen, you can't teach.
When a teacher fails, it's the students who pay.	When a student fails, the teacher still gets paid.
Students think everything is about race.	I use racialized language to see if teachers are capable or willing to talk about it—I'm testing them.
Students take advantage of you if you try to be their friend.	I won't work for teachers I can't relate to socially, but they shouldn't pry or try to be too chummy too soon.
I won't connect with you if you won't learn.	I won't learn from you if you won't connect with me.
I mean well; therefore, my actions and interpretations must be right.	There is no benefit of the doubt. The only thing that matters is what you do. And your intentions don't mean squat when you're wrong.
Students don't understand what's really happening in this school or classroom.	Teachers don't understand what's really happening in this school or classroom.

that administrators, counselors, school psychologists, and social workers will also recognize these interpretive gaps. When these gaps are allowed to persist and possibly to widen through neglect or ignorance, I have observed that students tend to respond with increasing (mis)behavior and withdrawal. In short, interpretive gaps provoke student (and educator) resistance.

When we repeatedly misinterpret student (mis)behavior in the ways suggested by table 11.1, we risk making students feel unheard, unknown, and misunderstood and thereby inciting their resistance. And if their resistance includes behaviors like withdrawing from relationships with us or purposely underperforming in school, these interpretive gaps can very quickly become achievement gaps. Therefore, simply knowing our students, how they think, what they feel, and how they envision an ideal learning community is a very effective way of preventing their resistance.

Promising Practices: Reading and Restoring Relationships with Students Who Resist

Relatively new to the United States but with a much longer history in Britain, Australia, and New Zealand, one approach holds incredible potential to radically shift how we engage youth resistance and (mis)behavior. It's called restorative justice. Inspired by the work of the Truth and Reconciliation Commission led by Archbishop Desmond Tutu in South Africa after the end of apartheid, restorative justice seeks to end the cycle of transgression-retribution-reprisal that characterizes so much of Western-style "accountability." For centuries, schools have used punitive if not retributive models to address student misconduct. They have resorted to paddling (still legal in nineteen U.S. states), detentions, suspensions, and expulsions, ostensibly to "teach the student a lesson."[27] Current punitive measures include humiliating students by having them wear prison jumpsuits when they violate the dress code, stigmatizing repeatedly truant students by forcing them to wear GPS devices on their ankles, and staffing schools with full-time police officers who have the authority to arrest students for offenses that may have only incurred trips to the office in decades past.[28] Though less extreme, many teachers use retributive, relational measures such as embarrassment, shame, and fear to coerce students into compliance.

Unfortunately, the data on the effectiveness of these methods is rarely encouraging.[29] Punishments tend to intensify rather than mitigate problems between the individual student and the school. In the eyes of students, punishments often

transform caregiving and supportive educators into enemy enforcers, pain inflic-
tors, or the organizers of social ostracism. This directly undermines if not destroys
the very relationships students most require if they are to understand the impact
of their actions and formulate different responses in the future. The results include more resistance, eroded trust, increased indignation and withdrawal, and
greater risk of push-out.

Restorative-justice methods, on the other hand, seek to shift this dynamic
not by using *power over* people but by using *relationships with* them.[30] When a
student commits some sort of violation of community norms (e.g., abusive language, bullying, theft, violence), the community rallies around both the victims
and the transgressor who committed the injurious act. People care for victims by
immediately focusing attention on the impact of the event and providing specific
structured opportunities for them to express their needs and feelings as well as
suggest ways the situation might be ameliorated. The transgressors are then confronted both by authorities and by peers in a way that brings the transgressors
deeper into the community rather than banishes them from it. Conflict, in this
case, is used as a catalyst to deepen community and interpersonal connections.
Practically, the transgressor is often asked to sit and listen to the victims' experiences of the event and their feelings about it while experienced facilitators (typically educators who have been trained in restorative methods) work with both
sides to make sure the students are listening to one another, thinking about the
effects of their words and actions, and staying focused on the goal of restoration
instead of retribution.

The point in these interactions is not to legalistically clarify what did or did
not happen. Far too many disciplinary discussions get bogged down in the investigation phase, while determinations of the impact of the event or full analyses
of the pros and cons of various responses are often shortchanged. The goal of
restorative justice is instead to describe the *impact* of the event so that victims feel
heard and the transgressor is held relationally accountable. The point is also not
to shame transgressors or to make them feel bad, but to confront them with the
consequences of their actions and appeal to their desire to belong, to be trusted,
to have good relationships, and to move with purpose toward behaviors that are
productive rather than destructive.

Restorative justice works, often beautifully, for students and educators alike.
It helps to keep relationships with students from devolving, holds all actors accountable, reduces or eliminates the factors that lead to push-out, and demolishes
the school-to-prison pipeline. But implementation is no cakewalk. Brenda Morrison and Dorothy Vaandering write that "the need to shift attention from a focus

on an individual's aberrant behavior within institutions to addressing relational needs within communities [is often not] an easy shift for institutions entrenched in policies and practices that value control and compliance over relational ecologies that nurture growth and well-being." The authors describe how educators readily embrace the restorative-justice "premise that relationship is more important than the behavioral incident," but the authors also warn that many educators remain "reluctant to let go of the option to punish and exclude."[31]

The immense benefits of restorative justice cannot be realized if we and our schools retain punitive, exclusionary disciplinary procedures and prohibit students from taking active roles in the creation and maintenance of healthy learning communities. Our reluctance to let go of those old, counterproductive, and often discriminatory practices can be tough to overcome, given how deeply rooted behaviorist and normative assumptions are within society and education. Therefore, part of any movement toward restorative justice should include the questioning of those base assumptions along with an analysis of their effects. If we do the hard, collaborative, exploratory, professional work of examining the causes and effects of resistance and (mis)behavior in school, and if we recalibrate our practices according to restorative rather than retributive objectives, powerfully liberating learning communities can emerge.

Panther Points

Ms. Kasdan is pleased with how well her honors biology students have done on the recent high-stakes test, but in the last few weeks, she has found it hard to keep them focused. It is springtime, and while she has heard many other faculty explain that students' increasingly ornery behaviors are the result of hormones, she isn't sure that is the reason. Ms. Kasdan thinks it is more likely the posttest academic doldrums she has seen every May since the state's testing program began.

Now eight months into a nine-month school year, her kids have become progressively more reluctant to start projects in class, less willing to apply their best effort, and overly social whenever it is time for classwork. Back in February and March, they mostly applied themselves rather dutifully when it came to prepping for the big test, but now they are acting as if the rest of the year were a wash. This disappoints Ms. Kasdan because some of her favorite units to teach occur in the late spring, when the students have developed the sophistication to really apply content in some exciting ways.

But the students aren't having it. After Ms. Kasdan faces several consecutive days of off-task behaviors, lots of requests for bathroom breaks and pencil sharpening, and what feels like a hundred reminders to put their cell phones away, she stops the class and reprimands the kids for their poor work ethic and what seems like their inadequate desire to learn.

To these admonishments, one of her star students actually replies, "This stuff isn't gonna be on the test 'cause the test is already done, so what's the point? Can't we just chill?"

When several colleagues express the same frustrations at a faculty meeting, the principal and his leadership team respond with an email asking all faculty to ramp up their use of Panther Points." These are the tickets faculty and staff are supposed to give out whenever kids exhibit good behaviors or demonstrate strong academic effort.

Though Panther Points are designed to motivate students to want to do good things, Ms. Kasdan is growing disillusioned with their impact. Lately, she feels as if everything she asks her kids to do is immediately followed by them asking, "Will I get any Panther Points for that?" Increasingly, her students act as if nothing is worth doing unless they immediately get a reward they can cash in for candy, pizza, or a chance to win a trip to a nearby amusement park.

So midway through her loud and boisterous fifth-period class, she decides to try something else. She has been trying to get her kids to complete a worksheet for over twenty minutes, circulating among the desks to prod students to get to work, hovering over them so they'd simmer down, announcing, "Hang in there while we get through this chapter," and monitoring their progress to make sure that they will do their best. But it isn't working. They are talking, passing notes, sharing answers, and generally looking for any opportunity to giggle about something—anything other than biology.

That's when she offers this: "I'll give a Panther Point to everyone who finishes their worksheet by the end of the period. And if you keep the noise level to a dull roar once you're done, I won't assign any homework tonight. You can have a little chill time as long as it's quiet. Do we have a deal?"

CHAPTER 12

"Is It My Fault?"

How We Provoke Resistance in the Classroom

TO MEET THE challenges presented by resistance, some educators rely on classroom management techniques to coerce students into obedience, while others use mainstream labels, narratives, and metaphors to frame youth resistance as "bad" so that students will discipline themselves. This chapter won't do either of those things. Instead, it begins with an assertion that may be difficult to accept: *it's largely our fault that students resist in school.* Of course we are not responsible for the countless social, political, and economic factors outside our control that negatively influence student achievement and behavior, and of course we cannot be expected to overcome problems within the community, family, and student. But at school, between the bells, we are the ones most accountable for what happens. We're the adults. We're the professionals. And we don't always get it right.

In this chapter, I outline some of the things we do to provoke student resistance. There is a risk in my doing this. Working as an educator in the twenty-first century too often entails dodging and deflecting a barrage of insults, complaints, and accusations from those who think (to my mind, erroneously) that our schools are mediocre and the professionals in them are lost. Far too much of what passes for conversations about education in the United States ends up blaming educators for everything wrong in schools, while elected representatives, appointed leaders, district officials, businesses, and the media seem to forever escape culpability. This chapter should not be read as another voice in that chorus. The point here is not to show our guilt in various malpractices, but to reveal how much power we have to change the conditions that tend to incite student opposition in the first place.

Resisting Being Manipulated

Students can be pretty manipulative. They use compliments, subterfuge, favors, gifts, and threats to compel their teachers, counselors, and administrators to bend to their will. Most educators are aware of this possibility and therefore approach some student behaviors with suspicion. Encountering a behavior whose agenda may not be clear, we sometimes ask ourselves, "Okay, what's this student trying to get me to do right now? And should I allow it?" But if we're honest with ourselves, we educators do a lot of manipulating too. We too use compliments, subterfuge, favors, deceit, gifts, and threats to compel students to bend to *our* will. And just like us, the students ask themselves questions when they encounter our manipulations: "What's this person trying to get me to do right now? Should I comply?" In both cases, the student's need for agency can collide with our need for control. This begs an important question: What rationalizations are we willing to accept for prioritizing *our* control over *their* agency? Or, as Henry Giroux puts it, how do we distinguish between "socially necessary authority and authoritarianism"?[1]

Most schools in the United States tend to answer that question using behaviorist assumptions. First developed by the psychologist B. F. Skinner, behaviorism was understood to be *the* "scientific control of human behavior" for much of the last half of the twentieth century. As an all-encompassing explanation of what drives human activity, behaviorism may not be as popular or as accepted in the scientific community as it once was, but it still exerts a strong influence on how we theorize rewards, punishments, reinforcements, conditioning, and the control of others' behaviors. Unfortunately, this influence produces some of our worst manipulations and our most authoritarian responses to student (mis)behavior.

The theory of behaviorism casts humans mainly as selfish, competitive, satisfaction-seeking organisms that respond to external stimuli primarily to maximize pleasure and minimize pain. Though other models and societies view humans as naturally cooperative, community-oriented, compassionate, and even selfless (see the material on restorative justice in chapter 11), U.S. schools largely adopted behaviorism because its assumptions fit well with a rapidly industrializing, capitalist economy and a culture of individualism and competition that was dominant through most of the twentieth century (and remains dominant today).

The theory stipulates that good behaviors can be successfully reinforced through rewards, and bad behaviors can be successfully curtailed either through the withholding of rewards or through the administration of some sort of pain. In Skinner's laboratory, animals were given food rewards or horrific electrical shock punishments to condition them to do what the researcher wanted. Likewise, schools were instructed to deliver rewards through praise, candy, gold stars, grades, free time, and parties and to deliver pain through raps on the knuckles with rulers, paddling, humiliation (remember the dunce cap?), exclusionary discipline, and the removal of privileges like recess or going to the prom. Today's positive behavioral interventions and supports programs are strongly influenced by behaviorist assumptions.[2]

The chief problem with behaviorist theory is not that we tend to react positively to rewards and negatively to punishments (we do). The problem is that humans respond to a far wider range of influences than just rewards and punishments. These influences cannot and should not be captured by a simplistic theory like behaviorism, which depends on a fairly bleak view of human nature and a series of laboratory experiments involving the torture of animals. Critics of behaviorism point out that humans are capable of altruism, sacrifice, empathy, justice, and love not solely because those responses get us what we want but because they make the world better for others besides ourselves. And we are equally capable of horrible things even when we know punishment or other personally negative outcomes are a foregone conclusion. Humans are not simple input-output machines, as behaviorism makes us seem.

So then why do we organize so many of our actions in schools—especially those devoted to manipulating and controlling student resistance—using behaviorist tenets? We do it because rewards and punishments often work in the short term. Student does X (mis)behavior, we respond with Y manipulation, and X (mis)behavior ceases. We think that's all the evidence we need to conclude that our approach is working. But just as it would make little sense to judge a movie by looking at only a few frames, it makes little sense to assess the merits of behaviorism only by looking at what a student does right after a reward or punishment is given. Far more important are the effects of those behaviorist interventions over time. And what we see when we take that view is not so good.

By and large, when you take away the punisher or the rewarder and you remove the possibility that rewards or punishments will be associated with a particular action, the motivation for the individual to act in a "conditioned" manner will tend to diminish. In other words, you can only manipulate the behavior as long as the manipulations and the manipulators are present. Take the student out of that context and out of those relationships, and the favored and disfavored activities will commence on the individual's terms, not the manipulator's. If we want lifelong learners, empathetic neighbors, and self-sacrificing citizens, behaviorism is not the method we should choose.

But the predictable decline of behaviorist manipulations aren't even the worst part. When a student is trained to respond to extrinsic and coercive incentives, to comply with an all-powerful authority at the expense of the child's own autonomy, and to have to think constantly about how to game the system to get gold stars and avoid paddling, the relationship the child forms with superiors is characterized by dependence, mistrust, resentment, and resistance. Forget to give students lollipops when they do something good but instead give candy to others for doing something only marginally good, and those forgotten students will no longer want to do the good thing anymore. Punish students unfairly or neglect to catch them when they do something they shouldn't have, and they won't look for ways to be good the next time. They will, however, seek to defy the system of manipulation that is attempting to control them.

We educators often try to plug these holes in the system even when our plugs make the system more authoritarian. For example, we might install an extensive apparatus of surveillance (video cameras, walkie-talkies, school security, metal detectors) to monitor behavior in all spaces at all times. We might cultivate informants (recruiting "snitches" or using divide-and-conquer techniques) and devise greater and greater threats (assertive-discipline approaches, zero-tolerance policies, police stationed in schools) to catch our students (mis)behaving and punish them for perceived wrongdoing. Practices like these typically alienate students who are already complying and force those who aren't to seek growth opportunities in arenas that are less coercive. Again, this is a recipe for provocation and push-out.

In addition, if student (mis)behaviors that supposedly warrant a punishment stem from lagging social-emotional skills or from environments that are themselves harming the child, no punishment is going to help. Students aren't learning any new skills when they are being punished; nor are they being given the kinds of support they need to change their circumstances. Punitive responses in these cases are just harm added to harm. Not surprisingly, then, student resentment and resistance often rise after punishments are given, and more punishment corresponds with less achievement (even though punishments are often rationalized as if they will improve students' relationships with their educators and with schools).[3] And if educators adopt the language of "consequences" in an attempt to distance themselves from behaviorist practices but persist in causing unrelated pain or suffering whenever a transgression has occurred (e.g., "Because of your graffiti, you will not be allowed to go to the prom"), it's still behaviorist manipulation.

Yes, behaviorist manipulations do often achieve short-term goals and may sometimes coerce students not to do things we want them to avoid. But at what cost? Though students rarely feel as if they have been taught a lesson when they are punished, many pedagogical messages are still being conveyed through behaviorist coercion. For example, punished students rightfully reach the following conclusions:

- Educators can cause pain more than they inspire growth.
- Educators will only support students when they comply but will seek to hurt students when they don't.
- Agency is only experienced outside of relationships with educators.
- The way to get others to do what you want is to manipulate them with threats and gifts.
- Getting things from others is more important than giving.
- Behavioral mistakes will result in retribution provided by those who claim to be your caregivers.
- Nothing is worth doing unless it comes with a reward (preferably an immediate one).
- Being watched and being threatened are proper ways for the state to engage its citizenry.
- Punishments are painful, and difficult tasks or projects can be painful; therefore, difficult tasks or projects should probably not be undertaken, because they feel like punishments—so a student should stick with the easy stuff and avoid anything demanding.

Students do sometimes ask for rewards—clamor for them, even—especially the students who are best positioned to receive the rewards. But in doing so, they are *not* clamoring for knowledge, challenge, compassion, restitution, growth, collaboration, and justice. They're being trained in a get-mine ethic in which selfishness, manipulation, and advantage become their own reward. By committing so much time, energy, and talent to carrots-and-stick systems, we overlook other commitments that may be far more academically inspiring if not life-sustaining. These are not the lessons we want our students to adopt. These are manipulations that provoke their resistance. We can do better.

The Student Handbook as Resistance Manual

At some point, we need rules. Rules keep us safe when we're driving on the road. They undergird contracts and property lines and keep three-year-olds out of the ballot box. Rules are the reason games are games. They serve a valuable purpose in any community, relationship, or activity. But educators can get carried away with rules, so much so that a learning community supposedly secured by its rules can end up feeling like a police state. Consequently, an overemphasis on rules can make educators feel safe and in control, but it may only provoke resistance in students.

Teachers, counselors, school psychologists, social workers, and administrators often seek to manage youth behavior with codes of conduct or standards of behavior that are typically assembled and presented in a student handbook. A handbook can make a lot of sense. It establishes a single source for behavioral expectations and sends clear community-wide messages about how a school will respond to disobedience. But there is a danger here, too. If the handbook's codification of rules and the institution's enforcement of them become more important than the rules' responsiveness to adolescent needs and cultural differences, schools may be foreclosing important opportunities for inquiries and adaptations that might otherwise promote the engagement and prosocial behavior of students.

Though student handbooks may have been generated through community outreach in the past, they can seem to be written in stone if no one is allowed to challenge them or if processes for revising them do not exist. Students, families, and community stakeholders need a say in which school rules are worth having and how they might best be enforced. Put more bluntly, dictated rules tend to provoke insubordination; community-generated standards and democratic processes for revising them, on the other hand, inspire cooperation.

In their analysis of school rules and disciplinary procedures, Brenda Morrison and Dorothy Vaandering observe that "traditional institutional practices can generate defiance, undermining an individual's capacity and willingness to cooperate":

> Within a formalized regulatory system of social control, the implicit belief is that clear rules and laws within the architecture of the system, backed up by clear and consistent sanctions, will elicit the desired behavior. The basic assumption is that students are rational actors, who will uniformly respond to codes of conduct and laws; yet, there is now clear evidence that traditional sanction-based rational actor models ignore the science of how individuals, groups, and society function. [What we need instead is] a pedagogy and praxis of engagement, development, and integrity at both individual and institutional levels.[4]

The "praxis" Morrison and Vaandering reference begins with the recognition that rules exist within a relational, developmental, ideological, and political ecology. They reflect a decision made by a person or group at a particular point in time, within a specific set of influences. But people, time, and circumstances change, and uniform agreement about a rule and its mode of enforcement is rare. When somebody said, "This will be the rule" and then codified it, dissent probably existed, whether it was acknowledged or not. People either inside the inner circle or outside it probably had experiences or desires that conflicted with the version voted on or mandated by the empowered. In this way, rule-making doesn't just constrain behaviors; it silences dissent.

If dissent is the lifeblood of a healthy democracy, then dissent is not something schools ought to be silencing. Suppress it, and you provoke resistance. Integrate it, and you invite critical thinking, collaboration, responsiveness, contribution, invention, and flexibility. But when the codification of rules is seen as an endpoint, allegedly resulting in quelled dissent and final documentation written in stone, dissenters will feel alienated from the process and the product. "Those may be *your* rules," they might say, "but they're not *mine*." This alienation can cause students to lose respect for the rules and for the rule enforcers. In this situation, even with crystal-clear descriptions and strong enforcement, rules will not build community. Educational philosopher Barbara Stengel puts it this way: "Rules cannot repair a quality of relation that does not exist."[5]

How might the way we reference school rules undermine the quality of our relationships with students? What might we do to provoke their resistance? Here are some possibilities:

- Whenever we say "Do as I say, not as I do" (as if being brazenly hypocritical adds to our credibility or trustworthiness)
- Whenever we respond to a student's rejection of a rule's legitimacy with a comment like "Rules are rules" (as if rules are not invented, rationalized, and enforced by people with the agency to do something different, if they cared to do so)
- Whenever we respond to a student's question about why a rule must be obeyed with a simple "Because I said so" (as if a raw power move that commands those of lower rank to obey for obedience's sake will ever accomplish anything other than resentment and resistance)
- Or worse, whenever we say to the student who complains that the rule or its enforcement is unfair, we respond, "Well, life is unfair" (read: "Welcome to adulthood, where constant confrontation with injustice demands a survival tactic of either cynicism or resignation")

Whenever we say and do these things, we are essentially telling adolescents that their experience is invalid, their critical skills are unwelcome, their resistance pointless. Again, responses like these seldom produce better relationships and more positive behaviors; they merely provoke opposition.

In addition, educators sometimes make rules that force youth to obey seemingly obvious behavioral standards as if those standards are clearly understood and accepted by everyone. They often aren't. For example, a commonly posted rule in middle and high school classrooms is "Use polite and appropriate language." What does that mean? According to whom? What criteria should we use when judging whether an action was polite or appropriate? You can't make a rule to obey a disputed concept unless you're also willing to admit that you're intentionally silencing dissent and alienating those who have different constructions of the term. The terms *polite* and *appropriate* refer to contested manners of behaving, especially in a multicultural society. To make a rule based on those terms without first working with a community to coestablish (and revisit, reform, and modify) their meaning and application is a perfect way of instituting culturally subtractive discipline and of guaranteeing resistance, particularly from marginalized students. Politeness can only be determined relationally, and appropriateness depends on culture. Think of it this way: "normal behavior" is most likely to be deemed polite and appropriate, whereas "different" behaviors are most likely to be labeled impolite and inappropriate. In dominant culture, who is most often labeled normal? And who is most likely to be understood as different? Questions like these remind us that if we're not careful, our rules will reinforce hierarchies of status. When educators admit this, they can begin cocreating rules *with* youth—rules that focus on sustaining community, dialogue, and justice, not just control.

To do this, educators need to view the establishment of a code of conduct not as an endpoint but as the beginning of a community-based process of negotiation and reinvention. Educational scholar and activist K. Wayne Yang recommends that "schools should not invest in a great discipline policy, but rather in a genuine discipline praxis." This praxis of discipline is the tricky but invaluable work of keeping alive the question "How are we to interact with one another here?" To start this process, Yang recommends two things. First, a school community engaged in discipline praxis should seek to develop educators, not to protect them from students. Because rules are frequently used to limit students' agency (often for reasons of safety, but sometimes oppressively), the goal in a discipline praxis is to prepare adults in schools to think critically, act with more cultural awareness, and pursue justice when using their power. Yang's second recommendation, that "discipline praxis must involve sustained, serious self-critique and reflection," is aligned with this objective.[6] Developing rules and articulating how they should be enforced (and by whom) can be a powerful exercise for educators, especially those who want (or need) to be more than controllers of people. And framing rule-making as a collaborative, iterative process makes the rule makers and rule enforcers more open, transparent, and willing to adjust—qualities that students typically relish in their educators.

Skeptics will rightly point out that we don't want such an iterative process when it comes to things like red lights at intersections. But a red light is not a community norm—it's a safety measure. By comparison, chemistry teachers absolutely should make the rule that everyone wears protective eyewear at all times in a lab. That rule should not be subject to negotiation, and there's no need to have a community discussion about it. Safety first. But just because necessary and (mostly) non-debatable safety measures exist does not mean that all rules are self-evident and culturally agnostic. Most rules require community deliberation. The question of which ones do and which ones don't is worth exploring in a learning community if for no other reason than to help clarify how rule makers and rule enforcers should use their authority to protect and promote "good" behaviors as opposed to dominate and control "bad" ones.

Provoking Mediocrity: Bargaining for Compliance

Responding to student resistance every day can be exhausting. Analyzing student behaviors, listening to their critiques, thinking about our own blind spots and assumptions, revising our methods, and deciding whether a certain (mis)behavior needs a strong hand or a good ear can take its toll on our energy levels and patience. Some days, it would be nice if we could just do our jobs and not have to deal with all this pushback. While this chapter has so far demonstrated that much student resistance really is our fault—that we provoke it—this section looks at the flip side. In other words, to accurately, effectively, and equitably engage student resistance in school, we sometimes need to realize how we relent.

Faced with resistance in the classroom, many teachers bargain with their students to garner greater compliance. Teachers will lower their academic expectations, inflate grades, give less work, and permit a range of low-level (mis)behavior if students will agree to obey more and resist less. This bargain benefits the short-term needs of the teacher by providing predictable calm, but it severely undercuts the students' long-term prospects by encouraging mediocre effort. These teachers' classrooms may be enjoyable, relaxed spaces where students like to hang out, but under the teachers' unstated or explicit permissiveness—their so-called style—and lack of academic rigor, students perform far below their potential. Some teachers who make such bargains may do so, as Yang points out, "in the name of creative exploration, or youth empowerment, or democratizing pedagogy, or some child-centered theory of learning," but the outcomes rarely if ever achieve anything close to these intentions.[7] To obscure these diminished outcomes, or possibly to try to compensate for them, the teacher may hang posters of inspirational anti-oppressive leaders or powerful quotes about learning, accomplishment, and social justice, or the teacher might assign readings about such subjects. Though the intent may be to signal the teacher's awareness of inequity or his or her presumed status as a "down" teacher, the incessant bargaining reveals these symbols to be little more than a facade.

The teacher may have multiple reasons for bargaining with students to lower the kids' resistance. He or she may fear chaos, want to be liked, lack skills in classroom management, worry about being perceived as oppressive in telling students what to do, or fundamentally doubt the academic capabilities of students. Regardless of the motivation, the teacher's establishment of an I-won't-mess-with-you-if-you-won't-mess-with-me ethic rarely proceeds through grand gestures. The bargaining is subtle, a game of inches. Consider some things bargaining teachers sometimes say:

- "Okay guys, if I can just get your attention so we can get through this, then I won't assign any homework tonight."
- "If everyone's quiet and on task during our library and computer lab days, we will have a pizza party on Friday and watch *Freedom Writers*."
- "Thirty percent of your grade is participation."
- "I accept late work anytime—just get it to me when you can."
- "I'll make you a deal, Johnny: if you stop disrupting my class, then I'll stop harassing you for your homework."

Some examples of practices that bargaining teachers often enact are:

- Seats are not assigned, because they're "too restricting and the students want to sit next to their friends."
- Privileges like being allowed to listen to one's iPod during silent sustained reading or while taking a test are granted liberally.
- Concessions like letting students text in class "as long as it doesn't interrupt learning" are granted to avoid conflict.
- Free time is amply awarded for "achievements" like finishing work early (as opposed to doing said work with exemplary effort and accomplishment).

In each of the preceding examples, the bargaining teacher typically rationalizes the reduction in academic demand by noting how the students were the ones who requested it. "I'm just giving them what they said they wanted," the teacher might say. Then later, when students underperform or fail, the teacher shames the students for choosing socializing or distractions over academics. This entire process is a setup.

Teachers who do this need help. Like the student who is underperforming because he doesn't want to try too hard only to fail, teachers who bargain with students to attain a "chill" classroom need to be pushed. They need to see the patterns described above and realize their complicity in them. They need critical colleagues who care enough about them and the students to have tough conversations about the severe liabilities with low-risk, low-return pedagogies. They need specific skills and targeted plans for how to change the culture of their classroom and eliminate the permissiveness in their "style." Basically, bargaining teachers need to see how their reactions to student resistance don't just allow mediocrity, but may actually provoke it.

The Seduction of Bad Ideas

When we misunderstand students, the lack of understanding can contribute a great deal to their decision to resist. It turns out, the same can happen when we misunderstand our own work. Education, like all other professions, is replete with bad ideas and lurking agendas that may not serve the purposes they seem to target. For example, the natural appeal of the images of "no child left behind" and everyone striving to "race to the top" in education are hard to resist both rhetorically and in terms of policy. The federal reauthorization of the Elementary and Secondary Education Act that gave rise to the No Child Left Behind (NCLB) and Race to the Top (RTTT) initiatives has radically shifted public school curricula, funding, assessment, and accountability since 2002, partly because the legislation relies on so many "commonsense" arguments.

Despite the seductive promises in the legislation's titles and programs and the grand rhetoric about how it will provide equity and excellence in K–12 education, problems with these reforms have been myriad.[8] As documented in countless publications, NCLB and RTTT have forced schools to devote inordinate amounts of time to test preparation and to allocate resources to the students whose scores will most likely improve (at the expense of those who struggle the most). As students shuffle from one test remediation program and intervention to the next, they are stigmatized as failures, pulled away from closer relationships with educators, and disallowed deeper engagements with curricula, all to focus solely on getting ready for the next standardized assessment. Tragically, while this may have helped some to race to the top, many have been left behind.

Under NCLB and RTTT, content areas not assessed in the standardized tests, such as social studies, art, music, and physical education, have seen their classes shortened as more time in the school day gets dedicated solely to the tested subjects. The notion of teaching as a profession has been systematically eroded as scripted curricula have become mandated, course content has become standardized, and pacing calendars now dictate the scope and sequence of a class more than teacher expertise and student interest. And because of massive lobbying efforts, the federal designation of what constitutes a highly qualified teacher now includes recruits from such corporate-sponsored programs as Teach For America, which prepares educators for the neediest classrooms by giving them only five weeks of training.

In the NCLB and RTTT accountability regime, when a school's yearly progress is insufficient, its funding can be reduced. This punishment further degrades a school's capacity to serve struggling populations of students. Because schools that are already under-resourced are the most likely to underperform on standardized tests, accountability measures like these effectively reward the privileged and punish the impoverished. The disparity can make some communities desperate for a change at the same time that more privileged communities increase their efforts to protect the status quo. Gert Biesta writes that "if, for example, schools are rewarded for high exam scores, they will increasingly try to attract only 'motivated' parents and 'able' children and will try to keep 'difficult students' out. Ultimately, this results in a situation where the primary question is no longer what schools can do for their students but what students can do for their school."[9]

These circumstances also create separate and highly unequal schools. Students, families, and educators in the underfunded schools sometimes find themselves immersed in glossy brochures, stirring multimedia advertisements, and compelling sales pitches from for-profit companies that claim they will better manage "underperforming" schools either by taking them over or by opening charters. As the collective commitment to a truly *public* education begins to wane, arguments for the privatization of public education soon take hold, and a balkanized, antidemocratic "this school for me, that school for you" system takes root.

What do these policies and programs have to do with student resistance? In short, neoliberal reforms like NCLB and RTTT constrain educators and students alike, forcing both to teach and learn within a normalizing, competitive, market-driven set of expectations. These expectations, and the "failing" labels and punishments they produce when compliance is perceived to be lacking, actually worsen many if not most of the resistance-inspiring practices this book has been exploring. For example, the accountability measures undertaken since 2002 have created performance-oriented cultures in schools; suppressed imagination and exploration in favor of information delivery and regurgitation; created incentives for cheating and dropout as a way of raising scores; prioritized extrinsic over intrinsic motivators; and reinforced the use of dominant rather than culturally responsive curricula. Furthermore, these accountability regimes constructed a powerful auditing apparatus that examines, classifies, ranks, and punishes students, educators, and schools for scores on tests that nearly everyone agrees fail to capture what communities most want their students to know and be able to do. And so, resistance is virtually guaranteed.

Measured, sorted, and remediated, students are provoked into resistance because they are being denied what they most desire—a more human connection and a more humane set of circumstances in which to learn. Students want to know and be known by their teachers. Students want to connect with their peers and with ideas. They want to negotiate what and how they learn and then ask questions and pursue interests that thrill and challenge them. When these desires are not met, student resistance rises. Because students are typically unprepared to criticize complex federal policies or abstract ideological agendas (and besides, with all the testing, who has time to teach that stuff?), they tend to resist the immediate and real-life people who are called upon to sustain the regime—their educators.

These educators, however, have been forced to acquiesce to normalizing practices so their school doesn't lose its ranking and funding. They have to approach student resistance as a threat to the students' and the school's future possibilities. Anything that may lower a test score is subjected to remediation or repression. Compliance and expediency soon trump critique and deliberation, even though the latter two practices are far more important to a healthy democracy than the former. As a result, student resistance is rarely understood as the outcome of a standardizing, normalizing, and homogenizing situation. Instead, one of two things happens: either the students themselves are blamed for their recalcitrance and failure, or educators' inability to impose sufficient discipline and maintain adequate standards is deemed the primary cause of school underperformance. Unfortunately, the real problem here is not student (or even educator) resistance but the context against which that resistance responds.

When the problem is successfully misidentified and its causes are suitably mistaken, the inevitable calls for stricter discipline, zero-tolerance policies, greater accountability (read: punishments), and a back-to-basics approach all become seductive "solutions." These solutions appeal to a public that has been told it should think of its school as a shopper thinks of a mall: as a product to be consumed, a resource to be acquired, an item to be compared with other items, a commodity that the market will evaluate and trade, a place where one should always ask, "What's in it for me?" Questions about collective well-being, justice, equity, diversity, purpose, and democracy are eclipsed. Competition, we are told, will force "bad" schools to improve. Innovations developed in less regulated charter schools, we are led to believe, will inspire traditional public schools to reform and recover (or those schools will be closed). Merit pay, they tell us, will motivate teachers to work harder and inspire greater achievement. And it's explained to us that giving parents vouchers or the ability to send their children to whatever school they choose, public or private, in the neighborhood or far outside of it, will force schools to make their programs more appealing to a wider range of students.

Though each of these contentions has been roundly questioned if not disproved in the last decade or so, these market-based reforms continue to seduce. Even those of us who are ready to resist the status quo and are hungry for something better can sometimes find the logic in these measures enticing or at least hard to debate. They seem to just make sense. The problem is, rather than listen to the insights and critiques of those with the greatest stake in the system's success (i.e., our students, their families, and the professional educators who serve them), and rather than align ourselves with those who have been least served by the system's triumphs and reforms (i.e., the students, particularly those who are marginalized because of who they are), we have deferred to powerful corporate and governmental interests to tell us what most needs fixing. In this context, resistance is more a solution than a problem.

Does this mean all of this is our fault? To the extent that we educators are forced to adhere to legislation and policies that constrain our work and our students, the answer is no, it's not our fault. But to the extent that we *accept* and *support* these agendas, the answer is most certainly yes. We work within a system that necessitates compromise, but at some point, we either will or will not let these things happen. We either participate in the pathologizing, punishing, and silencing of opposition in school so that the market can have its way, or we join the resistance. The current reform agenda that dominates most school-improvement efforts in this country has been and will continue to be neither a recipe for school enhancement nor a remedy for community appeasement. These so-called reforms are a provocation. Consequently, they will—and they should—generate more resistance.

Tracking and Resistance

Like the market-driven, neoliberal reforms described above, tracking too is a seductive "solution" that provokes student resistance. Nearly every school in the United States practices some form of tracking or ability grouping. The chief premise supporting this practice is that students will learn best and excel the most when they are put in homogenous groups so that instruction can be tailored to their particular needs. That premise rests on several assumptions we now know are wrong. First, students do not learn best when surrounded by learners who look, think, sound, and act like they do. Nor do they learn best when everyone around them is at the same skill level. Learners tend to learn the most and with the greatest efficiency when they are exposed to a wide range of peers, skill levels, cultures, and ways of thinking. The diversity of the learning environment—not its uniformity—is what most inspires the most growth. Second, the assumption that tailored instruction is only possible when students are homogenously grouped has nothing to do with how students best learn. This claim is a bait and switch. The real underlying agenda here is to make it easier for the educator.

The argument that we should track classes to better serve the students is disingenuous. Good teachers are forever differentiating their instruction and personalizing their approaches to make sure each student is achieving success. But as states and districts allow class sizes to grow bigger and bigger each year, the need for dependable and efficient means to educate ever-larger groups of students grows too. While segregating students by ability does nothing to help struggling learners, it does make the teacher's job easier. When a particular lesson can dependably and efficiently reach the majority of learners in the room, the teacher has less work to do to make sure struggling learners are ready to move on. Leaving aside for the moment whether or not the assessments we use to determine students' rankings are culturally biased or methodologically flawed (they are often both), we do know that all learners struggle on occasion. Academic learning and cognitive development rarely progress at a measured pace; they move in fits and starts, depending on the contexts and relationships that support it.[10] To divert struggling students into separate tracks based on some assessment that purports to capture their ability at a single moment in time essentially stigmatizes struggle even though struggle is a natural and desirable part of learning.

Ability grouping therefore labels some students as low expectancy and broadcasts to them—and to everyone else—that we have given up trying to teach them alongside other students who, at least at one point in time, were progressing more swiftly. This practice diminishes struggling learners' aspirations and motivations, which in turn leads to lower achievement, which in turn reinforces outsiders' perspectives that the low-track label actually describes (rather than delimits) students' potential. Tracking accomplishes this cyclical disadvantage at the same time that it legitimates social and economic advantages for those who were lucky enough not to struggle when the evaluation took place.

Confusing merit with advantage, tracking makes it look as though some students' high-expectancy label was earned (rather than merely an outcome of their privilege or an artifact of the dominant cultural capital they possess). Add to this the pervasiveness of White middle-class norms that distort what communities and schools (and tests and curricula) understand to be a good student, and it becomes clear that the tracks we create "to help the struggling learner" actually function as educational ruts, particularly for racially, ethnically, socioeconomically, and linguistically marginalized students. Is it any wonder the strongest resistance we see from students in school tends to come from those in the lower tracks?

Some will respond to these critiques by arguing for the value of remediation, claiming that the extra and more targeted instruction that struggling students supposedly receive in the lower tracks helps them to catch up so that they can eventually join their peers in the higher tracks. Responding to that assertion, researchers note how incredibly rare it is that students who have been diverted to lower classes ever "jump tracks." For every one of those exceptions we may be able to find, how many more students prove the rule? Numerous studies demonstrate that tracking students into different instructional groups produces unequal learning environments that typically widen achievement gaps rather than narrow them. Low-expectancy students receive less rigorous content, endure repetitive drill and practice routines, and accumulate isolated bits of information they are expected to absorb and replicate on reductive assessments. Higher-tracked classes, on the other hand, are more likely to be driven by inquiries, projects, essential questions, and explorations. Lower-tracked classes are more often taught by novice educators or those teaching outside their credential, whereas higher-tracked classes are reserved typically for experienced educators who have distinguished themselves as content or pedagogical experts and are therefore rewarded with the "good" kids.[11]

Because of pressures from families of high-expectancy students (and sometimes their teachers) not to "dumb down" the content in the upper-tracked classes just for the "slow kids," administrators and counselors often combine low-expectancy students with English language learners, those who qualify for special education services, and students identified as having anti-academic behaviors. These groups are combined sometimes with little or no additional support for the teacher, even though the practice directly contradicts the original argument for tracking (the supposed value of homogenous learning environments). Sometimes this grouping is intentional, and other times it may be accidental. For example, some students may only be grouped into one lower-track math class, but because of the way school schedules are built, the students in that single class then follow the same group of peers through the rest of their school day—and, probably, their school year. This situation creates a de facto system of schoolwide segregation even if it is not named as such.

As previous chapters have demonstrated, whenever we emphasize ability differences and label students as deficient or defective, we create learning environments that shut down risk taking, inhibit help seeking, decrease motivation, diminish future aspirations, threaten meaningful relationships with educators, increase avoidance behaviors, elevate self-handicapping, and promote push-out. Tracking creates these disadvantages. Accordingly, where there is tracking, there is injustice, and where there is injustice, there will be resistance.

Promising Practices: Curtailing Our Provocations

If the causes of student resistance are sometimes our fault, then we don't have to work very hard to figure out who is responsible for fixing things: it's us. When recognition of fault turns into levying of blame, however, folks tend to shut down and retreat. No one likes to be shamed for having caused a reprehensible outcome. But people generally do like to be credited with having solved a problem. So admitting fault is perhaps the best first step if it is immediately followed by a search for and enactment of solutions. Many solutions are suggested throughout the book, but here are a few that specifically target the provocations detailed in this chapter.

Employing Cooperative Grouping

The ability to plan and facilitate group activities is a highly developed skill. Many of the misunderstandings explained in this chapter are provoked by poorly constructed or badly managed group activities. In these problematic groups, students are being asked to work together across cultural, racial, class, and linguistic boundaries, in a setting in which their performance is being watched and will at some point be evaluated for a grade. The stakes are high even when the points in the gradebook may be small.

Too often, teachers who attempt cooperative activities in their classrooms will make understandable and perfectly forgivable mistakes that virtually guarantee underwhelming outcomes or outright failure. And sometimes, the mistakes can provoke student resistance, withdrawal, and even rage. Maybe roles were ill defined or not assigned at all (roles work because folks know what they need to do, how they can contribute, and how they need to rely on others). Or timing cues weren't provided or were too long or short (timing cues keep things moving and raise the level of concern so that students stay focused without getting stressed). Perhaps the task itself wasn't group-worthy (just because kids are put in groups doesn't make it a cooperative activity). At other times, maybe the students were allowed to pick their own groups (a recipe for tension, disappointment, hurt feelings, and ostracism if there ever was one). Or students might never have been shown or weren't given time to practice the social-emotional skills needed to successfully interact with peers in a task-oriented situation (just as we teach toddlers how to play in the sandbox, teens need instruction on how to share, negotiate, listen, respond, and collaborate).

In these circumstances, not only are students likely to resist, but the teacher may also incorrectly conclude that the kids can't handle group work because they're too immature. Or worse, the teacher may believe that students can't do cooperative activities because they just don't care about learning. But the truth is, highly skilled facilitators can get any group of kids to do pretty much anything. The success of the activity depends on the educator. If it goes well, it's because the teacher did things right. If it fails, it's the teacher's fault.

So, if we experience student resistance or (mis)behavior during group activities (or we know someone who does), we need to learn how to make those activities better before we blame our students for responding "inappropriately" to a context we set. We can ask a colleague who we know is good at cooperative grouping to observe us and provide suggestions. We can read books about effective techniques or go online and search for videos of successful approaches shared by skilled educators. We can contact classroom management instructors from nearby teacher education programs to ask for insights and recommendations. Whatever we do, we need to commit to our own development and learning and practice, practice, practice—just as we expect our students to do when they encounter difficulties.

Using Seating Charts

To address many of the problems identified in this chapter and throughout the book, I strongly recommend the following practice: use seating charts; assign seats; switch them around every quarter or so; and don't apologize for it. We're not dominating our students when we do this; we're helping them. Permitting students to sit anywhere may feel like we're supporting them, but for most students, the practice is experienced as a form of abandonment. There are bullies, cliques, subcultures, and divisions in our schools, and open seating allows the worst parts of those phenomena to flourish. To have to walk into a class each day and be forced to navigate racial, gender, class, linguistic, and sexual dynamics just to find a seat, and then deal with the distractions of neighborhood alliances, significant others, and popularity issues, can provoke students to (mis)behave. Giving them a dependable seat that's always there for them and *always theirs* provides predictability and safety amid the social demands of adolescence.

Too many teachers start the year allowing students to choose their own seats as a way of establishing the teacher's coolness. When students invariably oversocialize or get distracted by gossip or intergroup conflicts while they're supposed to be on task, those same teachers often blame the kids for not having the maturity or commitment to learning they are assumed to possess. And then seating charts are deployed as a punishment for their (mis)behavior. This is a setup.

Sure, some student will inevitably ask, "Can't I just sit next to my friends?" followed by that kid's friends saying, "Yeah, can we?" But ask the majority of the kids *not* at the top of the popularity contest or *not* in the privileged mainstream what they think about this idea (out of earshot from their dominating peers), and they will tell you "Please, just assign us seats." Keep in mind that those who publicly plead to sit next to their friends may be using that request to broadcast to the rest of the room that they have friends, that they deserve to have a classroom dedicated to their desires, that "others" can fend for themselves in figuring out where to sit, and that the classroom really only belongs to a privileged few.

No one wants to be the person who mistakenly takes the popular kid's seat and is reprimanded or mocked for doing so; who has to sit alone because no one will sit nearby; who has to move to a new school midyear and on the first day has to choose a seat among a room of scrutinizing strangers; or who comes to class last and has to awkwardly if not painfully locate some desk amid snickering peers. These situations provoke withdrawal, despair, and rage in many students, especially those who are socially marginalized. But we can stop this from happening. We can do this by thinking of the marginalized students first and then placing them where they will be protected and supported. On most days and in most circumstances, the popular and privileged kids will be just fine no matter where we seat them.

When we do assign seats, we should tell students why we're doing it. We can explain that we want them to learn to work with anyone and everyone in the room and that our job is to create with them a learning environment that facilitates productive interactivity. We should also explain that we reserve the right to relocate a few students here and there if for some reason the arrangement is not working—we're the adults in the room with the degree, the training, and the experience, so we get to make that call. And we can move people around to maximize heterogeneity, promote intercultural collaboration, prevent distraction, and guarantee exposure to multiple ways of thinking and acting. Basically, we use our seating charts to make the equitable and culturally responsive world we need, not to reinforce the hierarchies and oppressions we already have.

Partnering with School Psychologists, Social Workers, and Counselors

School psychologists, social workers, and counselors are experts in conceptualizing a broad array of factors that influence student decision making. These professionals are ideal partners to consult when we are trying to figure out what's at stake for a student who is demonstrating resistant behaviors at school. Though they are often stretched as thin as classroom teachers can be, with caseloads, meetings, paperwork, and such, they are an invaluable resource in our communities because they have been trained to see the environment around the person rather than him or her in isolation. Depending on their training and experience, these professionals know how to ask about and observe interpersonal, intrapersonal, political, cultural, and other issues that can interfere with students' ability to prioritize academics. Reaching out and asking them for help when a student's behavior confuses us is one of the best things we can do to help the student and help ourselves.

Taking a Stand Against Tracking and Neoliberal Reforms

As educators, many of us understand that our work doesn't stop at the end of the school day. Not only do we use our evenings and weekends to grade homework, place phone calls to parents, and make plans for the next day or the next week, but we also spend time advocating for our students, our profession, and our schools. We rave about how great our students are and defend them when folks use stereotypes about "kids these days" to dismiss or disparage youth. We share with friends and acquaintances the good things we do in our schools and the positive outcomes we produce. And we speak passionately about the value of public education and the need to protect it from those who would dismantle it. Our voices matter, and we make sure we're heard.

But as described in this chapter, our voices may need to get louder. Legislators, policy makers, and district officials have been seduced by some pretty bad ideas in the last few decades, ideas that have negatively impacted much of what we do in schools. To be an effective educator inside and outside school, we sometimes need to leverage our professional knowledge and social capital to inform the decision makers or resist them when necessary.

Luckily, educators have a long and impressive legacy of successful resistance on which to build. Communities across the nation have been well served by "loud," "uppity," and "impetuous" school-based professionals and activist researchers who refused to allow myopic policies or draconian budget cuts to undermine the promise of public education. For example, more and more attention is being paid to the profoundly negative impact that tracking has on students and communities, and research-informed activism along with community collaborations are making a positive difference. Powerful local and regional movements are afoot to eliminate the de facto segregation that occurs in ability-grouping regimes, with many schools moving to de-track their classes with terrific results.[12] And since the advent of NCLB and its strengthening in RTTT, countless teachers, administrators, school psychologists, counselors, social workers, and even ivory tower academics—with middle and high school students right alongside them—have made their voices heard about reductive and culturally biased standardized testing, counterproductive accountability measures, and dangerous market-driven agendas. Parents and teachers have demonstrated against overtesting, districts have opted out of state-mandated accountability systems, and students have walked out to protest budget cuts. Many organizations have been formed to raise awareness, organize, and convince legislators to reverse the direction of these problematic agendas. These actions too are making a difference.

If we are to adequately address the many ways we provoke student resistance and sometimes set students up for failure, we need to consider the interpersonal and classroom-based problems we sometimes create. But we need to go beyond these internal issues. To change things for the better, we need to also examine the institutional, societal, and policy-based problems that are created for us. Agreeing to comply with authorities' orders to institute policies and establish practices we know produce harm may be a salute, but it's not a solution. We need to change ourselves *and* the system. Luckily, none of us have to do this work alone. Our most resistant students and colleagues are already doing it. It's time we join them.

CHAPTER 13

Conclusion

Resistance Is Hope

The paradox of education is precisely this—that as one begins to become conscious one begins to examine the society in which he is being educated. The purpose of education, finally, is to create in a person the ability to look at the world for himself, to make his own decisions, to say to himself this is black or this is white, to decide for himself whether there is a God in heaven or not. To ask questions of the universe, and then learn to live with those questions, is the way he achieves his own identity. But no society is really anxious to have that kind of person around. What societies really, ideally, want is a citizenry which will simply obey the rules of society. If a society succeeds in this, that society is about to perish. The obligation of anyone who thinks of himself as responsible is to examine society and try to change it and to fight it—at no matter what risk. This is the only hope society has. This is the only way societies change.

—James Baldwin

Student Resistance Is Not Opposition to Learning

John Dewey once wrote, "Reality is what we choose not to question at the moment." To a significant extent, I have adopted this assertion in the preceding chapters. I have questioned or outright rejected various taken-for-granted realities about what student resistance represents, why it happens, and how educators should respond to it.

The theoretical approaches in part I helped cultivate a healthy suspicion about public education's capacity to function as a meritocracy and underscored the need for critique, deliberation, and resistance in the struggle for greater equity. Part II illuminated psychological and environmental factors that shape students' decisions to engage, apply effort, and comply—or do the opposite. These chapters helped us see the powerful undercurrents of motivation, cognition, and emotions that drive adolescent (mis)behavior in school. Part III's analysis of the political and sociocultural foundations of student resistance demonstrated how pervasive and problematic our misreading of student opposition can be. We saw how none of us is immune to the distortions that emerge from intercultural misunderstanding and systemic oppression. These chapters also showed how, if the distortions remain unaddressed, our relationships with youth provide ample justification for student resistance, particularly for marginalized youth. Finally, part IV looked at the pedagogical roots of student resistance. These chapters showed that many of our "commonsense" interpretations and techniques in schools are the very practices that provoke our students' opposition. The main takeaway there is that despite our noblest intentions, we may cause more student opposition than we alleviate.

Throughout these chapters, the goal has been to convince you, the reader, to consider the possibility that the unquestioned realities governing how we view student resistance are in fact due for some major revision. The need for that revision may be captured in this assertion: *all students—every last one—want to learn and grow but they will resist in school when the conditions of their learning and growing are less than optimal.*

If we accept this assertion as true and we also accept many of the findings and implications of the previous chapters, then we no longer need to invest our time and energy into locating what's supposedly wrong with our students. Rather, the Deweyan reality we need to question is the efficacy of our methods, the equity of our systems, and the conditions we establish in which we expect our students to learn. In short, once we change the way we think about resistance, we need to change the way we do our work.

Unfortunately, many will respond to the above assertion with statements like "You don't know my kids," or "I can name students who clearly don't care about school." Certainly, every school, classroom, and student is different, and no doubt some students have determined there is little point in applying themselves in school. But I stand by the observation that there is no such thing as a student who doesn't want to learn. Much of the research cited in this book reveals this deficit belief to be a fallacy, and a dangerous one at that. We can commit innumerable forms of pedagogical malpractice when we blame victims for reacting against their circumstances or when we fail to recognize that the context in which student resistance occurs is what ought to be resisted.

Though students may disrupt an activity or purposefully fail an academic assignment, this behavior is not evidence that they don't want to learn. It more likely suggests that students don't want to learn *this knowledge*, don't want to learn *in here*, or don't want to learn *from us*. When we ignore or dismiss these nuances, the only individuals who truly display an unwillingness to learn are those who refuse to see student resistance as a resource.

Student Resistance Is an Attempt to Alter the Terms of the Learning Environment

At some level, it's sort of amazing that we can get away with saying to students, "Sit still, be quiet, and comply," while we simultaneously claim that some of them have bad attitudes when they express displeasure with school or try to do something else in the classroom. Of course they want to be active rather than passive, to make decisions rather than take orders—good for them! Adolescents have enormous cognitive powers and equally potent emotional and social needs that will never be fully satisfied in overdetermined, control-oriented, punitive settings. For deep and long-lasting learning and growth to occur, some components of school need to be established on the students' terms. The learning environment needs to be *theirs*.

This doesn't mean an educator has license to abandon youth to their own devices and blame them when things go awry (that would be a setup), but an educator does have to learn to see student resistance for what it is: an attempt to negotiate the circumstances in which they are expected to learn. When we recognize student resistance as an exercise of agency, a struggle for ownership, a reaction against oppression, and an attempt at freedom, we can see how students' rebelliousness, recalcitrance, and insubordination are anything but character flaws. If the students are mature and brave enough to try to make the conditions of their learning better, then we need to be mature and brave enough to respect that and respond to it productively.

Student Resistance Is a Form of Engagement

Student resistance takes many forms, but perhaps the simplest and most direct way of characterizing the phenomenon is to call it engagement. When students attempt to participate in making something different, something better, they're engaging. Even when student (mis)behaviors are perceived by educators to be destructive or distracting, the kids' purpose may be to convey a complaint or suggest an improvement. That our adolescent students are young, can be impulsive, have underdeveloped interpersonal skills, and may speak in tones and with words derived from cultures or subcultures with which we are not very familiar does not mean their grievances or their disruptions aren't worth engaging. If the message the student is sending is "I need something different here," we need to heed it, regardless of the style of its delivery.

But there's a caveat. When student resistance is an attempt to make their relationships and learning contexts more responsive to their needs, and educators respond to such forms of resistance by suppressing, dismissing, or maligning those attempts, student resistance can very quickly morph into forms of withdrawal and destruction best understood as *dis*engagement. Withdrawal is often the student's attempt to avoid troubling circumstances, whereas acts of destruction (abusive language, put-downs, bullying, vandalism, fighting) may represent students' reprisals or preemptive strikes that were designed to counter hurtful or oppressive situations they may have been forced to endure. Though not acts of engagement per se, these oppositional deeds can clue us into the types of engagement the student may need. In general, students need to feel competent, connected, and autonomous for learning to be optimized, and when those experiences are lacking, they will look for ways to pull or push back.

Either way, students are taking an active (just not always productive) role in their education and in their learning community when they resist. It takes imagination for a student to say "I want something else" or to creatively subvert dominant behavioral norms, and it takes even greater imagination for many educators to meet the challenges of student resistance with patience, curiosity, and humor. But we need to see that opportunity and seize it. The benefits of doing so are clear. After all, resisting student resistance typically produces only more struggle between adults and adolescents, whereas engaging student engagement can produce greater understanding and collaboration between them.

Student Resistance Is a Symptom of a Problem, Not the Problem Itself

An effective solution can only come from an accurate read of the problem. Blindly and unreflectively throwing techniques or labels at something (even "commonsense" ones that supposedly everybody uses or nobody questions) without analyzing causal relationships and the full ecology in which all behavior is generated will rarely yield the results both students and educators need. We have to work smarter than that. The theoretical, psychological, and political analyses in this book have made it clear that we cannot ignore the potential for public schooling to reproduce if not worsen the many gaps between the advantaged and the disadvantaged. A significant proportion of our students' resistance can be traced to the tendency for schools to reproduce social hierarchies, and we are rarely innocent in the perpetuation of that tendency. When we pathologize resisters within a context of oppression we reinforce unearned advantage. Our students can tell when this is happening, and they're right to get mad when it does. And when we discipline marginalized students for objecting to or interrupting our practices, we teach them to expect inequity. The problem isn't the presence of those "others," nor is it their supposedly "inappropriate" or "rebellious" behavior. The problem is the othering process and the exclusionary assumptions that are allowed to persist. Resistance is the symptom of that problem, not the problem itself. Table 13.1 summarizes how this symptomatic shift can change the rhetoric about students and, ultimately, transform our schools.

If all behavior is an attempt to get our needs met, then resistance is also a symptom of unmet expectations. Anger, disruption, frustration, willful defiance—these behaviors and more may be compensations for the experience of being insufficiently challenged, socially rejected, or being named as abnormal or unwelcome. Resilience and survival often depend on resistance, particularly for the chronically marginalized. When hailed as deficient, deviant, or "other," students often resist not to exacerbate those perceptions or to escalate the situation but to cope in some way with the psychological and social damage experienced when they are labeled and excluded. In this way, resistance doesn't produce dysfunction—it attempts to guard against it.

Student Resistance Should Be Engaged

Because resistance is an expression of individual and collective agency, it will always reveal the limits of control. This is because all human systems, to a greater or lesser extent, depend on the assent of those who are supposed to obey. Legislatures depend on compliance with laws, superintendents depend on fidelity to their directives, principals depend on consistent observance of schoolwide norms, and teachers depend on student obedience to classroom rules and procedures. When assent is not forthcoming, the system is usually quick to discipline, but slow to ask why the resistance is occurring in the first place. But a commitment to *engaging* resistance, not just punishing it, can help slow the disciplinary response and open space, time, and relationships to the possibility that something might be gained by listening to opposition.

TABLE 13.1　Changing our minds

	Suppressing resistance	Engaging resistance
Assumption	Resistance is the problem.	Resistance is a *symptom* of the problem.
Rhetoric	· They have a bad attitude. · They don't want to learn. · They're rejecting the value of education. · We're trying to save them. · Our intentions are pure.	· What are they resisting? · Why are they resisting? · What's going on around the students such that resistance makes sense to them as a viable response? · What is the larger problem here?
Response	They don't deserve to be here.	What can we do to change this larger problem?
Outcomes and practices	· Severing relationship · Holding only kids accountable · Testing and sorting · Labeling and tracking · Bribing and threatening · Detentions, suspensions, expulsions · Removing support · Diverting resources to "those who want to learn" · Lowering expectations · Blaming kids and shaming families · Humiliation · Marginalization · Push-out · Prison pipeline · Underperforming schools	· Enhancing relationship · Holding everyone accountable · Questioning and listening · Integrating families as partners · Enacting cultural responsiveness · Prioritizing belonging and agency · Providing support · Dedicating resources to those who need the most help · Elevating expectations · Building on strengths · Assessing learning environments · Consulting research · Collaborating across differences · Increasing student voice · Transforming schools

Student Resistance Is Good for Educators

One theme carried throughout this book has been that resistance is often good for students. The same is true for educators. Nevertheless, the resources communicated in student resistance cannot be made available for pedagogical use unless we actually engage them. Detentions, referrals, and suspensions squander that resource. The best alternative to suspending students is to suspend our assumptions about what constitutes bad behaviors and to examine what we are doing in students' social, developmental, political, cultural, and pedagogical environments to actually encourage their resistance. For those who cling to the belief that schools are meritocracies and our methods, curricula, and policies somehow sit above racist, classist, sexist, and heterosexist societal trends, this shift in focus can be difficult. Part of the work in engaging resistance productively is to help our professional colleagues realize that cultivating a critical instead of an expedient relationship with student resistance isn't just good for kids—it's also really good for us.

If we do it well, engaging resistance will make us better educators. It will help us see how oppression may be operating in the institution and in relationships. It will alert us to systemic inequities that might otherwise go undetected. It will tell us, "Something is not right here," so that we can ask, "What is it?" Through an active and analytic engagement with resistance, educators will better understand their students and their own successes and failures. The only way to get better at what we do is to examine where we falter, and student resistance points the way.

Student Resistance Is Good for Schools, Communities, and the Rest of the World

Paolo Freire once wrote: "One of the most important tasks of critical educational practice is to make possible the conditions in which the learners, in their interaction with one another and with their teachers, engage in the experience of assuming themselves as social, historical, thinking, communicating, transformative, creative persons; dreamers of possible utopias, capable of being angry because of a capacity to love."[1]

Dreamers and revolutionaries often possess a powerful fusion of anger and love: anger at lost opportunities, wasted possibilities, and unjust circumstances, and love for equity, compassion, and human flourishing. This powerful fusion of anger and love is frequently expressed in individuals' resistance.

When it comes to adolescents, their idealism and imagination, combined with their burgeoning critical faculties, can produce forms of resistance that may be hard to accept and even harder to engage, especially for those of us responsible for keeping order. But engage them we must, not just because it's good for them or for us but because it's essential for healthy communities to listen to anger and look for love. Put differently, the utopias our students imagine and try to enact through their resistance are the realities we might one day build. And the annoyances and injustices they rail against are the policies and oppressions we might need to dismantle on our way to those new realities.

Adolescent argumentativeness and the righteous indignation of youth may not be fun to endure every day, but those expressions are signs of a future engaged citizenry that promises to be as attentive to what *is* happening as to what *should* be. Youth no doubt have a lot to learn and may be terribly naive about how the world works and what classrooms, school, communities, and nations need to function optimally. That's why we have schools. But if we mark their journey into adulthood with dismissiveness, control, reprimands, ridicule, and exclusion, then we are virtually guaranteeing that we will never exceed the status quo. We need their anger and their love. We need their resistance.

Preparing Ourselves for Student Resistance

If learning communities are to benefit from resistance, the educators within them have to cultivate a willingness to look beyond the immediacy of student (mis)behaviors to the interests and agendas that lie underneath. This doesn't mean we have to accept all forms of student resistance. Nor does it require us to stop everything whenever a student expresses even the slightest bit of displeasure or withdrawal. As I explained in chapter 1, our work lies somewhere between demanding that students comply and complying with student demands. Finding that middle ground likely requires us to pay attention to students differently than we may have been taught. We have to look for pushback and listen for defiance, not to put out fires or target insurgents for removal but to identify opportunities where we can learn about student perspectives and appreciate their experiences. Unfortunately (and fortunately), there is no blueprint for this work. Each educator and student needs to find his or her way into the relationship and build bridges between each other's perspectives and expectations. Engaging resistance is a good way to build that bridge.

But we can't build a bridge to something we can't see, and we can't see something we won't look at. As this book has demonstrated, to prepare ourselves for student resistance, we need to recognize the potential validity of the student's opposition. Deficit discourses and pathologizing rhetoric won't help. Nor will racism, classism, sexism, heterosexism, and any other systemic pollutants we may internalize as we navigate the mainstream. We need to concede that sometimes, our students are right to resist. And we may also need to admit that the questioning, critiquing, investigating, and relating we must do to engage resistance aren't always promoted in today's standardized, competitive, and assessment-obsessed schools. Engaging resistance in this era may therefore be countercultural, which means that to protect the spaces and relationships needed to do this work, we may have to do some resisting ourselves.

To sustain that countercultural stance, we may find it helpful to remember that students will want to learn with us when they are confident they won't have to capitulate or disappear in the process. They will (mis)behave less when they are involved in preserving their learning community. By fostering our own humility, analyzing how we compensate for vulnerability, working critically and collaboratively with other stakeholders, and demonstrating to students our capacity for reciprocal accountability, we actually strengthen the learning environment, not weaken it. Students who know they can bring their full selves to academic challenges and who trust that any difficulties will be handled judiciously and compassionately will be more motivated to invest the level of effort required for academic success. Therefore, engaging resistance doesn't mean lowering standards or giving up control; it means giving up the belief that our current standards and level of control should remain undisputed.

Not Taking Student Resistance Personally (Even When It Is)

The stakes are high both for the student and the teacher when resistance is misunderstood and mishandled in the classroom. The vulnerabilities students experience in school are myriad, but the same is true for us adults. Educators take endless orders from above and are expected to carry out those orders with audiences that are often reluctant or outright defiant. On top of that, many of us are then hired, evaluated, and fired on the basis of how well we manage those populations to produce measurable gains in achievement, even though that achievement is mostly a product of factors far beyond our control. And that's to say nothing of the internal difficulties these situations can create. Frustration and disappointment are common when we spend hours preparing for our work with youth only to have it casually dismissed in seconds by a few supposed troublemakers or ne'er-do-wells. For these reasons and more, our work with youth can be frustrating, their rejections of us can sting, and their resistance can feel like a slap in the face.

The key to successfully handling these perceived slights, however, is precisely *not* to take them personally—even though they may be! We need to be big enough to see beyond a perceived insult. Even when students are reacting against social forces like racism or classism or when they refuse institutional mandates they consider unfair, they typically do so by resisting the educators in their immediate presence. We become a target for their opposition not necessarily because we represent what's wrong (though sometimes we do) but because we're the one standing there when students have finally had enough. Their impulsivity in expressing their resistance and their immaturity in deciding to make us its target are developmentally and politically appropriate, because they're young. They're exactly where they should be. Some of the best work we can do with resistant students is to help them articulate what's wrong and identify the best channels for their opposition while we remind ourselves not to take their expressions personally.

When student resistance is expressed as a personal condemnation, we can be tempted to respond in a way that will render us blameless. Many of us are quite skilled at using our enhanced interpersonal skills and our decades of experience—not to mention our power as an institutionally credentialed professional—to deflect culpability elsewhere (e.g., on the students). To truly engage student resistance, however, we have to stop doing this. We need to demonstrate a reciprocal accountability that may feel personally destructive before it becomes pedagogically productive. That is, if we let student resistance sink in, it may expose us to the possibility that our methods are unfair and unwanted—that we blew it. This awareness can threaten our self-perception as a "good person" and make us want to withdraw from those who make us feel that way.

And the truth is, nobody gets out of an active engagement with resistance intact. To engage resistance, we have to give up our assumptions, admit our inadequacies, acknowledge our biases, and relate to others with more vulnerability. But if, as Audrey Thompson puts it, "we insist, in advance on an outcome that guarantees that we will feel good about ourselves—that guarantees we will feel growth without loss," then we are the ones unwilling to learn.[2] Any time we manipulate things to create a supposedly secure, untroubled position where we think we can respond to resistance with impunity, that position comes at a price: we probably bought it by denying the legitimacy of student insights, by remaining blind to their lack of agency, by perpetuating norms that exclude them, and by wasting the resources contained within their resistance. Predictably, our attempts to remain blameless only reinforce our students' desire to resist us. This is why I agree with Thompson when she asserts that "the first major step towards change is giving up the need to control meaning."[3] We ask students to do that all the time, so it's only fitting that we agree to do it ourselves once in awhile.

Finding Hope in Resistance

As a final illustration of the power of engaging student resistance, I want to recount an actual event, one that underscores the assertion in James Baldwin's quote that opened this chapter.

While I was writing this book, the teachers in Portland, Oregon, where I live, were preparing to strike. After decades of budget cutbacks, school closings, and layoffs, the teachers were fed up with being asked every year to do more with less. They had given up ten days of pay in 2003 to keep the district from having to shorten the school year, and they relinquished promised salary increases at least three times in the last decade to keep the district from laying off more teachers or cutting instructional days. Having amply demonstrated that they weren't in it for the money, the teachers argued in their contract negotiations that the single greatest threat to their ability to do their jobs well was the fact that some class sizes were now swelling to forty. Noting that Oregon had the third-largest class sizes in the nation in 2013, the teachers made the untenable class sizes their central bargaining issue, the thing they would resist the most.

Unfortunately, mainstream media and district officials painted the teachers as greedy and deceptive as if they were focused solely on raises and benefits during an era that called for fiscal austerity. Media reports, opinion letters, and district statements claimed that the teachers' demands were unrealistic if not impossible, given the financial struggles of the district. Some commentators even declared that the teachers' proposed changes to the contract would disproportionately affect low-income minority students even though all the data suggested that those populations had the most to gain with smaller class sizes. Because of these mischaracterizations and manipulations, in the court of public opinion, the teachers were losing the fight.

But just when the teachers felt the most beleaguered and misunderstood and began preparing to capitulate at the bargaining table to appease a public that seemed aligned against them, youth added their voice. High school students from around the city mobilized their peers and neighbors, staged rallies, held marches, scheduled walkouts, conducted social media campaigns, produced lawn signs and posters, uploaded YouTube videos, and formed their own student union. They resisted, beautifully and powerfully. Low-income and minority students organized English language learner forums to help spread the truth about the need to hire more teachers to reduce class sizes. Students drew up a compelling list of reforms in a document they titled "The Schools Portland Students Demand" and distributed it around the city. And as the strike date drew near, students kept the momentum and prepared for the worst. They coordinated babysitting for those on the picket lines and planned teach-ins for their peers in lieu of school. They even packed a school board meeting, during which they waved posters, chanted, and gave speeches indicating their frustration with the district's unwillingness to listen to or prioritize the students' concerns and those of their teachers. The board's response was to walk out of its own session rather than stay, listen, and engage. This evasion only emboldened the students' resolve.

Largely because of the students' resistance and the relationships, awareness, passion, and activism it fostered, the tide began to turn. The students' pressure and organizing galvanized the city. With public sentiment now overwhelmingly behind the teachers, the district was forced to stay at the bargaining table the night before the strike and eventually agreed to hire 150 new faculty, to reduce class sizes to where they were in 2010, to provide more planning time for teachers, to allow teachers to determine what materials they would use for day-to-day instruction, and to bar the use of standardized tests as the basis for teacher hiring, transfers, layoffs, remuneration, and firing. It was a resounding victory—utterly unimaginable were it not for the students' resistance.

The Portland example and countless others like it show us that student resistance is a way of actualizing hope. It does this by interrupting the status quo, by informing superiors that all is not well, by suggesting alternatives, and by energizing others to join the opposition. When officials won't listen, resistance only intensifies because it offers experiences of agency and the prospect of change. Though large, coordinated, and strategic forms of resistance can and will produce change, even the simplest and seemingly least productive oppositional behaviors can transform relationships and promote hope if they're engaged rather than ignored or punished. Whether we're open to that transformation and hope is an important question. Regardless of how we answer it, we have to admit that examples like the one in Portland reveal that our resistance and our destinies are tied up with those of our students. They will take care of us when we take care of them.

Therefore, when we tell students to do something and they challenge us to "make me," their response isn't just impudence, rudeness, or disrespect. It's an opportunity to enter into a more authentic and just relationship, to improve the context for learning, to recognize that we can be better educators. Essentially, it is an invitation for us to be made too.

Let's accept the invitation. What have we got to lose?

NOTES

Chapter 1

1. All the names used in this book have been changed to protect the individuals' privacy.

Chapter 2

1. Horace Mann, "Horace Mann on Education and National Welfare, 1848 (Twelfth Annual Report of Horace Mann as Secretary of Massachusetts State Board of Education), Tennessee Criminal Law Resource, accessed July 14, 2014, www.tncrimlaw.com/civil_bible/horace_mann .htm.

2. Woodrow Wilson, "The Meaning of a Liberal Education," address to the New York City High School Teachers Association, January 9, 1909; *High School Teachers Association of New York* 3 (1908–1909): 19–31; and *Papers of Woodrow Wilson* 18: 593–606, available at http:// en.wikisource.org/wiki/The_Meaning_of_a_Liberal_Education.

3. David F. Labaree, *Someone Has to Fail: The Zero-Sum Game of Public Schooling* (Cambridge, MA: Harvard University Press, 2010); David F. Labaree, "School Syndrome: Understanding the USA's Magical Belief That Schooling Can Somehow Improve Society, Promote Access, and Preserve Advantage," *Journal of Curriculum Studies* 44, no. 2 (2012): 143–163.

4. Nevertheless, communities the least served by public education had long doubted such assertions. One need only examine the history of schools on American Indian reservations or in racially segregated areas throughout the nation to find evidence of students, families, and communities that were and are deeply suspicious of any meritocratic claims.

5. For example, Titles I, VII, and IX of the Elementary and Secondary Education Act, Section 504 of the Rehabilitation Act, the Individuals with Disabilities Education Act, and the Indian Education Act.

6. See, for example, Jean Anyon, "Social Class and School Knowledge," *Curriculum Inquiry* 11, no. 1 (1981): 3–41; Ronald F. Ferguson, "Teachers' Perceptions and Expectations and the Black-White Test Score Gap," *Urban Education* 38, no. 4 (2003): 460–507; P. Gándara et al., "English Learners in California Schools: Unequal Resources, Unequal Outcomes," *Education Policy Analysis Archives* 11, no. 36 (2003); Anne Gregory et al., "The Relationship of School Structure and Support to Suspension Rates for Black and White High School Students," *American Educational Research Journal* 48, no. 4 (2011): 904–934; Jennifer L. Hochschild, "Social Class in Public Schools," *Journal of Social Issues* 59, no. 4 (2003): 821–840; Jeannie Oakes, *Keeping Track: How Schools Structure Inequality*, 2nd ed. (New Haven: Yale University Press, 2005); Ray C. Rist, "Student Social Class and Teacher Expectations: The Self-Fulfilling Prophecy in Ghetto Education," *Harvard Educational Review* 70, no. 3 (2000): 257–301; Daniel G. Solórzano et al., "Latina Equity in Education: Gaining Access to Academic Enrichment Programs," *Latino Policy*

and Issues Brief 4 (2003): 1–4; Rubén A. Gaztambide-Fernandez, *The Best of the Best: Becoming Elite at an American Boarding School* (Cambridge, MA: Harvard University Press, 2009).

7. Henry A. Giroux, *Theory and Resistance in Education: Towards a Pedagogy for the Opposition* (Westport, CT: Bergin & Garvey, 2001), 46.

8. This analysis was adapted from Mary E. Clark, "Skinner vs the Prophets: Human Nature & Our Concepts of Justice," *Contemporary Justice Review* 8, no. 2 (2005): 166.

9. See, for example, Anyon, "Social Class and School Knowledge"; Jean Anyon, *Ghetto Schooling: A Political Economy of Urban Educational Reform* (New York: Teachers College Press, 1997); Jay MacLeod, *Ain't No Makin' It: Aspirations and Attainment in a Low-Income Neighborhood* (Boulder, CO: Westview Press, 1995); Jeannie Oakes, *Multiplying Inequalities: The Effects of Race, Social Class, and Tracking on Opportunities to Learn Mathematics and Science* (Santa Monica, CA: Rand Corporation, 1990); Oakes, *Keeping Track.*

10. Paolo Freire, quoted in Ken McGrew, "A Review of Class-Based Theories of Student Resistance in Education," *Review of Educational Research* 81, no. 2 (2011): 252.

11. See, for example, Rubén Gaztambide-Fernández, "Bullshit as Resistance: Justifying Unearned Privilege Among Students at an Elite Boarding School," *International Journal of Qualitative Studies in Education* 24, no. 5 (2011): 581–586; Laura M. Ahearn, "Language and Agency," *Annual Review of Anthropology* 30 (2001): 109–137; Clive Harber, "Schooling as Violence: An Exploratory Overview," *Educational Review* 54, no. 1 (2002): 7–16; Jane Van Galen, "School Reform and Class Work: Teachers as Mediators of Social Class," *Journal of Educational Change* 5, no. 2 (2004): 111–139; Lesley Bartlett and Bryan McKinley Jones Brayboy, "Race and Schooling: Theories and Ethnographies," *The Urban Review* 37, no. 5 (2005): 361–374; Melissa S. Abelev, "Advancing Out of Poverty: Social Class Worldview and Its Relation to Resilience," *Journal of Adolescent Research* 24, no. 1 (2009): 114–141; Eric Toshalis, "From Disciplined to Disciplinarian: The Reproduction of Symbolic Violence in Preservice Teacher Education," *Journal of Curriculum Studies* 42, no. 2 (2010): 183–213.

12. For perhaps the most comprehensive and detailed analysis of the ongoing debates about the significance and originality of Willis's work, see McGrew, "Class-Based Theories of Student Resistance."

13. See, for example, James Collins, "Social Reproduction in Classrooms and Schools," *Annual Review of Anthropology* 38, no. 1 (2009): 36.

14. Giroux, *Theory and Resistance in Education*, 59.

15. Another major shortcoming of this scholarship is its inaccessibility. Many of the primary works that most inform this field are highly academic, overly esoteric, and simply difficult to read. Too often, the scholars in these fields are writing for a narrow audience, ethnographers writing for ethnographers, anthropologists writing for anthropologists, and philosophers writing for philosophers. When educators try to access such scholarship, they are often turned away by its tone, style, and jargon, despite the importance of the content to educators' work. Few if any school-based professionals with whom I have collaborated in the past two decades have ever named any of the theorists and theories surveyed in this chapter. This omission may be partly due to the technical (as opposed to the intellectual) nature of their graduate preparation, in which case the causality of this inaccessibility may be traced partly to their university professors and programs. But because most social reproductionists write primarily for other social reproductionists, the field suffers from its own reproductive circularity. If scholars truly believe that theory informs practice (and vice versa), they need to publish in journals that educators can easily access and they need to write in styles that educators appreciate. Much of the important scholarship produced in these fields is locked up behind online paywalls and restrictive subscription policies that require university affiliation for access. As a result, the people that are

best positioned to make the changes these scholars often recommend are the very ones who can never access that literature. If any part of social reproduction theory is actually (rather than theoretically) a closed system, this may be it.

16. Michael W. Apple, "Theory, Research, and the Critical Scholar/Activist," *Educational Researcher* 39, no. 2 (2010): 152.

17. Paul Willis, quoted in McGrew, "Class-Based Theories of Student Resistance," 248.

18. The National School Reform Faculty, at www.nsrfharmony.org, is a terrific resource for CFG training and support.

Chapter 3

1. Perhaps the most comprehensive, well-researched, and compelling analysis is Ken McGrew, "A Review of Class-Based Theories of Student Resistance in Education," *Review of Educational Research* 81, no. 2 (2011): 234–266.

2. Ibid., 250.

3. Henry Giroux, "Theories of Reproduction and Resistance in the New Sociology of Education: A Critical Analysis," *Harvard Educational Review* 53, no. 3 (1983): 290.

4. This analysis is derived from Leo van Lier, "Agency in the Classroom," accessed May 6, 2012, www.dilit.it/allegati/LeoVanLierScrittaParte.pdf.

5. Michael J. Nakkula and Eric Toshalis, *Understanding Youth: Adolescent Development for Educators* (Cambridge, MA: Harvard Education Press, 2006).

6. For an insightful analysis of how adolescent risk-taking may be read as authoring or coauthoring experiences, see Cynthia Lightfoot, *The Culture of Adolescent Risk-Taking: Culture and Human Development* (New York: Guilford Press, 1997).

7. Mary Haywood Metz, "Teachers' Ultimate Dependence on Their Students," in *Teachers' Work: Individuals, Colleagues, and Contexts*, ed. Judith Warren Little and Milbrey Wallin McLaughlin (New York: Teachers College Press, 1995).

8. Ibid., 109.

9. This list is derived from the one provided in Michael Newman, *Teaching Defiance: Stories and Strategies for Activist Educators* (San Francisco: Jossey-Bass, 2006), 124–125.

10. Henry A. Giroux, *Theory and Resistance in Education: Towards a Pedagogy for the Opposition* (Westport, CT: Bergin & Garvey, 2001), 47.

11. Michel Foucault, quoted in Brent L. Pickett, "Foucault and the Politics of Resistance," *Polity* 28, no. 4 (1996): 458.

12. I use the construction *(mis)behavior* to suggest that some of what is traditionally considered misbehavior is actually students' response to real or perceived injustice. The parenthetical breaking of the term is also meant to signal the contested nature of the behavior, to remind the reader that the evaluation of resistance depends on the eye of the beholder.

13. Kathleen M. Nolan, "Oppositional Behavior in Urban Schooling: Toward a Theory of Resistance for New Times," *International Journal of Qualitative Studies in Education* 24, no. 5 (2011): 564.

14. Giroux, "Theories of Reproduction and Resistance," 292.

Chapter 4

1. Jean Piaget, *Genetic Epistemology*, trans. Eleanor Duckworth (New York: Columbia University Press, 1970).

2. Here, I am paraphrasing Deborah Britzman's observation that a theory of knowledge "must begin with the tensions exercised when the knowledge offered through pedagogy meets the knowledge brought to pedagogy" (Deborah P. Britzman, *Lost Subjects, Contested Objects: Toward*

   a Psychoanalytic Inquiry of Learning (Albany, NY: State University of New York Press, 1998), 5.
3. Ibid., 24.
4. Charles Bingham, "Let's Treat Authority Relationally," in *No Education Without Relation*, ed. Charles Bingham and Alexander M. Sidorkin (New York: Peter Lang, 2004), 31.
5. Britzman, *Lost Subjects, Contested Objects*, 32.
6. Maxine Greene, *Teacher as Stranger: Educational Philosophy for the Modern Age* (Belmont, CA: Wadsworth, 1973), 141.
7. George Slavich and Philip Zimbardo, "Transformational Teaching: Theoretical Underpinnings, Basic Principles, and Core Methods," *Educational Psychology Review* 24, no. 4 (2012): 574.
8. Though these discoveries have accelerated in recent years with advances in imaging technologies, and President Obama was dedicating $70 million worth of research grants to support systems-based neurotechnology in 2014, there are growing concerns that neuroscientists (and journalists who poorly summarize the research) may be overstating their findings. Knowing what areas of the brain "light up" under specific laboratory-based simulations is not the same thing as knowing the meaning the brain is making of those stimuli. Nor does it mean we know how that meaning might be integrated with prior memories, experiences, and feelings. Consider an analogy: just because I can show someone on a map where Paris is located and describe its basic geography doesn't mean I can explain the city's history, inhabitants, culture, and what a proper French baguette ought to taste like. Neuroscientists are getting clearer and clearer pictures of the cellular landscape on which cognition occurs, but we are far from understanding the great array of networks that give shape and depth to our thinking. Consequently, educators should be careful not to move too quickly from neuroscientific explanations to classroom applications. See, for example, L. Anderson, "What Every Teacher Should Know: Reflections on 'Educating the Developing Mind,'" *Educational Psychology Review* 24, no. 1 (2012): 13–18, doi: 10.1007/s10648-011-9189-0; D. Brooks, "Beyond the Brain," *New York Times*, June 18, 2013, A25; R. M. Jordan-Young, *Brain Storm: The Flaws in the Science of Sex Differences* (Cambridge, MA: Harvard University Press, 2010); R. A. Poldrack and A. D. Wagner, A. D., "What Can Neuroimaging Tell Us About the Mind?" *Current Directions in Psychological Science* 13, no. 5 (2004): 177–181, doi: 10.1111/j.0963-7214.2004.00302.x; R. A. Poldrack, "Can Cognitive Processes Be Inferred from Neuroimaging Data?" *Trends in Cognitive Sciences* 10, no. 2 (2006): 59–63, doi: 10.1016/j.tics.2005.12.004; J. Schenck, *Teaching and the Adolescent Brain* (New York: W.W. Norton & Co., 2011); D. T. Willingham, *Why Don't Students Like School? A Cognitive Scientist Answers Questions About How the Mind Works and What It Means for the Classroom* (San Francisco: Jossey-Bass, 2010); J. Willis, "The Neuroscience of Joyful Education," *Educational Leadership Online* 64 (summer 2007), www.ascd.org/publications/educational-leadership/summer07/vol64/num09/The-Neuroscience-of-Joyful-Education.aspx.
9. Daniel Kahneman, *Thinking, Fast and Slow* (New York: Farrar, Straus and Giroux, 2011).
10. This explanation and those that follow is partly adapted from Freeman Dyson, "How to Dispel Your Illusions," review of *Thinking, Fast and Slow*, by Daniel Kahneman, *New York Review of Books* 58, no. 20 (December 2011): 40–43.
11. For a comprehensive review of executive function and its importance in education, I highly recommend Lynn Meltzer, *Executive Function in Education: From Theory to Practice* (New York: Guilford Press, 2007).
12. There is, however, significant evidence that even these accounts should be disputed. Gottfried Leibniz probably invented calculus before Newton, and multiple scientists and philosophers were at work on similar problems in physics at the same time that Newton was experimenting and publishing on such matters. That Newton may have borrowed ideas and used them

without credit further refutes the spontaneous appearance of brilliance. Human brains typically yield genius only after hard work, lots of time, and significant dedicated cognitive resources. Whether it was Newton or Leibniz who crossed the finish line first is a matter for historians to settle, but the fact that it took centuries of intellectual labor to lay the necessary groundwork so that a theory of gravity could emerge in the mind of one thinker suggests just how power-fully and how slowly system 2 functions. For a complete explication of the Newton vs. Leibniz controversy, see: Hall, A. Rupert, *Philosophers At War: The Quarrel Between Newton and Leibniz* (Cambridge, UK: Cambridge University Press, 1980).

13. Eric Amsel, "Hypothetical Thinking in an Adolescent: Its Nature, Development, and Ap-plications," in *Adolescent Vulnerabilities and Opportunities: Developmental and Constructivist Perspectives*, ed. Eric. Amsel, and Judith G. Smetana (New York: Cambridge University Press, 2011), 107.

14. Ibid., 87.

15. Peter McLaren, *Schooling as a Ritual Performance: Toward a Political Economy of Educational Symbols and Gestures*, 3rd ed. (Lanham, MD: Rowman & Littlefield, 1999), 159.

16. As quoted in: Kirsten Olson, *Wounded By School: Recapturing the Joy in Learning and Standing Up to Old School Culture* (New York: Teachers College Press, 2009), 36.

17. Amsel, "Hypothetical Thinking in an Adolescent: Its Nature, Development, and Applications," 97.

18. Laurence Steinberg, "Adolescent Risk-Taking: A Social Neuroscience Perspective," in *Adolescent Vulnerabilities and Opportunities: Developmental and Constructivist Perspectives*, ed. Eric Amsel and Judith G. Smetana (New York: Cambridge University Press, 2011), 43.

19. For an insightful analysis of the more social aspects of adolescent risk-taking, see Cynthia Light-foot, *The Culture of Adolescent Risk-Taking: Culture and Human Development* (New York: Guil-ford Press, 1997); Lynn Ponton, *The Romance of Risk* (New York: Basic Books, 1997).

20. Ibid., 45.

21. Peter McLaren, "Multiculturalism and the Postmodern Critique: Towards a Pedagogy of Resis-tance and Transformation," *Cultural Studies* 7, no. 1 (1993): 137.

Chapter 5

1. Deborah P. Britzman, *Lost Subjects, Contested Objects: Toward a Psychoanalytic Inquiry of Learn-ing* (Albany, NY: State University of New York Press, 1998), 32.

2. Jennifer Logue, "Reading Resistance Psychoanalytically," *Philosophy of Education* (2010): 334.

3. This sentence and several that follow are paraphrased from the clinical psychologist Herbert J. Schlesinger's description of the response he recommends therapists provide to a resistant patient, an apt analogy for classroom educators: "But recognizing that the patient is resisting should at the very least tell us that the patient is frightened. Something has just happened that intimates threat. Thus to the therapist resistance should be no more a nuisance or inconvenience than is pain to a physician when it occurs in the course of a physical examination. Both the resistance and the pain tell the doctor that something important is going on in that area. We are therefore interested in resistance and would like to know more about it, why the patient needs to behave in that way. Note the paradox: Although the resisting patient may be attempting to thwart us, to withhold information, to deny cooperation, or more subtly to avoid collaborating in the therapeutic task, the resisting patient is also conveying a good deal of information" (Herbert J. Schlesinger, "Resistance as Process," in *Resistance: Psychodynamic and Behavioral Approaches*, ed. Paul L. Wachtel [New York: Plenum Press, 1982], 27).

4. Though the list of pertinent publications is long, here are a few of the more notable ones: Carol S. Dweck, "Mind-Sets and Equitable Education," *Principal Leadership* 10, no. 5 (2010): 26–29;

Carol S. Dweck, *Mindset: The New Psychology of Success* (New York: Random House, 2006); Carol S. Dweck, *Self-Theories: Their Role in Motivation, Personality, and Development* (Philadelphia: Psychology Press, 1999); Claudia M. Mueller and Carol S. Dweck, "Praise for Intelligence Can Undermine Children's Motivation and Performance," *Journal of Personality and Social Psychology* 75, no. 1 (1998): 33–52; Heidi Grant and Carol S. Dweck, "Clarifying Achievement Goals and Their Impact," *Journal of Personality and Social Psychology* 85, no. 3 (2003): 541–553; Jennifer A. Mangels et al., "Why Do Beliefs About Intelligence Influence Learning Success? A Social Cognitive Neuroscience Model," *Social Cognitive and Affective Neuroscience,* no. 2 (2006): 75–86; Melissa L. Kamins and Carol S. Dweck, "Person Versus Process Praise and Criticism: Implications for Contingent Self-Worth and Coping," *Developmental Psychology* 35, no. 3 (1999): 75–86.

5. The notion of grit has been brilliantly researched and described by Angela Duckworth and her colleagues. For example, see Angela Lee Duckworth, "Self-Discipline Is Empowering," Phi Delta Kappan 90, no. 7 (2009): 536–536; and the following articles by Angela Lee Duckworth et al.: "Self-Regulation Strategies Improve Self-Discipline in Adolescents: Benefits of Mental Contrasting and Implementation Intentions," *Educational Psychology* 31, no. 1 (2010): 17–26; "Grit: Perseverance and Passion for Long-Term Goals," *Journal of Personality and Social Psychology* 92, no. 6 (2007): 1087–1101; "Deliberate Practice Spells Success Why Grittier Competitors Triumph at the National Spelling Bee," *Social Psychological and Personality Science* 2, no. 2 (2011): 174–181.

6. This insight and several that follow are adapted from Juliane C. Turner et al., "The Classroom Environment and Students' Reports of Avoidance Behaviors in Mathematics: A Multi-Method Study," *Journal of Educational Psychology* 94, no. 1 (2002): 89.

7. Ibid.

8. Barry J. Zimmerman, "Self-Efficacy: An Essential Motive to Learn," *Contemporary Educational Psychology* 25, no. 1 (2000): 86.

9. Slavich and Zimbardo, "Transformational Teaching." 578.

10. Ibid.

11. K. Ann Renninger, "Interest and Identity Development in Instruction: An Inductive Model," *Educational Psychologist* 44, no. 2 (2009): 105–118.

12. For further evidence of the importance of this concept to adolescent achievement motivation and classroom resistance, see Jacquelyn S. Eccles and A. Wigfield, "In the Mind of the Achiever: The Structure of Adolescents' Academic Achievement–Related Beliefs and Self-Perceptions," *Personality and Social Psychology Bulletin* 21 (1995): 215–225; Jacquelynne S. Eccles and Allan Wigfield, "Motivational Beliefs, Values, and Goals," *Annual Review of Psychology* 53, no. 1 (2002): 109–132; Allan Wigfield, "Expectancy-Value Theory of Achievement Motivation: A Developmental Perspective," *Educational Psychology Review* 6, no. 1 (1994); Allan Wigfield and Jacquelynne S. Eccles, "Expectancy-Value Theory of Achievement Motivation," *Contemporary Educational Psychology* 25, no. 1 (2001): 68–81.

13. For a complete explication of the research supporting self-determination theory, see Edward L. Deci et al., "Motivation and Education: The Self-Determination Perspective," *Educational Psychologist* 26, no. 3–4 (1991): 325–46; Richard M. Ryan and Edward L. Deci, "Self-Determination Theory and the Facilitation of Intrinsic Motivation, Social Development, and Well-Being," *American Psychologist* 55, no. 1 (2000): 68–78; Richard M. Ryan and Edward L. Deci, "Intrinsic and Extrinsic Motivations: Classic Definitions and New Directions," *Contemporary Educational Psychology* 25, no. 1 (2001): 54–67.

14. There is an important caveat to this claim, however. Researchers Idit Katz and Avi Assor, "When Choice Motivates and When It Does Not," Educational Psychology Review 19, no. 4 (2007):

437, describe how freedom, liberty, human rights, democracy, and happiness are specifically Western, individualist values that are not universally held: "Westerners strive to perceive themselves as possessing unique attributes that enables them to stand apart and be distinct from others around them. One important normative imperative for such individuals is to become independent from others and to discover and express their unique attributes. Accordingly, they strive to achieve independence and autonomy." But collectivist cultures often favor an interrelated set of values that prioritize collaboration, cooperation, unity, deference, community, family, and lineage. "Thus, their focal point is not their inner self but rather their relationship with others." In collectivist cultures, autonomy can therefore "challenge the sense of relatedness and belonging to one's in-group, as well as threaten the need to be accepted and loved by important authority figures." Consequently, we must consider the cultural orientation of individual students before assuming that autonomy will always enhance their motivation to engage and achieve.

15. Candice R. Stefanou et al., "Supporting Autonomy in the Classroom: Ways Teachers Encourage Decision Making and Ownership," *Educational Psychologist* 39, no. 2 (2004): 101.
16. To explore how educators might best accomplish this, see Eric Toshalis and Michael J. Nakkula, "Motivation, Engagement and Student Voice," The Students at the Center Series, April 2012, www.studentsatthecenter.org/sites/scl.dl-dev.com/files/Motivation%20Engagement%20Student%20Voice_0.pdf.
17. Allen N. Mendler, *Motivating Students Who Don't Care: Successful Techniques for Educators* (Bloomington, IN: National Educational Service, 2000), 7.
18. As quoted in Jeb Schenck, *Teaching and the Adolescent Brain* (New York: W.W. Norton & Co., 2011).
19. Ibid., 165–171.

Chapter 6

1. Robert Balfanz et al., "Preventing Student Disengagement and Keeping Students on the Graduation Path in Urban Middle-Grades Schools: Early Identification and Effective Interventions," *Educational Psychologist* 42, no. 4 (2007): 224.
2. This explanation of self-handicapping is a blending of definitions provided in Tim Urdan and Carol Midgley, "Academic Self-Handicapping: What We Know, What More There Is to Learn," *Educational Psychology Review* 13, no. 2 (2001): 115–138, esp. 116 and 118.
3. Tim Urdan et al., "The Role of Classroom Goal Structure in Students' Use of Self-Handicapping Strategies," *American Educational Research Journal* 35, no. 1 (1998): 116.
4. Urdan and Midgley, "Academic Self-Handicapping," 121.
5. Carol Midgley and Tim Urdan, "Predictors of Middle School Students' Use of Self-Handicapping Strategies," *Journal of Early Adolescence* 15, no. 4 (1995): 391–392.
6. James Dillon, quoted in Allison M. Ryan et al., "Avoiding Seeking Help in the Classroom: Who and Why?" *Educational Psychology Review* 13, no. 2 (2001): 95.
7. Ibid.
8. Ibid., 99.
9. Ibid., 106.
10. Juliane C. Turner et al., "The Classroom Environment and Students' Reports of Avoidance Behaviors in Mathematics: A Multi-Method Study," *Journal of Educational Psychology* 94, no. 1 (2002): 89.
11. Ryan et al., "Avoiding Seeking Help in the Classroom," 101–102.
12. Ibid., 103.
13. Ibid., 98.

14. I have written more extensively on this topic in Eric Toshalis, "A Question of 'Faith': Adolescent Spirituality in the Public Schools"; in *Adolescents at School: Perspectives on Youth, Identity, and Education*, ed. Michael Sadowski (Cambridge, MA: Harvard Education Press, 2008); and with my coauthor Michael J. Nakkula, chapter 12 in *Understanding Youth: Adolescent Development for Educators*, (Cambridge, MA: Harvard Education Press, 2006).

15. Deanna Kuhn and Amanda Holman, "What Are the Cognitive Skills Adolescents Need for Life in the Twenty-First Century?" in *Adolescent Vulnerabilities and Opportunities: Developmental and Constructivist Perspectives*, ed. Eric Amsel and Judith G. Smetana (New York: Cambridge University Press, 2011), 70.

16. Ibid.

17. This phenomenon has been explored in more detail in the following publications by Eric Toshalis and Michael J. Nakkula: "Motivation, Engagement and Student Voice," The Students at the Center Series, April 2012, www.studentsatthecenter.org/sites/scl.dl-dev.com/files/Motivation%20Engagement%20Student%20Voice_0.pdf; "Prioritizing Motivation and Engagement: The Future of Student-Centered Learning," in *Anytime, Anywhere: Student-Centered Learning for Schools and Teachers*, ed. Rebecca E. Wolfe, Adria Steinberg, and Nancy Hoffman (Cambridge, MA: Harvard Education Press, 2013).

18. Jeb Schenck, *Teaching and the Adolescent Brain* (New York: W.W. Norton & Co., 2011), 111.

19. For more comprehensive investigations of self-regulation, see Angela Lee Duckworth et al., "Self-Regulation Strategies Improve Self-Discipline in Adolescents: Benefits of Mental Contrasting and Implementation Intentions," *Educational Psychology* 31, no. 1 (2010): 17–26; Barry J. Zimmerman, "Attaining Self-Regulation: A Social-Cognitive Perspective," in *Self-Regulation: Theory, Research, and Applications*, ed. M. Boekaerts, Paul Pintrich, and M. Seidner (Orlando, FL: Academic Press, 2000); Barry J. Zimmerman, "Developing Self-Fulfilling Cycles of Academic Regulation: An Analysis of Exemplary Instructional Models," in *Self-Regulated Learning: From Teaching to Self-Reflective Practice*, ed. Dale H. Schunk and Barry J. Zimmerman (New York: Guilford Press, 1998); Cynthia A. Cooper and Jennifer Henderlong Corpus, "Learners' Developing Knowledge of Strategies for Regulating Motivation," *Journal of Applied Developmental Psychology* 30, no. 4 (2009): 525–536; Deborah L. Butler, "Individualizing Instruction in Self-Regulated Learning," *Theory into Practice* 41, no. 2 (2002): 81; Monique Boekaerts and Lyn Corno, "Self-Regulation in the Classroom: A Perspective on Assessment and Intervention," *Applied Psychology: An International Review* 54, no. 2 (2005): 199–231; Scott G. Paris and Alison H. Paris, "Classroom Applications of Research on Self-Regulated Learning," *Educational Psychologist* 36, no. 2 (2001): 89–101.

20. Kenneth A. Kiewra, "How Classroom Teachers Can Help Students Learn and Teach Them How to Learn," *Theory into Practice* 15, no. 5 (2002): 71–72.

21. That said, a growing chorus of scholars have valid criticisms of the middle-class biases, assimilative tendencies, and compliance-obsessed aspects of self-regulation research. Many have noted that the so-called self-regulated learner is the easily managed worker and that self-regulation is a thinly veiled effort to institutionalize and valorize middle-class culture over working-class modes of working and collaborating. Critics observe that too often, self-regulation aims to place all the responsibility for lack of learning on the individual student's capacity to focus rather than on the environmental, social, pedagogical, political, and relational ecology that may make such focus impossible or problematic. Critics of self-regulation research argue that if self-regulation changes only the student, not the context, the practice may participate in oppressive systems that reproduce social inequities rather than dismantle them. And yet, social change and social justice are unachievable without some level of self-discipline, intellectual rigor, and

sustained engagement with complex tasks. All students needs to move from emulation to regulation when learning a new skill or when creating new knowledge, so some self-regulation may make sense as long as it does not prioritize obedience and control over agency and autonomy. If students are given choices, opportunities for both self-control and context control, and ample opportunities to collaborate and negotiate across differences, then self-regulated learning can still be liberating and can help move students toward greater academic achievement. For further critiques of self-regulation, see Allyson F. Hadwin, "Response to Vassallo's Claims from a Historically Situated View of Self-Regulated Learning as Adaptation in the Face of Challenge," *New Ideas in Psychology* 31, no. 3 (2013): 212–115; Mary McCaslin and Heidi Legg Burross, "Research on Individual Differences Within a Sociocultural Perspective: Coregulation and Adaptive Learning," *Teachers College Record* 113, no. 6 (2011); Stephen Vassallo, "Considering Class-Based Values Related to Guardian Involvement and the Development of Self-Regulated Learning," *New Ideas in Psychology* 31, no. 3 (2013): 202–211; Stephen Vassallo, "Critical Pedagogy and Neoliberalism: Concerns with Teaching Self-Regulated Learning," *Studies in Philosophy & Education* 32, no. 6 (2013): 563–580; Stephen Vassallo, "Observations of a Working Class Family: Implications for Self-Regulated Learning Development," *Educational Studies* 48, no. 6 (2012): 501–529.

22. Idit Katz and Avi Assor, "When Choice Motivates and When It Does Not," *Educational Psychology Review* 19, no. 4 (2007): 438–439.

23. For example, Kathleen Cushman, "Students Solving Community Problems: Serious Learning Takes on a New Look," *Challenge Journal: The Journal of the Annenberg Challenge* 4, no. 1 (2000); Kathleen Cushman, *Fires in the Bathroom: Advice for Teachers from High School Students* (New York: New Press, 2003); Dana L. Mitra, "Student Voice in School Reform: Reframing Student-Teacher Relationships," *McGill Journal of Education* 38, no. 2 (2003): 289–304; Alison Cook-Sather, "'Change Based on What Students Say': Preparing Teachers for a Paradoxical Model of Leadership," *International Journal of Leadership in Education* 9, no. 4 (2006): 345–358; Michael Fielding, "Beyond 'Voice': New Roles, Relations, and Contexts in Researching with Young People," *Discourse* 28, no. 3 (2007): 301–310; Susan Yonezawa and Makeba Jones, "Student Co-Researchers: How Principals Can Recruit, Train, and Enlist the Help of Students to Examine What Works and Does Not Work in Their Schools," *NASSP Bulletin* 91, no. 4 (2007): 322–342; Dana Mitra, "Student Voice in School Reform: From Listening to Leadership," in *International Handbook of Student Experience of Elementary and Secondary School*, ed. Dennis Thiessen and Alison Cook-Sather (Dordrecht, The Netherlands: Springer, 2007); Susan Yonezawa and Makeba Jones, "Using Students' Voices to Inform and Evaluate Secondary School Reform," in *International Handbook of Student Experience of Elementary and Secondary School*; Kathleen Cushman, and Laura Rogers, *Fires in the Middle School Bathroom: Advice for Teachers from Middle School Students* (New York: New Press, 2008); Dana L. Mitra, *Student Voice in School Reform: Building Youth-Adult Partnerships That Strengthen Schools and Empower Youth* (Albany, NY: SUNY Press, 2008); Ben Kirshner, "'Power in Numbers': Youth Organizing as a Context for Exploring Civic Identity," *Journal of Research on Adolescence* 19, no. 3 (2009): 414–440; Dana L. Mitra and Steven Jay Gross, "Increasing Student Voice in High School Reform: Building Partnerships, Improving Outcomes," *Educational Management Administration & Leadership* 37, no. 4 (2009): 522–543; Tim Fredrick, "Looking in the Mirror: Helping Adolescents Talk More Reflectively During Portfolio Presentations," *Teachers College Record* 111, no. 8 (2009): 1916–1929; Dana L. Mitra, "Strengthening Student Voice Initiatives in High Schools," *Youth & Society* 40, no. 3 (2009): 311–335; Dana L. Mitra, "Student Voice and Student Roles in Education Policy Reform," in *AERA Handbook on Education Policy Research*,

ed. D. Plank et al. (London: Routledge, 2009); Susan Yonezawa and Makeba Jones, "Student Voices: Generating Reform From the Inside Out," *Theory into Practice* 48, no. 3 (2009): 205–212; Laurie B. Hanich, "Using Student Interviews to Understand Theories of Motivation," *Teaching Educational Psychology* 3, no. 3 (2009): 1–5.

24. For a full explication of this spectrum of student-voice oriented activity, see Eric Toshalis and Michael J. Nakkula, "Motivation, Engagement and Student Voice," The Students at the Center Series, April 2012, www.studentsatthecenter.org/topics/motivation-engagement-and-student -voice.

Chapter 7

1. A. Rae Simpson, "Ten Tasks of Adolescent Development," Massachusetts Institute of Technology, MIT Work-Life Center, accessed July 14, 2014, http://hrweb.mit.edu/worklife/raising -teens/ten-tasks.html.

2. This gloss of moral development theories is adapted from Diane Goodman, "Motivating People from Privileged Groups to Support Social Justice," *Teachers College Record* 102, no. 6 (2000): 1073.

3. Carol Gilligan, *In a Different Voice: Psychological Theory and Women's Development* (Cambridge, MA: Harvard University Press, 1993); Lawrence Kohlberg and Carol Gilligan, "The Adolescent as a Philosopher: The Discovery of the Self in a Postconventional World," *Daedalus* (fall 1971): 1051–1086; Lawrence Kohlberg, *The Psychology of Moral Development: The Nature and Validity of Moral Stages*, 1st ed. (San Francisco: Harper & Row, 1984).

4. Robert L Selman, *The Promotion of Social Awareness: Powerful Lessons from the Partnership of Developmental Theory and Classroom Practice* (New York: Russell Sage Foundation, 2003); Robert L. Selman et al., "Assessing Adolescent Interpersonal Negotiation Strategies: Toward the Integration of Structural and Functional Models," *Developmental Psychology* 22, no. 4 (1986): 450–459; Robert L. Selman, *The Growth of Interpersonal Understanding: Developmental and Clinical Analyses*, Developmental Psychology Series (New York: Academic Press, 1980).

5. William Damon and Anne Gregory, "The Youth Charter: Towards the Formation of Adolescent Moral Identity," *Journal of Moral Education* 26, no. 2 (1997): 117–130; William Damon, *Moral Development* (San Francisco: Jossey-Bass, 1978); William Damon, *The Moral Child: Nurturing Children's Natural Moral Growth* (New York: Free Press, 1988).

6. Joan F. Goodman, "Teacher Authority and Moral Education," *Education Week*, March 20, 2002), available at Teaching Tolerance Web page, www.tolerance.org/supplement/teacher -authority-and-moral-education.

7. William Damon et al., "The Development of Purpose During Adolescence," *Applied Developmental Science* 7, no. 3 (2003): 121.

8. Ibid., 124.

9. Ibid., 121.

10. I have written about this dynamic with its moral, ethical, pedagogical, and spiritual dimensions elsewhere, including Eric Toshalis, "A Question of 'Faith': Adolescent Spirituality in the Public Schools," in *Adolescents at School: Perspectives on Youth, Identity, and Education*, ed. Michael Sadowski (Cambridge, MA: Harvard Education Press, 2008); Michael J. Nakkula and Eric Toshalis, *Understanding Youth: Adolescent Development for Educators* (Cambridge, MA: Harvard Education Press, 2006), ch. 10, 201–230.

11. Ibid.

12. Dia N. R. Sekayi, "Intellectual Indignation: Getting at the Roots of Student Resistance in an Alternative High School Program," *Education* 122, no. 2 (2001): 421; Dia N. R. Sekayi, "Student Resistance to Culturally Irrelevant Curriculum and Pedagogy: The Role of Critical

Consciousness," in *Urban Teacher Education and Teaching: Innovative Practices for Diversity and Social Justice*, ed. Rovell P. Solomon and Dia N. R. Sekayi (Mahwah, NJ: Lawrence Erlbaum, 2007), 175.

13. Alice J. Pitt, "Qualifying Resistance: Some Comments on Methodological Dilemmas," *International Journal of Qualitative Studies in Education* 11, no. 4 (1998): 546.

14. Harter's work is described in K. Ann Renninger, "Interest and Identity Development in Instruction: An Inductive Model," *Educational Psychologist* 44, no. 2 (2009): 110.

15. For a full review of the research on shyness, see Louis A. Schmidt and Arnold H. Buss, "Understanding Shyness: Four Questions and Four Decades of Research," in *The Development of Shyness and Social Withdrawal*, ed. Kenneth H. Rubin and Robert J. Coplan (New York: Guilford, 2010).

16. For a complete listing and explanation of these related outcomes, see Kenneth H. Rubin et al., "Social Withdrawal in Childhood and Adolescence: Peer Relationships and Social Competence," in *The Development of Shyness and Social Withdrawal*, ed. Kenneth H. Rubin and Robert J. Coplan (New York: Guilford, 2010); Kenneth H. Rubin et al., "Social Withdrawal in Childhood," *Annual Review of Psychology* 60, no. 1 (2009): 141–171; Mary Ann Evans, "Language Performance, Academic Performance, and Signs of Shyness," in *The Development of Shyness and Social Withdrawal*, ed. Kenneth H. Rubin and Robert J. Coplan (New York: Guilford, 2010).

17. Rubin et al., "Social Withdrawal in Childhood," 149–151.

18. Ibid., 153.

19. See, for example, Jeremy D. Finn, "Withdrawing from School," *Review of Educational Research* 59, no. 2 (1989): 117–142; Michelle Fine, *Framing Dropouts: Notes on the Politics of an Urban Public High School* (Albany, NY: SUNY Press, 1991); George Jerry Sefa Dei, *Reconstructing "Drop-Out": A Critical Ethnography of the Dynamics of Black Students' Disengagement from School* (Toronto: University of Toronto Press, 1997); R. W. Rumberger, "The Economics of High School Dropouts," in *International Encyclopedia of Education*, ed. Penelope Peterson, Eva Baker, and Barry McGraw (Oxford: Elsevier, 2010); Russell W. Rumberger, *Dropping Out: Why Students Drop Out of High School and What Can Be Done About It* (Cambridge, MA: Harvard University Press, 2011); Jessica Ruglis, "Mapping the Biopolitics of School Dropout and Youth Resistance," *International Journal of Qualitative Studies in Education* 24, no. 5 (2011): 627–637; Robert B. Stevenson and Jeanne Ellsworth, "Dropouts and the Silencing of Critical Voices," in *Beyond Silenced Voices*, ed. Lois Weis and Michelle Fine (Albany, NY: SUNY Press, 1993).

20. Isabelle Archambault et al., "Student Engagement and Its Relationship with Early High School Dropout," *Journal of Adolescence* 32, no. 3 (2009): 651–770; Louie F. Rodríguez and Gilberto Q. Conchas, "Preventing Truancy and Dropout Among Urban Middle School Youth," *Education and Urban Society Education* 41, no. 2 (2009): 216–247; Olson, *Wounded by School: Recapturing the Joy in Learning and Standing Up to Old School Culture*; Robert Balfanz et al., "Preventing Student Disengagement and Keeping Students on the Graduation Path in Urban Middle-Grades Schools: Early Identification and Effective Interventions," *Educational Psychologist* 42, no. 4 (2007): 223–235.

21. The Editors of Education Week, "Diplomas Count 2013: Second Chances: Executive Summary," *Education Week*, May 31, 2013, www.edweek.org/ew/articles/2013/06/06/34execsum.h32.html?intc=EW-DC13-LNAV.

22. Research has demonstrated that such involvement can compensate for initial shyness and help build confidence and competence in social situations. For more on this, see Kenneth H. Rubin et al., "Social Withdrawal in Childhood," *Annual Review of Psychology* 60, no. 1 (2009): 162.

Sick of It

1. This anecdote is partly inspired by an episode from HBO's *Middle School Confessions* series that was originally broadcast in 2002. The episode, on violence, is now available at www.youtube .com/watch?v=aKkgTWz6pWw and focuses on a student named Jesse who shares many of William's experiences and responses. I use the video in my classroom management course to help explain how the antecedents of bullying are often misunderstood. I also use it to demonstrate how easily we can miss and misinterpret classist interactions in school and how they warp relationships and hurt both students' psychological well-being and their academic achievement.

Chapter 8

1. David Berliner, "Effects of Inequality and Poverty Vs. Teachers and Schooling on America's Youth," *Teachers College Record* (2014).
2. James Collins, "Social Reproduction in Classrooms and Schools," *Annual Review of Anthropology* 38, no. 1 (2009): 43.
3. Stephanie Jones and Mark D. Vagle, "Living Contradictions and Working for Change: Toward a Theory of Social Class-Sensitive Pedagogy," *Educational Researcher* 42, no. 3 (2013): 130.
4. Ibid., 129.
5. Ibid., 131.
6. Jill Barshay, "PISA Math Score Debate Among Education Experts Centers on Poverty and Teaching," *Education by the Numbers Blog*, December 12, 2013, http://educationbythenumbers .org/content/pisa-math-score-debate-among-education-experts-centers-poverty-teaching_758/.
7. Organisation for Economic Co-operation and Development, "PISA 2012 Results," accessed July 14, 2014, www.oecd.org/pisa/keyfindings/pisa-2012-results.htm.
8. U.S. Census Bureau, "Poverty: Highlights," accessed July 14, 2014, www.census.gov/hhes/www/ poverty/about/overview/.
9. National Center for Children in Poverty, "Child Poverty," accessed July 14, 2013, www.nccp.org/ topics/childpoverty.html.
10. Sophia Addy et al., "Basic Facts About Low-Income Children: Children Aged 12 Through 17 Years, 2011," National Center for Children in Poverty, January 2013 www.nccp.org/publications/ pdf/text_1075.pdf.
11. Robert Balfanz et al., "Preventing Student Disengagement and Keeping Students on the Graduation Path in Urban Middle-Grades Schools: Early Identification and Effective Interventions," *Educational Psychologist* 42, no. 4 (2007): 225.
12. Summary statistics available at National Center for Education Statistics, Institute of Education Sciences, "Percentage of High School Dropouts Among Persons 16 Through 24 Years Old (Status Dropout Rate), by Income Level, and Percentage Distribution of Status Dropouts, by Labor Force Status and Years of School Completed: 1970 through 2011," accessed July 14, 2014, http://nces.ed.gov/programs/digest/d12/tables/dt12_129.asp.
13. For an exhaustive and poignant summary of decades of research on this matter, see American Psychological Association, "Effects of Poverty, Hunger and Homelessness on Children and Youth," accessed July 14, 2014, www.apa.org/pi/families/poverty.aspx?item=1#.
14. Berliner, "Inequality and Poverty Vs. Teachers and Schooling."
15. Cynthia Hudley, "Education and Urban Schools," *SES Indicator*, May 2013, www.apa.org/pi/ ses/resources/indicator/2013/05/urban-schools.aspx.
16. The scholarship examining the problems Teach For America creates rather than solves is growing every year. See, for example, Linda Darling-Hammond, "Who Will Speak for the Children? How 'Teach for America' Hurts Urban Schools and Students," *Phi Delta Kappan* 76, no. 1

(1994): 21; Tyrone C. Howard, "Who Receives the Short End of the Shortage? Implications of the U.S. Teacher Shortage on Urban Schools," *Journal of Curriculum and Supervision* 18, no. 2 (2003): 142–160; Linda Darling-Hammond et al., "Does Teacher Preparation Matter? Evidence About Teacher Certification, Teach for America, and Teacher Effectiveness," *Education Policy Analysis Archives* 13, no. 42 (2005): 1–51; Lorene C. Pilcher and Donald C. Steele, "Teach For America and Regularly Certified Teachers: Teacher Efficacy, Teaching Concerns, Career Aspirations, and Teaching Effectiveness," in *Research on Alternative and Non-Traditional Education*, ed. Julie Rainier Dangel and Edith M. Guyton (Lanham, MD: Scarecrow, 2005); Heather G. Peske and Kati Haycock, "Teaching Inequality: How Poor and Minority Students Are Shortchanged on Teacher Quality: A Report and Recommendations by the Education Trust," *Education Trust* (2006); Linda Darling-Hammond, "A Future Worthy of Teaching for America," *Phi Delta Kappan* 89, no. 10 (2008): 730–35; Barbara Torre Veltri, "Teaching Or Service? The Site-Based Realities of Teach for America Teachers in Poor, Urban Schools," *Education and Urban Society* 40, no. 5 (2008): 511–542; Betty Achinstein et al., "Retaining Teachers of Color: A Pressing Problem and a Potential Strategy for 'Hard-to-Staff' Schools," *Review of Educational Research* 80, no. 1 (2010): 71–107; Kevin K. Kumashiro, "Seeing the Bigger Picture: Troubling Movements to End Teacher Education," *Journal of Teacher Education* 61, no. 1–2 (2010): 56–65; David F. Labaree, "Teach For America and Teacher Ed: Heads They Win, Tails We Lose," *Journal of Teacher Education* 61, no. 1–2 (2010): 48–55; Beverly Falk, "Ending the Revolving Door of Teachers Entering and Leaving the Teaching Profession," *New Educator* 8, no. 2 (2012): 105–108; Lydia Bentley, "Teach for America's Mission, Vision, and Core Values: A Closer Look," *Teachers College Record* (2013), www.tcrecord.org/content.asp?contentid=17126.

17. See, for example, Sebastián J. Lipina and Jorge A. Colombo, *Poverty and Brain Development During Childhood: An Approach from Cognitive Psychology and Neuroscience* (Washington, DC: American Psychological Association, 2009); J. Luby et al., "The Effects of Poverty on Childhood Brain Development: The Mediating Effect of Caregiving and Stressful Life Events," *JAMA Pediatrics* 167, no. 12 (2013): 1135–1142; Anandi Mani et al., "Poverty Impedes Cognitive Function," *Science* 341, no. 6149 (2013): 976–980; Sendhil Mullainathan and Eldar Shafir, *Scarcity: Why Having Too Little Means So Much* (New York: Times Books, 2013).

18. Sendhil Mullainathan and Eldar Shafir, "Freeing Up Intelligence," *Scientific American Mind* 25 (2014): 58–63.

19. For an example of a methodological critique, see Jelte M. Wicherts and Annemarie Zand Scholten, "Comment on "Poverty Impedes Cognitive Function," *Science* 342, no. 6163 (2013): 1169.

20. Mani et al., "Poverty Impedes Cognitive Function," 980.

21. Ibid.

22. See, for example, Berliner, "Inequality and Poverty Vs. Teachers and Schooling"; Ellen A. Brantlinger, *The Politics of Social Class in Secondary School: Views of Affluent and Impoverished Youth* (New York: Teachers College Press, 1993); Jennifer L. Hochschild, "Social Class in Public Schools," *Journal of Social Issues* 59, no. 4 (2003): 821–840; Mary Metz, "How Social Class Differences Shape Teachers' Work," in *The Contexts of Teaching in Secondary Schools: Teachers' Realities*, ed. Milbrey Wallin McLaughlin, Joan E. Talbert, and Nina Bascia (New York: Teachers College Press, 1990); Ray C. Rist, "Student Social Class and Teacher Expectations: The Self-Fulfilling Prophecy in Ghetto Education," *Harvard Educational Review* 70, no. 3 (2000): 257–301; Michelle Fine and April Burns, "Class Notes: Toward a Critical Psychology of Class and Schooling," *Journal of Social Issues* 59, no. 4 (2003): 841–860; Tommy M. Phillips and Joe F. Pittman, "Identity Processes in Poor Adolescents: Exploring the Linkages Between Economic Disadvantage and the Primary Task of Adolescence," *Identity: An International Journal*

of Theory and Research 3, no. 2 (2003): 115–129; Peter Demerath et al., "Decoding Success: A Middle-Class Logic of Individual Advancement in a U.S. Suburb and High School," *Teachers College Record* 112, no. 12 (2010): 2935–2987.

23. Annette Lareau, "Invisible Inequality: Social Class and Childrearing in Black Families and White Families," *American Sociological Review* 67, no. 5 (2002): 747–776; Annette Lareau, *Home Advantage: Social Class and Parental Intervention in Elementary Education*, 2nd ed. (Lanham, MD: Rowman & Littlefield Publishers, 2000); Annette Lareau, *Unequal Childhoods: Class, Race, and Family Life*, 2nd ed. (Berkeley: University of California Press, 2011).

24. Lareau, "Invisible Inequality," 774, is careful to note that "It is a mistake to see either [of these orientations] as an intrinsically desirable approach. As has been amply documented, conceptions of childhood have changed dramatically over time. Drawbacks to middle-class childrearing, including the exhaustion associated with intensive mothering and frenetic family schedules and a sapping of children's naiveté that leaves them feeling too sophisticated for simple games and toys remain insufficiently highlighted. Another drawback is that middle-class children are less likely to learn how to fill 'empty time' with their own creative play, leading to a dependence on their parents to solve experiences of boredom."

25. Fine and Burns, "Class Notes: Toward a Critical Psychology of Class and Schooling," 850.

26. Lareau, "Invisible Inequality," 773.

27. Wendy Luttrell, "Becoming Somebody in and Against School: Toward a Psychocultural Theory of Gender and Self-Making," in *The Cultural Production of the Educated Person: Critical Ethnographies of Schooling and Local Practice*, ed. B. Levinson, D. Foley, and D. Holland (Albany, NY: SUNY Press, 1996), 94.

28. La Paperson, "A Disrupting Darkness: Youth Resistance as Racial Wisdom," *International Journal of Qualitative Studies in Education* 24, no. 7 (2011): 812.

29. Duane E. Thomas et al., "Racial and Emotional Factors Predicting Teachers' Perceptions of Classroom Behavioral Maladjustment for Urban African American Male Youth," *Psychology in the Schools* 46, no. 2 (2009): 186.

30. Paul Corrigan and Simon Frith, quoted in Ken McGrew, "A Review of Class-Based Theories of Student Resistance in Education," *Review of Educational Research* 81, no. 2 (2011): 245.

31. Paperson, "Disrupting Darkness," 809.

32. I owe this insight to Peter McLaren, *Schooling as a Ritual Performance: Toward a Political Economy of Educational Symbols and Gestures*, 3rd ed. (Lanham, MD: Rowman & Littlefield, 1999), 147: "Here students would scoff at and deride the accepted syntax of communication. The antistructure of resistance was a dialectical theatre in which meanings were both affirmed and denied simultaneously. Whatever sense of identity was stripped from the student during class time was returned through the torn seams, fissures and eruptions of the resistant and liminal self. In both subtle and overt ways, recusant students exhibited actions which undermined the consensually validated norms and authorized codes of the school."

33. Jonathan G. Silin et al., "Rethinking Resistance in Schools: Power, Politics, and Illicit Pleasures," *Occasional Paper Series, Bank Street College of Education* 14 (2005): 35.

34. Ibid., 33–34.

35. Ibid., 33.

36. Daniel A. McFarland, "Student Resistance: How the Formal and Informal Organization of Classrooms Facilitate Everyday Forms of Student Defiance," *American Journal of Sociology* 107, no. 3 (2001): 665.

37. Ellen A. Brantlinger, *Dividing Classes: How the Middle Class Negotiates and Rationalizes School Advantage* (New York: RoutledgeFalmer, 2003), 38–39.

38. Mollie K. Galloway, "Cheating in Advantaged High Schools: Prevalence, Justifications, and Possibilities for Change," *Ethics & Behavior* 22, no. 5 (2012): 378–399.
39. See, for example, Melissa S. Abelev, "Advancing Out of Poverty: Social Class Worldview and Its Relation to Resilience," *Journal of Adolescent Research* 24, no. 1 (2009): 114–141; Ann S. Masten, "Resilience in Individual Development: Successful Adaptation Despite Risk and Adversity," in *Educational Resilience in Inner City America*, ed. Margaret C. Wang and Edmund W. Gordon (Hillsdale, NJ: Erlbaum Associates, 1994).
40. This list is derived from the research and recommendations contained in the following publications: Elizabeth Bondy et al., "Creating Environments of Success and Resilience: Culturally Responsive Classroom Management and More," *Urban Education* 42, no. 4 (2007): 326–348; Caroline S. Clauss-Ehlers, "Sociocultural Factors, Resilience, and Coping: Support for a Culturally Sensitive Measure of Resilience," *Journal of Applied Developmental Psychology* 29 (2008): 197–212; Craig A. Olsson et al., "Adolescent Resilience: A Concept Analysis," *Journal of Adolescence* 26 (2003): 1–11; American Psychological Association, "The Road to Resilience," accessed January 9, 2014, www.apa.org/helpcenter/road-resilience.aspx#; Saundra Murray Nettles and Joseph H. Pleck, "Risk, Resilience, and Development: The Multiple Ecologies of Black Adolescents in the United States," in *Stress, Risk, and Resilience in Children and Adolescents: Processes, Mechanisms, and Interventions*, ed. Robert J. Haggerty (New York: Cambridge University Press, 1994); John Hoffman, "Kids Can Cope: Parenting Resilient Children at Home and at School," accessed July 14, 2014, www.psychologyfoundation.org/pdf/publications/ResilienceChildrenBooklet .pdf; Mark Hassinger and Lee A. Plourde, "'Beating the Odds;: How Bilingual Hispanic Youth Work Through Adversity to Become High Achieving Students," *Education* 126, no. 2 (2005): 316–327.
41. Jones and Vagle, "Social Class-Sensitive Pedagogy," 129.
42. Ibid., 137.

Chapter 9

1. Anne Gregory and Rhona S. Weinstein, "The Discipline Gap and African Americans: Defiance or Cooperation in the High School Classroom," *Journal of School Psychology* 46, no. 4 (2008): 456.
2. Anne Gregory et al., "The Achievement Gap and the Discipline Gap: Two Sides of the Same Coin?" *Educational Researcher* 39, no. 1 (2010): 59.
3. Ibid., 60.
4. U.S. Department of Justice, and U.S. Department of Education, "Dear Colleague Letter on the Nondiscriminatory Administration of School Discipline," January 8, 2014, www2.ed.gov/ about/offices/list/ocr/letters/colleague-201401-title-vi.pdf, 3–4.
5. Center for Effective Discipline, "U.S.: Corporal Punishment and Paddling Statistics by State and Race," accessed February 20, 2014, www.stophitting.com/index.php?page=statesbanning.
6. Ibid., 1. The Web site where all related documents, guidelines, webinars, statistics, and resources may be found is U.S. Department of Education, "School Climate and Discipline," accessed July 14, 2014, www2.ed.gov/policy/gen/guid/school-discipline/index.html.
7. Shi-Chang Wu et al., "Student Suspension: A Critical Reappraisal," *Urban Review* 14, no. 4 (1982): 245–303.
8. Pamela Fenning and Jennifer Rose, "Overrepresentation of African American Students in Exclusionary Discipline: The Role of School Policy," *Urban Education* 42, no. 6 (2007): 540.
9. Daniel J. Losen and Jonathan Gillespie, "Opportunities Suspended: The Disparate Impact of Disciplinary Exclusion from School," Center for Civil Rights Remedies at the Civil

Rights Project, August 2012, http://civilrightsproject.ucla.edu/resources/projects/center-for -civil-rights-remedies/school-to-prison-folder/federal-reports/upcoming-ccrr-research/losen -gillespie-opportunity-suspended-2012.pdf, 32.

10. R. J. Skiba et al., "The Color of Discipline: Sources of Racial and Gender Disproportionality in School Punishment," *Urban Review* 34, no. 4 (2002): 317–342, doi: 10.1023/A:1021320817372, 332.

11. Gregory and Weinstein, "Discipline Gap and African Americans," 461.

12. U.S. Department of Justice and U.S. Department of Education, "Dear Colleague Letter," 4.

13. See, for example, S. Fordham and J. U. Ogbu, "Black Students' School Success: Coping with the Burden of 'Acting White,'" *Urban Review* 18, no. 3 (1986): 176–206; Margaret A. Gibson and John U. Ogbu, *Minority Status and Schooling: A Comparative Study of Immigrant and Involuntary Minorities* (New York: Garland, 1991); John U. Ogbu, "Class Stratification, Racial Stratification, and Schooling," in *Race, Class, and Gender in American Education*, ed. L. Weis (Albany: SUNY Press, 1988); John U. Ogbu, "Minority Status and Literacy in Comparative Perspective," *Daedalus* 119, no. 2 (1990): 141–168; John U. Ogbu, *Minority Education and Caste: The American System in Cross-Cultural Perspective* (New York: Academic Press, 1978); John U. Ogbu, "Minority Education in Comparative Perspective," *Journal of Negro Education* 59, no. 1 (1990): 45–57; John U. Ogbu, *Black American Students in an Affluent Suburb: A Study of Academic Disengagement* (Mahwah, NJ: L. Erlbaum Associates, 2003); John U. Ogbu, "Collective Identity and the Burden of 'Acting White' in Black History, Community, and Education," *Urban Review* 36, no. 1 (2004): 1–35; John U. Ogbu, *Minority Status, Oppositional Culture, and Schooling* (New York: Routledge, 2008); John U. Ogbu and Herbert D. Simons, "Voluntary and Involuntary Minorities: A Cultural-Ecological Theory of School Performance with Some Implications for Education," *Anthropology & Education Quarterly* 29, no. 2 (1998): 155–188.

14. There are multiple problems with the concepts of involuntary minorities and voluntary minorities. For example, our nation manipulates international markets and The World Bank to devalue foreign currencies and to render foreign goods too expensive to sell in our markets. The United States then forces other nations to accept economic "help" whereby American factories capitalize on cheap foreign labor, the lack of environmental and workplace safety regulations, and the scarcity of unions. When "voluntary minorities" who live in those contexts come across our borders looking for better work, are they truly voluntary? Likewise, should the refugees who are fleeing political or military situations the United States had a direct role in creating (Vietnamese, Guatemalans, Iraqis, and Afghans, to name only a few) be considered voluntary? Might some of these "voluntary" immigrants enter the country with the same deep suspicions that Ogbu's "involuntary minorities" theoretically possess?

15. Garvey F. Lundy, "The Myths of Oppositional Culture," *Journal of Black Studies* 33, no. 4 (2003): 459–460.

16. Antwi A. Akom, "Reexamining Resistance as Oppositional Behavior: The Nation of Islam and the Creation of a Black Achievement Ideology," *Sociology of Education* 76, no. 4 (2003): 307.

17. See, for example, ibid.; James W. Ainsworth-Darnell and Douglas B. Downey, "Assessing the Oppositional Culture Explanation for Racial/Ethnic Differences in School Performance," *American Sociological Review* 63 (1998): 536–553; Diane A. M. Archer-Banks and Linda S. Behar-Horenstein, "Ogbu Revisited: Unpacking High-Achieving African American Girls' High School Experiences," *Urban Education* 47, no. 1 (2012): 198–223; David A. Bergin and Helen C. Cooks, "High School Students of Color Talk About Accusations of 'Acting White,'" *Urban Review* 34, no. 2 (2002): 113–134; Philip J. Cook and Jens Ludwig, "Weighing the 'Burden of "Acting White"': Are There Race Differences in Attitudes Toward Education?" *Journal of Policy Analysis and Management* 16, no. 2 (1997): 256–278; John B. Diamond, "Are We Bark-

ing Up the Wrong Tree? Rethinking Oppositional Culture Explanations for the Black/White Achievement Gap," *The Achievement Gap Initiative at Harvard University* (2006); Douglas B. Downey and James W. Ainsworth-Darnell, "The Search for Oppositional Culture Among Black Students," *American Sociological Review* 67, no. 1 (2002): 156–164; George Farkas et al., "Does Oppositional Culture Exist in Minority and Poverty Peer Groups?" *American Sociological Review* 67, no. 1 (2002): 148–155; Douglas Foley, "Ogbu's Theory of Academic Disengagement: Its Evolution and Its Critics," *Intercultural Education* 15, no. 4 (2004): 385–397; Anthony Graham and Kenneth Anderson, "'I Have to be Three Steps Ahead': Academically Gifted African American Male Students in an Urban High School on the Tension Between an Ethnic and Academic Identity," *Urban Review* 40, no. 5 (2008): 472–499; Angel L. Harris, "I (Don't) Hate School: Revisiting Oppositional Culture Theory of Blacks' Resistance to Schooling," *Social Forces* 85, no. 2 (2006): 797–834; Angel L. Harris, *Kids Don't Want to Fail: Oppositional Culture and Black Students' Academic Achievement* (Cambridge, MA: Harvard University Press, 2011); Erin M. Horvat and Kristine S. Lewis, "Reassessing the 'Burden of Acting White': The Importance of Peer Groups in Managing Academic Success," *Sociology of Education* 76, no. 4 (2003): 265–280; Erin McNamara Horvat and Carla O'Connor, eds. *Beyond Acting White: Reframing the Debate on Black Student Achievement* (Lanham, MD: Rowman & Littlefield, 2006); Kathleen M. Nolan, "Oppositional Behavior in Urban Schooling: Toward a Theory of Resistance for New Times," *International Journal of Qualitative Studies in Education* 24, no. 5 (2011): 559–572; Gary L. St. C. Oates, "An Empirical Test of Five Prominent Explanations for the Black–White Academic Performance Gap," *Social Psychology of Education* 12, no. 4 (2009): 415–441; Jason Osborne and Brett Jones, "Identification with Academics and Motivation to Achieve in School: How the Structure of the Self Influences Academic Outcomes," *Educational Psychology Review* 23, no. 1 (2011): 131–158; Louie Rodríguez, "Struggling to Recognize Their Existence: Examining Student-Adult Relationships in the Urban High School Context," *Urban Review* 40, no. 4 (2008): 436–453; Margaret Beale Spencer et al., "Identity and School Adjustment: Revisiting the 'Acting White' Assumption," *Educational Psychologist* 36, no. 1 (2001): 21–30; Karolyn Tyson et al., "It's Not 'a Black Thing': Understanding the Burden of Acting White and Other Dilemmas of High Achievement," *American Sociological Review* 70, no. 4 (2005): 582–605.

18. Dorinda Carter, "Achievement as Resistance: The Development of a Critical Race Achievement Ideology Among Black Achievers," *Harvard Educational Review* 78, no. 3 (2008): 466–497; Prudence L. Carter, *Keepin' It Real: School Success Beyond Black and White* (Oxford: Oxford University Press, 2005).

19. Lundy, "Myths of Oppositional Culture," 463.

20. Karolyn Tyson, "Weighing In: Elementary-Age Students and the Debate on Attitudes Toward School Among Black Students," *Social Forces* 80, no. 4 (2002): 1179.

21. Ibid., 1181.

22. Ibid., 1180.

23. Karolyn Tyson, "Notes From the Back of the Room: Problems and Paradoxes in the Schooling of Young Black Students," *Sociology of Education* 76, no. 4 (2003): 326.

24. Tyson, "Weighing In," 1184.

25. Ibid., 1175.

26. Richard Rothstein, "For Public Schools, Segregation Then, Segregation Since: Education and the Unfinished March," Economic Policy Institute, August 27, 2013, www.epi.org/publication/unfinished-march-public-school-segregation/.

27. For more information, see Carolyn J. Marr, "Assimilation Through Education: Indian Boarding Schools in the Pacific Northwest," University of Washington Digital Collections, accessed July 14, 2013, http://content.lib.washington.edu/aipnw/marr.html#positives; Donna Deyhle,

"Navajo Youth and Anglo Racism: Cultural Integrity and Resistance," *Harvard Educational Review* 65, no. 3 (1995): 403–445; Gilberto Conchas et al., "Acculturation and School Success: Understanding the Variability of Mexican American Youth Adaptation Across Urban and Suburban Contexts," *Urban Review* 44, no. 4 (2012): 401–422; The Children of the Camps Project, "Children of the Camps: Internment History," PBS, accessed July 14, 2014, www.pbs.org/childofcamp/history/index.html?PHPSESSID= 032e01e0d9275e2e1d447e604074cc9c.

28. David E. Kirkland, "Acting White: The Ironic Legacy of Desegregation," *Teachers College Record* (2011).

29. Ibid.

30. Lundy, "Myths of Oppositional Culture," 460–461.

31. Some of the best explications of the phenomenon of subtractive schooling include Angela Valenzuela, *Subtractive Schooling: U.S.-Mexican Youth and the Politics of Caring* (Albany: SUNY Press, 1999); Russel Rumberger and Patricia Gándara, "The Schooling of English Learners," in *Crucial Issues in California Education*, ed. Elizabeth Burr, Gerald Hayward, and Michael Kirst (Berkeley: Policy Analysis for California Education, 2000); Guadalupe Valdés, "Heritage Language Students: Profiles and Possibilities," National Foreign Language Center, University of Maryland, accessed July 14, 2014, www.nflc.org/REACH/documents/valdes.pdf; Angela Valenzuela, "Reflections on the Subtractive Underpinnings of Education Research and Policy," *Journal of Teacher Education* 53, no. 3 (2002): 235–241; Aimee V. Garza and Lindy Crawford, "Hegemonic Multiculturalism: English Immersion, Ideology, and Subtractive Schooling," *Bilingual Research Journal* 29, no. 3 (2005): 599–619; Beth Hatt-Echeverria, "Beyond Biology and Ability: Understanding Smartness as Cultural Practice" (paper presented at the annual meeting of American Educational Research Association, San Francisco, 2006); Harris, *Kids Don't Want to Fail*.

32. Asians too experience subtractive schooling. According to Mary E. Clark, "Skinner vs the Prophets: Human Nature & Our Concepts of Justice," *Contemporary Justice Review* 8, no. 2 (2005): 172, "Asian cultures—based on Confucianism, Taoism, and Buddhism—are most concerned with social harmony and the mutual connectedness of everything. An individual's primary aim is to give support to the group, and to feel accepted by it. Relationships take precedence over personal aspirations, and self-aggrandizement is frowned upon. Conflict—at least at local levels—tends to be resolved by intermediaries, with the reduction of hostility and restoration of harmony as the primary social goal." Therefore the common expectation in schools that everyone will conform to the values of Western individualism may feel alienating.

33. This is a paraphrasing of Stephen Vassallo's observation that "adaptation is a mechanism of control, subordination, and domination because the focus of change is on the consciousness of the oppressed, not the situation that oppresses them" (Stephen Vassallo, "Critical Pedagogy and Neoliberalism: Concerns With Teaching Self-Regulated Learning," *Studies in Philosophy & Education* 32, no. 6 [2013]: 566).

34. Perhaps the most concise and most compelling summary of the multiple failings in and lack of empirical support for Ogbu's theories can be found in Diamond, "Are We Barking Up the Wrong Tree?" For other more detailed critiques, both empirical and theoretical, see Jennifer O Burrell et al., "Race-Acting: The Varied and Complex Affirmative Meaning of 'Acting Black' for African-American Adolescents," *Culture & Psychology* 19, no. 1 (2013): 95–116; Tiffani Chin and Meredith Phillips, "The Ubiquity of Oppositional Culture" (paper presented at the annual meeting of the American Educational Research Association, San Francisco, 2005); Cook and Ludwig, "Weighing the 'Burden of "Acting White"'"; Downey and Ainsworth-Darnell, "Oppositional Culture Among Black Students"; Farkas et al., "Does Oppositional Culture Exist?"; Foley, "Ogbu's Theory of Academic Disengagement"; Kevin Michael Foster, "Coming to Terms:

A Discussion of John Ogbu's Cultural-Ecological Theory of Minority Academic Achievement," *Intercultural Education* 15, no. 4 (2004): 369–384; Nolan, "Oppositional Behavior in Urban Schooling"; Rodríguez, "Struggling to Recognize Their Existence"; Kitae Sohn, "Acting White: A Critical Review," *Urban Review* 43, no. 2 (2011): 217–234; Spencer et al., "Identity and School Adjustment."

35. Bergin and Cooks, "High School Students of Color Talk," 113.

36. Graham and Anderson, "'I Have to Be Three Steps Ahead," 493.

37. Harris, *Kids Don't Want to Fail*, 824.

38. Horvat and Lewis, "Reassessing the 'Burden of Acting White,'" 275–276.

39. Recent scholarship that demonstrates this point includes Lorri J. Santamaria, "Culturally Responsive Differentiated Instruction: Narrowing Gaps Between Best Pedagogical Practices Benefiting All Learners," *Teachers College Record* 111, no. 1 (2009): 214–247; Robin DiAngelo and Özlem Sensoy, "'OK, I Get It! Now Tell Me How to Do It!': Why We Can't Just Tell You How to Do Critical Multicultural Education," *Multicultural Perspectives* 12, no. 2 (2010): 97–102; H. Richard Milner, *Start Where You Are but Don't Stay There: Understanding Diversity, Opportunity Gaps, and Teaching in Today's Classrooms* (Cambridge, MA: Harvard Education Press, 2010); Mardi Schmeichel, "Good Teaching? An Examination of Culturally Relevant Pedagogy as an Equity Practice," *Journal of Curriculum Studies* 44, no. 2 (2011): 211–231; Danielle Moss Lee, "Creating an Anti-Racist Classroom," *Edutopia*, blog, January 12, 2012, www.edutopia.org/blog/anti-racist-classroom-danielle-moss-lee; Rae Shevalier and Barbara Ann McKenzie, "Culturally Responsive Teaching as an Ethics- and Care-Based Approach to Urban Education," *Urban Education* 47, no. 6 (2012): 1086–1105; Django Paris, "Culturally Sustaining Pedagogy: A Needed Change in Stance, Terminology, and Practice," *Educational Researcher* 41, no. 3 (2012): 93–97; Özlem Sensoy and Robin J. DiAngelo, *Is Everyone Really Equal? An Introduction to Key Concepts in Social Justice Education* (New York: Teachers College Press, 2012); Kristy S. Cooper, "Safe, Affirming, and Productive Spaces: Classroom Engagement Among Latina High School Students," *Urban Education* 48, no. 4 (2013): 490–528; Barry M. Goldenberg, "White Teachers in Urban Classrooms: Embracing Non-White Students' Cultural Capital for Better Teaching and Learning," *Urban Education* 49, no. 1 (2014): 111–144.

40. Peter McLaren, "Multiculturalism and the Postmodern Critique: Towards a Pedagogy of Resistance and Transformation," *Cultural Studies* 7, no. 1 (1993): 139.

41. Howard C. Stevenson, "Fluttering Around the Racial Tension of Trust: Proximal Approaches to Suspended Black Student-Teacher Relationships," *School Psychology Review* 37, no. 3 (2008): 357.

42. With regard to doing collective readings on whiteness, several articles articulate well what's at stake in this work and how it might best be done: Beverly Daniel Tatum, "Teaching White Students About Racism: The Search for White Allies and the Restoration of Hope," *Teachers College Record* 95, no. 4 (1994): 462–476; Alice McIntyre, *Making Meaning of Whiteness: Exploring Racial Identity with White Teachers* (Albany, NY: SUNY Press, 1997); Henry A. Giroux, "White Squall: Resistance and the Pedagogy of Whiteness," *Cultural Studies* 11, no. 3 (1997): 376–389; Kathy Hytten and John Warren, "Engaging Whiteness: How Racial Power Gets Reified in Education," *International Journal of Qualitative Studies in Education* 16, no. 1 (2003): 65–89; Audrey Thompson, "Tiffany, Friend of People of Color: White Investments in Antiracism," *International Journal of Qualitative Studies in Education* 16, no. 1 (2003): 7–29; Nancy P. Gallavan, "Helping Teachers Unpack Their 'Invisible Knapsacks,'" *Multicultural Education* 13, no. 1 (2005): 36–39; R. Patrick Solomon et al., "The Discourse of Denial: How White Teacher Candidates Construct Race, Racism and 'White Privilege,'" *Race Ethnicity and Education* 8, no. 2 (2005): 147–169; Nado Aveling, "'Hacking at Our Very Roots': Rearticulating White Racial

Identity Within the Context of Teacher Education," *Race Ethnicity and Education* 9, no. 3 (2006): 261–274; Özlem Sensoy and Robin DiAngelo, "Developing Social Justice Literacy: An Open Letter to Our Faculty Colleagues," *Phi Delta Kappan* 90, no. 5 (2009): 345–352; Bree Picower, "The Unexamined Whiteness of Teaching: How White Teachers Maintain and Enact Dominant Racial Ideologies," *Race Ethnicity and Education* 12, no. 2 (2009): 197–215; Robin DiAngelo and Özlem Sensoy, "Getting Slammed: White Depictions of Race Discussions as Arenas of Violence," *Race Ethnicity and Education* (2012): 1–26.

Chapter 10

1. A team of leading researchers in ethnic and racial identity development recently recommended that scholars and practitioners use the inclusive term *ERI* rather than separately employing either *race* or *ethnicity*. A full explication of the research and theoretical bases for that recommendation can be found in Adriana J. Umaña-Taylor et al., "Ethnic and Racial Identity During Adolescence and into Young Adulthood: An Integrated Conceptualization," *Child Development* 85, no. 1 (2014): 21–39.

2. Studies that confirm these observations include W. David Wakefield and Cynthia Hudley, "Ethnic and Racial Identity and Adolescent Well-Being," *Theory into Practice* 46, no. 2 (2007): 147–154; Sabine Elizabeth French et al., "The Development of Ethnic Identity During Adolescence," *Developmental Psychology* 42, no. 1 (2006): 1–10; Lisa Kiang et al., "Change in Ethnic Identity Across the High School Years Among Adolescents with Latin American, Asian, and European Backgrounds," *Journal of Youth and Adolescence* 39, no. 6 (2010): 683–693; Kate C. McLean and Monisha Pasupathi, "Processes of Identity Development: Where I Am and How I Got There," *Identity* 12, no. 1 (2012): 8–28; Anthony D. Ong et al., "Measurement of Ethnic Identity: Recurrent and Emergent Issues," *Identity* 10, no. 1 (2010): 39–49; Adriana J. Umaña-Taylor et al., "Developing the Ethnic Identity Scale Using Eriksonian and Social Identity Perspectives," *Identity* 4, no. 1 (2004): 9–38; Umaña-Taylor et al., "Ethnic and Racial Identity During Adolescence."

3. Umaña-Taylor et al., "Ethnic and Racial Identity During Adolescence," 31.

4. These theories are not without their enduring disagreements and controversies. ERI development is an active field with new discoveries and modifications to previous models happening all the time. I am presenting here a generalization of decades of research involving scores of scholars working across multiple areas of inquiry. My intent is to be conversant with that research rather than try to be comprehensive. Note also that psychology itself has a long history of racist and scientifically dubious conclusions pertaining to ethnically and racially marginalized subjects, including eugenics, racialized theories of intelligence, and various models of cultural deprivation. The following titles capture some of the main critiques of psychology in general and developmental psychology in particular and are worth consulting as you weigh the utility of these explanations in work with ethnically and racially marginalized youth: Ali Rattansi, and Ann Phoenix, "Rethinking Youth Identities: Modernist and Postmodernist Frameworks," *Identity: An International Journal of Theory and Research* 5, no. 2 (2005): 97–123; Asa G. Hilliard III, "Psychology as Political Science and as a Double Edged Sword: Racism and Counter Racism in Psychology," *Psych Discourse* 29, no. 5–6 (1998): 7–15; Barbara Beatty, "Rethinking Compensatory Education: Historical Perspectives on Race, Class, Culture, Language, and the Discourse of the 'Disadvantaged Child,'" *Teachers College Record* 114, no. 6 (2012): 1–11; Jean S. Phinney, "Ethnic Identity in Late Modern Times: A Response to Rattansi and Phoenix," *Identity* 5, no. 2 (2005): 187–194; Robert V. Guthrie, *Even the Rat Was White: A Historical View of Psychology*, 2nd ed. (Boston: Allyn and Bacon, 1998).

5. See, for example, J. E. Helms, *Black and White Racial Identity: Theory, Research, and Practice* (Westport, CT: Greenwood Press, 1990); Tina Q. Richardson and Timothy J. Silvestri, "White Identity Formation: A Developmental Process," in *Racial and Ethnic Identity in School Practices*, ed. Rosa Hernandez Sheets and Etta R. Hollins (Mahwah, NJ: Lawrence Erlbaum, 1999); Rita Hardiman and Molly Keehn, "White Identity Development Revisited: Listening to White Students," in *Asian American Racial Identity Development Theory*, ed. Charmaine Wijeyesinghe and Bailey W. Jackson (New York: New York University Press, 2012).

6. For a chart in which a series of these models are presented in comparison, see Michael J. Nakkula and Eric Toshalis, *Understanding Youth: Adolescent Development for Educators* (Cambridge, MA: Harvard Education Press, 2006), 133. Recent scholarship surveying various ethnic identity development models in an attempt to ascribe a single common model includes Charmaine Wijeyesinghe and Bailey W. Jackson, *New Perspectives on Racial Identity Development: Integrating Emerging Frameworks*, 2nd ed. (New York: New York University Press, 2012); Deborah Rivas-Drake et al., "Ethnic and Racial Identity in Adolescence: Implications for Psychosocial, Academic, and Health Outcomes," *Child Development* 85, no. 1 (2014): 40–57; Ong et al., "Measurement of Ethnic Identity"; Umaña-Taylor et al., "Developing the Ethnic Identity Scale."

7. Some relatively recent and well-regarded models can be found in Angela R. Gillem et al., "Black Identity in Biracial Black/White People: A Comparison of Jacqueline Who Refuses to Be Exclusively Black and Adolphus Who Wishes He Were," *Cultural Diversity and Ethnic Minority Psychology* 7, no. 2 (2001): 182–196; Angela-MinhTu D. Nguyen and Verónica Benet-Martínez, "Biculturalism Unpacked: Components, Individual Differences, Measurement, and Outcomes," *Social and Personality Psychology Compass* 1, no. 1 (2007): 101–114; Jean S. Phinney and Mona Devich-Navarro, "Variations in Bicultural Identification Among African American and Mexican American Adolescents," *Journal of Research on Adolescence* 7, no. 1 (1997): 3–32; W. S. Carlos Poston, "The Biracial Identity Development Model: A Needed Addition," *Journal of Counseling & Development* 69, no. 2 (1990): 152–155.

8. Again, different theories of racial and ethnic identity development name this phase or its corollary differently. Examples of these differently titled and differently understood developmental eras include *internal quest, consequence, awakening, redirection, search/moratorium*, and *resistance and denial*.

9. Geneva Gay, "Implications of Selected Models of Ethnic Identity Development for Educators," *Journal of Negro Education* 54, no. 1 (1985): 47.

10. Ibid., 51.

11. See, for example, April Harris-Britt et al., "Perceived Racial Discrimination and Self-Esteem in African American Youth: Racial Socialization as a Protective Factor," *Journal of Research on Adolescence* 17, no. 4 (2007): 669–682; Wakefield and Hudley, "Ethnic and Racial Identity"; Frank C. Worrell and Donna L. Gardner-Kitt, "The Relationship Between Racial and Ethnic Identity in Black Adolescents: The Cross Racial Identity Scale and the Multigroup Ethnic Identity Measure," *Identity* 6, no. 4 (2006): 293–315; Matthew D. Jones and Renee V. Galliher, "Ethnic Identity and Psychosocial Functioning in Navajo Adolescents," *Journal of Research on Adolescence* 17, no. 4 (2007): 683–696.

12. Derald Wing Sue et al., "Racial Microaggressions in Everyday Life: Implications for Clinical Practice," *American Psychologist* 62, no. 4 (2007): 273.

13. Though Sue and his colleagues primarily describe the way therapist-client relationships are undermined when microaggressions occur, the researchers' observations apply just as readily to educator-student interactions.

14. Both of these examples are adapted from vignettes provided by ibid., 281.

15. Ibid., 279.
16. Ibid.
17. Daniel G. Solorzano et al., "Critical Race Theory, Racial Microaggressions, and Campus Racial Climate: The Experiences of African American College Students," *Journal of Negro Education* 69, no. 1–2 (2000): 60–73.
18. Elizabeth A. Pascoe and Laura Richman Smart, "Perceived Discrimination and Health: A Meta-Analytic Review," *Psychological Bulletin* 135, no. 4 (2009): 531–54; Frederick X. Gibbons et al., "The Erosive Effects of Racism: Reduced Self-Control Mediates the Relation Between Perceived Racial Discrimination and Substance Use in African American Adolescents," *Journal of Personality and Social Psychology* 102, no. 5 (2012): 1089–1104; Gene H. Brody et al., "Perceived Discrimination and the Adjustment of African American Youths: A Five-Year Longitudinal Analysis with Contextual Moderation Effects," *Child Development* 77, no. 5 (2006): 1170–1189; Harris-Britt et al., "Perceived Racial Discrimination and Self-Esteem in African American Youth"; Lucas Torres et al., "Discrimination, Acculturation, Acculturative Stress, and Latino Psychological Distress: A Moderated Mediational Model," *Cultural Diversity and Ethnic Minority Psychology* 18, no. 1 (2012): 17–25; Melissa L. Greene et al., "Trajectories of Perceived Adult and Peer Discrimination Among Black, Latino, and Asian American Adolescents: Patterns and Psychological Correlates," *Developmental Psychology* 42, no. 2 (2006): 218–36; Ronald L. Simons et al., "Incidents of Discrimination and Risk for Delinquency: A Longitudinal Test of Strain Theory with an African American Sample," *Justice Quarterly* 20, no. 4 (2003): 827–854.
19. Wakefield and Hudley, "Ethnic and Racial Identity," 152. See also: Umaña-Taylor et al., "Ethnic and Racial Identity During Adolescence."
20. The benefits of these home spaces both inside and outside school are beautifully described in Jennifer Pastor et al., "Makin' Homes: An Urban Girl Thing," in *Urban Girls: Resisting Stereotypes, Creating Identities*, ed. Bonnie J. Ross Leadbeater and Niobe Way (New York: New York University Press, 1996).
21. Janie Victoria Ward, "Uncovering Truths, Recovering Lives: Lessons of Resistance in the Socialization of Black Girls," in *Urban Girls Revisited: Building Strengths*, ed. Bonnie J. Ross Leadbeater and Niobe Way (New York: New York University Press, 2007), 245.
22. Ibid., 246.
23. Ibid., 251.
24. Sofia Villenas and Melissa Moreno, "To *Valerse Por Si Misma* Between Race, Capitalism, and Patriarchy: Latina Mother-Daughter Pedagogies in North Carolina," *International Journal of Qualitative Studies in Education* 14, no. 5 (2001): 671.
25. Ward, "Socialization of Black Girls," 247.
26. Ronald L. Simons et al., "Supportive Parenting Moderates the Effect of Discrimination upon Anger, Hostile View of Relationships, and Violence Among African American Boys," *Journal of Health and Social Behavior* 47, no. 4 (2006): 373–389. Italics added.
27. Duane E. Thomas et al., "Racial and Emotional Factors Predicting Teachers' Perceptions of Classroom Behavioral Maladjustment for Urban African American Male Youth," *Psychology in the Schools* 46, no. 2 (2009): 187.
28. Ward, "Socialization of Black Girls," 246.
29. Tara J. Yosso, "Whose Culture Has Capital? A Critical Race Theory Discussion of Community Cultural Wealth," *Race Ethnicity and Education* 8, no. 1 (2005): 80.
30. See, for example, Pepi Leistyna, "Racenicity: Understanding Racialized Ethnic Identities," in *Multi/Intercultural Conversations*, ed. Shirley R. Steinberg (New York: Peter Lang, 2001); Jean S. Phinney, "Understanding Ethnic Identity," *American Behavioral Scientist* 40, no. 2 (1996):

143–152; Janet E. Helms and Regine M. Talleyrand, "Race Is Not Ethnicity," *American Psychologist* (1997): 1246–1247.

31. For poignant analyses of how the racial designator *White* has morphed depending on regional, social, cultural, political, legal, and economic circumstances, see Karen Brodkin, *How Jews Became White Folks and What That Says About Race in America* (New Brunswick, NJ: Rutgers University Press, 1998); Noel Ignatiev, *How the Irish Became White* (New York: Routledge, 2009); Ian Haney-López, *White by Law: The Legal Construction of Race* (New York: New York University Press, 1996).

32. These statistics come from Umaña-Taylor et al., "Ethnic and Racial Identity During Adolescence," 32.

33. National Center for Education Statistics, Institute of Education Sciences, "English Language Learners: Fast Facts," accessed July 14, 2013, https://nces.ed.gov/fastfacts/display.asp?id=96

34. Daniel J. Losen and Tia Elena Martinez, "Out of School and Off Track: The Overuse of Suspensions in American Middle and High Schools," Center for Civil Rights Remedies at the Civil Rights Project, April 8, 2013, http://civilrightsproject.ucla.edu/resources/projects/center-for-civil-rights-remedies/school-to-prison-folder/federal-reports/out-of-school-and-off-track-the-overuse-of-suspensions-in-american-middle-and-high-schools/OutofSchool-OffTrack_UCLA_4-8.pdf, 1.

35. K. Wayne Yang, "Discipline or Punish? Some Suggestions for School Policy and Teacher Practice," *Language Arts* 87, no. 1 (2009): 51.

36. See, for example, Wu et al., "Student Suspension: A Critical Reappraisal"; Christine Bowditch, "Getting Rid of Troublemakers: High School Disciplinary Procedures and the Production of Dropouts," *Social Problems* 40, no. 4 (1993): 493–509; Tara M. Brown, "Lost and Turned Out: Academic, Social, and Emotional Experiences of Students Excluded from School," *Urban Education* 42, no. 5 (2007): 432–455; Fenning and Rose, "Overrepresentation of African American Students in Exclusionary Discipline"; Jenna K. Chin et al., "Alternatives to Suspensions: Rationale and Recommendations," *Journal of School Violence* 11, no. 2 (2012): 156–173; Pamela A. Fenning et al., "Call to Action: A Critical Need for Designing Alternatives to Suspension and Expulsion," *Journal of School Violence* 11, no. 2 (2012): 105–117.

37. Yang, "Discipline or Punish?" 49.

38. Chin et al., "Alternatives to Suspensions," 158.

39. Anne Gregory and Pharmacia M. Mosely, "The Discipline Gap: Teachers' Views on the Over-Representation of African American Students in the Discipline System," *Equity & Excellence in Education* 37 (2004): 18–30; Anne Gregory et al., "The Relationship of School Structure and Support to Suspension Rates for Black and White High School Students," *American Educational Research Journal* 48, no. 4 (2011): 904–934; Edward W. Morris, "'Tuck in That Shirt!': Race, Class, Gender, and Discipline in an Urban School," *Sociological Perspectives* 48, no. 1 (2005): 25–48; H. Richard Milner, "Why Are Students of Color (Still) Punished More Severely and Frequently Than White Students?" *Urban Education* 48, no. 4 (2013): 483–489; Russell J. Skiba et al., "The Color of Discipline: Sources of Racial and Gender Disproportionality in School Punishment," *Urban Review* 34, no. 4 (2002): 317–342; Russell J. Skiba, "Are Zero Tolerance Policies Effective in the Schools? An Evidentiary Review and Recommendations," *American Psychologist* 63, no. 9 (2008): 852–862; Russell Skiba, "When Is Disproportionality Discrimination? The Overrepresentation of Black Students in School Suspension," in *Zero Tolerance: Resisting the Drive for Punishment in Our Schools*, ed. William Ayers, Rick Ayers, and Bernardine Dohrn (New York: New Press, 2001).

40. Perhaps the most impressive is the "Solutions Not Suspensions" campaign directed by the group Dignity in Schools, now active in twenty-one states and in the District of Columbia. The work

of this campaign is described in Dignity in Schools, "Solutions Not Suspensions: A Call for a Moratorium on Out-of-School Suspensions," Dignity in Schools web page, accessed September 19, 2014, www.dignityinschools.org/solutions-not-suspensions-call-moratorium-out-school-suspensions. The Model School Code the organization proposes to replace suspension-oriented policies may be found at Dignity in Schools, "A Model Code on Education and Dignity: Presenting a Human rights Framework for Schools," The Dignity in Schools Campaign, revised October 2013, www.dignityinschools.org/our-work/model-school-code.

41. Fenning and Rose, "Overrepresentation of African American Students in Exclusionary Discipline," 538.

42. Ibid., 551–552.

Chapter 11

1. Gert Biesta, "'Mind the Gap!' Communication and the Educational Relation," in *No Education Without Relation*, ed. Charles Bingham and Alexander M. Sidorkin (New York: Peter Lang, 2004), 12–13.

2. See, for example, Jacquelynne S. Eccles et al., "Development During Adolescence: The Impact of Stage-Environment Fit on Young Adolescents' Experiences in Schools and in Families," *American Psychologist* 48, no. 2 (1993): 90–101; Jacquelyn S. Eccles and A. Wigfield, "In the Mind of the Achiever: The Structure of Adolescents' Academic Achievement Related-Beliefs and Self-Perceptions," *Personality and Social Psychology Bulletin* 21 (1995): 215–225; R. W. Roeser et al., "School as a Context of Early Adolescents' Academic and Social-Emotional Development: A Summary of Research Findings," *Elementary School Journal* 100 (2000): 443–471; Robert A. Gable et al., "Cognitive, Affective, and Relational Dimensions of Middle School Students," *Clearing House* 79, no. 1 (2005): 40–44; Nicole Zarrett and Jacquelynne Eccles, "The Passage to Adulthood: Challenges of Late Adolescence," *New Directions for Youth Development* 111 (2006): 13–28; Carrie Furrer and Ellen Skinner, "Sense of Relatedness as a Factor in Children's Academic Engagement and Performance," *Journal of Educational Psychology* 95, no. 1 (2003): 148–162.

3. Studies and analyses that make this point are abundant. Here are two that do it quite convincingly: Kirsten Olson, *Wounded by School: Recapturing the Joy in Learning and Standing Up to Old School Culture* (New York: Teachers College Press, 2009); Diane Ravitch, *The Death and Life of the Great American School System: How Testing and Choice Are Undermining Education* (New York: Basic Books, 2010).

4. Erik H. Erikson, *Identity, Youth, and Crisis* (New York: W. W. Norton, 1968); Mary McCaslin, "Co-Regulation of Student Motivation and Emergent Identity," *Educational Psychologist* 44, no. 2 (2009): 137–146; Robert W. Roeser et al., "Identity Representations in Patterns of School Achievement and Well-Being Among Early Adolescent Girls," *Journal of Early Adolescence* 28, no. 1 (2008): 115–152; Susan P. Hall and Marla R. Brassard, "Relational Support as a Predictor of Identity Status in an Ethnically Diverse Early Adolescent Sample," *Journal of Early Adolescence* 28, no. 1 (2008): 92–114.

5. This phrasing is derived from Mayer et al., who define trust as "the willingness of a party to be vulnerable to the actions of another party," as quoted in Kate Phillippo, "'You're Trying to Know Me': Students from Nondominant Groups Respond to Teacher Personalism," *Urban Review* 44, no. 4 (2012): 446.

6. A. Gregory and M. B. Ripski, "Adolescent Trust in Teachers: Implications for Behavior in the High School Classroom," *School Psychology Review* 37, no. 3 (2008): 337–353; Anne Gregory and Rhona S. Weinstein, "The Discipline Gap and African Americans: Defiance or Cooperation in the High School Classroom," *Journal of School Psychology* 46, no. 4 (2008): 455–475;

Anthony S. Bryk and Barbara L. Schneider, *Trust in Schools: A Core Resource for Improvement* (Cambridge, MA: Russell Sage Foundation, 2002); Catherine D. Ennis and M. Terri McCauley, "Creating Urban Classroom Communities Worthy of Trust," *Journal of Curriculum Studies* 34, no. 2 (2002): 149–172; Howard C. Stevenson, "Fluttering Around the Racial Tension of Trust: Proximal Approaches to Suspended Black Student-Teacher Relationships," *School Psychology Review* 37, no. 3 (2008): 354–358.

7. The concept of relational pace comes from Phillippo, "'You're Trying to Know Me,'" 460.

8. Ibid.

9. Ibid., 452.

10. See, for example, Elizabeth Bondy et al., "Creating Environments of Success and Resilience: Culturally Responsive Classroom Management and More," *Urban Education* 42, no. 4 (2007): 326–348; H. Richard Milner and F. Blake Tenore, "Classroom Management in Diverse Classrooms," *Urban Education* 45, no. 5 (2010): 560–603; Anne Gregory et al., "The Relationship of School Structure and Support to Suspension Rates for Black and White High School Students," *American Educational Research Journal* 48, no. 4 (2011): 904–934; L. Janelle Dance, *Tough Fronts: The Impact of Street Culture on Schooling* (New York: RoutledgeFalmer, 2002); H. Jerome Freiberg and Stacey M. Lamb, "Dimensions of Person-Centered Classroom Management," *Theory Into Practice* 48, no. 2 (2009): 99–105; Johnmarshall Reeve, "Why Teachers Adopt a Controlling Motivating Style Toward Students and How They Can Become More Autonomy Supportive," *Educational Psychologist* 44, no. 3 (2009): 159–175; William L. Sterrett, "From Discipline to Relationships," *Educational Leadership* 70, no. 2 (2012): 71–74; Carol Ann Tomlinson, "Rising to the Challenge of Challenging Behavior," *Educational Leadership* 70, no. 2 (2012): 88–89.

11. Duane E. Thomas et al., "Racial and Emotional Factors Predicting Teachers' Perceptions of Classroom Behavioral Maladjustment for Urban African American Male Youth," *Psychology in the Schools* 46, no. 2 (2009): 185.

12. This insight is derived from the analysis provided in K. Wayne Yang, "Discipline or Punish? Some Suggestions for School Policy and Teacher Practice," *Language Arts* 87, no. 1 (2009): 52.

13. L. Janelle Dance, *Tough Fronts*, 52.

14. Ibid., 60.

15. Carol Tavris, quoted in Michael Newman, *Teaching Defiance: Stories and Strategies for Activist Educators* (San Francisco: Jossey-Bass, 2006), 55. Italics in original.

16. Ibid., 55–56.

17. Angel L. Harris, "I (Don't) Hate School: Revisiting Oppositional Culture Theory of Blacks' Resistance to Schooling," *Social Forces* 85, no. 2 (2006): 813.

18. Russell J. Skiba et al., "The Color of Discipline: Sources of Racial and Gender Disproportionality in School Punishment," *Urban Review* 34, no. 4 (2002): 336.

19. Thomas et al., "Racial and Emotional Factors," 185.

20. Harris, "I (Don't) Hate," 813.

21. Ibid.

22. Thomas et al., "Racial and Emotional Factors," 185.

23. Skiba et al., "Color of Discipline," 336.

24. Thomas et al., "Racial and Emotional Factors," 186.

25. Heather K. Alvarez, "The Impact of Teacher Preparation on Responses to Student Aggression in the Classroom," *Teaching and Teacher Education* 23 (2007): 1114.

26. Thomas et al., "Racial and Emotional Factors," 192.

27. Alyssa Morones, "Corporal Punishment Persists in U.S. Schools," *Education Week*, October 22, 2013, www.edweek.org/ew/articles/2013/10/23/09spanking_ep.h33.html.

28. For a thorough and compelling analysis of these and other measures that are used to punish and instill fear in students, see Aaron Kupchik, *Homeroom Security: School Discipline in an Age of Fear* (New York: New York University Press, 2010).

29. Alfie Kohn, *Beyond Discipline: From Compliance to Community*, 2nd ed. (Alexandria, VA: Association for Supervision and Curriculum Development, 2006); Clive Harber, *Schooling as Violence: How Schools Harm Pupils and Societies* (New York: RoutledgeFalmer, 2004); Cynthia E. Mader, "'I Will Never Teach the Old Way Again': Classroom Management and External Incentives," *Theory into Practice* 48, no. 2 (2009): 147–155; Mary E. Clark, "Skinner vs the Prophets: Human Nature & Our Concepts of Justice," *Contemporary Justice Review* 8, no. 2 (2005): 163–176; Pedro A. Noguera, "Schools, Prisons, and Social Implications of Punishment: Rethinking Disciplinary Practices," *Theory into Practice* 42, no. 4 (2003): 341–350; Ronald E. Butchart, "Punishments, Penalties, Prizes, and Procedures: A History of Discipline in U.S. Schools," in *Classroom Discipline in American Schools: Problems and Possibilities for Democratic Education*, ed. Ronald E. Butchart and Barbara McEwan (Albany, NY: SUNY Press, 1998).

30. See, for example, Patricia Leigh Brown, "Opening Up, Students Transform a Vicious Circle," *New York Times*, April 3, 2013, www.nytimes.com/2013/04/04/education/restorative-justice-programs-take-root-in-schools.html?smid=pl-share; Nirvi Shah, "'Restorative Practices': Discipline but Different," *Education Week*, October 16, 2012, www.edweek.org/ew/articles/2012/10/17/08restorative_ep.h32.html?qs=restorative+issues; Matt Davis, "Restorative Justice: Resources for Schools," *Edutopia*, October 4, 2013, www.edutopia.org/blog/restorative-justice-resources-matt-davis; Centre for Justice and Reconciliation, "Class Room," *Restorative Justice Online*, accessed July 14, 2014, www.restorativejustice.org/other/schools; Centre for Justice and Reconciliation, "Class Room," *Restorative Justice Online*, accessed July 14, 2014, www.restorativejustice.org/other/schools/outcome-evaluation; Restorative Justice 4 Schools, home page, accessed July 14, 2014; www.restorativejustice4schools.co.uk/; Oakland Unified School District, "Restorative Justice," last modified April 25, 2014, www.ousd.k12.ca.us/restorativejustice. See also the following academic resources: Brenda E. Morrison and Dorothy Vaandering, "Restorative Justice: Pedagogy, Praxis, and Discipline," *Journal of School Violence* 11, no. 2 (2012): 138–155; Jeanne B. Stinchcomb et al., "Beyond Zero Tolerance: Restoring Justice in Secondary Schools," *Youth Violence and Juvenile Justice* 4, no. 2 (2006): 123–147; Pamela A. Fenning et al., "Call to Action: A Critical Need for Designing Alternatives to Suspension and Expulsion," *Journal of School Violence* 11, no. 2 (2012): 105–117; Sally Varnham, "Seeing Things Differently: Restorative Justice and School Discipline," *Education and the Law* 17, no. 3 (2005): 87–104; Wesley G. Jennings et al., "Localizing Restorative Justice: An In-Depth Look at a Denver Public School Program," in *Restorative Justice: From Theory to Practice*, ed. Holly Ventura Miller (Bingley, UK: Emerald Group Publishing, 2008).

31. Morrison and Vaandering, "Restorative Justice," 148.

Chapter 12

1. Henry A. Giroux, *Theory and Resistance in Education: Towards a Pedagogy for the Opposition* (Westport, CT: Bergin & Garvey, 2001), 31.

2. Brenda E. Morrison and Dorothy Vaandering, "Restorative Justice: Pedagogy, Praxis, and Discipline," *Journal of School Violence* 11, no. 2 (2012): 149; Jenna K. Chin et al., "Alternatives to Suspensions: Rationale and Recommendations," *Journal of School Violence* 11, no. 2 (2012): 160.

3. K. Wayne Yang, "Discipline or Punish? Some Suggestions for School Policy and Teacher Practice," *Language Arts* 87, no. 1 (2009): 51.

4. Morrison and Vaandering, "Restorative Justice," 141.
5. Barbara Stengel, "Facing Fear, Releasing Resistance, Enabling Education," *Philosophical Studies in Education* 39 (2008): 74.
6. Yang, "Discipline Or Punish?" 59.
7. Ibid., 55.
8. An abbreviated list of sources from a much larger array of empirical and theoretical critiques is supplied here: Audrey Amrein-Beardsley and David C. Berliner, "An Analysis of Some Unintended and Negative Consequences of High-Stakes Testing," *Educational Policy Studies Laboratory*, January 1, 2002, http://epicpolicy.org/publication/an-analysis-some-unintended-and-negative-consequences-high-stakes-testing; Enrique G. Murillo and Susana Y. Flores, "Reform by Shame: Managing the Stigma of Labels in High Stakes Testing," *Educational Foundations* 16, no. 2 (2002): 93–108; Gert J. J. Biesta, "Education, Accountability, and the Ethical Demand: Can the Democratic Potential of Accountability Be Regained?" *Educational Theory* 54, no. 3 (2004): 233–250; Steve Turley, "Professional Lives of Teacher Educators in an Era of Mandated Reform," *Teacher Education Quarterly* 32, no. 4 (2005): 137–156; Margaret Smith Crocco and Arthur T. Costigan, "High-Stakes Teaching: What's at Stake for Teacher (and Students) in the Age of Accountability," *The New Educator* 2, no. 1 (2006): 1–13; Sharon L. Nichols et al., "High-Stakes Testing and Student Achievement: Does Accountability Pressure Increase Student Learning?" *Education Policy Analysis Archives* 14, no. 1 (2006): 1–172; Doug Selwyn, "Highly Quantified Teachers: NCLB and Teacher Education," *Journal of Teacher Education* 58, no. 2 (2007): 124–137; Linda Darling-Hammond, "Race, Inequality and Educational Accountability: The Irony of 'No Child Left Behind,'" *Race Ethnicity and Education* 10, no. 3 (2007): 245–260; Margaret S. Crocco and Arthur T. Costigan, "The Narrowing of Curriculum and Pedagogy in the Age of Accountability: Urban Educators Speak Out," *Urban Education* 42, no. 6 (2007): 512–535; Geneva Gay, "The Rhetoric and Reality of NCLB," *Race Ethnicity and Education* 10, no. 3 (2007): 279–293; Mark W. Ellis, "Leaving No Child Behind Yet Allowing None Too Far Ahead: Ensuring (In)Equity in Mathematics Education Through the Science of Measurement and Instruction," *Teachers College Record* 110, no. 6 (2008): 1330–1356; J. S. Wills and J. Haymore Sandholtz, "Constrained Professionalism: Dilemmas of Teaching in the Face of Test-Based Accountability," *Teachers College Record* 111, no. 4 (2009): 1065–1114; Heinrich Mintrop and Gail L. Sunderman, "Predictable Failure of Federal Sanctions-Driven Accountability for School Improvement—and Why We May Retain It Anyway," *Educational Researcher* 38, no. 5 (2009): 353–364; Heinrich Mintrop and Gail L. Sunderman, "Why High Stakes Accountability Sounds Good But Doesn't Work—and Why We Keep on Doing It Anyway," Civil Rights Project at UCLA, April 2009, http://civilrightsproject.ucla.edu/research/k-12-education/nclb-title-i/why-high-stakes-accountability-sounds-good-but-doesn2018t-work2014-and-why-we-keep-on-doing-it-anyway/mintrop-high-stakes-doesnt-work-2009.pdf; Diane Ravitch, *The Death and Life of the Great American School System: How Testing and Choice Are Undermining Education* (New York: Basic Books, 2010); Gary D. Fenstermacher and Virginia Richardson, "What's Wrong With Accountability?," *Teachers College Record*, May 26, 2010, www.tcrecord.org/PrintContent.asp?ContentID=15996; Jason M. Smith and Philip E. Kovacs, "The Impact of Standards-Based Reform on Teachers: The Case of 'No Child Left Behind,'" *Teachers and Teaching* 17, no. 2 (2011): 201–225; Iris C. Rotberg, "Is Anyone Listening? Policy Versus Research on Test-Based Accountability and Charter Schools," *Teachers College Record*, June 19, 2012, www.tcrecord.org/Content.asp?ContentID=16798; Barbara Tomlinson and George Lipsitz, "Insubordinate Spaces for Intemperate Times: Countering the Pedagogies of Neoliberalism," *Review of Education, Pedagogy, and Cultural Studies* 35, no. 1 (2013): 3–26.

9. Biesta, "Education, Accountability, and the Ethical Demand", 240–41.

10. Kurt Fischer's work in cognitive development and skill theory has been particularly enlightening on this matter: Kurt W. Fischer, "A Theory of Cognitive Development: The Control and Construction of Hierarchies of Skills," *Psychological Review* 87, no. 6 (1980): 477–531; Kurt W. Fischer and Mary Helen Immordino-Yang, "Cognitive Development and Education: From Dynamic General Structure to Specific Learning and Teaching," in *Traditions of Scholarship in Education*, ed. Ellen Lagemann (Chicago: Spencer Foundation, 2002); and Kurt W. Fischer and Samuel P. Rose, "Growth Cycles of Brain and Mind," *Educational Leadership* (1998): 56–60.

11. The research revealing the enormously negative impact of tracking is substantial. Notable titles include Jeannie Oakes, *Multiplying Inequalities: The Effects of Race, Social Class, and Tracking on Opportunities to Learn Mathematics and Science* (Santa Monica, CA: Rand Corporation, 1990); Linda Harklau, "'Jumping Tracks': How Language-Minority Students Negotiate Evaluations of Ability," *Anthropology & Education Quarterly* 25, no. 3 (1994): 347–363; Jeanne Oakes and Gretchen Guiton, "Matchmaking: The Dynamics of High School Tracking Decisions," *American Educational Research Journal* 32, no. 1 (1995): 3–33; Susan Yonezawa et al., "Choosing Tracks: 'Freedom of Choice' in Detracking Schools," *American Educational Research Journal* 39, no. 1 (2002): 37–67; Ellen A. Brantlinger, *Dividing Classes: How the Middle Class Negotiates and Rationalizes School Advantage* (New York: RoutledgeFalmer, 2003); Betty Achinstein et al., "Are We Creating Separate and Unequal Tracks of Teachers? The Effects of State Policy, Local Conditions, and Teacher Characteristics on New Teacher Socialization," *American Educational Research Journal* 41, no. 3 (2004): 557–603; Jeannie Oakes, *Keeping Track: How Schools Structure Inequality*, 2nd ed. (New Haven: Yale University Press, 2005); Daryl G. Smith and Gwen Garrison, "The Impending Loss of Talent: An Exploratory Study Challenging Assumptions About Testing and Merit," *Teachers College Record* 107, no. 4 (2005): 629–653; R. Mickelson, and B. Everett, "Neotracking in North Carolina: How High School Courses of Study Reproduce Race and Class-Based Stratification," *Teachers College Record* 110, no. 3 (2008): 535–570; Maika Watanabe, "Tracking in the Era of High Stakes State Accountability Reform: Case Studies of Classroom Instruction in North Carolina," *Teachers College Record* 110, no. 3 (2008): 489–534; Lynn M. Mulkey et al., "Keeping Track or Getting Offtrack: Issues in the Tracking of Students," in *Springer International Handbooks of Education*, ed. Lawrence J. Saha and A. Gary Dworkin (New York: Springer, 2009); Jo Worthy, "Only the Names Have Been Changed: Ability Grouping Revisited," *Urban Review* 42, no. 4 (2010): 271–295; George Ansalone, "Tracking: Educational Differentiation or Defective Strategy," *Educational Research Quarterly* 34, no. 2 (2010): 3–17; David F. Labaree, "School Syndrome: Understanding the USA's Magical Belief That Schooling Can Somehow Improve Society, Promote Access, and Preserve Advantage," *Journal of Curriculum Studies* 44, no. 2 (2012): 143–163.

12. See, for example, Yonezawa et al., "Choosing Tracks"; Carol Corbett Burris and Kevin G. Welner, "Closing the Achievement Gap by Detracking," *Phi Delta Kappan* 86, no. 8 (2005): 594–598; Nora E. Hyland, "Detracking in the Social Studies: A Path to a More Democratic Education?" *Theory into Practice* 45, no. 1 (2005): 64–71; Doris Alvarez and Hugh Mehan, "Whole-School Detracking: A Strategy for Equity and Excellence," *Theory into Practice* 45, no. 1 (2005): 82–89; Carol Corbet Burris et al., "Accountability, Rigor, and Detracking: Achievement Effects of Embracing a Challenging Curriculum as a Universal Good for All Students," *Teachers College Record* 110, no. 3 (2008): 571–607; Beth Rubin, "Detracking in Context: How Local Constructions of Ability Complicate Equity-Geared Reform," *Teachers College Record* 110, no. 3 (2008): 646–99.

Chapter 13

1. Paulo Freire, *Pedagogy of Freedom: Ethics, Democracy, and Civic Courage*, Critical Perspectives Series (Lanham: Rowman & Littlefield Publishers, 1998), 45

2. Audrey Thompson, "Tiffany, Friend of People of Color: White Investments in Antiracism," *International Journal of Qualitative Studies in Education* 16, no. 1 (2003): 23.

3. Ibid., 22.

ACKNOWLEDGMENTS

This book exists only because many, many people supported me in writing it. Its genesis occurred while I was working with Janie Victoria Ward as a doctoral candidate and research assistant at Harvard in the early 2000s. Janie's nuanced analysis of Black students' resistance in school, its foundations in truth telling and parenting strategies designed to raise resisters, its connection to community activism and feminist and womanist pedagogies, and her four-step process of reading, naming, opposing, and replacing racial oppression informed much of my early curiosity about and research into youth resistance in the classroom. In capturing resistance the way she did, Janie named for me what I find most thrilling about working with educators and youth, and she helped frame why I believe adolescents are so frequently misread in schools and classrooms. She also woke me up to my own ignorance and privilege as well as my participation in systemic racism. Janie once asked me why I didn't like John Ogbu's acting-White theory, and I stumbled to frame an answer that made sense. I hope this book is a better explication of my response.

Michael Sadowski was the first to express interest in seeing my ideas about resistance expressed as a book. I am indebted to him for his encouragement and guidance as this project moved from conception to reality. Likewise, I am forever thankful for Caroline Chauncey's enthusiasm for the book and her shepherding of it through the various phases of production. Caroline's priceless suggestions for improvements, along with Patricia Boyd's careful and incisive copyediting, made the work stronger and clearer.

I am grateful to Scott Fletcher, Dean of the Graduate School of Education and Counseling at Lewis & Clark College, and Janet Bixby, Associate Dean, and then-Chair of the Teacher Education Department. Their commitment to protecting time for scholarship and their granting of my sabbatical provided the necessary conditions in which I could sustain focus and complete this book. Likewise, I am indebted to my Lewis & Clark faculty colleagues, especially those who encouraged me to prioritize this work and who picked up the slack in my absence. In particular, thank you to my colleague and mentor Vern Jones for his sage advice, for opening the field of classroom management to a greater awareness of the contexts that surround all behavioral decisions, and for helping so many educators recognize that threats of punishment are never as successful at encouraging prosocial behaviors as communities of support. And a big thanks to Kasi Allen and Dyan Watson, my genius collaborators in Rogers Hall who manage to take the occasional frustrations, disappointments, and glaring inequities in our work and gracefully turn them into progress, power, and justice.

Thanks go to Ranger Derek Lohuis of Channel Island National Park for listening to me blather on about this stuff while traipsing over all those trails, cliffs, canyons, slopes, and alpine switchbacks. Turns out our long hikes were pretty good for my thinking.

To Mike Nakkula, mentor, teacher, theorist, therapist, developmentalist, wordsmith, coach, Dylanophile, and friend: your hermeneutic orientation toward applied developmental work with youth made it possible for me to believe that adolescents sometimes resist for good reasons, even when that resistance may be mystifying to us adults. Like everything else, resistance is a matter of interpretation, and I have you to thank for that core insight, plus about a billion others.

Thank you to my teachers at Ottawa Elementary, Sand Creek Elementary, Pinewood Elementary, North Side Junior High, Central High, and Helix High. I learned a lot by testing you and watching how you responded. I know now how fortunate I am to have been educated by professionals who let me push back without cutting me off.

To my former students at Santa Barbara Junior High, Santa Barbara High, Jonata School, Goleta Valley Junior High, and Cambridge Rindge and Latin School, I must apologize for not knowing how to engage your resistance more productively back in the day. You were right to resist then, and I hope you still do.

To my graduate students and student teachers at University of California–Santa Barbara, in the Harvard Teacher Education Program, at the Massachusetts Institute for New Teachers, at Cal State Channel Islands, and in Lewis & Clark's Middle Level/High School M.A.T. Program: may this book better capture what I've been trying to say these many years.

And to my parents, sister, mother-in-law, father-in-law, and sibs-in-law, thank you for your consistent enthusiasm and support. I hope this work somehow benefits Mason, Sam, Elwood, and Henry.

And finally, I am immeasurably grateful to Sarah Sentilles. Since we first met, you have demonstrated daily the courage that is required, the benefits that may be gained, and the costs that must be paid by those who contest the mainstream.

In your scholarship, teaching, writing, activism, art, and companionship, you make justice and peace possible because you refuse to let things default to the norm, and in so doing, you make it clear to everyone, especially me, why resistance is necessary. Thank you for this. Thank you for everything.

ABOUT THE AUTHOR

ERIC TOSHALIS received his Bachelor of Arts, Teaching Credential, and Master of Education degrees from the University of California, Santa Barbara; a Master of Theological Studies degree from Harvard Divinity School; and a Doctorate in Education from the Harvard Graduate School of Education. He is the co-author, with Michael J. Nakkula, of *Understanding Youth: Adolescent Development for Educators* (Harvard Education Press, 2006) and its companion Web site, Understanding-Youth.com. He is on the faculty of the Teacher Education Department in the Graduate School of Education and Counseling at Lewis & Clark College in Portland, Oregon, where he directs the Summer Middle Level/High School M.A.T Program and teaches courses in adolescent development and classroom management.

For over two decades, Eric has served public education in a variety of roles, including middle and high school teacher, coach, mentor teacher, union president, community activist, teacher educator, curriculum developer, researcher, author, professor, and consultant. His primary focus has been to study and practice what it takes to ensure that students flourish in school, particularly those students who are often marginalized by mainstream practices and contexts. He received the Human Relations Award by Santa Barbara County for his antiracist efforts at his middle school, was recognized as Teacher of the Year by his school district, and was awarded the Certificate of Distinction in Teaching by Harvard College. He consults with educators, nonprofits, and after-school professionals across the country. For more information, please visit EngagingResistance.com.

INDEX

agency (*continued*)
   framing of power as a relationship and, 51
   inevitability of resistance due to, 48
   myth of pure agency, 55–56
   teachers' dependence on student assent, 48–49
   understanding resistance using, 49
Akom, Antwi A., 210
Althusser, Luis, 24–27, 42, 52
Amsel, Eric, 78, 80
Anderson, Kenneth, 216
angry students. *See* indignation
apartheid, 272
Apple, Michael, 35
Arendt, Hannah, 50
Arizona, 218
assessments
   educators' complicity in the accountability system, 290
   educators' forced acquiescence to standardizing practices, 289–290
   problems with NCLB and RTTT, 287–288
   schools' contribution to the logic of self-handicapping, 127–128
   test-prep activities versus hypothetical thinking, 79–80
assimilation. *See* acting-White hypothesis; identity and opposition
Assor, Avi, 143
autonomy
   current prioritizing of order over, 112–113
   factors that motivate students to achieve in school, 110–112
   help avoidance and the adolescent desire for, 130
   practices that increase, 144
   resistance's relation to suppression of, 111–112
   supporting in order to encourage engagement, 144
   supporting in the classroom, 112

availability bias, 73
avoidance of help
   adolescent desire for autonomy and, 130
   adoption of as a self-protective measure, 182
   changing the performance- and status-goal orientation of students, 131–132
   counter-productiveness of teachers asking for questions, 132
   help's role in enhancing learning, 129
   maladaptive nature of, 129
   prevalence of performance goal over mastery goal conditions and, 130
   quality of teacher-student relationships and, 131
   rationale for not seeking help, 129–130, 131

Baldwin, James, 299, 309
Balfanz, Robert, 124
bargaining for compliance, 285–287
behaviorism theory, 278–279
Bergin, David, 216
Berliner, David, 178
Biesta, Gert, 254, 288
Bingham, Charles, 66
Bloom's Taxonomy, 75
Bourdieu, Pierre, 27–29, 52
Bowles, Samuel, 30
brain system 1. *See also* cognition and imagination
   adolescent risk taking and, 82–83
   applicability to learning, 73–74
   availability bias due to emotional reactions, 73
   characteristics of, 69, 72
   coding of memories and, 73
   drawbacks to, 72
   multitasking and, 137
   school cultures' role in student responses, 74
   specificity of areas of the brain, 69

promising practices for countering,
36–38
reinforcement of social inequities by
schools, 22
sailboat analogy of defaulting to following the system, 34
school ideology's affect on pedagogical
approaches, 26
schools' allocation of students to meet
society's needs, 22
schools' justification of class-based
differentiation, 30
schools' mirroring of the economy's
structure, 30
schools' representation of mainstream
society and, 203–204
social hierarchies view of schools, 20,
27
society's acceptance of prevailing ideology of schools, 25
state versus ideological state
apparatuses, 24–25
steps toward a structural view of education, 35
structural analysis of what causes social
inequity, 23–24
a teacher's feeling of a collective deter-
mination to fail, 17–18
view of lower SES students, 176
socioeconomic reasons for resisting school
achievement gap between wealthy and
poor students, 176
adolescent focus on status, 181
adolescents' awareness of opportunity
disparities due to income, 185
adoption of avoidance as a self-
protective measure, 182
deficiencies in low-income-serving
schools, 178–179
deficit orientation of views on poverty,
196
deficits in current research, 180–181
disproportionality of discipline in
schools and, 205

dropout or push-out rate of students,
178
influence of class on typical adolescent
concerns, 181–182
inward manifestations of students'
resistance to classism, 193–196
logic behind student resistance to
education-as-self-betterment
messages, 184–185
misalignment between low-income
students' experiences and those of
school adults, 183
neuroscientific-based view of low
performance, 179–181
outward manifestations of students'
resistance to classism, 186–193
poverty rate for children in U.S., 177,
178
promising practices against classism,
196–199
relationship between poverty and
cognition, 179–180
segregation by income in the U.S., 178
sense of alienation felt by low-income
students, 183, 184–185
sense of belonging felt by middle-class
students, 182–183
SES as a predictor of academic success,
176–177
shame felt by socioeconomically marginalized youth, 182
social and academic effects of living
with low income, 177–179
social reproduction theory's view of
lower SES students, 176
students' choosing of resistance over
compliance, 185–186
students' interpretation of messages to
"better themselves," 183–184
tracking's stigmatizing of status, 185
vignette about SES differences in
schools, 173–174
state versus ideological state apparatuses,
24–25